PRINCIPLES OF POLITICS AND
GOVERNMENT

PRINCIPLES OF POLITICS AND
GOVERNMENT

SIXTH EDITION

Edwin M. Coulter, Professor Emeritus
Clemson University

Brown & Benchmark
PUBLISHERS

Madison, WI Dubuque Guilford, CT Chicago Toronto London
Mexico City Caracas Buenos Aires Madrid Bogotá Sydney

Book Team

Executive Editor *Ed Bartell*
Acquisitions Editor *Scott Spoolman*
Project Editor *Stan Stoga*
Developmental Editor *Marsena Konkel*
Publishing Services Coordinator *Peggy Selle*
Proofreading Coordinator *Carrie Barker*
Production Manager *Beth Kundert*
Design and New Media Development Manager *Linda Meehan Avenarius*
Production/Costing Manager *Sherry Padden*
Visuals/Design Freelance Specialist *Mary L. Christianson*
Marketing Manager *Kirk Moen*
Copywriter *Sandy Hyde*

Basal Text *10/12 Palatino*
Display Type *Palatino Bold*
Typesetting System *Macintosh™ QuarkXPress™*
Paper Stock *50# Restore Cote*
Production Services *Shepherd, Inc.*

Executive Vice President and General Manager *Bob McLaughlin*
Vice President, Business Manager *Russ Domeyer*
Vice President of Production and New Media Development *Victoria Putman*
National Sales Manager *Phil Rudder*
National Telesales Director *John Finn*

A Times Mirror Company

Cover design by Cunningham & Welch Design Group, Inc., Madison, WI

Cover photograph © Jane Sterrett/The Image Bank

Copyedited by Anne Scroggin; Proofread by Barb Callahan

Library of Congress Catalog Card Number: 96–84171

ISBN 0–697–23762–1

Printed in the United States of America by Times Mirror Higher Education Group, Inc.,
2460 Kerper Boulevard, Dubuque, IA 52001

10 9 8 7 6 5 4 3 2 1

In memory of my father, Homer Preston Coulter

Contents

PREFACE   xi

**1   POLITICS, GOVERNMENT, AND POLITICAL
        SCIENCE**   1
Defining My Terms   **1**
Early Approaches to Political Science   **2**
The Traditionalists Versus the Behavioralists   **5**
Research Methods in Political Science   **7**
Points to Ponder   **8**

2   BASIC CONCEPTS OF POLITICS   9
Political Activity   **9**
Power   **11**
Legitimacy and Authority   **13**
Political Culture and Socialization   **14**
Politics   **16**
Political and Egalitarian Democracy   **17**
The Time of Sovereignty   **21**
Other Definitions of Politics   **23**
Points to Ponder   **26**

3   THE STATE   27
The Origins of the State   **27**
The Feudal State and the Nation-State   **33**
Sovereignty   **38**
Nationalism   **41**
Whither the State?   **53**
Points to Ponder   **54**

4   THE NATURE OF GOVERNMENT   **55**
Ways of Classifying Governments   **55**
The Unitary Form   **59**
The Confederal Form   **59**
The Federal Form   **61**
Two Principles of Federalism   **66**
The American Presidential System   **69**
The Parliamentary System   **72**
Coalition Parliaments   **78**
Points to Ponder   **82**

5   THE FUNCTIONS OF GOVERNMENT   **83**
Legislatures   **84**
Executives   **88**
The Judiciary   **93**
The Regulators   **95**
Points to Ponder   **101**

6   THE NATURE OF LAW   **103**
Normative and Positive Law   **103**
What Is Law?   **104**
Classification of Laws   **106**
Law Enforcement   **109**
Legal Concepts   **111**
Legal Systems of the Western World   **116**
The Evolution of Legal Systems   **116**
Roman Law   **118**
Anglo-Saxon Common Law   **119**
Judicial Selection   **122**
Changes in British Law   **127**
Equity Law   **128**
The Structure of Legal Systems   **130**
Points to Ponder   **134**

7   THE NATURE OF IDEOLOGY   **135**
Ideological Terms and Their Origins   **135**
Political Democracy   **141**
The Prerequisites for Political Democracy   **142**
Majoritarianism   **147**
Democracy or Guardianship?   **148**
A Warning to Americans   **151**
Authoritarian Government   **152**
Totalitarianism   **154**
The Evolution of Ideology   **159**
Points to Ponder   **162**

8 LIBERALISM, CONSERVATISM, SOCIALISM, COMMUNISM, AND FASCISM   163
Liberalism   163
Conservatism   172
Modern Conservatism   177
Socialism   180
Communism   185
Fascism   197
Points to Ponder   201

9 POLITICAL PARTIES AND INTEREST GROUPS   203
The Origin of Political Parties   203
European Political Parties   208
The American Approach to Political Parties   209
Interest Groups and Their Role in Politics   211
Points to Ponder   214

10 ADMINISTRATION AND THE BUREAUCRACY   215
The Evolution of American Bureaucracy   217
Bureaucratic Organization and Procedure   218
The Bureaucratic Problem   224
Points to Ponder   226

11 PROBLEMS IN POLITICAL DEMOCRACY   227
Who Should Vote and How?   227
Voting Behavior   232
Bases of Representation   236
Bicameralism and Unicameralism   239
Single-Member Districts Versus Proportional Representation   241
Single-Member Districting and the Electoral College   246
Qualifications and Characteristics of Legislators   249
Representation and Population   251
Legislation by Committee   253
The Future of Representative Democracy   256
Points to Ponder   258

12 INTERNATIONAL POLITICS   259
Foreign Policy and the National Interest   259
National Security   261
Diplomacy   270
Third Party Diplomacy and the Settlement of Disputes   272
International Law   274
The Balance of Power   278
International Organizations   279
War and Terrorism   285
International Politics and the Future   287
Points to Ponder   288

CONTENTS

GLOSSARY 289

SELECTED BIBLIOGRAPHY 299

INDEX 305

Preface

Why another introduction to politics book? The answer is the reason I decided to write this book. Most of the existing works on the subject begin by assuming that the student is already intellectually well into the field. More often than not, this is simply not the case. My purpose herein is to enable the beginning student to understand what politics and government are about (and what they aren't about).

Most American college freshmen and sophomores have been ill taught or are generally ignorant about politics and government. I have bemoaned students' myths and misconceptions for two decades in large and small colleges and universities. I have attempted to help them to "unlearn" the myths and to teach the basic realities of political science. We in the profession have all too often assumed that they already know these realities.

This book attempts to teach students to better understand the world environment in which government operates; to acquire a theoretical and analytical structure in which to approach questions about government; to relate western political democracy to other governmental alternatives; to clarify the verbiage of political discourse; to examine the problems of achieving political democracy at the end of the twentieth century; and to gain a historical perspective with regard to the age-old dilemma of achieving order without servitude.

It provides that basic level of understanding necessary before one can fruitfully embark on a political science curriculum of American Government, Political Methodology, Comparative Government, Public Administration, Public Law, or International Relations. This book is where all of these things must begin. It can and should be supplemented by works that emphasize other aspects of the discipline, but it lays the groundwork for almost any of these endeavors. Whereas the traditional introductory subjects of political culture, political socialization, and voting behavior are each addressed separately as subsections of chapters, they are also integrated, along with other standard concepts, into a more general and systematic approach to politics and government. My goal was to interrelate as many of the facets of the subject as possible into a relatively jargon-free explanation of the major political systems of the world and the principles under which they operate.

This book also assumes a traditional, historical, and normative stance toward the study of politics. It assumes that politics is rooted in a system of conciliation, however misapplied. It argues that good government is political government and that the political process should be defended from the assaults of power, nationalism, and ideology. It suggests that any government made by human beings can be improved and that to this end value judgments are necessary. Thus, in this book there are many value judgments rendered. They are not offered as self-evident truths, but as points for reflection, discussion, and debate.

Finally, law is viewed as essentially positive and subject to humanity's will, whether or not that will serves the ends of politics and good government. I make no apologies for this overall approach and point of view. I only hope that those who read and use this book will understand the material within it and profit from its descriptions and the organization of its basic concepts.

In the second edition of the book, I added a chapter on the origins and evolution of political science. Particular emphasis was given to the tension between the traditional approach to political science and the behavioralist approach to the discipline. Further, in response to several critics, I added to the end of the chapter on the basic concepts of politics a section entitled "Other Definitions of Politics," which takes into account those writers whose definition of politics varies with my rather narrow and normative definition.

In the third edition, I expanded the chapter on ideology to address the question of democracy versus guardianship; updated all references to party politics to take into account the possible political realignments in America and elsewhere since 1980; added a section on the relationship between law and truth; expanded the section on regulation; included a glossary; and, most important, added a new and separate chapter on administration and bureaucracy.

In the fourth edition, I added a chapter on international politics, which included the material on international law previously found in chapter 5 along with other relevant principles. This chapter can serve as a follow-on chapter to chapter 3. I also updated the material in the governmental, ideological, and political parties sections to reflect events since 1985.

The fifth edition reflected the revolutionary change in the international community brought on by the emancipation of the Eastern European states, the reunification of Germany, and the collapse of the Soviet Union. Those events impacted directly on theories of ideology, nationalism, and international politics. Much that had been written in the past few years was already out-of-date. Much change still lies ahead, which will no doubt bedevil even this new edition.

This, the sixth edition, addresses the continuing evolution of American party politics. The realignment that began in the 1980s proceeds apace with more clarity than it had a few years ago. I have also thought it helpful to add a section on national security and war in the new age and the lesser problem of terrorism. In addition, attention is given to the reemergence of the United Nations as an instrument for world peace. I have also expanded the discussion of ideology to include new forms of conservatism and the concept of majoritarianism. I have updated references and illustrations throughout the book. Finally, at the end of each chapter, I have added a list of "Points to Ponder," which will both review important points and draw comparisons to political realities in non-American settings.

Most of these changes were made in response to my most helpful critics, for, in the final analysis, no textbook author can stand alone as the singular organizer of a subject. With that in mind, I would say to some who have found certain sections of this book to be somewhat compressed and occasionally lacking in expanded commentary that there are two reasons for this. First, I wish to give the instructor wide latitude for his or her own interpretation of the subject. Second, I want to provide for the student some basic information relevant to many different organizational approaches to the subject. This book is not so much designed for a single kind of course as it is an outline and anchor for many different kinds of introductory courses. I hope that this new edition will prove to be even more useful and timely than the last five versions.

ACKNOWLEDGEMENTS

The publisher would like to thank the following people for their assistance in reviewing this and previous editions of *Principles of Politics and Government:* William Burns, West Chester University; Robert Doane, Christopher Newport University; Elizabeth Normandy, Pembroke State University; Hassan Tajalli, Southwest Texas State University; Blaine Benedict, Houghton College; Bertil L. Hanson, Oklahoma State University; Allen Hartter, Parkland College; Craig Heneveld, Hillsborough Community College; Lewis E. Moore, Jr., Columbia State Community College; Thomas Oberlink, Kalamazoo Community College; and Robert Wood, North Dakota State University.

1 | Politics, Government, and Political Science

DEFINING MY TERMS

This book is primarily about politics and government, two related concepts that will be examined in great detail in the next chapter. The student who reads this book will most likely do so in conjunction with an introductory course in political science.

Political science is a broad discipline that includes many different but related subfields. A basic subfield is American government. This is the study of our national governing structure, our state governments, and local (municipal) governance. The study of American government involves, sometimes as separate courses, such major areas as the Constitution and its evolution; federalism; political parties; the bureaucracy; elections; and an analysis of the three major organs of our system: the executive, legislative, and judicial branches. Other subfields concern comparative government— the study of the forms of government found in other countries, both democratic and nondemocratic.

There is a group of subfields concerning nation-states and their interactions. These subfields include international politics, international law, international organizations, and foreign policy. Public law is a subfield of considerable interest to those students interested in going to law school. This study is usually divided into constitutional law in general and a concentration on civil rights. Public administration is a major subfield useful to future bureaucrats and other government workers. Future politicians will want to study the political dynamics of parties, campaigns, pressure groups, and the media. One can also study the judicial, executive, and legislative processes as separate bodies of knowledge. Political theory is a major subfield. This can be approached from a historical, philosophical, or methodological point of view. One can also study the politics of geographical areas such as Western Europe, South Asia, or Latin America. One of the newer areas of political science is national security policy, which is the study of national defense and how best to achieve an acceptable level of security in the world. Even this survey does not include all the subfields of political science, as it spills over into psychology, sociology, geography, and history. Nevertheless, all these aspects of political science require an overall orientation or approach, and there are several possibilities.

The approach herein is traditional. It is also *normative,* which is to say that it deals not only with what *was* and *is* but also with several views of what *ought to be.* Furthermore, the approach is theoretical, historical, and institutional. In other words, it examines the historical record of ideas about government and the structure of the institutions of government, and it tries to illuminate the basic theoretical assumptions behind them.

This is my approach to political science. There are others, and, since the reader who carries his or her studies further into the field will encounter different approaches along the way, the others should be at least partially defined.

EARLY APPROACHES TO POLITICAL SCIENCE

Political science began as political speculation for the most part. Ideas about how to govern humanity are as old as governments themselves, and no one knows for sure how old *they* are. Early nonwestern political thought can be found in the *Arthashastra,* a book believed to have been written by a Brahman advisor to an Indian king in the fourth century B.C. It is full of pragmatic advice on how to govern successfully, and it bears a remarkable resemblance to a sixteenth-century western work, *The Prince,* written for a similar purpose by Niccolo Machiavelli, an Italian statesman and scholar. The writings of Confucius (551–478 B.C.) are also a good example of nonwestern political theory.

Early Western studies of government include *The Republic* by Plato and *Politics* (as well as other works) by Aristotle, two Greek philosophers of the fourth century B.C. As in the *Arthashastra,* the approach of these studies is essentially practical and theoretical. Roman writers, such as Cicero (106–43 B.C.), also emphasized the practical aspect of government, especially in the areas of administration and law. Later, during the medieval period, when the church became the locus of much of what passed for government, the approach became extremely normative, blending together both government and theology in the writings of such theologians as St. Thomas Aquinas (1227–1274).

The Renaissance produced a return to the emphasis on the pragmatic side of the political order, creating the first serious attempt since Aristotle to discover a political "science." One of the least known but most illustrative works of the period was *The New Science* by Giovanni Battista Vico, published in the 1740s. Also, after the Reformation, there was a return to the more theoretical approach common to the Age of Reason. This flowered in the writings of Hobbes, Locke, Rousseau, and Bodin, some of which will be examined later. Most of the books of the period focused to some extent on the best forms and structures of government for the evolving nation-states of Europe.

America's beginnings as an independent state were couched in both the practical and theoretical ideas of Jefferson, Madison, Hamilton, and others among our founding fathers. *The Federalist Papers* illustrate the state of the art at that time. These "papers" were, in reality, a series of eighty-five lengthy letters to newspapers written in 1787–88 explaining in detail the theory and operation of the new government proposed under the Constitution of 1787. The authors, James Madison, Alexander Hamilton, and John Jay, sought, thereby, to influence the voters of New York to ratify the Constitution.

About fifty years later, the formal teaching of government entered the higher classes in schools through such books as *The Political Class Book*, written in 1831 by William Sullivan, a Massachusetts attorney, for use in the high schools of that state. It bears a remarkable resemblance to modern political science texts except for its addition of moral philosophy to the now standard American style of theory and pragmatism, resulting in a generally normative approach to the subject.

This overall approach continued, from the creation of the first chair in political science, established at Columbia University in 1857, on into the late nineteenth century, when political science emerged as a distinct discipline in most centers of higher learning. Woodrow Wilson's great work, *Congressional Government* (1885), is typical of the genre of that period.

By the end of World War II, a basic change had begun to occur in what had become the traditional approach to the subject. In retrospect, the antecedents of the change appear to have included Darwin's theory of evolution; the scientific socialism of Karl Marx; and the advent, in 1904, of what geographer Sir Halford Mackinder called "geopolitics" (a combination of geographical realities and their effect on the distribution of political power). In addition, just as the advent of the twentieth century saw a greater use of empirical methods of observation, survey, and quantitative measurement in the natural sciences, so, too, were these methods being borrowed by many younger political scientists. The advent of the atomic bomb, which had elevated nuclear physicists to a position of prominence within the military, also had the effect of bringing together other natural and social scientists. For instance, one now needed to know, with some precision, the various elements that went into the achievement of nuclear deterrence, a concept based on the psychological as well as the material aspects of defense structures. Political scientists joined with mathematicians and psychologists to search for answers to new problems of national security. Their studies were influenced by ideas such as game theory, a new way of thinking about human interactions, developed in part by John von Neumann and Oskar Morgenstern.

In a parallel development of the 1940s, the writings of John Maynard Keynes had given birth to a new national economic policy wherein it was argued that governments, by manipulating such variables as taxes, spending, and the supply of money, could keep the entire economy on an even keel. The Keynesians all seemed to know something tangible and real. For instance, these new economists seemed to be able to calculate the effect of a given tax cut on jobs and economic growth with precision. Political scientists felt that they had to learn to do similar things that could be applied to political activities.

One of the most dramatic applications of this new approach to politics was a pioneering study of voting behavior in Ohio during the election of 1940. Thereafter, voting statistics became a staple form of data for certain kinds of political analysis. By the 1960s, it became possible to predict or explain elections with a high level of accuracy in most cases. Other forms of group behavior were subjected to ever greater depths of analysis as political scientists moved toward a closer working relationship with other disciplines, especially economics, geography, sociology, anthropology, psychology, biology, ecology statistics, and communication. All of this ultimately evolved into what has become known as the behavioral approach to political science.

Unlike the older traditional approach, which emphasized institutions of government, behavioralism focused on individuals and their behavior in social circumstances. It continues to see politics and governments as operational systems made up of various subsystems, which can be studied, measured, and evaluated in terms of their operational qualities. An early version of the behavioral approach might involve a study, using exit polls at election time, aimed at determining how people voted on a particular referendum such as a tax increase for public schools. The voters would then be divided by sex, age, occupation, place of residence, economic level, and number of children. Analysis of these numbers would then suggest which groups were more likely to support such tax increases. With that data, supporters of such initiatives in the future could target groups more likely to be in their favor and work to get out the vote among such groups. Thus the older search for immutable political norms was increasingly challenged by a search for a more precise understanding of present realities. The preferred method of measure and evaluation in the new era became more and more mathematical, and the evolution of the math model as a device for description and explanation of political phenomena has become quite prevalent in the literature of political science.

A comparison of the two methods of approach to political science might be seen in a consideration of neoisolationist tendencies in the American Midwest. A traditionalist might approach the problem by studying the history of the area, the ethnic origins of its inhabitants, their political values, and their voting record on issues of foreign policy. Finding that a strong isolationist tendency tends to dominate opinions of this type throughout the area, it might be concluded that these people can be expected to continue to oppose a rigorous involvement by America in foreign affairs. From there, the traditionalist might try to argue that this is a beneficial or a detrimental attitude based on a set of values that the analyst feels are relevant to contemporary foreign policy and to suggest avenues of change if such is desired.

A behavioralist approach does not differ fundamentally from any of this. Rather it seeks to go beyond the "what is" of the situation to a deeper question of "why it is," and what are the strongest elements in the "why" of it. Factors such as the Republicanism in the area, its rural character, its third-generation German-Irish stock and the distance of a particular area from the East and West coasts would be analyzed. This is called multivariate analysis. A set of data would then be constructed based on the percentage of people in each of the identified variables and the degree of distance from the sea coast compared to geographical areas with less isolationist tendencies. Then a comparison of the impact of each variable on the overall isolationist tendency might be attempted. The overall result would then focus on what factors seem to be the most important in producing the tendency. From this data, a math model (or paradigm) would be constructed and applied as a measure of predicting the degree of isolationist tendencies in other parts of the country. The model would be evaluated as to its relevance and similarity in structure (isomorphic quality) to other environments and whether it has true qualities. Thus, each approach produces knowledge that can be used in different ways.

THE TRADITIONALISTS VERSUS THE BEHAVIORALISTS

With the advent of behavioralism came controversy and confusion. Indeed, the definition of political science fell into disarray, leading one despairing observer to note as early as 1953 that the discipline has become "a device, invented by university teachers, for avoiding that dangerous subject, politics, without achieving science."[1] Certainly, as traditionalists confront behavioralists, no single definition of the subject has gained general currency. Perhaps, to the teachers anyway, what we teach is, in the words of Alfred de Grazia, "political science as I would like it to be."

Even the movement toward behavioralism is beset by problems of nomenclature. Is behavioralism, as applied to political science, any different from the scientific method in general? If so, how? Are we speaking of a mere intellectual tendency or a whole new academic movement? Are behavioralists the true social scientists, or are we all social scientists with different approaches? The student should be aware at the outset that we are dealing with a phenomenon (behavioralism) that is still evolving and about which no single definition seems to exist—only different points of view.

Traditionalists counterattacked the behavioral revolution almost from the beginning. They cited the complexity of human behavior and the near impossibility of fully explaining how political decisions are actually made. They also questioned whether total objectivity (required by empirical

---

[1]Cobban, A. 1953. "The Decline of Political Theory." *Political Science Quarterly* 48:335.

approaches) can be sustained when political scientists are attempting to measure things about which they, by virtue of their own orientation, are apt to hold strong views. In addition, the increasingly narrow focus of the behavioral approach nettled some traditionalists who were used to thinking in terms of large organizations and structured power relationships. The charge was made that behavioralists spend too much time measuring inconsequential aspects of government and that they offer no practical advice on how to govern *better*. Further, they were labeled as logical positivists, who, by definition, limit the scope of inquiry to observable behavior. The caveat was raised that "when one undertakes to quantify, one can only study that which is quantifiable."

By the late 1950s, many traditionalists had gravitated toward University of Chicago professor Leo Strauss, who had led the traditionalist counterattack from the beginning, giving the label "Straussian" to the older, institutional, and normative school of political science. Strauss objected to the moral relativism of the behavioralists, and he asserted that the fundamental purpose of the study of government remains to help people better understand government institutions and processes so as to operate them for the benefit of all and for the preservation of traditional values such as freedom. In other words, he seemed wedded to a concept of a political philosophy, which he contrasted with the political science, of the behavioralists. In his later years, this strong normative approach of Strauss gained him as many traditional critics as behavioral ones.

Especially in the area of national security, critics of the behavioralists have come to decry what they term the false appearance of precision that numbers tend to suggest, when the real variables are all too often people and their various idiosyncrasies, intertwined with complex institutional settings and unpredictable events. Indeed, to some at least, the war in Vietnam stands as a grotesque monument to certain presumptions of the math modelers; to others, certain aspects of the strategic (nuclear) arms race between the United States and the former Soviet Union illustrates the problem.

Behavioralists respond in various ways. They argue that measuring with numbers and symbols does not necessarily reduce what is measured *to* numbers and symbols. Rather, numbers and measurements enable one to view governmental phenomena in new ways and not in *substitute* ways. They assert that *all* knowledge is valuable, however derived, and note that it is far too early to evaluate fully what can be learned from the still relatively new techniques. Behavioralists note that the scientific method is accepted in other disciplines within the social sciences (especially psychology and sociology) and that some behavior is inherently amenable to measurement and quantification. They seek not only to measure and predict but mostly to explain. Further, political science, throughout its history, has lacked a unique methodology and needs one in order to advance beyond the limitations of the traditional approach, which still seems to borrow mostly from the historian and the philosopher.

The debate goes on. One side fears that the behavioralists will either reduce political science to nothing more than a mathematical exercise or, conversely, gain some new kind of arcane power with which to manipulate the minds, decisions, and actions of others. The other side fears that the methods of the traditionalists do not provide the kind of precise information needed by mass societies of infinite complexity with problems unanticipated by older assumptions. One should begin his or her study of political science with a traditional grounding in the basic concepts of the discipline and then proceed to a more behavioral approach as quickly as possible, gaining as many mathematical skills (and especially a knowledge of computer usage) as one can develop so as to achieve the highest level of contemporary knowledge one can.

RESEARCH METHODS IN POLITICAL SCIENCE

Despite the apparent, though entirely unnecessary, incompatibility between the traditionalists and behavioralists, they have managed to coexist within the confines of a single discipline that operates under the same basic research methodology in spite of one's own orientation. Thus, some mention should be made about the techniques of inquiry germane to political phenomena.

Be the approach one of historical inquiry, philosophical speculation, or empirical and quantitative research, the approach to research remains essentially the same. First, an area of study is selected and a tentative **hypothesis** (however arrived at) is stated. Then comes observation (through reading, interviews, polling, experiments, etc.), followed by gathering data (in the form of facts, numbers, ideas, etc.), and the classifying and/or organizing of it in such a way as to relate it in some meaningful way to the hypothesis. Next comes analysis and interpretation of the data. Finally, conclusions are reached (by deductive or inductive reasoning) based on the logic (verbal or mathematical) of the data, and the hypothesis is either supported, modified and re-tested or analyzed, or abandoned.

In all research dealing with social phenomena, but with political science in particular, one is beset by several stumbling blocks, whose effects, if recognized early, can be lessened if not done away with entirely. Such problems include the complexity of political events; the bias of the researcher; the difficulties of measuring such things as motivations or intents; the tendency toward oversimplification in constructing verbal or mathematical models; and, in many cases, the impossibility of realistic experimentation on which to base or test the refined hypothesis.

Finally, despite the existence of alternative approaches to the study of political science, one must keep in mind that no one has ever succeeded in constructing a general theory of politics to serve political science in the way that the theories of Sir Isaac Newton (and later, Albert Einstein) served the subject of physics. All approaches are valid as long as they take reasonable care to avoid, as much as possible, the research pitfalls mentioned previously and allow their various hypotheses to be challenged by other researchers in a spirit of humility and common interest. When these conditions are met, our storehouse of knowledge is increased.

POINTS TO PONDER

Why are you studying political science, and what utility do you see for it in your future?

In what applications would you see the greater value of the traditional approach to political science as opposed to the behavioral approach and vice versa?

In doing research in political science, which methods do you see yourself using most often? Why?

2 | Basic Concepts of Politics

POLITICAL ACTIVITY

From the beginning, human beings have usually managed to find themselves in some sort of mess in their attempts to both satisfy their wants and live in peace with their neighbors. Aristotle, an ancient Greek philosopher and educator, noted that, while men and women are by nature gregarious (they have an instinct to live with their fellows in order to be fully human), they are also by nature quarrelsome, selfish, and a bit greedy. It was in the service of this dilemma that government was born. Government's first (and still most basic) job was to balance the needs of harmony and peace with the darker side of humankind, which still tends toward disharmony and violence. For Aristotle, whose book *Politics* remains one of the most comprehensive treatments of the subject, the highest and most civilized form of government is *political government*. This form of government requires a knowledge of politics. Indeed, Aristotle felt that the science of politics is the master science on which all other aspects of civilization depend.

What does all of this mean for contemporary men and women in the latter stages of the civilized twentieth century? Let's begin by reducing our encounter with the elements of government to its simplest level. Let's imagine two young children, John and David, who are playing in a room. There is one red truck on the floor. Both want to play with it—now. Here we have gregarious humanity and its inevitable conflict with its fellows. There are three possible kinds of outcome to this (and indeed any) human conflict:

1. The children can fight about it, and to the victor go the spoils. This is not very civilized, and it has little to do with politics or government.
2. They can attempt to ignore or transcend the conflict (i.e., find something else to do). This really doesn't solve the problem, and it can produce tensions, ulcers, and other pathological side effects, but it is better than fighting.
3. They can compromise their dispute, with John getting the truck for thirty minutes, followed by David's playing with it the next thirty minutes. This is the civilized way. This is the beginning of politics.

Politics (partially defined): The peaceful resolution of human disputes through compromise.

Actually, there is much more to politics and government than this, but at least this is a good place to begin. For instance, what is a compromise? Would you say that, in the illustration, it is a 50/50 sharing of a resource, value, or desire? Actually, it wasn't a 50/50 arrangement at all. John got more than David, at least from a child's point of view. He got the truck FIRST. Therein lies an important point. A compromise (a political solution) does not have to be exactly equal for all concerned (and seldom is). It must, however, be acceptable to the major participants as an alternative to fighting or ignoring the dispute.

When John and David made the compromise, they were not only practicing politics, they were playing a game called *government*, albeit on a primitive level. Actually, the level of our illustration is too primitive, and the outcome described is unlikely, considering the nature of children. Let's back up and introduce another character into the scenario—the parent.

As the tension mounts in the playroom, it is probably accompanied by considerable noise, which attracts parental attention. Upon surveying the scene, it is he or she who probably *imposes* the compromise in order to resolve the dispute peacefully. Now we're really playing the game of government.

Government: An institution(s) whose purpose is to solve human disputes through law and enforce those solutions or laws through superior power (i.e., government is a regulator of society).

What is this stuff about law? Well, let's back up again. The parent, of course, illustrates government in our little saga. He or she imposes a compromise solution after hearing and weighing the needs and desires of the principals involved. Thus, she has ordained a solution, which emerges in the form of a decree, which is a form of law. A *law* is often nothing more than a solution to a public conflict. Actually, most contemporary laws anticipate the conflict and impose a solution before the conflict occurs.

This can be seen in an everyday occurrence. Two automobiles approach each other at perpendicular angles at an intersection. Whether the drivers realize it or not, there is a potential conflict inherent in the situation. Which one will clear the intersection first? As in any human conflict, as we have observed, there are three possible outcomes. Both drivers can accelerate and try to push the other out of the way (fight); each can transcend the issue by turning around and proceeding by another route (ignore the dispute); or the two can stop, get out of their cars, and negotiate the dispute (compromise). That is, however, a ridiculous way to compromise such a conflict, especially one that is apt to recur many times.

Fortunately, government has already compromised this recurring dispute for drivers by anticipating the whole affair and resolving it in advance. It has instituted a law that places a stoplight at the intersection, letting drivers know who "wins" and who "loses" the conflict. The law is a kind of compromise in that the loser has a chance to win next time, and he or she still gets a feeling of safety even when losing. (We'll explore the concept of law further in chapter 6.)

Returning to our earlier illustration involving the two boys and the red truck, we note that the parent (government) has the power to enforce his or her decision (law). Thus, because of that power, he or she fulfills the criteria for government in our definition. Taking this a step further, if John and David's wishes are heard by their parent, and if the decision is made in such a way as to conciliate them as much as possible, then the compromise is met in the spirit of *politics*. It need not be, however.

Suppose that the parent likes John more than he or she likes David. Indeed, suppose that the parent really can't stand David at all! When he or she seeks to resolve the dispute, the parent might ignore David altogether and give John the truck while banishing David from the room. Now where are we? Well, for one thing, the criteria for our definition of government have still been met. The dispute has been resolved peacefully by an enforced decree. But you might protest, "It wasn't fair." You might more accurately have said, "It wasn't political." You would be right. Government need not be conciliatory or political. It is just that we have come to identify *good government* as political in nature and to demand some sort of compromise in it. Many governments are not political, and most of them seem to work to some extent.

The task for the more civilized among us has always been to make government political. The alternative is to have government that solves public issues in ways that do not measure up to what we instinctively describe as acceptable compromises. Government may successfully emanate from a king, a dictator, an oligarchy, a priest, or a totalitarian party, all of whom dictate the outcomes of conflict (laws) through conformity to a variety of idiosyncratic motivations. We call these governments *authoritarian.* What these diverse governments share is that none of them are apt to pay much attention to transitory public opinion concerning the issues involved. Their laws simply anticipate possible disorders or describe acceptable conduct (acceptable to the government, that is). The laws are still laws, and the governments govern. Peace and order are kept. Society is regulated. The way these and other governments enforce their laws is through power that must be superior to any other power within the society.

POWER

Power is an often misunderstood concept. It may be defined as follows:

Power: The capacity to cause a thing to happen that would not happen without that capacity.

To put it another way, power is the ability to make people do something they really do not want to do such as obeying laws (stopping at stop signs, paying taxes, keeping off the grass, etc.). What is this capacity? For our purposes, there are at least three kinds of power. This can be seen by another illustration.

Joe and Pete are standing in the middle of a field on a hot day. Joe has a shovel, and he wants Pete to dig a ditch across the field. Pete does not care to do it. How does Joe get Pete to dig the ditch (i.e., how can he exercise power over Pete)? Three answers suggest themselves, revealing three types of power:

1. Joe can threaten Pete with bodily harm if he does not get to work. This is *military power* or force. Actually, in this and most cases, this is not a very reliable kind of power because Joe ultimately must give the shovel to Pete, who might bash Joe over the head with it and walk off. The result can be that, by attempting to apply military power, Joe winds up without achieving his goal and, indeed, he is worse off than when he started—a sore head and no ditch. (This warning transcends the immediate purpose of our story.)

2. Joe can offer Pete $100 to dig the ditch. Pete still does not want to dig the ditch, but he wants the money more than he does not want to work. The money gives Joe·*economic power* over Pete. This is a more reliable kind of power. There are reciprocal advantages here. Joe gets the ditch dug, while Pete gets richer. However, economic power still has disadvantages. While it is more reliable than military power, it is elastic. One never knows how much is adequate for one's purposes or how far it will "stretch." For instance, Pete might get halfway across the field and decide that the work is too hard for $100 and demand $200 to continue. If Joe has no more money, he has lost his power over Pete. We see myriad examples of this every day in labor disputes wherein workers go on strike for more pay. Economic power is not the ultimate answer either.

3. Joe can say to Pete: "You're looking sickly today. If you dig this ditch I have proposed, you will regain your health and be better off. Also, the purpose of the ditch is to drain a mosquito-infested swamp near town, and the townspeople will admire you for your public service." Pete doesn't want to dig the ditch, but now he sees a reason to do so, and, being convinced of the desirability of doing the undesirable, he proceeds with enthusiasm to dig the ditch. What has happened? Joe has used a more subtle and effective type of power—*psychological power*. The motivation is intangible but keenly felt within the psyche of the person on whom the power is being used. The results are often extraordinary.

Governments, too, have available to them all three types of power. Citizens can be jailed, tortured, or killed by police; citizens can be bribed by social programs or bread and circuses; they can be fined for nonobedience; or people can be induced by some psychological bond between them and their governments to obey laws because they have become convinced that it is good to do so. Which approach makes the most sense? The last one, of course. If psychology fails, there are always the other two methods to fall back on, but *most governments depend, most of the time, on psychological power.* This includes authoritarian regimes as well as political governments.

LEGITIMACY AND AUTHORITY

How does one achieve psychological power over people? To put it another way, what will be the basis of the psychological bond between the government and the people? Here we confront two new concepts: *legitimacy* and *authority.*

> **Legitimacy:** The popular perception of a justifiable and acceptable use of public power.
> **Authority:** The right to use public power deemed to be legitimate.

To establish the critical psychological bond between a government and its people on which a willing obedience to law depends, that government must be considered legitimate by its citizens. Why should they perceive it so? On what is this legitimacy based? Why is the use of power deemed just and acceptable? In order to achieve legitimacy, a government must have a reason for claiming it. History reveals many such reasons:

Religion: When Samuel, the priest of God, anointed King Saul as the first king of ancient Israel, Saul claimed to exercise his power as an agent of God. To believe in God was to accept Saul as God's legitimate agent on earth. To obey Saul was to obey God. That gave Saul his authority to rule. He thus used the religion of the Hebrew people to justify his use of temporal power. To this day, most divine right monarchs have achieved legitimacy in this manner. This is true of the government of Iran.

Wisdom: In Plato's *Republic,* we have a hypothetical example of a government by "Philosopher Kings," whose use of power is legitimized by virtue of their long education and training for government. In more primitive societies, an old sage can gain authority by virtue of the tribe's perception of the sage's wisdom.

Force: Hitler, Attila the Hun, Genghis Khan, and other conquerors ruled through the stark rationale of power. There was no one with superior power to challenge them. They achieved obedience primarily through military power, but, in a sense, the day-to-day psychological legitimacy of their rule rested on the sheer power of force, their proven willingness to use it, and the sense of fear that it induced. The same has been true of many modern dictators although authority derived through fear may be short lived if the dictator is ever perceived as weak.

Bloodline: With European royalty, after the beginning of the feudal period, kings and queens were obeyed and bonded to their subjects by virtue of being the sons or daughters of royal persons. The bloodline thus gave legitimacy to the use of power. This has been true of other societies as well.

Ideology: This is a form of legitimacy through wisdom, but it is a special case in the modern world. Nations such as China and North Korea have seen government leaders claim legitimacy on the basis of their ability to understand and carry out the programs and tenets of communism. The effectiveness of this claim may be doubted when one considers the number of occasions such governments resort to force. Indeed, when ideology is used to legitimize a totalitarian regime, it does not automatically follow that the society is in absolute agreement with those who define the ideology. The society might be governed simply because the people are apathetic or confused.

What is the source of legitimacy in the western world? More especially, what is the source in our own country? From whence does our government gain authority? How are we led into a psychological oneness with our government that leads us to support its laws and institutions? Neither religion, wisdom, force, bloodlines, nor ideology seem to be the central cause. The answer is both subtle and profound. It is also terribly important in terms of the future of our type of government. In a sense, the source of our government's legitimacy is *politics.* We obey our laws, follow our leaders, and support our institutions because all of these things are the result of a process that involves *us,* however indirectly. We obey because we are participants in a kind of government called political democracy (about which I shall say a great deal in the following sections). The key to the successful achievement of this legitimacy (as well as to the creation of any of the legitimacies already noted) is found in a process called **socialization.** This process involves the creation of a public value system within the society, which, in turn, creates and supports the psychological bond that gives most governments their authority and thus makes them work.

POLITICAL CULTURE AND SOCIALIZATION

Every society has a common culture that includes some judgment about its form of government. This culture is derived from a common knowledge of the governing system and the set of values and assumptions that underscores it. These values and assumptions, in turn, are rooted in the society's history, traditions, ideological outlook, and self-image. We are literally born into a society, therefore, we are also born into such a cultural system.

A part of a society's common value system is called (incorrectly in most cases) its *political ethos,* although all such public ethics are not political in their makeup. A better term might be *public ethos.* This consists of the society's public attitudes, moral code, and customary habits. The public ethos of a society produces a behavior pattern that is supposed to be repeated by most members of that society in a fairly regular manner. It is this regularity of public behavior that government wishes to establish in conjunction with the establishment of its legitimacy, thus producing the prerequisite psychological bonds on which its authority is based.

What government wishes to accomplish by way of a public governmental culture and ethos can be seen in the following illustration. You are in an automobile, hurrying to arrive at your destination. Before you looms a stop sign. No one is around, and there doesn't seem to be anyone coming from any adjacent direction. Why do you stop (if you do)? Since there is no immediate sense of danger, it must be something else that makes you stop. Is it fear of being shot by the police (military power)? Probably not; they aren't around, anyway. Is it fear of a fine (economic power)? Again, arrest seems doubtful. In most cases it is probably a subconscious reaction to a deeply planted value within your psyche. You stop because you know that you are supposed to stop. The question now is, why and how did you know that?

This is where socialization comes in. Somehow you have been carefully taught that it is a good thing to stop at stop signs. Even if you are, at that moment, unpersuaded, and you continue moving through the stop sign, chances are that you were taught sufficiently for you to feel a tiny twinge of guilt about your disregard of the norm. This feeling is a result of being socialized into a repetitive pattern of behavior at some point during your life.

Socialization is achieved by many methods in various societies. It is achieved by interactions with family, neighbors, teachers, and other public groups during the earliest years of one's existence. It is reinforced by peer values, media exposure, experiences, and public events (such as patriotic observances) as one grows older. In more advanced societies, many of the better efforts are made through what passes for public education. This can, in totalitarian societies, be little more than collective brainwashing by propaganda. In such systems, a distinction is understood to exist between public education, which is for the purpose of socialization, and training, which is designed for a career of service to the state.

In societies like our own, we see something of the same phenomenon. Public education devotes a lot of time to teaching civics, or the responsibilities of citizenship, through direct and indirect methods. We are taught that our government is of the best kind, that our founding fathers were almost god-like, that our economic system is the most rational and successful, that our laws are just, and that our history is one of unblemished excellence. Of course, we are supposed to learn other things as well, but the government is probably getting its money's worth if we are at least socialized to its norms. If, somehow, we happen to become truly educated as well, then that's nice too.

This is not meant to be a cynical observation. The principle involved is one of complete pragmatism. We will outgrow a lot of the simplicities of our early school years through further education and our real-life experiences. It is assumed that, in our more mature years, the shock of reality will not radicalize us too much, and it usually doesn't. The point is to plant the seeds of the psychological bond early in our lives and to provide at least an opportunity for education to occur within the confines of a compulsory school system.

In the U.S. Supreme Court case of *Wisconsin* v. *Yoder*, in 1972, which concerned the issue of religious rights versus compulsory education, the government's case contained the argument that public education through the eighth grade was provided and required for the purpose of: (1) the preservation of the political system, (2) economic survival, and (3) the socialization of young people. Here, at least, was an unabashed recognition of the value of the public schools for achieving public socialization first and foremost.

Other countries do this in both similar and dissimilar methods. Thus is our assimilation into the body politic achieved (to the extent that it is). In societies seeking political democracy, the process of socialization and the propagation of public values stress the ideas and principles of politics. The hope is that the instinct for politics will not only bind the people to the government but also show them how government should be carried out. We will now examine the principles we are supposed to learn. (It might be useful for the reader to proceed to "A Warning for Americans" found at the end of the section entitled Political Democracy in chapter 7.)

POLITICS

I am indebted to a British political scientist, Bernard Crick, for the ideas in this section.[1] Politics arises from accepting the fact of the simultaneous existence of different groups of people, with different interests and traditions, all within the same society. This condition is deemed to be more desirable than life in a monistic system dominated by single orthodoxies and lifestyles.

Within the diversity of political society, questions and conflicts arise that are of concern to many individuals. These call for public resolutions to determine who gets what, when, and how. In a political society, men and women are free to respond to these questions and conflicts. *Political governments grant legal status to all relevant viewpoints and spokespersons.* There is a feeling of security on the part of the various advocates, who fear no reprisal because of their opinions.

Furthermore, *a political society provides a means of articulation—a forum for expressing ideas:* a free press, freedom of speech, a parliamentary body, and so on. Whether the viewpoints are being expressed directly, or indirectly through representative spokespersons, *the purpose of government is to listen to as many ideas as is practical* and then *to deliberately conciliate as many factions as possible.* This conciliation takes the form of compromises on public questions.

[1]Crick, B. 1962. *In Defense of Politics.* London: Weidenfeld and Nicolson.

No single view prevails; most participants get some satisfaction. There is an emphasis on plural interests as opposed to single truths. In cases where an either/or situation exists and no compromise is possible, as in elections, *the decisions of government in a political society at least have the saving grace of being temporary.* Indeed, all political outcomes are temporary. Issues may be reconsidered at any time. Nothing is forever closed. These five principles (italicized) lie at the core of the concept of politics.

Politics, then, is the public actions of free men and women intent on being heard and involved in public questions. Political governments open themselves to all relevant opinions and seek conciliatory compromises, which emerge as temporary laws or decisions. Politics is an activity—a means to an end. It can take place in simple or complex structures. It is a normal human process. It is civilized humanity in the fullness of its public being.

POLITICAL AND EGALITARIAN DEMOCRACY

To some, the previous discussion may sound something like **democracy,** a word hitherto undefined. This is a difficult term to apply because it is so widely misunderstood and misused. Indeed, I will devote a major section to that murky subject later on. For the present, let's acknowledge that there *is* a relationship between politics and democracy. This relationship can be illustrated by figure 2.1.

Several things are evident from figure 2.1. Politics may occur outside of democratic governmental organizations altogether (in churches, schools, etc.). Compromise, conciliation, and temporary outcomes are possible within these frameworks, as well as within the governments of states.

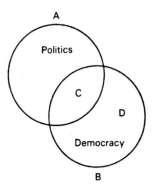

Circle A encompasses the world of politics.
Circle B encompasses democracy.
Area C is the world of political democracy.
Area D is the world of egalitarian democracy.

FIGURE 2.1   The Relationship Between Politics and Democracy

Furthermore, there are two approaches to democracy, the political and the egalitarian. Westerners are often taken aback by the sincere insistence of the North Koreans or the mainland Chinese that they are democratic societies. They are in the egalitarian sense, which is to say that their governments assert the absolute equality of all persons within their societies. Let's compare the two forms of democracy.[2]

We can say at the outset that **egalitarian** democracy, as practiced by the People's Republic of China, and North Korea to some extent, differs from the more familiar political democracy, which we are used to, in four particulars:

1. In an egalitarian democracy, government is for the people. In a political democracy, government is of, for, and by the people.
2. In an egalitarian democracy, there is an enforced standard of equality. In a political democracy, there is an equal opportunity to achieve any standard.
3. In an egalitarian democracy, the emphasis is on output. In a political democracy, the emphasis is on input.
4. In an egalitarian democracy, participation is enforced. In a political democracy, participation is encouraged but optional.

FOR THE PEOPLE

Egalitarian democracy is the kind of government that is *for* the people. It envisions its role as serving the vast majority of the people within the national boundaries. It proposes to meet the needs of its people as it sees those needs.

In contrast, political democracy, using the words of Abraham Lincoln, is not only *for* the people but *by* and *of* the people. The difference is found in the way the needs of the people are perceived. In a political democracy, the people perceive their own needs and create and/or order their government and control its response to those needs. Thus, political democracy is *by* the people who perceive their own needs. It arises from or *of* the people through elected representatives and, thus, translates their perceptions into actions. Like egalitarian democracy, political democracy is also *for* the people, but it is much more a product of the people than the government of an egalitarian state.

APPROACHES TO EQUALITY

A second difference is found in the concept of equality. Egalitarian democracy takes its name from the word *equal,* and indeed there is, within an egalitarian democracy, an enforced standard of equality. Again, the government

[2]Some people may have difficulty with the term *democracy* as applied to egalitarian/totalitarian states. However, one must attempt to deal somehow with the claims of communist parties, groups, and governments to be "people's republics" or "democratic movements." Just calling them liars does not seem to be an adequate response.

defines the standard of equality. This standard is generally manifested in the material realm in terms of equal housing, equal wages, equal food and clothing, equal living conditions, and sometimes equal education. Whatever standards the government of an egalitarian democracy sets are enforced upon the people in such a way as to create a kind of uniformity in the society.

In a political democracy, equality is manifested somewhat differently. There is an *opportunity* to achieve any standard of material, educational, social, or spiritual life. What is equal is the opportunity. In a political democracy, unnecessary barriers such as religion, race, or economic position should be reduced to the extent that any person can compete equally with any other person in achieving whatever level of material comfort or social achievement that person wishes to accomplish. Society in a political democracy shows no favoritism when it comes to allowing individuals to seek their own goals. The emphasis is on equal opportunity, and differences of outcome are accepted.

INPUT VERSUS OUTPUT

A third difference between the two forms of democracy is seen in what we might call the input-output concept of government.[3] As seen in figure 2.2, we may consider government to be a large box into which flows certain inputs: ideas of various people, resources, money, labor, and so forth, and the power to cause things to happen. The outputs (what comes out of the box) take the form of laws, other kinds of decisions, and material or public institutions (hospitals, agencies). The connection between the input and output sides of the box is called *feedback*. Feedback is the response to the output by the public or by officials responsible for reviewing the performance of government. The third difference is that, in an egalitarian democracy, the emphasis is on what comes out—the laws, policy decisions, and particularly the material institutions (hospitals, schools, highways, a government monopoly that makes clothing, or a collective farm that grows food). These outputs must be made equal insofar as possible for all people. The concentration by government officials in such a government is on some abstract decision as to what the citizen's equal portion of these outputs should be.

In a political democracy, the concentration is on the input. As we have seen before, politics should represent as many ideas as possible. The resources of the nation should also be considered in terms of who owns them. The power input is generated through a majority decision of those people with ideas or control over the resources. People in a political democracy concentrate, then, on an opportunity for a proper input into the process

[3]The input-output concept was pioneered by David Easton in his article entitled "An Approach to the Analysis of Political Systems" in the April 1957, edition of *World Politics*, volume 9 and in his numerous books and articles since that time. It has become a standard approach to a systems analysis of government.

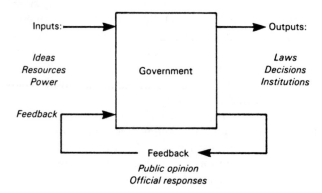

FIGURE 2.2   An Input-Output Concept of Government

of government. If the input is properly determined, then there is no need to worry so much about the output—the laws, the policy decisions, the material, and the public institutions. These things are unpredictable because the precise nature of compromises reached by the government cannot be anticipated. One can only be confident, if the theory is properly observed, that the government will provide acceptable compromises of ideas, resources, and power and that these will result in laws, institutions, and decisions that are temporary and, therefore, changeable.

A corollary to this third difference involves feedback. In an egalitarian democracy, feedback is often merely official response to the output situation. That is to say, though the public may have an opinion with regard to the output, the public's opinion is only fed into the governmental process through officials who choose whether or not to take note of public response, and often they do not choose to take such notice. On the other hand, in a political democracy the feedback is very often strongly motivated by public opinion, and that public opinion becomes a portion of the new ideas that become new inputs, which result in new decisions. This makes political democracy more flexible and more susceptible to public response.

PARTICIPATION

A fourth difference between the two forms of democracy may be found in the area of participation. In an egalitarian democracy, participation by citizens is not only encouraged, it is enforced. Strong pressures may be placed upon the public to vote in elections that have a dubious relationship to free choice because the candidates represent only the views of the government. Furthermore, mass demonstrations of support for the government are also enforced to the extent that, for example, participation in a mass demonstration for a new leadership group in the People's Republic of China, becomes necessary if one wishes to maintain his or her position within the society.

On the other hand, in a political democracy, participation is encouraged, but it is optional. No one has to vote. No one has to celebrate a national holiday or participate in any other manner concerning the way the government is run. Again, the emphasis is on opportunity. There is an opportunity to participate. There is an opportunity to demonstrate. There is no obligation for a uniform or mass response to government, which is so characteristic of egalitarian democracies. One can even opt out altogether by freely leaving the country and going to live elsewhere.

THE TIME OF SOVEREIGNTY

Having defined, however briefly, the elements of government, (power, authority, legitimacy, and politics) and having seen the differences between political and egalitarian forms of democracy, we are still left with one final question as to the nature of politics. That question arises very often in the form of a commonsense inquiry into the future of a political form of democracy when it is beset by certain challenges that do not seem to be manageable within the context of a system of deliberate decision making, conciliation, temperance, and thought. In other words, does the theory of political democracy lead to an institution of government that will ultimately disintegrate? This would happen if there were an internal and general breakdown of consensus on important issues or if the state were faced by a sudden peril from without that required some form of instant response. In answering, the theory of political democracy anticipates such a situation.

Again in reference to the writing of Bernard Crick, there is a special time that comes to most political democracies, with varying frequency. This time may be defined as a time of sovereignty. The concept of sovereignty (which is the absolute, indivisible, and complete power of the government of a nation-state over the people of that state) will be discussed at length in chapter 3. Suffice it to say that we are dealing with the kind of power necessary to rule in a crisis. The theory of the time of sovereignty is that, when civil breakdown or an outside emergency or threat arises in *genuine* form (and here one must be careful to note that the threat must be unmistakable), then certain extraordinary actions may be allowed, and even be required, by the government of a political democracy. What distinguishes a political democracy from some other form of government at such a time is not so much the actions taken but the *way* in which they are taken.

Perhaps the best way to illustrate a time of sovereignty would be to repeat the legend told of the early days of the Roman Republic, when that government was still attempting an early experiment in political democracy. In that case, there was a military threat to Rome by the Aequi and the Volsei. The Roman Senate, which was the popularly accepted institution of government, could not decide on the issue of whether to go outside the gates of Rome with an army and meet the enemy head-on or to fight a defensive battle within the walls of Rome. No answer was forthcoming from the normal process of government or from the consuls who were the titular leaders. Therefore, in some exasperation, the leaders of the Senate went out into the fields south of Rome and met with a retired general of the Roman army, whose name was Cincinnatus. They asked Cincinnatus to do an extraordinary thing. They asked him to come to Rome and become a dictator. The Senate would obey whatever commands he gave, and he alone would lead Rome during the crisis. Roman law allowed for this possibility.

In the story, Cincinnatus was ploughing his field when the delegation approached, and, having heard the request, he left his plough where it was and went to the city of Rome. He took over the reigns of government; he sent out scouts to determine the nature and makeup of the enemy; he made the decision to go out of the city of Rome to fight; he organized the army; he organized the internal situation within the city; and he proceeded to take on the enemy. Cincinnatus was victorious and returned to Rome in triumph. A grateful Senate and population placed a wreath upon his head and decided that henceforth he would remain dictator of Rome. However, Cincinnatus was a wise man. He took off the wreath, rejected the power, and reminded the Senate that they had asked him only to respond to the crisis. The crisis (which had lasted sixteen days) was now over; it was time to return to more normal circumstances. Cincinnatus then left the Senate and Rome, went back to his farm, and, as the story goes, picked up the plough where he had left it and continued ploughing.

In this simple story are the elements of a time of sovereignty. In a civil war such as we experienced in the mid-nineteenth century, or in the world war of the 1940s, leaders of political democracies such as Abraham Lincoln, Winston Churchill, and Franklin Roosevelt took upon themselves extraordinary powers and issued extraordinary orders to populations whose instinct for inputs and discussion was abandoned for the moment. At the end of these emergencies, the instinct for political democracy returned, and the people picked up the concepts and practices of political democracy and put them back into operation as they were before the crisis arose. This is the answer to those who say political democracy is weak because it cannot face a challenge.

The prerequisites of the time of sovereignty are twofold. First, the emergency or civil breakdown must be clearly apparent to the vast majority of the citizens. If it is not, then the seizure of power, generally by the executive part of the government, will not be supported. President Richard Nixon perceived a crisis in the United States in the early 1970s with regard to civil disturbances related to the Vietnam War and the civil rights movement. The public failed to share Nixon's perception, and his attempts to use extraordinary power were rejected by the Congress, which moved to impeach him. Having thus lost his legitimacy, he resigned the presidency before he was impeached.

On the other hand, although there was great criticism of Lincoln's excessive use of power during the Civil War, and some criticism of both Winston Churchill and Franklin Roosevelt during World War II, these criticisms reflected a distinct minority. In the cases of Lincoln and Roosevelt, both died before having an opportunity to voluntarily relinquish their powers. There is general agreement that in all likelihood they would have done so. In the case of Winston Churchill, as soon as the crisis was over, insofar as Great Britain was concerned, his national government was voted out of office. These particular events illustrate the second prerequisite of the time of sovereignty, namely that the leaders who use extraordinary powers during a time of sovereignty must be prepared, as was Cincinnatus, to relinquish those powers and return government to the people as soon as the crisis has apparently passed.

OTHER DEFINITIONS OF POLITICS

This book argues that politics is essentially an activity that leads in some way to deliberate conciliation of differing viewpoints in the quest for nonviolent resolutions of human conflict and that this view of politics is sometimes confused with other uses of the word *politics*. The issue is sometimes raised that such a definition ignores power politics and political violence. Further, some may find my definition of politics to be normative and narrow. However, one of the basic purposes in writing this book has been to restate the traditional principles of politics and government in modern and relevant terms and to distinguish those things that are truly political from those that are merely governmental.

This *is* a normative judgment, but it is an ancient one as well. Aristotle's solution to the search for good government, found in his book *The Nicomachean Ethics*, is to recognize the claims of the many and the homogenization of those claims into public policy, or "distributive justice," as he puts it. To Aristotle, the whole point of politics is not so much how to rule as it is how to rule well. The thrust of his argument is that good laws can help make good people and that good government makes good laws only through politics. This is not a bad place to *begin* the study of political science.

With regard to politics as power or the politics of violence, let Bernard Crick speak to the point: "Why call a struggle for power 'politics' when it is simply a struggle for power [wherein] . . . the contestants will regard *any* compromise as a mere tactic of breathing-space on the way to the complete victory of one faction and the suppression of the other." Consider Fidel Castro's remark to a reporter in 1961: "We are not politicians. We made our revolution in order to get the politicians out. We are social people. This is a social revolution."[4] In this recognition, he was a better political scientist than some who claim the title, as it is a generally held position that "power politics is pseudopolitics."

[4]Crick, B. 1962. *In Defense of Politics*. London: Weidenfeld and Nicholson, p. 16.

It is necessary, because of the normative character of this book, to remind the reader that the word *politics* also means other things to other people. Although the understanding of these other definitions is necessary if one is to relate to the other authors and teachers in the field of political science, they sometimes tend to emphasize attitudes and values that are at odds with the central thesis of this work.

One of the most basic problems with the word *politics* stems from its coupling with the word *science*, giving us the modern concept of political science. This has had an increasing tendency to detract from the human element—the art—of politics and to emphasize instead the methodological aspect of the governing process. The serendipitous political "art of the possible" and ethical compromise becomes instead the hard science of the expedient and the material; politics becomes **realpolitik.** One who emphasizes the behavioral approach too much often abandons the complexities of the political process and its proper concerns with practical and humane problem solving and confines oneself instead to the world of government, while insisting that the two are the same. Government can be political, as we have seen, but, if it is not, it is still government if it contains a monopoly of power over a society and effectively enforces its mandate to rule that society under some claim to legitimacy.

Political science is becoming more scientific every day. Knowledge of the governing process is increasingly based on observation and experience. More and more, it produces hypotheses that become quantitatively verifiable and applicable to real-life situations. Furthermore, as seen in chapter 1, predictions and explanations are made, which, within limits, are then seen to be sufficiently accurate for application. (Predicting election returns is the best-known version of this phenomenon, but application of the predictive and explanatory aspects of the discipline are prevalent in a variety of settings.) One may still ask if this new science has any necessary relationship to politics, or is it mostly about government or even broader social phenomena such as the determination of public tastes?

Politics, like beauty, apparently exists mostly in the eye of the beholder. Thus, the concept seems to have meant various things to various people at different times. Some have said it is essentially a process designed to allocate things desired by people (as in Harold D. Lasswell's famous definition, "who gets what, when and how"[5] or in David Easton's statement that "politics is the authoritative allocation of values"[6]). Others seem to relate politics to a selfish struggle for personal gain at the expense of others or of society as a whole. Thus, when a seemingly undeserving person is placed in a position of power and prestige primarily through the successful manipulation of some structural system, we say, "Well, that's politics!"

---

[5]Lasswell, H. D. 1936. *Politics: Who Gets What, When and How.* New York: McGraw-Hill.

[6]Easton, D. 1965. *A Framework for Modern Political Analysis.* Englewood Cliffs, N.J.: Prentice-Hall, p. 57.

Is it? Here the mistake seems to be one of confusing the structure (government) with the process and of accepting *any* outcome of government as political with no regard for the purpose served by the outcome nor for the precise way in which it was achieved.

Politics is also seen as simply the process of making governmental policies. This is true only if the process is one of conciliation in an open environment. Governments can make policies by means other than political ones.

Of course, in political government, as in any other kind of government, decisions *are* made (and they are binding). It is for this reason that the word *politics* is also applied to those who make such decisions—the *politicians*. It is important to understand clearly two things. First, not all governmental decisions are made by politicians. In fact, most are made by such public officials as civil servants, bureaucrats, judges, administrators, and the police, and through such people we are governed for good or ill. Second, when public decisions *are* made by politicians, they are made by persons (usually in the legislative or executive organs of the government) who generally place the goals of conciliation and openness on a high level (along with self-interest, to be sure). Far from being a label of disapprobation, the term *politician* should connote a person of high social responsibility and enormous utility in a pluralistic society that desperately needs him or her to work out the compromises of good government necessary to help keep a humane peace in the society. It is a measure of our public misunderstanding of the concept of politics that we don't see politicians this way, nor honor them for it when we do.

Finally, the basic reason for limiting the approach to politics in this book is that seeing politics in its essential form enables one to understand where it begins. To do so is to suggest where it should go. One needs not only to understand the prerequisites of political democracy, but also to understand what political democracy is for. Otherwise, it may perish, either from an excess of method over substance or by an excess of cynicism about its utility in a complex world (or both).

These, then, are the basic concepts of government that relate to the broader concept of politics. They are as interrelated as they are important. To approach government purely through the concept of power is to miss the point of government. To divorce law from legitimacy is to have no law at all. To ignore authority in the process of socialization would dilute that process to meaninglessness. To attempt to encompass all of these concepts by the label *democracy* is to say almost nothing. A clear understanding of the precise meaning of these concepts and of how they fit together is necessary for the fullest understanding of government.

The greatest concept of all is politics. It is the quest of rational men and women who aspire to govern well. To hear, to conciliate, and to govern in a spirit of change, rejecting finality as a goal, is to govern in the interests of civilized people everywhere. Politics is the measure that will be applied to a variety of governments in the pages to follow.

POINTS TO PONDER

Why does the government of China have so much trouble establishing its legitimacy in Tibet?

On what does the current government of Russia base its legitimacy? Do you think that it is sustainable?

Can you foresee any set of circumstances in the United States that could lead to a "time of sovereignty"?

Civics is taught in most Western European schools as a requirement for a high school diploma. Religion, on the other hand, is seldom mentioned. What does that suggest about differences in the process of socialization between Europe and the United States?

Many contemporary American politicians seem to want to divide people into single issue groups and then coalesce as many of those groups as possible into an electoral majority. How does this square with the author's definition of politics?

3 | The State

We have now begun to understand the basic concepts of politics, power, and government. Although politics, power, and even government may exist outside of the context of what is called the **state,** people generally associate these phenomena with the state. What is the state, and where does it come from? Most people have a general understanding of the state in terms of a relatively well-defined piece of territory inhabited by a group of people who have been traditionally associated with that territory. These people have been governed by some institution to which they ascribe varying degrees of loyalty, and they recognize to some extent its authority over them. Thus, we have the three basic ingredients of the state: (1) a roughly bounded *territory,* (2) a unified *population,* and (3) a *government* that extends its power over most of the people in most areas of the territory.

THE ORIGINS OF THE STATE

Having said this, we are still left with the question of the origin of the state. This subject has occupied the time of a great number of political scientists and others. There are several theories concerning the origin of the state. Most of these theories in some way show the theorist's understanding of the nature of the state and the kind of state he or she would like to see.

THE DIVINE THEORY

Perhaps the oldest theory of the origin of the state is the *divine theory.* In short, this theory states that God created the state and that He had a reason for doing so. The early Hebrews subscribed to the theory that God created their state in order that the Hebrew nation might fulfill God's will. This same concept of the religious origin of the state carried over into the Christian religion as manifested by such writers as St. Augustine, who declared that obedience to the state even when ruled by unjust men and women is a divine remedy for sin, in that God created the state as a chastisement for original sin. Thus, salvation was attainable only by obedience to the state during one's time on earth. Thomas Paine observed in his famous 1776 pamphlet *Common Sense* that "government like dress is the badge of lost innocence," reflecting again the idea that God created the state so that men and women might be controlled in the context of their original, sinful nature.

In the medieval period, the divine theory gave way to the concept of divine right rule, which is to say that, if God created the state, God also created the government and decided who should govern. God generally chose kings or queens, because monarchy was most like God's authority in heaven. People obeyed the monarchy not simply because of the authority of the bloodline but also because God had placed him or her on the throne. The divine theory has appeared in many forms, not only in the ancient Jewish state and in the feudal state of the medieval period but also in such theocratic states as old Tibet under the leadership of the Dalai Lama, present-day Iran under Islamic religious leaders, and perhaps to some extent in other countries of the Middle East. This theory, however, does not advance the cause of political democracy. Instead, it suppresses the impulse, so we will move on to another theory of the origin of the state.

THE CHARISMATIC THEORY

A second theory, almost as popular as the divine theory, is the *charismatic theory*. According to this theory, the state comes about by virtue of a superior being or group of beings who enforce their will over other people. These strong-willed people decide to create an institution for their own purposes, and they bind the people together through force (either physical or psychological). The leaders define the territory, sometimes through war, and create a mystique around the government. The government's authority is derived from that mystique. Charlemagne (742–814) and his Frankish state is an ancient example. Adolf Hitler is perhaps the most dramatic modern manifestation of a charismatic theory statist. He, in fact, defined not only himself but a whole race of Aryan peoples as inherently superior to the rest of humankind. As such, they had a license through their own force, either through war or through other forms of coercion, to create a new superstate that would encompass the bulk of Europe and would last for a thousand years.

There are other illustrations of charismatic leaders and the states they have created. Generally, these are people that history finds rather unattractive, people such as Genghis Khan, Attila the Hun, or perhaps Napoleon Bonaparte. There is, however, a simplicity to the concept of the charismatic theory that seems to suggest not only how certain empires came about in history but also that these states are rather temporary, depending mainly on the success of the individual group who created it. We must go beyond the charismatic theory of the state in order to have some idea of where *our* concept of the state arises.

THE NATURAL THEORY

Aristotle suggested a rather benign theory, which is called the *natural theory.* The natural theory is perhaps the simplest of all. Aristotle suggested that the state is nothing more than a stage in the evolution of human society. First came men and women, then came the horde, next came the family, then the tribe, and ultimately the state as a natural evolutionary order in the context of a linear progression of knowledge including organization, war, and other talents such as the building of great structures and the further development of culture. Again, we are left somewhat unsatisfied in coming to grips with the nature of the types of states that we see today. The divine theory, the charismatic theory, and the natural theory all seem to suggest that the state is the result of some human action or reaction, but that is about all.

THE SOCIAL CONTRACT THEORY

Having said all this, what about the United States of America? What about Great Britain? What about most of the states that we know? Did God will them? Did some super individual or group create them? Did they simply evolve for natural reasons of their own? None of this seems satisfactory.

There is another theory of the state that is more helpful. It is somewhat complex because there are at least three different versions of it. It is called the *social contract theory.* A **social contract** is an agreement among people that creates a state and its government. The three versions are those of Thomas Hobbes (1588–1679), John Locke (1632–1704), and Jean-Jacques Rousseau (1712–78). Each proceeded in different directions to explain how the state came to be though they suggested the same dynamic of contractural origins. The result of each person's speculations yields a different philosophy of what the state should be.

According to Hobbes

Let's begin with the first of these versions in order to establish the common ingredients of all three. Thomas Hobbes was a British philosopher who sought both to justify the claim to absolute rule of King Charles I of Great Britain and to describe the nature of monarchy. He attempted to do this at a time when the British people (at least the upper classes) were leaning toward a more limited government with some degree of representation. Hobbes began his theory with the assertion that in early days people lived in a primitive society that he called "the state of nature." He defined the state of nature in very dreary terms. It was a time and place where everyone was at war with everyone else. Greed and violence so undermined the hope for stability that people fell into a state of despair. Life, said Thomas Hobbes in his book *The Leviathan* (1651), was "nasty, brutish and short." There was no relief within the state of nature from the actions of evil people.

Certain more rational individuals sensing the hopelessness of the situation came together at some unknown time and decided to do something. They made a contract in which one individual was selected to rule over the rest. The contract was rather one-way. The people would agree to obey the ruler in all cases. The ruler, in turn, owed the people only the requirement to rule—the requirement to resolve conflicts for the people through law and through force if necessary and, thus, to make life livable. The people gave up all future political rights. Why would people make such a one-way contract with a ruler? According to Hobbes they had no choice. Without the ruler, and by implication without an absolute monarch, they would lapse again into the state of nature, where life was intolerable. However, with the rule of the sovereign monarch, or whatever the ruler might be called, there was at least hope that sufficient order could be created wherein people could have families, homes, farms, and some means of livelihood that would not arbitrarily be taken away. Hobbes in effect said that people created the state, under an authoritarian ruler, in a social contract. They did so because they had no choice. Fear was the major motivation. The fear of violence, in effect, civilized humanity by causing people to create a monstrous, but God-like state.

According to Locke

This rather pessimistic view of the social contract was later challenged by another British philosopher, John Locke. John Locke was attempting to explain how a king of Great Britain had been deposed during the Glorious Revolution of 1688, and the parliament (as it was in those days) had put limitations on future kings. How does one explain this to a population that either suspects that God created the state or subscribes to the views of Thomas Hobbes? Locke explained the situation by retelling the story of men and women in the state of nature and the contract that they made with their fellow humans.

In Locke's version of the story, the state of nature was not quite as bad as Hobbes would have it. There were dangers, but there were rational people as well. These rational people acted less out of fear than out of a sense of practicality. They, too, realized the need for order, law, predictability, and a monopoly of power under some organized structure. When they made their contract with the monarch, however, it was a two-way contract. The people would obey the monarch, keep the law, pay their taxes, and do other reasonable things that the monarch decreed. On the other hand, the monarch owed something to the people. He or she owed them, specifically, protection for their lives, their liberties, and their property. We define *liberty* as the right to be heard by government without fear of reprisal, the right to be represented before government, and the right to live as one chooses within the confines of the law. Thus, the contract called for obligations on the part of both the monarch and the people. The monarch could punish the people if they broke the law. How, though, would the people punish the monarch if he or she acted in such a way as to undermine life, liberty, and property? Locke suggested that, in the latter case, the monarch could and should be deposed, by force if necessary. In effect, in John Locke's view of the social contract, the monarch, by breaking the contract, gives the people the right of revolution. Many will begin to suspect that this has something to do with the American view of the origin of the state, and indeed it does.

When he drafted the Declaration of Independence, Thomas Jefferson used the theory of John Locke extensively. This can be found in the preamble to the declaration, in which Jefferson discusses such things as the inalienable rights of the American colonists to life, liberty, and the pursuit of happiness; in which he alludes to government as an institution designed to protect these rights; and, finally, when he suggests that, after the monarch (in this case George III) has abused these rights for a sufficient length of time, the people (in this case, the American colonists) have the right to break the contract and to establish a new form of government. Keep in mind, however, that John Locke, when he wrote this theory in his celebrated *Second Treatise of Government* (1690), allowed for monarchy. When the American colonists revolted in 1776, they sought to go beyond Locke's theory, which included a king, and to make a contract among themselves that involved a representative government without a king. Where did we get this idea?

According to Rousseau
Here we must go to the third social contract theorist, Jean-Jacques Rousseau, a Frenchman. Rousseau's social contract theory is more difficult to understand than the theories of Hobbes and Locke,[1] and there is much controversy concerning its exact meaning. For our purposes, we can say that Rousseau, in his book *The Social Contract* (1750), also began with the state of nature. However, he differed markedly from Hobbes and Locke in that, in his state of nature, life was rather pleasant. The state of nature in Rousseau's vision was simply a state of unstructured humankind. A "noble savage" inhabited this rational and pleasant world, and that savage was a rather kind, generous, and altogether good person. Rousseau argued that it was the material progress of civilization that created the phenomena of greed, lust, and violence that so beset society both in his time and in our own. The coming of the nation-state had made things worse. It was time for a new social contract, in which citizens of a new kind of state would agree to meet and discuss any public difficulty. Out of this discussion, in which all would participate, there

[1]Rousseau differs from Hobbes and Locke in that his state of nature exists in the future as well as in the past.

would arise a consensus that would be called the General Will. Once the General Will was known, it was sovereign. That is to say, the sovereign of Rousseau's contracted state was not a person but an idea—the consensus of the population on any issue. Of course, in the vision of Rousseau, the state had to be rather small, for all had to participate in the creation of the General Will, and having created it, all would know it and obey it. Thus, men and women would return to a more pleasant society, somewhat like the one they had enjoyed in the past.

Rousseau, unfortunately, was rather vague on how all this was to come about. Certainly, he gave no clue of how such a society could come into existence, but he, at least, gave to the political philosophers of the United States the idea that government could exist by consent of the people without the necessity of having a king or queen. This idea, combined with John Locke's concept of the right of revolution and his overall concept of the social contract, led directly to the Declaration of Independence of 1776 and later to the establishment of the first of our nation's constitutions, the Articles of Confederation. Later they led to the current American Constitution. Both of the latter documents are nothing more than forms of the social contract. Indeed, one of the major contributions that the United States of America has made to political theory is the fact that we were the first to draft *actual* social contracts among people in general and to live under them. Our experience has been so successful that practically all nation-states have constitutions and adopt some form of social contract theory, although not always the combination of Locke and Rousseau.

It should not be surprising that we Americans put the social contract theory into effect first.[2] Actually, our political experience for over a century before they were written clearly led to the Articles of Confederation and the U.S. Constitution. A group of English dissenters, whom we now know as the Pilgrims, left Great Britain in 1620 in order to seek religious freedom and self-government in the colony of Jamestown in Virginia. Their intention was to try to live within their religious beliefs and outside of the criticism and hostility of the established Church of England. The *Mayflower*, the ship on which they traveled, got lost. Instead of Jamestown, it put in at what we now know as Cape Cod in Massachusetts. The captain of the ship did not know where Jamestown was, he did not know where he was, but he knew where England was and he decided to return. The Pilgrims had two choices. They could return with him to England or they could get out and create their own colony.

For the first time in history a group of civilized men and women were literally put out into a state of nature. There were savages around, and even though some were rather noble, there was no state; there was no government; there was no protection. Before disembarking from the *Mayflower*, the

---

[2]Some would argue that the Magna Charta was the first social contract. However, it was made by a small group of nobles and King John of England in 1215 for their mutual relationship, it affected the people very little, and it did not create a state.

instinct of the social contract prevailed, and the Pilgrims drew up a document known to history as the Mayflower Compact. In the compact are all the ingredients of a modern constitution: who shall rule, what the structure of government shall be, what the basic laws shall be. Having drawn up and signed the Mayflower Compact, they then proceeded to create the state it described. That state is now Massachusetts.

In similar fashion later, other colonies drew up other charters. In the case of the colony that became South Carolina, the charter, known as the "Fundamental Constitutions," was written in 1670 by none other than John Locke. By 1776, the instinct for contractual government describing some form of political order was widespread throughout the American colonies. The inevitable results, the Articles of Confederation and the U.S. Constitution, should, therefore, not be surprising. Hence, the social contract theory is the theory of the United States of America and of many other political states. It tells us that men and women created the state for specific reasons of their own, for specific purposes that they envisioned, and for specific conditions that they desired. Thus, men and women can *re-create* the state as they will from time to time.

THE FEUDAL STATE AND THE NATION-STATE

Having discussed various theories of the origin of the state, we are still left to ponder the varieties of the state and the existence of the present nation-state system. We know that historically there have been several kinds of states, starting probably with a tribal state found at the beginning of most cultures. The city-states of ancient Greece, ancient Rome, and other parts of the world also come to mind. Vast empire states are typified by the Roman Empire. We can move from theory to fact, however, when we raise the question of how we arrived at a situation today where something called the nation-state dominates the political geography of the world. We need not depend on theory so much as on the interpretation of history.

The modern nation-state derives its beginnings from the medieval feudal states or feudal kingdoms of Europe. These, in turn, developed because of the fall of the Roman Empire sometime between A.D. 500 and 700. The feudal kingdom remained the essential form of the state in Europe into the seventeenth century. Therefore, we must begin our historical excursion with the fall of Rome, which was a vast empire state.

Rome did not so much fall, for whatever reasons historians debate, as it rotted or disintegrated by degrees over a rather lengthy period of time. The Roman Empire in Europe contracted slowly, and, in those areas where it abandoned its rule, some form of the state was necessary to replace the old one. Prior to the decline of Rome, for a period of more than 200 years, Europe was blessed by a period known as the *Pax Romana*, in which most of Western Europe was under one code of law, under the protection of one military structure, enjoyed one form of money, and during the later Christian era practiced one form of religion. There was uniformity to some extent in the process of administration, there was a common language (Latin), and there was a general awareness of the unity of civilization. This period is less than adequately described in the written histories because it was a rather placid period, and historians are more often interested in the disruptive aspects of civilization. Nevertheless, this period of unity of civilization ended as the Roman Empire contracted back to what is now Italy, suffering the various invasions of the Goths, the Visigoths, and other Germanic tribes. A degree of uncertainty, fear, and danger was left behind.

The danger came primarily from the constant invasions of central and western Europe by hordes of Norsemen, Vikings, Danes, and other groups from the extreme northern part of Europe. There were also violent rivalries between local tribal chieftains and their emerging states. Something had to be done. Europe, during the sixth and seventh centuries A.D., was something akin to what Locke and Hobbes referred to as a state of nature. That is to say, there were people inhabiting a territory that was insecure because it lacked a uniform governmental structure.

In a rather stylized description, this is essentially what happened. Small groups of people banded together and chose a leader who would protect them. In exchange for his protection, the people gave the leader a portion of the produce of their farms or the fruits of the hunt. The leader, in turn, spent his time organizing defense and preparing for a possible encounter with invading forces. He usually built a stockade; equipped it with rudimentary weapons (swords, axes, slings, spears, and things of that nature); and, upon sight of an enemy, brought his people into the stockade. With their help (and perhaps under the leadership of his immediate family), the leader did what he could to protect them.

These leaders, who emerged early in the feudal period, eventually combined and chose from their number a greater leader, whose function was to protect the leaders by building a stronger fortress and by equipping it with more sophisticated weapons. The relationship between the greater leader and the lesser leaders was reciprocal. The lesser leaders owed the greater leader their combined efforts to protect the fortress on call. They also paid him part of their agricultural produce and whatever other wealth they controlled. The greater leader, in turn, owed the lesser leaders protection, not only from the outside invasion but also from possible insurrection from within their own small communities. Ultimately, the greater leaders consulted among themselves and chose a super leader. This super leader lived in a castle and in effect controlled the lesser leaders as well as the greater leaders under the same reciprocal relationship. The greater leaders shared their wealth with the super leader, and the super leader protected the greater leaders from both outside danger and insurrection from the lower leaders.

We can give these leaders names, and we can picture the emerging pyramidal relationship of what became known as the feudal state. As we see in figure 3.1, the lesser leaders, who controlled a group of farms and perhaps a

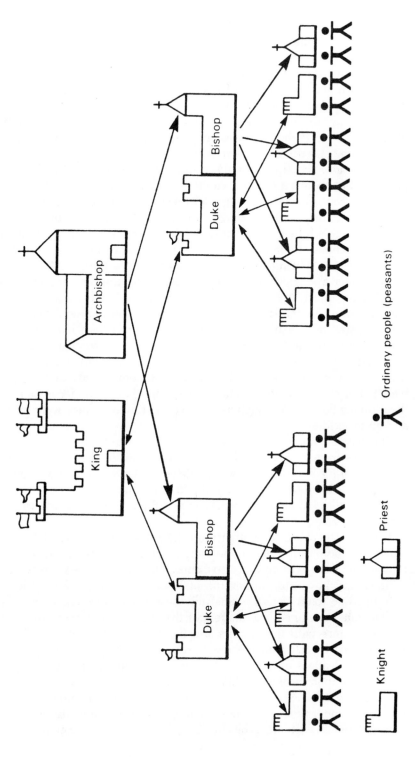

FIGURE 3.1 Feudal State Relationships

Ordinary people (peasants)

Priest

Knight

village, were called knights. They lived in manor houses and became the immediate controllers of their territory. They, in turn, were protected by a second level of leadership, which we might call, for illustrative purposes, dukes. The word *duke* comes from the Latin word *ducto*, meaning leader. The dukes controlled the combined territories of the knights, including many farms and several villages. They controlled something akin to what we call a county. They, in turn, were controlled by the super leader, who ultimately became the king. Perhaps he was not yet a king, but only an earl, or perhaps he bore some other title, but for our purposes let's call him a king and make one distinction. The king not only controlled the areas over which the dukes presided, but he also ultimately came to *own outright* the entire territory. The dukes had control from the king over their large holdings, but they did not own the land, nor did the knights own the land dominated by their manor house. Rather, all the land eventually fell under the ownership of the king, who could choose to parcel it out or reclaim it as he saw fit.

The question that remained was, how big could these consolidations of power under a single king become? How many dukedoms and earldoms could be organized under the rule of a single king? Two answers seem relevant to European **feudalism.** First, geography worked against the expansionist desires of British kings (the English Channel), French kings (the Pyrenees Mountains), and Scandinavian kings (the peninsular makeup of that area). Second, different kings showed different abilities to organize and control territory. Some, like the Hapsburgs, Hohenzollerns, and Romanovs, were better at this than the Italian, Polish, and Netherlander leaders. Thus, the ultimate boundaries (such as they were) of feudal states were transitory and quite accidental.

The people who originally selected the knights had, by so doing, removed themselves from the process of government and the possibility of politics shortly after the knights became established. Therefore, the only people who mattered in the feudal state were the knights, the dukes, and the kings. It was *their* interrelationship that determined the nature of the government of the feudal state.

However, there was one other important element in the feudal state. Not only were there individuals who were in peril with the contraction of the Roman Empire, but there was also a church left without the protection of the military and governing apparatus of Rome. The church had priests and buildings and some items of value, and these also required protection. As the feudal state developed, the leaders of the church, the priests and bishops, sought alliance with the knights and the dukes, and ultimately the kings. This alliance was similar to the reciprocal relationship that existed among the secular leaders of the feudal state. The relationship proposed by the church was this: the kings, dukes, and knights would protect the church buildings, watch over the priests in their travels, and encourage the people who lived under them to participate in religious activities (to tithe and pay indulgences). In exchange, the church would support the secular leaders. In particular, the church would instruct the people that the knights, dukes, and kings ruled through God's will. This was symbolized at the very highest levels by having the prominent archbishop in the kingdom place the crown upon a new king. It can be seen on the lower levels by the religious nature in which a new knight was ordained into knighthood, by making a vow not only to his leader on the next echelon and ultimately to the king, but by also making a pledge to God to uphold the Christian ethic and to behave at all times in a Christian way. Thus, the feudal state, as it emerged, involved a class of political people—knights, dukes, and kings—and a hierarchy of religious leaders—priests, bishops, and archbishops—who had combined to rule over the people in such a way as to completely remove most of them from what might be called public decisions. The people's obligation was to obey their local leaders and the king. The king provided justice through the application of the law. The church provided moral instruction for the salvation of the soul. The king ruled by divine right.

The kings were not completely free to do as they wished, however. There was always a representative of the church to tell them that they could not go to war under certain circumstances (especially against another Christian king) for an unjust cause. The church might also inform the king that he could not marry or divorce under certain circumstances. There were other points of conflict, and eventually a certain tension began to develop during the later medieval period over who should have ultimate rule. Should the king have the right to name the bishops and therefore control the church, or should the church have the right to control the kings and therefore participate in the rule over the state? Whereas there were many kings, there was only one pope. The question that arose was, where did his authority over kings end? By the sixteenth century, a period of great uneasiness had begun in central Europe. It was brought to a head by one of the most revolutionary movements in modern history. This was the **Reformation,** which began in 1517 and whose ultimate effect was to split the European Christian church into Protestant and Roman Catholic factions, each supported by groups of sympathetic kings and princes.

With a divided church, the kings and their subordinates now had a chance to win the battle for ultimate control of the state. The Reformation period, especially the Thirty Years' War, which began in 1618 and lasted until 1648, was ultimately a battleground not so much between the Protestant churches (inadvertently created by Martin Luther and John Calvin) and the traditional Catholic church, as it was a war between the secular rule of the feudal state and the spiritual, ecclesiastical rule of the church. After a long and bitter war, the central part of Europe was exhausted. It is estimated that upwards of 30 percent of the population of what is now Germany died during that thirty-year period from battles, disease, or famine.

The rest of Europe did not escape lightly, either. In 1648, in the small German town of Westphalia, the secular leaders of Europe met. The result of the meeting, the *Treaty of Westphalia,* was significant. The treaty's main purpose was the ending of the internal conflict between Protestant and Catholic versions of Christianity, but the *way* in which the conflict was ended created a whole new political order. The decision was that each king or prince who controlled a certain defined territory would decide which of the two aspects of Christianity would prevail within his kingdom. That, in turn, placed the king above the church. Catholic kings could then say to Catholic priests and bishops: "You need me to sustain the church in my kingdom. I will henceforth play a role in naming the bishops, and I will henceforth place what limitations I wish upon Canon law (church law) and how it shall affect my kingdom." Protestant kings, on the other hand, could say something similar. They could say that, for the Protestant religion to flourish against a possible Catholic resurgence, they would determine to what extent the Protestant church would affect secular affairs in their states. The transfer of absolute power to the kings was not wholly the result of religion and the Thirty Years' War. Before and during the period of religious conflict previously described, there had risen a wealthy middle class of businessmen, bankers, and traders and their various guild organizations in Europe. These people demanded a more efficient state for the expansion of their mercantile ambitions. They also encouraged the concentration of power in the hands of stronger and more secular kings who would protect local business and industry, money and trade. Their story goes far beyond the purposes of this book, but the end product of all such activities, religious, military, and economic, was the concept of sovereignty that emerged from the agreements at Westphalia.

SOVEREIGNTY

For the first time in western history, a state emerged that was led by single rulers, who recognized no higher authority than themselves. Let's discuss briefly the significance of this event, because it is the central fact that led to the transition from the feudal state to the modern nation-state.

Rulers throughout history have claimed extraordinary powers to rule. Prior to 1648 in most states in Europe, however, there was generally considered to be a limit beyond which kings, emperors, archons, or whatever the supreme rulers were called, could not go. The major exceptions to such limits have been the outlaw regimes of such historically abhorrent characters as Attila the Hun and Genghis Khan. In the famous Greek story of Antigone, King Creon claimed the right to rule without restraint. He was put to shame by his advisor, Haemon, and forced to face the fact that there is a natural order of things even greater than kings, a natural limitation to what rulers might aspire to do. Similar limitations existed in most historic states.

During the Roman Empire, there were the limits of the *Natural Law* (which will be described in chapter 6). In the case of divine right rule during the feudal period, there was the church. Even in Oriental bureaucratic states, there was always the concept of the bounds of rational excess, whether based on Confucianistic or Taoistic norms or the concept of "the Mandate of Heaven."

After the Treaty of Westphalia, by implication, there existed no limit to what kings could do. They literally had the power of life and death, the power to go to war as they pleased, to tax as they pleased, and to determine what the social order of their states would be, as they pleased. This led to a whole new concept of power, which had to be given a name. To this end came the concept of **sovereignty.** French philosopher Jean Bodin, in his book *De La Republique* (1576), had described sovereignty essentially as the absolute, indivisible, and complete power of the king or queen over the people in his or her territory. He argued that there should be no higher authority. Jean Bodin justified the concept of sovereignty as necessary to rational rule in order to prevent chaos. There are similarities between his concept of sovereignty and Thomas Hobbes' justification of absolute monarchy. Bodin's thinking had been inspired by an earlier event, the Peace of Augsburg in 1555. Some thirty-five years into the Reformation, and after some early fighting over it within the Holy Roman Empire, it had been decided in part that, in certain German states, secular territorial rulers could dictate whether their subjects' religion was to be Catholic or Lutheran. This concept was used later in drawing up the Treaty of Westphalia in 1648, as we have already seen. Thereafter ended the old feudal period of divine-right monarchy and began the period of absolute monarchy and the rise of the modern nation-state.

The state under the absolute monarch became enormously more powerful than most historic states up to this point and certainly more powerful than the feudal state that preceded it. It soon became known as the *nation-state.* Earlier in this chapter, I defined the state as having three elements: geographical boundaries, a people unified within those boundaries, and a government that rules over them within those boundaries. A fourth element needed to arrive at the nation-state is sovereignty. In the nation-state, the government is sovereign. There is no organization, no idea, no structure superior to the government of the state. What began as a concept of absolute monarchy emerges in modern times as the rather grandiose idea of the sovereign independence of a state's government over the people within that state and over any interference from outside the state.

During the nineteenth century in Europe, many kings lost their thrones to popularly elected parliaments. Although the kings were eliminated, the concept of sovereignty was not. It was retained by the government, to be wielded by those deemed to have legitimacy and authority from the people. There still was no religious or ideological superior power to that of the state, and the government, under whatever control, was still free to do as it pleased to the point of life and death. We are plagued with this concept of absoluteness that has now been inherited in varying ways by over 160 entities called nation-states.

How did it happen that a historical accident in Europe, the Reformation, which enabled kings to seize total control over feudal states and establish sovereign power over states, became a pattern for the rest of the world? Why didn't other parts of the world, with more traditional and limited concepts of the state, continue them? The answer is to be found in the coincidence that, as Europe evolved the nation-state, it also reached the technological level that enabled it to conquer the rest of the world through colonization. Thus it was that the nation-states of France, Britain, Germany, the Netherlands, Portugal, and Spain not only went through a two-century period of consolidation of sovereign power in the hands of kings but also, under that sovereign power, launched expeditions that ultimately colonized most of Africa and Asia and all of the western hemisphere. Here in America, where the power of King George III was so much an anathema, we did not forego the concept of sovereignty when we achieved our independence. Rather, we looked upon the concept of sovereignty as a means to maintain our independence vis-a-vis Great Britain or any other European power that might threaten us in the future. In the same fashion, all colonies that eventually gained their freedom maintained the concept of sovereignty.

Let's return to an idea discussed previously. During the days of the Roman Empire, there was only one government in most of Europe. There was also only one law, one tax, one language, and one culture. To a significant extent, this universality also characterizes the feudal period. Despite having a different set of nobles, most European people lived in a culture of economic, social, and religious commonality, speaking various forms of vulgar Latin or Germanic languages. With the advent of the sovereign nation-states, Europe was never to be united again. Rather, the coming into existence of a sovereign monarch over an established territory with his or her own laws, currency, church, and cultural aspirations served over the next two or three centuries to divide Europe into the polyglot states that now characterize it. Furthermore, through colonization and ultimately the freeing of the colonies during the twentieth century, the concept of nation-statehood, with its characteristics of sovereignty and cultural and linguistic differences, was transferred throughout the world.

Although the concept of sovereignty is a reality not likely to disappear, it is not necessarily an unmixed blessing. The power of sovereign governments to organize people in dramatic and radical ways has served to organize resources and ideas to bring about many of the achievements of the nineteenth and twentieth centuries. Unfortunately, the concept of sovereignty has also served to divide people and produce among peoples a competition that is artificial in many respects. Furthermore, sovereignty itself (that is to say, the concept of an absolute, indivisible, and complete power held by a single government of a single state) is, on the surface, a rather ridiculous idea. What government has the power to stop a hurricane, prevent a plague, or absolutely ensure the security of its state? Nation-states, although claiming sovereignty, constantly abandon the concept when faced with problems that require joint action. Wartime coalitions, international attempts to regulate disease and control natural disaster, and even some of the activities of the United Nations in the sharing of weather information, the control of aircraft, and the organization of postal and communications services constantly suggest that, though governments may claim the right to sovereignty, it is a right that should not necessarily be exercised in *all* cases and at *all* times. The big question is whether humankind is served at all by its continued exercise.

NATIONALISM

Although sovereignty can be seen to have evolved through an accident of history and to have served the purpose of dividing humanity, it had an offspring that has proven to be even more detrimental to human society. That offspring is **nationalism.** Again let's remember that under the Pax Romana and during the feudal age there was a united culture in Europe. A feeling of universality prevailed to the extent that, wherever one traveled in Europe, the Latin language, the political structure, and the religion kept people in some state of intimate familiarity with each other. With the coming of the modern **nation-state**, things began to change rather radically. All of a sudden, boundaries became more clearly demarcated, absolute, and enforced. One had to know now where the sovereignty of one monarch ended and that of another began. Within the confines of these stronger boundaries, the people began to identify with their own monarch and his or her own particular brand of culture. Travel and information did not flow as freely as before, and something called the national economy began to evolve. If your king or queen prospered in war, your nation's economy prospered. If your king or queen lost a war, he or she had to pay, which meant your taxes went up. Even the very language spoken by the people within the boundaries of a nation began over time to differ slightly from the same language spoken by other citizens of other states. Latin became vulgar Latin, and vulgar Latin became Italian, French, Spanish, Portuguese, Romanian, and other tongues. With the fall of Rome, new languages crept into the European society, primarily Germanic languages, and these were resurrected on the outer fringes of Europe so that a Danish monarch encouraged the speaking of Danish, a German monarch, German, and a Norwegian monarch, what became a Norwegian version of German and Danish. In Great Britain, where Latin never really had much of a hold anyway, the language of the Anglo-Saxons, French, and Danes combined with what was left of Latin into what we know as English.

People then really began to be divided by the religion of their monarch as opposed to the religion of another, by the language they began to speak, by their economic future as compared to the economy of other kingdoms, by a set of common aspirations imposed on them by their monarch, by the evolution of a common history of events within their own boundaries, and by a gradual awareness of *nationhood.* By the nineteenth century, it was apparent that French people differed from Germans, who in turn differed from Russians, who in turn differed from people in the Scandinavian states. The peoples of the states around the Mediterranean became Spanish, Italian, or Portuguese. Slavic peoples were brought under the rule of the Hapsburgs or Turks but recognized their own differences. Race, religion, language, economics, and history all served to divide what had been a fairly uniform group of people into a severely classified and differentiated European population.

That in itself might not have been so bad; after all, humankind does love diversity. With the coming of nationhood, however, it was not long before nationalism developed. This was especially promoted by the attempt of the French under Napoleon to destroy national instincts in other states of Europe, only to be repulsed by the emerging nationalistic outpourings of the emerging states of the nineteenth century. After 1814, there seemed to have evolved a solidification of national identity. This national identity grew stronger over the years.

THE EVOLUTION OF NATIONALISM

Nationalism has evolved through three historical periods. The first full flowering of nationalism was in the form of a liberating movement in which a group of people who felt themselves different from an outside ruler (such as Napoleon or the Turks in central Europe) rose up, united by their feeling of separateness, and seized their own government, becoming a new nation-state. The Greek rebellion of the 1820s was such an event. Thus, nationalism, outside of those early nation-states that produced it, was a liberating, self-governing force. Then came the nineteenth century, when, under the guise of national competition, various unorganized parts of Africa and Asia were colonized. These areas had imposed on them the national culture of the country that had taken them over. Finally, in the twentieth century, nationalism was the backbone of the anticolonial experience, which began to assert itself most prominently at the end of World War II and continued in varying degrees, especially among the former captive states of the former USSR. Again, because the nation-state system of Europe was transferred to the rest of the world through colonization, the colonies, as they became free, copied the nation-state, not only in terms of its claim to sovereign independence but also with regard to a felt necessity to create a single national and unified culture of their own.

PATRIOTISM AND ULTRANATIONALISM

Within the unified cultures of nationalism, two levels of response have evolved, and at this point it is necessary to make a distinction. A citizen of a nation-state may respond rationally to his or her nationhood and state by feeling supportive of it, appreciative of its own special attributes, respectful of its symbols, obedient to its laws, responsive to its taxation policies, and loyal in many other ways. One might even give one's life to defend the state and its people when they are seriously threatened or attacked. We call this rational response **patriotism.** It is generally considered to be a positive value. However, some may respond to nationalism in irrational ways. They may take the attitude that their country is the best in the world in all things, that all nations should be like their own; or that all other countries should bow to the will of their own. They literally worship the national symbols and demand obedience not only to the laws of the land but to all policies and values of the current government, without question. We call this irrational response **ultranationalism.**

PROBLEMS OF ULTRANATIONALISM

Ultranationalism has led to many problems in the twentieth century. These problems make solutions to the many basic difficulties besetting the nations of the world more difficult.

Briefly, these problems are

1. Egocentrism
2. Loss of objectivity
3. Confusion of terminology
4. Universal assertion of values
5. Overcommitment to secondary interests
6. Neotribalism
7. Enforced limitation on the growth of human personality[3]

Egocentrism
Egocentrism expresses itself in the propensity for nations to view the world from their own central perspective—to identify good and evil or right and wrong from the point of view of those things that are beneficial to their own nations, even though those same things may not be beneficial to others.

Loss of Objectivity
Many nations are unable to see other sides of a particular international question. The only side that is of importance to a nation-state is its own.

Confusion of Terminology
This may be illustrated by the concept of defense. A nation-state's own weapons are felt to be defensive, whereas the weapons of antagonists are always offensive. A nation-state claims to be peace loving in its attempt, through war, to achieve its goals, whereas other nations are always warlike in similar pursuits.

[3]Adapted from Hartmann, F. H., 1957. *The Relations of Nations.* New York: The MacMillan Company, pp. 33–34.

Universal Assertion of Values

The values of one state, be they economic, political, or cultural, are asserted as the proper values for all other states. Any state that rejects these values is deemed to be inferior to, a threat to, or perhaps even an enemy of the state whose values are rejected.

Overcommitment to Secondary Interests

This problem or result of nationalism is a bit more complex. All nations have groups of goals, interests, or values that fall under the collective label of the *national interest.* Generally, the national interest is divided into vital interests and secondary interests. **Vital interests** are loosely defined as those things that would primarily and fundamentally affect the nation-state's territory, people, government, and economy. Vital interests are so important that a genuine threat to any of them generally results in war. Nation-states do not lightly challenge vital interests of other states. However, there are other interests, values, and goals that nation-states pursue that are not necessarily vital to a nation-state's well-being. These are things a nation-state would *like* to see occur or to possess. These are **secondary interests.** They are, by definition, interests that may be compromised in some fashion. Half a loaf is better than none. Perhaps one secondary interest might be traded for another.

The rational and patriotic statesperson is careful to distinguish between vital interests that might result in war and secondary interests that are compromisable and require a sound diplomatic approach. Unfortunately, the nationalist, a person overcome with nationalistic fervor, is apt to be unable to distinguish between those things that are of a secondary interest and those things that are vital. To the ultranationalist, all interests are vital, and no national interest should be compromised. The ultranationalist is willing to go to war, or at least willing to risk war, for anything desired by the nation-state.

Neotribalism

A tribe is generally a primitive form of society in which there is a primitive set of laws. These laws are characterized by totems and taboos. A *totem* is something that must be done; a *taboo* is something that must not be done. Generally, a tribal code of totems and taboos is the result of fear of the unknown and fear of the future. This, in turn, is the result of ignorance. A totem might result from an ill person recovering after being given a certain fruit to eat. Henceforth, all members of the tribe must eat that particular fruit every day to protect their health. The tribal leaders do not know why the particular individual got well, but the fear of the disease is so strong that a simple totem is now decreed in order to protect against future occurrence. An example of a taboo would be if the tribal leader decides a particular pool must be cursed because a person swims in the particular pool and later dies; it is now taboo to swim in that pool. Thus, a taboo is born. The tribal leader may be unaware of the reasons for the death, which may have something to do with temporary pollution of the stream, but that is irrelevant. He does not know. He fears. Totems and taboos help maintain some degree of security in a world of fear and ignorance.

When a totem or taboo in a primitive society is broken, the general punishment is ostracism, or the casting out of the individual from the tribe, lest his or her flagrant behavior constitute a model for others and danger recur to the tribe. A tribe, then, is not a very happy place—a place where laws are rather straightforward. Actions are predetermined, and fear dominates the political environment.

Neotribalism resulting from nationalism is similar in its effects. Certain individuals living in a world of nation-states, all of which are sovereign and which at certain points may threaten other states, have similar fears with regard to their future. These fears are often based on a rather determined ignorance of the rest of the world. Therefore, in response to their fear of the world, they create totems and taboos for the national society. Totems might be required patriotic observances such as saluting the flag, singing the national anthem, behaving in accordance with the dominant economic philosophy, or things of that nature. Taboos might include the avoidance of international associations or of ideological philosophies that run counter to the dominant philosophy of the society.

The neotribalist says to his or her fellow citizens: "You must behave in a certain prescribed manner. You must not do certain things, and you must do other things or else you create a feeling of insecurity. If you break these totems and taboos, you should leave our nation-state and take up residence elsewhere." You have seen, no doubt, bumper stickers on many American automobiles that illustrate this phenomenon: "America, love it or leave it." In effect, this is a neotribalistic statement. It says to obey the general totems and taboos of our society or get out. Do not attempt to change ideas, values, or customs or even to question them.

Enforced Limitation on the Growth of Human Personality

This is one of the most interesting results of nationalism. Consider the evolution of the human personality. Sigmund Freud (1856–1939) described three levels of personality: the id, ego, and superego. Roughly stated, the id is the personality of the child. It is entirely self-centered. A baby can only conceive of itself and its wants. When it is wet or hungry, it cries out for immediate attention. It does not care at what cost the attention comes or who provides the attention; the important factor is the satisfaction of the need and instant satisfaction if at all possible.

Later, the child grows into a more aware state when the ego begins to manifest itself. In the ego state, the child is aware of others: parents, siblings, neighbors, the community, and ultimately his or her nation-state. The child realizes that, although he or she has wants, the society also has wants, and these must somehow be brought into harmony with each other. The child owes something to society, just as society owes something to him or her. The child knows who he or she is, but in relation to the rest of society.

The highest development of the personality is the superego. At this stage, the individual identifies not only with those with whom he or she is most familiar—family, community, and state—but also with humanity in general. He or she identifies with humankind in the past, present, and future. The individual is a member of a stream of human consciousness in which he or she owes allegiance to the past, devotion to the present, and concern for the future.

The nationalist says to the individual: "You must grow from the id to the ego stage and become a good citizen of the nation-state, but you must not proceed to the stage of the superego. It is wrong to identify with all human beings, because humanity consists of different cultures and different ideas, and people can never be united into a single life form." The ultranationalist imposes upon the citizens of the nation a limitation on the growth of the human personality. He or she does this because identifying with all human beings causes the ultranationalist to question the legitimacy of the nation. One must not be a citizen of the world. One must be suspicious of the United Nations. One must be suspicious of any international activities whose goal is the preservation of humanity as a whole rather than the preservation of the nation-state.

BENEFITS OF NATIONALISM

Nationalism has certain benefits if it is applied in the context of patriotism. It can unify a diverse population toward common and beneficial ends, such as the development of an economy or the organization of science and culture into high levels of progress. It can also be the basis for a common degree of concern for problems brought on by natural or economic disturbance. It can become part of a person's identity and help one understand one's own life in the context of the history of the society and its future goals. The problem comes when the unfortunate by-products of nationalism so exaggerate a person's identity as to make him or her essentially an antisocial and dangerous person.

Whether or not one approaches the results of nationhood in terms of patriotism and ultranationalism, we are all inevitably going to confront them. This is because in modern society nationalism is taught to people from the time they are born until the time they die. It is taught because it is a part of the human situation. It is taught in order to make good citizens (patriots) and in order to establish a psychological bond between the people of the nation-state and their government.

Nationalism is essentially an abstraction. It does not exist in the physical, measurable, or empirical world. The difference between an American and a Canadian cannot be measured concretely in terms of language, religion, culture, or ideology. A Canadian can easily pass for an American and an Australian for a Britain, and throughout Europe it is difficult to distinguish between Austrians and Germans or between some Swiss and French. In Africa, tribal identity is often much more manifest than national identity. The illustrations are numerous. The problem is that the nation-state system requires a concept of nationhood, whether or not that concept is real.

It is difficult to teach nationalism because it is an abstraction. Nationalism is taught the same way that other abstractions are taught—through symbols. A comparison might be made with religion. Most religions envision an ultimate, all-powerful creator in the form of God and yet different religions see God in different ways. Few people claim to have seen God, therefore religions use symbols to tell their believers something about their thoughts of God. To a Christian, a cross symbolizes much of what he or she thinks with regard to God and his relation to men and women. To a Buddhist, the statue of Buddha will suffice. To a Jew, much symbolism is found in the Star of David. In the Muslim religion, geometric forms may suffice. In primitive religions, there are totem poles and many other symbols with which we may be less familiar.

With nationalism, the symbols are better known and much more familiar to us. Perhaps the greatest symbol of the nation-state is its flag. Each nation has a flag that is differentiated from each other nation. On the flag are certain symbols that tell something about that nation. The American flag deals essentially with the coming together of thirteen original states into a federation and the increase of those states to fifty symbolized by the stars. The colors red, white, and blue also connote certain values that the United States holds dear. The British flag, which combines the cross of St. George with that of St. Andrew, symbolizes the coming together of similar groups of people into one nation.

In Canada, where nationalism was not always a strong element in the society, the citizens were quite content to adopt the flag of Great Britain, from whom came their independence in 1867. After 100 years of independence, Canadians sought their own symbol. It was important for some Canadians of French descent to have their French heritage displayed on the flag, as opposed to the continuation of a British symbol, that there were riots and arguments of great fervor for some time until a more neutral, and perhaps ultimately symbolic, answer came in the form of the maple leaf that now adorns that nation's flag.

To the French, the tri-color of the revolution has always symbolized their continuing effort at some form of representative government that can be changed in revolutionary fashion at any point.

To illustrate the importance of the symbolism of the flag, one need only remember the horror that went up in this country when, in symbolic protest to the Vietnam War, the American flag was burned by war protestors. Severe penalties were not only proposed in many states but were actually meted out for those who would dare assault nothing more than a symbol. The nation was never in danger when the flag was burned, but national sensibility certainly was. One is left with the question, was the response to an attack on a symbol a bit more than necessary in a nation that had always prided itself on free speech? The Supreme Court apparently agreed, in 1988, that flag burning *was* a legal expression of free speech, and this in turn has led to all manner of protests both within and without the government.

Other symbols are also important. National anthems are a common symbol of most nations. In the United States, we are unfortunate to have as our national anthem a song whose tune is derived from an Old English drinking song. One humorist has described this anthem as being written by Francis "Offkey" and singable only if suitably drunk. It does have an enormous range, and it is over long. However, any attempt to change the anthem either in its content or in the style of its presentation, inevitably evokes an angry, emotional response by some. Other national anthems are quite familiar and equally important to the citizens of the states to which they apply. The "Marseillaise" in France is a typical example.

Language has sometimes been a symbol of nationalism to the extent that the purity of the language is seen as a necessity for the continuation of national identity. The French, for example, have attempted to purge from their language any words, however useful, that were not of French derivation.

Popular slogans seem to symbolize, for many, the meaning of the state itself. Perhaps the best known is the French phrase "Liberty, equality, and fraternity." In the United States, a phrase with a rather unfortunate meaning has been around for some time, expressing a *very* nationalistic attitude. It is found in a famous nineteenth-century toast by Commodore Steven Decatur (1779–1820), in which he declared, "Our Country, in her intercourse with foreign nations, may she always be in the right, but our country right or wrong." This is a very revealing phrase or slogan in what it suggests. It is an *ultra*nationalistic expression, because it says in effect that whether the policies of the nation-state are right or wrong is quite irrelevant to the fact that they are the policies of the state. This seems to suggest that concepts of morality must take second place to the aspirations of the state. This is a blatant expression of the ultranationalistic point of view.

History is often taught to symbolize the state rather than to enlighten the student. National histories are little more than national myths in which all the good things that have happened are stated in glorious terms and all the bad things done by the state or its leaders are mostly ignored. Thus, we have our hero-worshipping stories about George Washington and Abe Lincoln and others while we ignore the fact that on occasion our nation has not necessarily performed perfectly.

Other symbols of nationalism are found in more subtle areas, the folklore of the nation, the patriotic observances that are frequently held, and even a twentieth-century habit of drawing maps in such a way that one's own nation-state occupies the center of the map and the rest of the world is shown in its relationship to that state. If one does this on a world map, with the United States at the center, as is often the case, one is forced to draw Asia twice, once on each side of the map, because of the geography involved. If you pay careful attention to maps drawn in this way, you will often discover that the world is somewhat distorted in its pictorialization in order for the United States to occupy the center of the map. Here is a classic example of a distortion of reality brought on by a nationalistic egocentrism that results in a loss of objectivity.

In conclusion, the symbols of nationalism are necessary in order to make the abstraction of nationhood real to people when it cannot be demonstrated by other means. The public school system is by far the most efficient tool in the teaching of nationalism, as it is in the teaching of loyalty to the government. Both nationalism (we hope in the patriotic context) and loyalty to the government are important, and one should not be overcritical of the use of symbols. The question is how to use them. Sir Walter Scott was no doubt correct when he declared in his celebrated poem "The Lay of the Last Minstrel," "breathes there the man with soul so dead that *never* to himself hath said, `this is my own, my native land.' " There is nothing wrong in the knowledge of one's country, one's heritage, and one's native land. The danger is found in the exaggeration of its symbols to the extent that humanity becomes the victim of irrational and violent actions that are ultimately detrimental to human life.

NATIONALISM IN TODAY'S WORLD

The Limits of Self-Determination

The problems associated with nationalism have become more and more dangerous in the world in which we find ourselves. For instance, can *all* groups of people who come to share common languages, cultures, races, or histories become nation-states? Must they? In other words, what are the limits of "national" determination? Should the French-Quebec citizens of Canada have their own nation-state? Should the Breton people of France have their state? What about the Ibo tribes of Nigeria who sought to create their state in the 1960s with resulting civil war and the death of hundreds of thousands of people? What are the limits of self-determination in a world that has made an important thing out of the consciousness of national identity and the quest for national sovereignty? How many people will have to die so that a national group, or a group that feels itself to be a national entity, might have a sovereign independence in its own state? These problems continue in the struggles, since 1991, of the former republics of the Soviet Union and in the former provinces of Yugoslavia as they seek to achieve sovereign independence. Likewise, around the world, the Basques, Welsh, Tamils, Punjabis and Native Americans express a desire for a state of their own.

Indeed, there are many such ethnic/national groups who could become the exploders of time bombs of the future, as the quest for nation-statehood becomes one of the most volatile issues of our time. After all, the history of the nation-state system demonstrates that nation-states do not disappear (as was thought by some during the Cold War) but actually multiply. The thesis of the current day is that nationhood demands sovereign statehood. Territory does not multiply and all current territory is claimed by an existing nation-state, therefore, each new state must come into existence at the expense of another state's lands. Thus, war will inevitably accompany the birth pangs of new nation-states.

Identifying a Nation

A second, similar problem is how to *identify* a nation. What is an American? This is a question with which Americans have had to deal throughout most of their history. In the beginning, when mostly of English or German descent, it was not difficult to know who the Americans were. However, with the coming of the Irish, the Italians, and the central European groups; with the emancipation of the black slaves; with the increase of Hispanics; and with the self-consciousness of Native Americans, suddenly a polyglot, multicultural group of people finds itself searching for a single national identity. The answer to the question in times past came in the form of the symbol of Uncle Sam. An American *was* Uncle Sam, who was white, Anglo-Saxon, and Protestant. The letters **WASP** came to connote just who an American either was or should be. Of course, a black person could not be white. A Catholic did not need to become a Protestant. An Italian did not need to attempt to change his or her physical characteristics to fit the Anglo-Saxon mold. Rather, the idea was that, if you acted white, if you suppressed your Catholic or non-Anglo-Saxon heritage, and if you took on the cultural pattern of the WASP population that dominated the government, then you could be an acceptable American.

The concept of the United States as a melting pot of many races and cultures was always somewhat fictitious. If we were a melting pot, we would have evolved by now a kind of cultural and physical individual who was indistinguishable from others. However we know our roots, we know our cultural differences, and indeed we often take pride in them. Rather, what America became was a kind of crucible or mold. The mold was the WASP. To the extent that one could fit the mold, to that extent he or she became an American. It has only been in the past several decades that a rediscovery of cultural diversity and a reappreciation of that diversity have begun to undermine 150 years of applying the WASP mold to all who came to this country. Perhaps this is a sign that Americans are beginning to feel that people become Americans because of the way they think, their political values, and their loyalty to our government and state, which support those ideals. If so, then this would make America a true melting pot.

The failure of the old Soviet Union to Russify or otherwise bring into a common identity its numerous ethnic minorities led to the break-up of that country in 1991. With the loss of the central government's legitimacy, because of the failure of communism, nationalistic feelings engulfed the peoples of the USSR and broke it into contending states.

The problem is less dramatic, but no less tragic, in many African nations. When European nations colonized Africa in the mid-nineteenth century, they paid scant attention to traditional tribal boundaries in drawing up their colonies. Within many of them, groups of traditionally competitive tribes were thrown together and administered by a single colonial government, often through the cooperation of a single favored tribe. When independence came, the favored tribe often took over and engaged in favoritism, cultural aggression, exclusion, or even genocide against other tribal groups. The Rwandan tragedy of 1993–94 is but one example of what happens when one tribe decides to take its revenge for another tribe's colonial sins. This is sometimes referred to euphemistically as "nation-building," but, by whatever label, the process of identifying nations is both acute and often heartbreaking.

National Boundaries

A third problem we face in the international community with regard to nationalism has to do with the drawing of boundaries around nation-states. As already noted, nation-states seem to require boundaries so that the sovereign rule of the government has a geographical limitation applied to it. However, when a national entity achieves independence, it is often impossible to include all the people who want to be governed by that entity and exclude all those who don't within the boundaries drawn. National boundaries tend to be drawn along rivers and the watersheds of mountains because of their obvious defense advantages. However, people do not always obey the laws of geography. A single cultural group often lives on both sides of a river. An entire mountain might be inhabited by an ethnic group, and, when the boundary becomes the middle of a river or the highest line of the mountain, certain people get left out. They must then face two unpleasant possibilities: They must give up their property and move across the river or to the other side of the mountain so as to be ruled by their own national group, or they must accept the rule of another national group and be considered a minority, often with diminished political rights.

The results of this have been mass migrations at the point of national independence or else extreme prejudice and sometimes suffering by ethnic minorities within newly created states. As nation-states have multiplied during this century, the boundary problem has created great difficulty and suffering for many people. One wonders whether these people appreciate the joys of the nation-state system as much as others seem to.

Irridentias

Another problem of the nation-state in the modern world can be referred to as **irridentia.** This is an Italian word describing the territory of the Trieste Peninsula, which at various times has been controlled by the Ottoman Turks, the Austro-Hungarian Empire, Italy, and Yugoslavia. The Italians lost this territory to Yugoslavia at the end of World War II. However, they coined a term for it, *Italia Irridentia*, or "unredeemed Italy."

The theory behind the term is this: Once a piece of territory falls under the sovereign control of a nation-state, no matter whether that territory is lost through war or other means, it nevertheless remains forever a part of its original sovereign government. The desire to reclaim that territory becomes a historic quest for that nation-state and can ultimately cause a war.

Examples of irridentias are not difficult to find in modern history. The two provinces of Alsace and Lorraine, in eastern France, have been under the control of either the French or the Germans since the days of Napoleon. As long as one country controlled the two provinces, the other country presumed them to be unredeemed territories. Perhaps World War II has finally settled this issue. There are many other examples. The Cyprus dispute, in a way, is an example of irridentia in that both Greece and Turkey see Cyprus as having once been, or what ought to have been, their territory. The peninsula of Gibraltar used to be Spanish and is now British. Spain wants it back. The Falkland Islands belonged to Argentina until Britain took them in the 1830s. In 1983 (150 years later), Argentina went to war to regain them (and lost). The present state of Kashmir in northern India is considered Pakistan irridentia by that government. The already numerous causes of war are too often increased by these concepts of irridentia, which, in turn, are outgrowths of exaggerated nationalism.[4]

Divided Nations

A further problem might be called that of the divided nations. What happens when a nation-state, with a clearly defined boundary under a single sovereign government, suddenly finds itself divided into two nation-states with two sovereign governments, one in each state, with markedly different approaches to politics and economics? There are several such cases. Germany was divided into East Germany and West Germany; Vietnam was artificially divided by the seventeenth parallel in 1954 and not reunited until 1975 after twenty years of bloodshed; and Korea was artificially divided at the thirty-eighth parallel. In all of these cases, citizens on one side of the border have had to decide to which government to give their loyalty and face either enforced emigration or the acceptance of a regime that they may not particularly enjoy.

There is a further problem in the divided nation situation. What if that nation becomes reunited, as in the case of Vietnam and, more recently, Germany? Suppose a citizen has supported a government that is now an anathema to the newly created, united government? What penalties must he or

---

[4]To our embarrassment, in 1917, a large portion of the southwestern United States was considered Mexico irridentia by some Mexican citizens. This prompted our entrance into World War I to some extent when Germany sought to provoke Mexico into pursuing the concept.

she pay? This question may appear academic to those uninvolved, but it could become quite real to those who must suffer the transition, as the turmoil in South Vietnam after 1975 illustrates so vividly.

Temptations Toward Aggression

Finally, there is the ultimate result of nationalism in a world of nation-states. If all nations are sovereign, if there is no higher authority or limitation on the desires and goals of a national government than the government itself, then there is the temptation to **aggression**—the temptation to go to war either for territorial expansion or to achieve some economic goal. Most of the wars of the twentieth century can ultimately be explained by such temptations. The quest for world government, or at least some degree of world order, is a constant response by more civilized nations or by nations not currently engaged in aggression. Thus, a world already beset by the difficulties of over one hundred sixty sovereign governments must also contend with the dangers of thoughtless or irresponsible actions brought about through the forces of nationalism.

WHITHER THE STATE?

As we have seen, the state has taken many forms throughout history: city-state, empire-state, feudal state, and the modern nation-state, to name a few. It should give us pause to consider that the nation-state as we know it, even though it has become the model for all of the world, is less than three-hundred years old in its most complete form. That is three hundred out of at least four thousand years of recorded human history. It is not entirely inconceivable that the nation-state, made up of a single national group within a definite territory and ruled by a single, sovereign government, will give way to some future form of the state.

Political theory, and indeed much of contemporary political literature, especially science fiction, is replete with suggestions as to where we might be heading in terms of the evolution of the state. George Orwell, in his book *1984*, envisioned perhaps the most popular prediction in this regard—a regional state. In his concept of Oceania, Eurasia, and Eastasia, he suggested a highly technological government that unites people formerly divided by their nationality into an enterprise of larger goals and greater economic unity. There are evidences of this tendency in the world today. The increasing concern about world economic interdependence illustrated by the rise of transnational corporations and the trend to unite economies through such organizations as the Organization of Petroleum Exporting Countries (OPEC) and the integrated West European economic structure of 1993.

The state system could also evolve into a single world state. There is, however, less support in terms of evidence or enthusiasm for this idea. Whether this state should come about through an evolution of the United Nations or through conquest is really quite immaterial. Most serious political scientists do not conceive of this possibility. It is, though, quite conceivable that other forms of the state not yet even envisioned might ultimately prevail.

The point is to understand that the nation-state and the nation-state system were not preordained in evolution to be the final setting for the governmental mechanism. Any alternative structure of government is possible. Certainly, the nation-state has served the interests of humanity in many instances, for example, in the areas of economic development, cultural achievement, and scientific achievement. We must also acknowledge, however, that these benefits have come at great cost in human lives, in terms of the effects on human psyche, and in the problems created among the nations of the world. Therefore, let's be more committed to a fuller understanding of the nation-state, its evolution, its problems, and the necessity for patience in the context of living within the system.

POINTS TO PONDER

Can a social contract be imposed upon a society such as that in Haiti or Russia?

Are all of the officially recognized nation-states of the world really sovereign given the increasing interdependence of today's world? What does this suggest about the definition of the concept of sovereignty?

Name five areas of the world wherein nationalism in some form is causing enormous difficulties. What can be done about it?

What problems do you see in trying to unite North and South Korea?

Which forces are stronger in today's world: Those of national integration or those of sovereignty and nationalism? Why?

4 | The Nature of Government

WAYS OF CLASSIFYING GOVERNMENTS

ARISTOTLE'S CLASSIFICATION

There has been, since Aristotle's time, a preoccupation with the idea that different kinds of government exist in the world and that they must be dealt with in terms of classifications whereby one can be compared with another. Aristotle's own attempt at such classification involved, as the major variable, the extent to which people participated in the governments. In viewing this aspect of government, Aristotle decided that there were three basic kinds of government: government based on rule by the one, government based on rule by the few, and government based on rule by the many. Aristotle's classification is seen in figure 4.1.

First we'll discuss *monarchy*, which is a government in which only a single ruler participates. The word is derived from the Greek words *mon* (one) and *archy* (rule). Aristotle described a monarchy as a government in which the monarch (or archon in the Greek city-state) rules for the benefit of the people. His or her concern is for good law, order, and social justice. There is also a perverse form of monarchy that Aristotle called **tyranny.** According to this form, the monarch rules not for the good of the subjects but rather to benefit his or her own ego, to accumulate wealth, and to satisfy a lust for power. Such a ruler is not legitimate, and the people of the society not only have the right, but also the duty, to do away with him or her.

	Rule by one	Rule by the few	Rule by the many
Proper forms	Monarchy	Aristocracy	Polity (democracy)
Perverse forms	Tyranny	Oligarchy	Democracy (mob rule)

FIGURE 4.1 Aristotle's Classification of Governments

Aristotle called his second classification of government *aristocracy*. This takes its name from the Greek words *aris* (best) and *archy*, which mean "rule by the best." In this form of government, quite a few people participate. They can number between ten and twenty, and they are considered the wisest, the most just, and the most honest people in the state. Together they make governmental decisions. Perhaps the old saying that "committees do not commit suicide" is a good explanation for the fact that Aristotle looked with favor on this form of government. Individuals may go amuck and do irrational things, but committees seldom do. They tend to be more contemplative and careful in their actions.

Rule by the best, under an aristocracy, is generally a good rule according to Aristotle. However, there is also a perverse form of this type of government. Aristotle called it *oligarchy*. Oligarchy, translated from the Greek, means "rule of the few (oli)." The implication here is that a few people, again perhaps ten to twenty, collectively take over the power of government not for the benefit of the people, not in the pursuit of wise and just government, but rather for their own material benefit and vainglory. This form of government is to be resisted, just as is tyranny. The problem is that it is harder to get rid of a governing group with its many supporters than it is to overthrow a single tyrant.

For Aristotle, the best possible form of government, although not always probable and indeed most difficult to achieve in any fashion, is *polity*. The word *polity*, as Aristotle used it in this case, is the origin of our word *politics*. A polity occurs when all relevant citizens of the state participate in the decision making through open discussion, compromise, and conciliation. Of course, polity was only possible in the small city-states that Aristotle knew so well. Again, the characteristics of this government are that justice is sought, the highest form of wisdom is distilled through compromise and conciliation, and government generally works for the benefit of all.

Aristotle was somewhat pessimistic about the possibilities of achieving a polity. He, therefore, noted a possible perversion of this form, which he called *democracy*. In Greek, this translates into "rule of the people (demos)." In his democracy, which we would call *mob rule* or **anarchy**, individual citizens go into the chambers of government not to do social justice or to try to achieve solutions to problems that will maximize public benefits, but rather to seek their own ends. Each is unwilling to compromise, and, generally, this causes a breakdown in the process of government. The result is that government collapses.

Over the years, especially after the Renaissance, when polity again began to attract the attention of those of our ancestors who resisted monarchy, the word *democracy* was elevated to the equivalency of Aristotle's polity, and *politics* became synonymous with representative government involving the people. We then relabeled his perverse form of polity either *mob rule* or *anarchy*.

Aristotle's conclusion to his analysis of governmental types was to suggest that humanity's best bet lay in combining the proper forms of aristocracy and polity in order to decrease the possibility of perversity in each. Thus, we derive the modern concept of representative democracy, wherein an aristocracy (of legislators and executives) is selected through the votes of the polity (people) in general. This has become the central characteristic of political democracies everywhere.

CLASSIFICATION BY CONSTITUTION

What we have today is a more specific system of classification in which constitutions seem to describe the basic points of division. As mentioned earlier, in the context of the social contract theory of the state, almost all nation-states have constitutions. It is within these constitutions that one can discern the real differences among most governments.

First, a word about **constitutions.** If a constitution is legitimate (and many are not, such as the constitution of the former Soviet Union, which did not fulfill the third criterion to follow), then the constitution serves three purposes:

1. It describes the basic organs of government.
2. It organizes the powers of government by describing where they shall exist and how they shall be used. (In effect, it defines the rules of the political game.)
3. It sets limits on the use of governmental power, including the use of sovereignty within the nation-state.

A functioning constitution will achieve all three purposes to some extent. However, not all governments with constitutions are limited in their governance. Of the three basic forms of government those governments that seek political democracy are most apt to be truly constitutional. The two other forms of government may have constitutions, but they may not establish effective constitutional limitations on their governance. One such form is authoritarian government. It is perhaps the most common form of government. The other form is totalitarian government. There are not many examples of this form, but it also presents us with an alternative pattern. Authoritarian and totalitarian governments will be discussed later. For the present, let's examine the possibilities of form within those constitutional governments that seek political democracy.

A political democracy with a written constitution still has choices to make in terms of the structure of the organs of government, the organization of power, and the rules of the game. These choices are basically two-fold. First a state must choose whether to divide the powers of government within a *federal* or a *confederal* structure or to unify those powers for the most part in a centralized or *unitary* government. Then (and separately) a state needs to choose between a *presidential* system of government, which separates the functions of government into different organs of government, or to more thoroughly combine those functions into a *parliamentary* system. Our American political

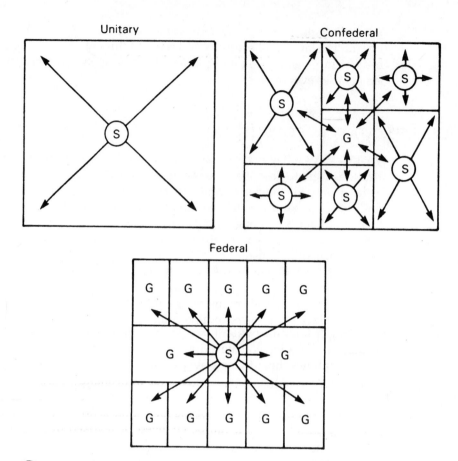

(S) = Sovereign government

G = Governing power

FIGURE 4.2   Three Forms of Government

democracy has chosen a federal form with a presidential system of government. These two choices have resulted in several separate organs of government and a very unusual organization (or division) of power. In fact, our federal union has been copied by comparatively few countries of the world, and our presidential system is rare among the modern western industrial societies.[1] Almost all important western industrial governments, which includes most of the political democracies, use a **parliamentary** system of government rather than our presidential system and most of them are unitary.

The first set of choices are illustrated in figure 4.2. They are the unitary form, the confederal form, and the federal form.

[1] France has a presidential system superimposed over a parliamentary system. Russia has a model somewhat similar but with more power given to the president.

THE UNITARY FORM

Most governments of the feudal period and the early nation-state period in Europe would be classified in terms of the **unitary** form. A model unitary government is one in which all governing power, including sovereign power, exists in a single government over the entire nation. Any public issue, any public service, and any public activity within the boundaries of the nation-state is under the direct control of the central, sovereign, unitary government. Such a nation-state may have subdivisions within its boundaries, such as the French departments, but these divisions are merely extensions or local offices of the central government. They do not have the power to make their own laws and regulations independent of the scrutiny of the national government. In fact, often these laws must be drawn up under the direct requirement of similarity with the laws of the national government.

Some unitary systems are not quite as severe as the French model. In Great Britain, for instance, sovereignty is still retained by the national parliament, and the national will prevails in all sectors of the country, but a degree of local autonomy is present nevertheless. Some county and municipal authority exists in areas of traditional independence, limited now to such things as traffic laws and local schools. In addition, both Scotland and Northern Ireland have achieved a particular relationship with the parliament that allows them to legislate (in the case of Northern Ireland) or run their own governmental departments (as in Scotland). Further, separation sentiments are sometimes voiced in both areas. However, the regime is still a unitary one in that the power of the local units is not only overseen by the National Ministries, but it can be changed or revoked by a single parliamentary act.

THE CONFEDERAL FORM

Prior to 1789, the major alternative to unitary government was a confederacy, or confederal government. In this form today, several sovereign states with unitary forms of government come together under a central government that is designed to make as uniform as possible the major laws of each of the parts of the confederation. Each unit, being sovereign, can choose to recognize the power of the confederacy, but it is also free to decide whether or not to abide by the general laws proposed by the central government. Thus the high degree of unanimity required to make a law stick tends to limit the effectiveness and breath of confederal laws. Such a confederacy was formed in ancient Greece and is known to us as the Athenian Confederacy. The Swiss cantons of the late medieval and Renaissance periods also formed a confederacy. We, perhaps, remember from our own national experience the attempt to establish a confederal government among the thirteen colonies during the period from 1781 to 1789. The southern states also attempted to revive the concept of confederacy during the Civil War.

The problem with confederacy is almost self-evident. General laws over sovereign entities are seldom satisfactory for all, and the central government generally lacks the power to make them prevail when sufficient numbers of sovereign subunits disagree with them. Further, history has shown that confederacies generally do not last long and break up through either war or apathy. Perhaps the best modern illustration of something approximating a confederacy would be the United Nations. This organization is made up of over one hundred seventy-five sovereign states that have agreed to attempt, through a rather weak governing structure, to arrive at general solutions or at least general policies in the conduct of certain affairs of the world. The lack of success in achieving significant unity is too well known to bear repeating.

When the United States of America broke away from the unitary rule of the British empire and sought to establish its own form of government, it was only natural that it should reject a single unitary government under which it had so recently been ruled and choose the only known alternative, confederacy. Thus, the Articles of Confederation, which was our first national constitution, came into effect in most of the colonies in 1781. The history of that confederacy is, again, well known. Each state, being sovereign, had its own currency, its own tariff laws against the trade from other states, its own contract law, and its own general set of civil and criminal laws. Each found little necessity or desire for being governed by the congress of the confederacy. In practice, this congress was made up of an equal number of representatives, who were also equally powerful, from each of the states and achieved very little in the way of unifying the thirteen colonies.

This is not to say that nothing was done. Such legislative examples as the Northwest Ordinance of 1787 show that some level of common government was achieved during this time. However, primarily because of economic difficulties, a new form of government was sought by the younger, more conservative eastern lawyers and businessmen who decried the powerful and divisive state tariffs, contract laws, and separate currencies, all of which restricted the growth of a national economy. Others among the older revolutionaries feared the collapse of the new nation through civil breakdown from within or through a military attack from without. After some preliminary discussions at Annapolis, Maryland, in 1787 the Congress called for a convention to revise the Articles of Confederation. When it met in Philadelphia, the convention decided early on to abolish the Articles and to devise a whole new national government. What resulted was that our founding fathers, during that convention, invented a third form of government, which fell between the extremes of unitary and confederal government. This is our current federal form.

THE FEDERAL FORM

At the time the Constitution was written, a central sovereign government over all the states was acknowledged to be necessary, but the states, which were previously sovereign, sought to maintain real power within their boundaries that was independent in many areas from the sovereign central government. The trick in the apparent contradiction between a sovereign center and a collection of independent lesser entities was to be found in the division of power. Let's remember that power is simply a capacity to cause things to happen that would not happen without it. Power is a flexible and relative concept. It can wax and wane, and it can exist in different degrees. I might have the power to overcome a 100-pound individual (like the states in a federation), but my power might be less than that of a 300-pound man (like the federal government), who can overcome me.

What the founding fathers did was to decide that there would be a central sovereign government that would have the power to make laws over the entire federal union but that this sovereign government would be limited to certain purposes. Most of the governing power, which would be less than sovereign but at least effective for all practical purposes, would remain in the states. The division of power decided upon in the Constitutional Convention of 1787 is illustrated in figure 4.3 in the box on the left.

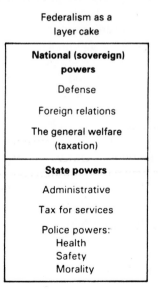
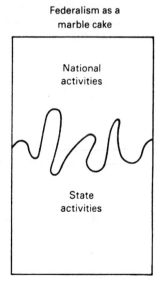

FIGURE 4.3 Two Views of Federalism

RESPONSIBILITIES OF THE NATIONAL GOVERNMENT

The theory of **federalism** that is contained in the U.S. Constitution suggests a layer cake in which the top layer is the national government. It is sovereign over all the rest of the federal union (or the cake). However, the sovereign power can only be used for three basic purposes:

1. National defense
2. Foreign relations
3. Promotion of the general welfare (and taxing for that purpose)

Unfortunately, the general welfare is a rather vague concept and quite debatable in its ultimate meaning. However, in 1787 it was generally thought that certain things would obviously be of general interest to thirteen separate states and easily distinguishable from things that were not. After all, that was a time when the purposes of governments were much more limited than they are now and when most governmental questions tended to concern local matters. Things of the general welfare were seen essentially as protective or economic: a single currency for the entire governmental society; a single set of contract laws so that citizens of one state might make a contract in another state and be protected by a sovereign central government; the protection of the nation from foreign invasion; and the desire to speak to other nations with one voice in foreign affairs. Included also under the general welfare would be a system of national canals, postal roads, and a postal system. Standard weights and measures needed to be set, copyrights and patents needed protection, and counterfeiting had to be punished. Finally, some regulation of interstate commerce was thought necessary. It was thought to be rather self-evident, then, what things would be of benefit and would affect the nation in general and what things were essentially and traditionally local in their impact upon the people. As we shall see later, in order to achieve the goals of the national government it was allowed to tax imports (tariffs); lay excise taxes on expensive things like gold and furs; and, if necessary, place a direct tax (head tax) on all citizens equally (and on three-fifths of slaves). Actually, tariff revenues sufficed for the majority of national functions until the end of the nineteenth century.

RESPONSIBILITIES OF THE STATE GOVERNMENT

As envisioned by the founding fathers, the lower half of the layer cake, the state government, even though it was not sovereign, would have rather extensive powers, also in three areas:

1. Administration
2. Supplying basic services through taxation
3. Protection of public health, safety, and morality

First, there was administrative power. Whereas the national government's structure, procedures, and limits were imposed in the national Constitution, a state government could be organized administratively in any fashion it saw fit, as long as it was republican, which meant essentially representative. Thus, a state government could follow a parliamentary system or a presidential system, or it could federalize its own lower institutions or leave them in a unitary construction, as most states did. It could organize its counties, subdivide them, or establish cities or other forms of government as it saw fit. It had total authority to administer itself under any structure or program it desired.

Second, since most services of government were deemed to come from the local government, the state governments had the power to tax for these services. Local roads, schools, sanitation projects, and other functions such as record keeping would be provided by the state government through whatever taxing system it wished to devise. As far as taxation was concerned, the national government was essentially limited to either a national tariff on imported goods or to a uniform direct tax on all citizens, applied equally, for its revenues. States, in turn, could tax property, income, or any other source of revenue they deemed relevant to their particular needs. Thus, most of the services and most of the taxation in the original plan would emanate from relatively independent state governments.

The third area of state activity fell under the category of police power. Police power was defined as the protection of the public health, safety, and morality. The states would provide what we call *police protection*, generally in the form of county sheriffs (municipal police forces not yet being a part of law enforcement). States would also take care of health needs through the establishment of county health departments, which would administer immunization and quarantine activities. The keeping of public morality in terms of the prevailing codes of the day would also fall under local law enforcement. Most crimes would be under the jurisdiction of the states, and most criminals would be tried in state courts and punished by state institutions.

There was to be no national police. The military part of the national government would confine itself to defending the nation, providing services to states, assisting in geographical exploration, protecting citizens in the territories outside of state jurisdictions, and suppressing internal rebellions. It would perform none of those normal police functions defined in terms of health, safety, and morality.

This, then, was the agreement worked out in the Constitution of 1787. Most government would remain in the hands of nonsovereign state institutions, but sovereignty would prevail over the national union for those purposes deemed necessary for the security and well-being of the entire society. Just what differences lay within the national government's responsibility for the general welfare as opposed to the state's responsibility for normal governance was left rather vague; it remains a great point of contention to this day.

NATIONAL VERSUS STATE

Our political history is replete with examples of great controversy as to the meaning of the national government's power to legislate in the general welfare. For instance, in response to the passage of the Alien and Sedition Acts by the national government in 1798 (which were designed to limit the effectiveness of the new Jeffersonian Democratic party), the states of Virginia and Kentucky passed resolutions saying, in effect, that they would not observe this national law. In fact, the law was so bad that few states sought to enforce it, but a precedent was set that suggested the possibility of a state refusing to accept sovereign national law when it did not fit the particular desires or inclinations of the state's citizens. Then, during the War of 1812, which was very unpopular in New England, both Massachusetts and Connecticut asserted their right to nullify any national law relevant to that conflict. Based on those precedents, in the 1830s John C. Calhoun issued his famous nullification doctrine, which said that national laws (especially those concerned with slavery) could be nullified in each state by a vote of the state's legislature. This challenge was accepted by President Andrew Jackson, who, after some lengthy maneuvering, was able to defeat the legitimacy of that doctrine. This, in turn, led ultimately to the Civil War, which constituted, along with the economic issues of the day (including the question of slavery), an attempt by the southern states to reassert the confederal form of government in fear of a national decree under the general welfare that would outlaw slavery. The Civil War was fought, then, not solely over slavery. In the mind of Lincoln and others the war contested the greater principle of federal versus confederal government, and it was no accident that the rebellious thirteen southern states formed a confederacy while the northern states pursued the goal of preserving the union.

One would have thought that after the Civil War the question of federalism and the rights of the national government to define the general welfare with tolerable distinction and make that decision acceptable to the states would have been resolved. However, as late as the 1950s and 1960s, during the civil rights controversy, governors of southern states were still attempting to defy national law with regard to desegregation of the public schools.

The question of where to draw the line between national activities and state activities has been further complicated by the intrusion of the national government into state affairs through the use of national monies to aid states to do what they are legitimately empowered to do. Although states have the right to administer schools and hospitals, they may accept federal money to build the buildings. This brings national regulation into an essentially state activity. As a result of this activity (most of which occurred after World War II), a myth has arisen in the United States that describes the national government as usurping state powers and growing to the extent that states no longer have the power accorded them under the Constitution.

This is indeed a myth, but, like many myths, it requires some lengthy explanation to divine the difference between truth and illusion.

The box on the right in figure 4.3 shows the national-state relationship not so much as a clearly defined layer cake, but as a mixed-up marble cake.[2] How did we get from layers to marble? The answer has to do with the tax structure. Around the turn of the century, national expenditures began to increase radically in order to pay for a large, two-ocean navy, expanded regulatory activities, and other services demanded by the public. Tariff revenues, which had, for the most part, sustained the national government thus far, would no longer suffice.

With the passage of the Sixteenth Amendment to the Constitution, enabling the national government to tax personal and corporate income on an unequal basis, and the gradual growth of those taxes, the bulk of tax revenues has flowed into the national treasury. The states, which had relied heavily on property taxes for a rather low level of state activities, found that when demands on their governments began to increase by the 1950s, the money to meet these new demands was not readily available. The national government had already managed to gain a firm grasp over where the money really was, which was in the income of people and corporations. Property taxes could only be raised so much, so the sales tax was invented as a kind of income tax where the expenditure of money rather than income was the point of taxation. Even these taxes and other forms of special taxes, such as those on alcohol, gasoline, tobacco, and state business licenses, could not meet the needs of newer and better schools, more hospitals, improved state roads, a state welfare system, state prison facilities (at a time when the crime rate began to expand), and other new state needs. The national government with its larger share of revenue came to the aid of the states in the form of federal grants-in-aid. In this fashion, money from the national treasury was transferred to state agencies, but with strings attached. Federal money had to be matched by state money according to a formula, federal standards over the quality of materials purchased with federal money were imposed over the states, and requirements with regard to the equitable distribution of federal monies were also imposed.

It appeared, on the surface, that the federal regulators of the grant in any specific program were, in effect, taking over a state function. This can be seen in the case of the Department of Education insisting on standards of school construction where federal funds are involved, on lists of publishers of schoolbooks purchased by federal money, or on the right of all citizens within the state to share equally in the educational institutions aided by the national government. This can appear to be a usurpation of the state power over the area of education. In reality, this is not the case at all. The state

[2]The layer cake/marble cake comparison was originated by Morton Grodzins in his 1961 article "Centralization and Decentralization in the American Federal System." In *A Nation of States*, ed. Robert A. Goldwin Chicago: Rand McNally and Company.

boards of education still run the schools, hire the teachers, pay the salaries, issue the regulations, and define the standards. However, if they wish to accept federal money they must make concessions to federal regulations.

Federal regulation is not equivalent either to federal control or to usurpation; it is rather a condition entered into voluntarily by states seeking federal financial resources in order to meet their particular service needs. No state is required to accept federal grants-in-aid, and no power is fully surrendered to the national government when federal aid is obtained. Rather, a marble-cake intertwining of federal regulation and state power has been the result of this new partnership between the two levels of government.

TWO PRINCIPLES OF FEDERALISM

The federal system of government has two major principles, both of which must exist simultaneously in order for it to be distinguished from unitary government or confederal government. The first principle is the division of power. Is the division of power real? Do the lower units of government have power that is essentially independent of the national government and under the control of the governing entities of the lesser units? Even in the new relationship prompted by the federal grants-in-aid and other forms of cooperative relationship between the national and state governments today, *no* power has been lost by state governments that cannot be reclaimed by them if they so desire. No new ability to coerce the states has been achieved by the national government. One can observe the subtle pressures that money can exert upon the states, as in the ability of the national government to reduce state highway speed limits to 55 MPH and state drinking ages to 21 years by threatening to cut off national highway funds during the 1970s, but one would be incorrect to describe that as a usurpation of power. Indeed, states such as Wyoming successfully defied the Department of Transportation with regard to the 55 MPH speed limit on rural interstate highways, ultimately forcing its increase to 65 MPH in 1987, and its subsequent abandonment in 1995.

The second principle of federalism concerns the boundaries of the local units. Can they be changed by the national government without the consent of the citizens within those boundaries? The answer to that question in our history is rather clear. They cannot. No state may be divided into other states without its consent, and no new state can be created out of territory without the consent of the representatives of that state in the Congress. It is true that during the Civil War the state of West Virginia, in effect, seceded from the state of Virginia, but that particular division can be accounted for by reasons having less to do with theory than with the fact of war, and in time of war some constitutional norms tend to be suspended.

Thus, the relationship between the governing units in the United States leaves most of the power of governing in the hands of state governments, with the national government finding new and very dramatic things to do within the original context of its mandate to exercise sovereign control over the general welfare. Most people's interaction with government in the United States, during the course of their lives, is an interaction with state government. From the time their birth certificates are issued by the state government, through their education even to and through the college level, when they are married, when they are divorced, when they break laws and are punished, when they get a business or professional license, and even when they die (death certificates are issued by state governments), it is the state government that records, regulates, or otherwise defines most of the particular interrelationship between people and government.

Municipal and county governments are creatures of the state in the context of the unitary model already described. Thus, these actions emanating from city or county councils and administrators, which so often affect our lives, are also examples of the *state's* continuing authority over us.

In the so-called Reagan Revolution of the 1980s, the *initiative* for many public policy decisions (particularly in education, social, and environmental issues) shifted back to the states, and, because of future budget constraints, it appears that it is likely to remain there for years. This particular movement was furthered in the late 1980s by growing state resistance to what was referred to as unfunded mandates, which emanated from the national government. The problem centered on regulatory agencies that imposed safety and environmental requirements on state activities but did not give the states the money they needed to fulfill the new requirements. A parallel problem was seen in the demands by the national government for some states to expand their welfare programs so that they would become more similar from state to state. A relatively minor 1993 unfunded mandate called the Motor-Voter law wherein states were required to register citizens to vote as they applied for welfare, got their driver's licenses or interacted in other small ways with the state government, sparked a revolt in 1995. The new Republican majority in the Congress took up the complaints of the states with the result that many of the older national intrusions into state activities are under fire, and the whole marble-cake model may undergo some major modifications.

Whatever the outcome with regard to the struggles over welfare reform or unfunded mandates in general, the national government continues to affect citizens directly at the point of the payment of the national income tax; the breach of those laws that are defined as national, such as interstate transportation of stolen goods or kidnapping; the violation of certain regulations with regard to the tax code; and a few other areas. Individuals are also affected directly if they are drafted into the armed forces during times of crisis. All other relationships with the federal government tend to involve a cooperative arrangement with business and state agencies involving the use of federal money on a voluntary basis or the control of business through national regulation for the public benefit. The federal relationship, as invented by our founding fathers, has been the essential pattern followed in this country since 1789. It is based on a formula of a *real* division of real governing power on at least two levels, no matter how the actual structure is defined.

OTHER APPROACHES TO FEDERALISM

There are approaches to federalism different from the American model. Since 1789, the federal system has been adopted by other nation-states, primarily because it serves the purpose of governing large geographical states with marked ethnic differences or traditions of local autonomy. (The latter part of the reason explains the rise of federalism in the United States, but the system also served our subsequent history of continental expansion and the immigration of large numbers of non-Anglo-Germans to our shores.)

Whereas about twenty nation-states claim to be federal in their governance, only five seem to meet the preconditions already discussed—division of power and local input into boundary changes. Besides the United States, they are Australia, Canada, Germany, and Switzerland. Each of the four non-American states differs in some respect from the United States in its application of the federal principle. In Australia, the division of power is such that the national government may legislate in many of the traditional areas of local government concurrently with the state governments. When there is a conflict between the two laws, the national law takes precedence. In Canada, there is a tendency for some national laws to be carried out by local (provincial) agencies of government. Provincial courts are even used to apply national laws. In Germany, the national government places local authorities in charge of the enforcement and administration of nearly all national laws, and the division of powers is more thoroughly spelled out in the German constitution than in our own. In Switzerland, most of the governmental employees are local employees, and the national government is quite small.

Regardless of these and many other deviations from the American norm (which comprise the substance of an interesting subdiscipline of political science called *comparative federalism*), all four of these countries are considered federal because (1) the division of powers between the sovereign center and the separate parts is a real division of real power that cannot be changed without constitutional amendment, requiring the consent of the governed, and (2) the boundaries of the parts cannot be significantly changed without the consent of the inhabitants therein. Other countries claiming federalism, such as Argentina, Brazil, India, Mexico, and Nigeria, fail to meet at least one of these two criteria. In other words, some governments are only quasi-federal yet, at the same time, are neither completely unitary nor confederal.

THE AMERICAN PRESIDENTIAL SYSTEM

The **presidential system** of government was not invented by our founding fathers. It was, in effect, a response to King George III of Great Britain and Montesquieu, a French philosopher (1689–1755). The personality and political record of George III was an anathema to our colonial ancestors, whereas the theories of Montesquieu were quite appealing to them. Montesquieu asserted that government could be improved and the citizens could be better protected if the functions of government were isolated into separate institutions. These functions included the making of laws, the application of the laws when there was dispute about them, and the general direction of government called **policy making.** Essentially, Montesquieu felt that there would be better government and greater safety if the monarch were restricted to making general policy, and if the laws that supported that policy were drawn up by an independent legislative organ.

In establishing our new national government in the Constitution of 1787, our forefathers wished to avoid the monarchical form of government they had so recently cast off. They decided to apply the theories of Montesquieu and create three separate and independent organs of government. The *presidency* would be under the control of a single individual, who would make policy (for example, request new laws or choose which ones to emphasize and to point the way in foreign and domestic pursuits). A *judiciary* would apply the law when it was broken and punish under those laws deemed necessary to be enforced. The *Congress* would be bicameral and would actually draw up the laws independent of the control of the executive. This system, which was explained by James Madison and others in *The Federalist Papers* as a system of checks and balances, seemed to meet the needs of those founding fathers who felt, like Jefferson, that the best government is the government that governs least.

The design of the presidential system of government as seen in figure 4.4 is a design for a government that is not supposed to work very well. In this endeavor, our forefathers succeeded far beyond their wildest expectations! The figure shows a triangulated sovereign government. It consists of the three organs (those previously mentioned). However, the relationship among those three organs is such that the use of sovereign power, which has been defined previously as indivisible, is tied to the necessity that all three organs of government be in general agreement that the use of sovereign power is proper. That is to say, the executive policy must be supported by legislative law, and the judiciary must feel that that law is proper (or constitutional) in its application.

The outline arrows linking the three separate organs of government in figure 4.4 show the balancing act out of which cooperation is possible. The executive recommends law or policy decisions to the legislature. It, in turn, writes laws that support executive policy. These laws instruct the judiciary, and the judiciary applies these laws and enforces them in cooperation with

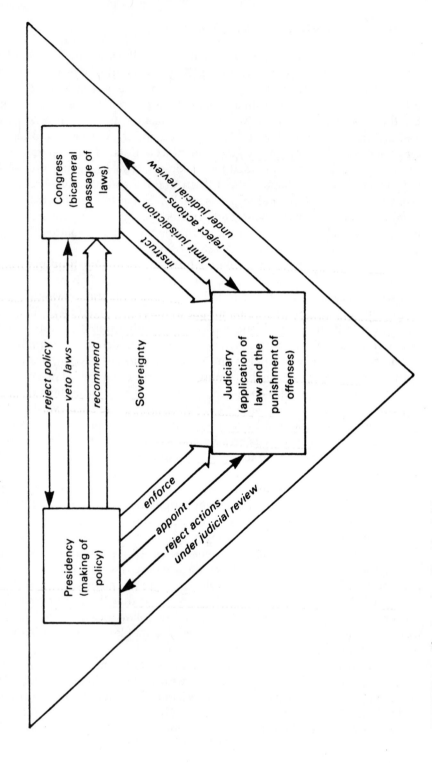

FIGURE 4.4 The American Presidential System

70

executive agencies. Thus, there is a balance of power, independently applied through common agreement by the three organs.

However, Madison also suggested that each of the organs could check the others, should there be an unwarranted use of power by any single organ. These relationships are shown in figure 4.4 as solid arrows linking the three branches. An executive may veto a law passed by the legislature, and it is very difficult for the legislature to override such a veto. On the other hand, an executive policy (a suggestion of law) may be rejected by the legislature, which may write its own ideas of policy into the law. In any of his or her actions, but especially in the areas of foreign policy and national defense, where he or she has enormous power to initiate change, the executive is also subject to the impeachment and removal powers of the legislature, however rarely they may be attempted. The judiciary may declare, through **judicial review,** that a law passed by the legislature is unconstitutional. (Judicial review is discussed in chapter 6.) The Congress in turn, may change the structure of the judiciary or limit its appellate jurisdiction, thus controlling its activities. Under judicial review, the executive branch may also be ruled unconstitutional in its actions, decrees, and policy decisions, but the executive retains the power to appoint judges to the court. During the Roosevelt, Nixon, and Reagan presidencies especially, the ideological orientation of the judiciary was changed through executive appointments.

Thus, figure 4.4 illustrates a system of government that divides its functions into three separate organs. This is to make more difficult the use of sovereign power in the attempt to protect or regulate the people. This is also a situation pregnant with the possibility of deadlock. As governmental decisions have become more complex, as governmental activity has expanded, and as new issues have arisen (such as obscenity, abortion, genetic research, religion in the public schools, and a host of other new problems), we have found an increasing propensity for our government to emphasize the checks rather than the balances.

We could be decades beyond the recognition of an energy problem in this country and still lack an effective energy policy. This should come as no surprise to anyone who understands the nature of our government. It was not designed for efficient response to broad problems such as energy or health care. When great movement in public policy has occurred over the years, what has happened has been either the ascendancy of Congress, as during the nineteenth century (not generally known as a period of excellence in government) or the ascendancy of the presidency, as during the twentieth century. This latter turn of events has also created problems, which ultimately came to an exaggerated form during the so-called Nixon imperial presidency. On a few occasions, there have even been periods in which neither the executive nor the legislature took the lead; rather, the courts led, as in the area of civil rights during the period of the Warren Court of the 1950s and 1960s. After the Congressional elections of 1994 and the perceived weakness of the Clinton presidency, many saw a return to the ascendancy of Congress over public policy.

Thus, dramatic and efficient government under the presidential system has occurred more often than not as the result of the ascendancy of one of the three branches rather than through the cooperative efforts of the three working in concert and harmony. Perhaps this is the reason the presidential system has not been a popular choice among countries that have sought to achieve political democracy. Most have chosen instead a system of government that evolved in Great Britain and that is quite dissimilar to the presidential system we know so well. Americans should realize that the word *government* to most of the western world means parliamentary organs and procedures and not the presidential system as we know it. We should not be surprised, therefore, that governmental decision making is far more efficient in those other western democracies, as well as being quite different from our own in its processes and assumptions.

THE PARLIAMENTARY SYSTEM

The parliamentary system, which prevails throughout Western Europe, is essentially the outgrowth of an evolution that began in the thirteenth century, when King John of Great Britain called together a few discreet knights and other nobles to advise him on the necessity and methods for tax collection. Later, these meetings were also used to advise the king on particular issues of public importance. This system slowly evolved through the centuries until such time that members of nobility (and later certain members of the upper-middle class) met on occasion with the monarch to advise him or her on law and taxation. These meetings were called *parliaments.*

When King George I (1660–1727) came to the throne of Great Britain, he could speak little English, being of German origin, and he was inclined to turn the tasks of governing over to his chief ministers or administrators. These ministers collected themselves into what is known as the **cabinet,** a kind of collegial executive group. The members of parliament were instructed and advised by the cabinet, and soon parliament and the cabinet became the government of Great Britain. To some extent, this precedent continued through the reign of King George II (1683–1760), also born in Germany. By the time of King George III (1738–1820), who was born in Great Britain and could speak very good English, the parliamentary system was already well established. Its modern manifestation in Great Britain, among other nation-states, is illustrated in figure 4.5.

The people elect, under the representative systems of the nineteenth and twentieth centuries, a group of individuals called *parliament,* who arrange themselves into a majority party, which is the party with the most members in parliament, or a minority party labeled for similar reasons. In turn, these two parties make up the totality of parliament. The majority party forms, from its leadership, a cabinet, which takes on the executive, or policy-making and law-recommending, functions. The legislative function, the shaping and passage of

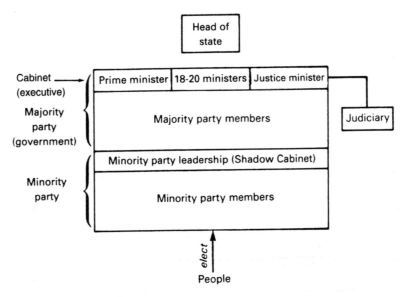

FIGURE 4.5 A Two-Party, Unicameral Parliment

law, is done not only by the rest of the members of parliament but also through the votes of cabinet members, who sit as members of parliament in a legislative capacity. The judiciary is essentially independent of parliament, though it is connected to it through a Ministry of Justice, as seen in figure 4.5.

CHARACTERISTICS

The best way to understand the essential differences between this system of government and the presidential system is to define the major characteristics of the parliamentary system and explain them. The characteristics of parliamentary government are

1. Fusion of the executive and legislative functions
2. Party responsibility
3. Indefinite term of office
4. Temporary irrelevance of the minority
5. Collegial executive
6. Separation of heads of government and state

Fusion of the Executive and Legislative Functions

The first and essential characteristic of a parliamentary government is the fusion of the executive and legislative functions into a single body. In figure 4.5, the majority party is referred to as the government. The government is the cabinet and the rest of the members of the majority party, along with the judiciary. There is an automatic majority, and most decisions are made from among these groups of people. Those who recommend legislation as members of the cabinet also vote on the same legislation as members of the governing legislature.

Party Responsibility

A second and very important characteristic of parliamentary government is party responsibility. It explains how the majority party can be considered the government in a parliamentary system. The political parties in a parliamentary system are quite different from our own in two respects. First, there is a platform that is clearly defined and on which the party's position on a wide variety of issues is clearly stated. The party platform is adhered to with as much consistency as possible. Second, party responsibility means that every member of the party will vote the same way on all major issues.

All members of the party in a parliamentary system must vote with the party leadership, as long as the issues relate in a fashion to the party platform. Thus, when a member of the cabinet suggests a piece of legislation that would fulfill a pledge made in the party platform, all members of the majority platform must vote for that particular law. Not to do so is to invite the wrath of the party and the subsequent failure to be nominated in the next election to run under that party's ticket. Therefore, the government in a parliamentary system has a built-in majority on most issues, and its will generally prevails.

The minority party may debate the issues, laws, and proposals, and they may even succeed in causing minor changes through suggested amendments. However, the minority can never defeat a bill initiated by the majority as long as the rule of party responsibility holds. It is rare for party responsibility to break down. This is a characteristic that is a particular concern to Americans, who take no great notice of party platforms and whose assumptions about significance of party labels are often misleading. We also seem to value the presumed right of an individual representative to vote his or her own conscience instead of merely following the party's leadership.

Indefinite Term of Office

A third characteristic of parliamentary government is indefinite term of office. In the British system, which is used as our model here, an election by the people of new members of parliament must be held at least every five years after the last election. In an election, the majority party may become the minority party and vice versa. However, the election for new members of parliament may be held at *any* time. There are several occasions when this might occur.

To illustrate one occasion, let's assume that the majority party leadership, which is in a position to govern pretty much as it sees fit in the context of an assured majority vote on the normal issues, suddenly takes a turn that moves the country in a different direction from that which the people expect. At that point, the population may express strong reservations about the direction taken. As a result, a resolution may be introduced into parliament by the minority party, expressing no confidence in the majority government. Should the new direction be unpopular with a sufficient number of majority party members, who then express their displeasure by voting against their own leadership, the vote of no confidence can pass and the government will fall. At that point, a new election must be called. This is referred to as a *loss on a vote of no confidence*. A vote of no confidence can also occur if there has been corruption or other wrongdoing by cabinet members. This can result in a breach of party responsibility also, in an attempt by regular party members to discipline or change their leadership.

A more frequent cause for a premature termination of a term of government in a parliamentary system is through a *loss of the majority through bye-elections*. **Bye-elections** occur when there is a death or resignation of a member of parliament. Soon thereafter, there must be an election in that member's district so that the people of that district may continue to be represented. If the majority party has a very thin majority (five votes or less) and sufficient numbers of deaths and resignations occur, public displeasure against the government may be expressed by returning to parliament members of the other party in the bye-elections. If enough of these members of the other party are elected, the government may lose its numerical majority. At that point, it falls and new elections must be held.

A third possibility for a premature end to a government majority can occur when a new issue that was not anticipated in the party platform rises to major importance and results in a split among the members of the majority party. Again the *loss of a majority vote on a major issue* causes the dissolution of parliament and new elections.

Finally, most leaders of majority parties try to anticipate at what point their popular strength may be greater than it was at the time when the last election was held. They may then *call for a new election* at a time when they feel their strength is at its maximum so as to increase the size of their majority. This is blatantly opportunistic and sometimes backfires through a public displeasure over such opportunism. This can result in a stunning reversal, installing the minority party as the new majority and thus forming a new government.

The minority party (or parties, if there are two or three parties in the minority) often has what is known as a **Shadow Cabinet.** This is its own leadership, standing by to become prime minister, minister of defense, minister of finance, and other important offices. Therefore, when one of these reversals occurs, the minority party can quickly organize a cabinet and begin to operate as the majority, and therefore as the government.

Temporary Irrelevance of the Minority

A fourth characteristic of parliamentary government has already been referred to. It may be labeled *the temporary irrelevance of the minority*. The party or parties that make up the minority in parliamentary governments can never hope to defeat the government on a major issue under normal circumstances. They are irrelevant in terms of the passage of laws and the making of policy decisions. One wonders, then, why they even show up during parliamentary debate. They do so because their irrelevance is temporary. Parliamentary debate is not so much intended to settle an issue as it is to provide the minority with an opportunity to express its opinion and to discuss its party platform position on the issue. In a parliament, there is also an occasion for questioning of the cabinet members by members of the minority on specific actions taken by the government. Whether debate is taking place or questions being asked, there are reporters from the news media in the parliament building who take note of the minority position and especially take note of criticism that seems to expose weakness or other organizational problems within the majority. In this way, the minority can communicate an alternative position to the public. Thus, when the next election comes, the minority, unable to govern or influence decisions to any appreciable extent, has at least become known for its alternative positions. By means of this information, which is disseminated to the public, may come the basis of a majority party shift in the next election.

Collegial Executive

A fifth characteristic of parliamentary government has also already been referred to, but it should be given a proper label as well. In a parliamentary government, the *executive is collegial,* or plural. Although the prime minister is the *chief* executive, he or she is not a singular executive, as is the president of the United States. The **collegial executive** is a collection of ministers (cabinet) who must make decisions as a group and must be in general agreement before legislation is recommended or policies are proposed. In Great Britain, it is common to refer to the prime minister as the first among equals. A cabinet generally numbers between twenty and twenty-five members. This seems a rather unwieldy group when it comes to making decisions, and it is. However, it is the group who must at least *ratify* decisions that are made by the prime minister and his or her close supporters.

What generally happens is this. A prime minister gathers what might be called an *innercabinet.* It is generally made up of very important ministers such as those concerned with defense, finance, foreign relations, and perhaps internal police. These important members, who are also senior party leaders, can generally find agreement among themselves rather easily. When a united front is presented by the innercabinet to the rest of the cabinet in weekly meetings, it is rather difficult for too many members of the full cabinet to disagree, although they may make suggestions and cause substantial changes in the policies or laws recommended. Then, when the entire cabinet concludes its weekly meeting, they speak with one voice or else a recalcitrant member resigns.[3] Therefore, the executive appears to the rest of parliament

---

[3]A ministerial resignation over principle is not uncommon in a parliamentary system. As long as such a person keeps the dissent to himself or herself, he or she is quite likely to be reappointed to a ministerial post in the future.

as a united group of senior administrators and party leaders who have collectively decided the great questions of policy and law.

The rest of the members of the majority party find it very easy, then, to follow this collective leadership. Some form of collective leadership is found in most governments of nation-states that are industrialized and important in world politics. That should give Americans pause when we consider that the president of the United States, because of the language of the U.S. Constitution, is primarily responsible for, and capable of causing changes in, our foreign policy and our national security policy. Although he or she has a cabinet, the president cannot be outvoted by it, and he or she does not even have to listen to it. Should a prime minister refuse the advice of his or her cabinet, the prime minister can be removed from the party leadership and office without any change in the government whatsoever. This has happened in the cases of both Great Britain and France during this century. One example (in November, 1990) was the forced resignation of Margaret Thatcher as British prime minister and her replacement by John Major. There is a degree of safety here that is lacking in the American system and irony in that attempting to create in America a limited government, we have inadvertently placed more initial power in the hands of one individual than is seen in any other democratic government in the world.

Separation of Heads of Government and State

A final characteristic of the parliamentary system is the separation of the head of government from the head of state. In the parliamentary system, the head of government is the prime minister (or first minister) or premier, who leads the cabinet and therefore leads the government. The prime minister's or premier's function is to make policy and suggest laws through his or her subordinates. There is another individual, called the head of state. This person in Great Britain is the queen or king. There are a few other constitutional monarchies in which a royal figure also serves as head of state (Netherlands, Denmark, and Japan). However, parliamentary countries that lack a constitutional monarchy will nevertheless have a separate head of state; this person is generally referred to as president. Italy and India are two examples. There are other titles for the office of head of state, but its functions are what concern us here.

One of the functions of the head of state is not to govern but to see that there is a government. When a crisis occurs, either through the breakdown of a coalition, which we will discuss later, or through some other national emergency, the head of state has the responsibility to select an individual or group of individuals to form a government and get on with the business of governing. Thus, it is said of the head of state, "He reigns but he does not rule."

The second and more important function of the head of state is in the area of ceremony. The head of state accepts ambassadors from other countries, presides at national holidays, and performs other ceremonial duties that symbolize the state to the people.

The head of state is the popular symbol of the government, though not the government itself. In the American presidential system, the American president is burdened by having to perform both as head of government, or chief executive, and also as head of state, or chief ceremonial figure. The American president could spend the entire four-year term, eight hours a day, doing nothing more than acting as head of state due to the ceremonial demands placed upon that office. Perhaps the parliamentary system has an enormous advantage in its division of the two functions.

COALITION PARLIAMENTS

Up to this point, we have discussed parliamentary government as if it were a two-party, unicameral phenomenon. The parliamentary principle may also be found at work in a two-house, or bicameral, legislature as well (although, in general, it is the lower house that is the key to the system, and the upper house serves merely as a brake or delaying device upon the wishes of the lower house). That need not concern us here. However, another version of the parliamentary system is of concern.

In some countries, especially Italy,[4] where there are many political parties, it is difficult for a single party to form the majority. What is generally found is a **coalition,** or grouping of several parties whose leaders combine into a single cabinet and whose members agree to vote in accordance with whatever common principles may exist among their collective platforms. Figure 4.6 illustrates this. In the figure, Parties A, B, C, and D have coalesced into a single group, which for all practical purposes becomes a single party. The prime minister is generally the leader of the largest party, while other important cabinet posts go to the leaders of the other parties in the coalition. All the members agree to vote as a bloc as long as issues relate to those aspects of public policy over which they are in general agreement.

The problem with a coalition government is two-fold. First, if issues that are not covered by general agreements arise, one or more of the parties may break with the coalition and vote with the minority. Second, the coalition itself cannot expect to rule for very long before some change takes place in the overall agreement on issues subject to general consensus. The result in either case is the fall of the government.

The role of the head of state in a multiparty coalition parliament is very important when a coalition government falls. He or she must decide which party leader to select to form a new coalition (and therefore form a government), and it is not always easy to determine which leader of which party is more capable of achieving consensus among other parties.[5] With the exception

---

[4]As of June 1995, Italy had had 54 governments since 1945.

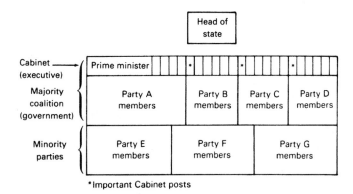

FIGURE 4.6   A Multiparty Coalition Parliament

of multiparty majorities, however, the multiparty coalition government operates much the same as the two-party system of Great Britain already described.

COMPARISON WITH THE AMERICAN PRESIDENTIAL SYSTEM

How does parliamentary government compare overall to our own presidential check and balance system?

Strength

First, the parliamentary system is a much stronger government. It is a government, in short, that governs. There is no doubt that laws proposed will be
passed and movement will occur. Furthermore, since the party platforms are
consistently adhered to, and party responsibility tends to guarantee that party
positions will prevail, the people have a much clearer idea of what they are voting for when they vote in a parliamentary election. They vote essentially for the
party rather than for the candidate because the candidate will vote in accordance with the party platform. In the United States, of course, one never knows
what a particular senator or representative may do on a particular issue, as
opposed to the British or other parliamentary system, where the idea of a political mandate is a reality rather than a meaningless term, as it is in this country.

Public Confidence

There is a degree of public confidence displayed in parliamentary governments that is lacking in our own system. The public is confident that the
party will perform as promised and that there are mechanisms to remove a

---

[5]The head of state appoints a party leader to try to find other parties that will join with the
leader's party to form a multiparty majority, which will then become a multiparty government.
If this attempt is not successful, the head of state may call for a new election, hoping that a particular party might gain enough strength to form a new and smaller coalition.

government from power should that performance not become manifest. In turn, there is on the part of the members of parliament a somewhat higher degree of what Walter Lippmann once described as a sense of "public philosophy," a concept of public service rather than of individual ego satisfaction. Indeed, to satisfy one's goals in a parliamentary system, one must vote with one's party and work one's way up through loyal service to that party in order to reach a position of public awareness. In the United States, a one-term congressperson, by performing in any bizarre fashion, may achieve a limelight position that does not do so much for the public good as it does for his or her own ego.

Flexibility

The parliamentary government is also much more flexible than our own. It has a built-in majority and can efficiently pass laws and move the country in whatever direction necessary. At the same time, we have already seen at least four ways a wrong step or false direction can be terminated by the indefinite term of office. These means generally give some pause to the leaders of a parliamentary government, lest they depart significantly from the public's expectations. Thus, the earmarks of parliamentary government are efficiency, confidence, flexibility, and a sense of mandate.

PROBLEMS

There are problems with the parliamentary system as well. Some of these problems are also found to some extent in presidential government.

Instability

There is, in the coalition version of parliamentary government, a problem of instability brought on by too much flexibility and too many governments, especially in multiparty states such as Italy. This results in public cynicism. Public cynicism is also a problem in the presidential system when the public notices deviations from stated positions by not only the president but also members of Congress. However, the presidential system of government with its two-year, four-year, or six-year terms of office tends to produce a stability that Americans seem to prefer to the flexibility of the parliamentary system.

Dominant Role of the Cabinet

Another problem with parliamentary government has been the increasingly dominant role of the cabinet. The cabinet has its own staff in each of the ministries and is better informed than the members of parliament in general. The members of parliament are often part-time parliamentarians, whereas members of ministries, who are the chief executives of the ministries, are in full-time positions. Therefore, they are better able to know what's going on. Then there is the complexity of the issues themselves, in which the expertise of the parliament minister is superior to that of the ordinary member. All of these factors combine to make the cabinet more and more the unquestioned ruler of the majority and, thereby, of the government itself. On the other hand, American cabinets are challenged by the knowledge, staff and experience of strong congressional committees, especially the chairperson of those committees and thus do not have the advantages of their parliamentary colleagues.

Distance Between Constituents and Representatives

A final problem with parliamentary government has to do with the distance that it tends to produce between the people and their own representatives. After all, as already stated, members of parliament are elected because of their party and not because of their own attributes. Therefore, the degree to which a member represents his or her constituency on local issues or provides help when problems arise may vary quite a bit from member to member. There is little of the careful scrutiny and concern for the constituents that is characteristic of the American presidential system. Even with these problems, in the late nineteenth and twentieth centuries, as the activities of government and the demands *for* public activity increased and as democracy came to the European states, their inclination was to choose the more efficient parliamentary form rather than the more restrictive and inefficient American presidential form.

It has often been suggested that the United States might be wise to consider the possibility of conversion to a parliamentary system. Unfortunately, the American political ethos or tradition does not contain the prerequisites for such a change. We still have a rather negative attitude about government; we still wish government to do as little as possible; and we are willing to pay the price of inefficiency. Individual members of our political parties are not party-responsible, and our political platforms are useful only for the period of a campaign. We demand that our representatives behave as individuals who, nevertheless, reflect the views of their immediate constituents rather than as members of a collective horde.

Perhaps in the future we will find a way to make our government more efficient by finding ways to emphasize the balances and cooperative relationships among our branches rather than their adversary-checking aspect. An improvement in political party structure and a superior degree of leadership would help serve these ends. In addition, perhaps a public understanding of the possibilities of parliamentary government might aid our collective leadership in attempting to provide more efficiency and, therefore, greater performance from our system of government.

In conclusion, governments that are called political democracies are characterized by constitutions, which describe either a federal or a unitary form of government and also describe organs of government that are parliamentary or presidential. The rules are laid out, the limits are placed, and the representative relationship between the people and those who exercise power is defined. It makes little difference in the long run what the forms, organs, or processes are. The process of political democracy has more to do with what is in the minds of the people who attempt to achieve it, and this will be the subject of a later chapter.

POINTS TO PONDER

Why would the "federation" of Western European governments today be more difficult to achieve than was the federation of U.S. state governments in 1789?

Why do you suppose that the American presidential system has been more popular in Latin America than in Europe?

Why do you suppose that judicial review is so weak in Germany and Japan even though their constitutions refer to it essentially in the same way that ours does?

Which do you feel is more "democratic"—parliamentary or presidential forms of government? Why?

Which feature of parliamentary government do you feel is most responsible for its success in Great Britain, and why do you think that?

5 | The Functions of Government

Having wrestled with the nature of politics, with the nature of the state, and with the structural options of government, it is now important to discuss the functions of government, no matter in what form they are structured. As far back as the eighteenth century, we find in the writings of Montesquieu a fairly clear description of the *proper* functions of government. As we noted in chapter 4, Montesquieu suggested that, if the functions of government were divided into separate organs, humanity was more likely to escape the trauma of absolute monarchy or the arbitrary government of any king. As has already been noted, Montesquieu became an important inspiration for the writing of the United States Constitution. What were the functions that Montesquieu envisioned as basic to government? What have we done with these functions over the succeeding two centuries to expand them and to create modern government?

First of all, there is the legislative function, which is to write the laws, to fashion conciliatory compromises, or simply to determine the wishes of the power structure. Second, there is the executive function, which is to make policy or to direct the state toward certain goals or interests. Third, there is the judicial function, which is to apply the laws when there is some dispute about those laws. Having said this, however, I have only scratched the surface of the functions of a modern government. I have completely ignored new functions that have evolved for the most part in this century, such as the regulatory functions contained in special agencies of enormous impact on our daily lives and the phenomenon of bureaucracy, which has grown apace with modern government. Therefore, in the following chapters we will examine the overall activity of government, going beyond the essential functions, and we will discuss what sometimes lies behind the activity described as government.

LEGISLATURES

Everyone generally agrees that legislatures serve the purpose of law making. Law makers, indeed, like to think of themselves as the center of the governmental process, and rightly so. Without those regulations of society that come from legislative bodies, there would be no common agreement as to the nature and direction of any government. However, legislators do more than simply write laws. The **legislature,** being the heart or center of government, contains at least six basic functions that go beyond the mere writing of statutory legislation:

1. Constitutional
2. Electoral
3. Executive
4. Judicial
5. Supervisory
6. Inquisitorial

CONSTITUTIONAL FUNCTION

In effect, the constitutional function means that it is the legislature, be it a congress or parliament, that ultimately either begins or completes the process of changing the basic, organic law of the land—the national constitution. In the United States, two-thirds of both the House and the Senate must separately agree, either to call a constitutional convention, which has not been done since 1787, or to propose a specific amendment to the Constitution. No other body may initiate this process. In Great Britain, it is seen more directly in the power of the British Parliament to change the British Constitution at any time simply by passing a major piece of legislation. While it is a myth to say that the British Constitution is unwritten (it is both written and unwritten), it is true that the British Constitution is the most changeable of the modern western political constitutions. Almost all parliaments contain within their basic structure some provision for proposing, and in many cases disposing of, constitutional amendments. Whether the amendment is ratified by a popular vote or by local governments, as in our own case, the process of initiation, and therefore the controlling process of constitutional change, lies within the legislature.

ELECTORAL FUNCTION

Electoral Function means that it is the legislature that will elect or select the executives of the national government. One might say that the United States is an exception to this rule, and, to a point, one would be correct. The Congress of the United States does not elect the president. Rather, the president is elected by a group of electors, who in turn have been selected by the popular vote. However, if the rather cumbersome and/or archaic process of presidential selection under which we now operate should break down, our Constitution places the residual power to elect the president in the hands of the House of Representatives, where, each state having one vote, the House shall select the president by a simple majority vote. This was done in 1824 when they chose John Quincy Adams over Andrew Jackson in an election wherein Jackson had more electoral votes than Adams, but not a majority. It is also possible for the House of Representatives to determine the legitimacy of disputed electors as they did in the election of 1876, finding that some of those who voted for Samuel J. Tilden were not legitimate. In parliamentary bodies, the selection of the executive by the legislative body is automatic in that the leadership in the majority party or coalition of parties together is designated to form the collegial executive of those kinds of government. Thus, the selection of the executive leadership is a legislative function in all parliaments and a residual function in our own presidential system.

EXECUTIVE FUNCTION

The **executive** function of legislatures is to make policy within the legislature, either in conjunction with the formal executive or in place of a firm leadership role by the executive. In our system again, we have within the Congress itself an executive leadership structure consisting of the Senate Majority Leader; the Speaker of the House; the Minority Leaders of both houses and the various assistants, called **Whips;** and other key figures such as committee chairpersons who constitute a policy-making body to steer the Congress in whatever direction they wish it to go. In normal times, these directions coincide with the suggestions of the president, especially if the president and Congress are of the same party or if the president maintains a close liaison with the executive leadership within the Congress. In parliamentary bodies, as we have already seen, within the Parliament lies the formal executive structure called the cabinet. Thus, the legislative Parliament fuses the executive and legislative power into the same organ insofar as the cabinet is concerned. Its members are both voting members of the legislature and policy-making members of the executive branch.

JUDICIAL FUNCTION

The judicial function consists of two kinds of activities, which, while engaged in only periodically, appear to make the legislature look as if it were a court. Again, using the United States as an example, we find that our Congress may act as a court in the impeachment and removal of members of the executive and judicial branches of government. The House of Representatives acts as a grand jury for purposes of indictment, which we call *impeachment,* and the

Senate serves as a court in terms of ascertaining facts and carrying out punishment, which is limited to the removal of the official from the office. Andrew Johnson was impeached by the House of Representatives in 1867, but he was acquitted by the Senate. The House of Representatives came perilously close to impeaching Richard Nixon in 1974, but he resigned from office before the process could be completed. The power of impeachment in the American government does not extend to the legislature itself.

There is another kind of legislative judicial power that does this. It is called *censureship*. We have seen examples of the legislature of the United States censuring its own members in the cases of Senator Joseph McCarthy in the 1950s, Congressman Adam Clayton Powell and Senator Thomas Dodd in the 1960s, and, more recently, Representatives Daniel Crane and Gerry Studds in 1983. The results of a censureship can include the denial of seniority privileges, the removal from committee chairpersonships, and the personal ostracism from the company of legislators. It seldom, if ever, includes the removal of a legislator from office. The assumption is that this decision is up to the voters in his or her constituency.

The power of impeachment and censureship exists in parliamentary bodies as well and is accompanied by the "vote of no confidence" in an entire executive leadership, which can result in the fall of an entire government and a new national election. Whereas the judicial powers of legislatures extend only to the removal of persons from power, the formal court system may follow this up by the application of relevant civil or criminal adjudications, out of which may come more serious punishment than mere removal from office.

SUPERVISORY FUNCTION

The supervisory function is a power often abused by the American government and only recently addressed in terms of past abuses. The rationale and definition of supervisory power is this: whenever a legislative body creates any new institution or activity that is to be supported by public funds, the legislative body retains the right to supervise the performance of that institution or activity. Thus, if Congress creates a regulatory agency, it may supervise the operation of that agency to see if it is meeting the goals set forth for it, if the money is being spent properly, and if the operation is being performed within the limits prescribed. This can also extend to such exotic things as the establishment of a foreign embassy or to the stationing of American troops at an overseas base. Having decided to undertake either activity, the United States Congress may send out a delegation of its own members to these embassies and military posts, ostensibly to ascertain whether the funds are being well spent and the mission is being accomplished. This has provided countless excuses for foreign travel by American legislators, many of whom have been defeated for reelection in November but whose terms do not expire until the end of December. We often observe a sudden interest in the military and diplomatic operations of Europe and the southern hemisphere by congressmen and -women when the weather is particularly bad in Washington or especially good in the area to be visited. These "supervisory" trips are called *junkets* and are held in some contempt by those who know what is going on. Reforms made during the 1970s now limit travel outside the United States at least by recently defeated congressmen and -women. Parliamentary bodies also have supervisory powers, but they are less apt to abuse them, at least insofar as the record shows, than are those members of the American Congress.

INQUISITORIAL FUNCTION

In effect, the inquisitoral function is the power to investigate. It can produce dramatic results on occasion. The premise under which this power operates is that, if the legislative body of a country is to write laws that are realistic and meaningful, it should have access to information about public problems and should be given the power to solicit this information wherever possible. This gives the legislative body the right to call people before it to give testimony as to conditions within the country on a variety of subjects. We know these occasions as congressional investigations, and we remember prominent examples such as the Senate Internal Security Investigation of alleged communist infiltration of the American government (and particularly the army) in the famous McCarthy hearings of the 1950s. More recent examples are Watergate, "Korea-gate," and the Iran-Contra investigations.

This seemingly innocuous power has certain dangers within it, however. The legislative investigation is not a trial but rather an attempt to gain information, therefore, the normal protections of the accused in a trial are not necessarily observed. This has proven to be a particularly disturbing problem. The Congress has the power to subpoena, to force a person to answer questions on any subject. That person must give factual information or else risk either perjury or contempt of Congress, either of which can land one in jail. In the past, a subpoenaed witness before a congressional committee could not have counsel, was not informed of questions to be submitted to him or her, and had limited control over the range of questions asked. If he or she chose to plead the Fifth Amendment and to refuse to give testimony that might be used against him or her in a criminal prosecution, the Congress had the power to grant that person immunity from subsequent trial for any activity he or she would discuss before the committee. This enabled the congressional committee to trade the enforcement of the law against small-time criminals for information that might lead to the prosecution of larger and more dangerous types of criminals or at least lead to laws under which they could be prosecuted. However, the potential for abuse remained.

After some embarrassments in the 1950s, when immunity was used to cover more offenses than Congress had desired, the concept of limited immunity began to be applied to congressional investigations. With limited immunity, witnesses are only immune from prosecution through evidence obtained in the hearings that was given in answers to specific questions asked by the committee or the designated committee counsel, but, beyond that, evidence not obtained in the hearings could result in prosecution of the witness for offenses related to the subject under investigation. The trick is to show that a witness was prosecuted only through other evidence and that that evidence would have been produced even if the witness had not appeared before the committee and given testimony. Such assertions by prosecutors have proven to be very difficult, if not impossible, to substantiate. This explains why both Marine Lt. Colonel Oliver North and Admiral John Poindexter managed, ultimately, to "beat the rap" in the Iran-Contra trials following the inquisitorial hearings on that murky subject. It appears that, henceforth, Congress should consider all immunities to be blanket immunities and decide that, if they want testimony from underlings or anybody else, then they should agree that future prosecution of those persons will be out of the question.

Despite periodic grants of congressional immunity, there have been occasions when the investigatory power of Congress was used less for the gaining of information than for the gaining of publicity for the leaders of the committees involved. This was accomplished through the abuse of witnesses who were embarrassed by the disclosure of facts that had little to do with the information sought. This was especially true of the McCarthy hearings. In order to gain as much publicity as possible, some investigations have exceeded the limits of propriety with regard to fairness toward the witness and an exaggeration of the problem being considered. Most of these abuses have been corrected in the American use of the inquisitorial power through such devices as allowing witnesses to have counsel and allowing for certain kinds of testimony to be given behind closed doors. Few of the aforementioned abuses have been noted in the use of similar power by parliamentary bodies of other nations, although these abuses are possible for any legislature in the use of this power.

When one considers that legislatures not only write statutory law but are the custodians of the constitutions of the nations they serve; that they are the ultimate determiners of the executive leadership and even, in many cases, of the governmental policies themselves; and that they possess within their overall power the ability to judge, to supervise, and to inquire into all aspects of national life, one begins to understand the assertion that it is the legislature that is usually the heart of the government of most political democracies.

EXECUTIVES

As previously noted, executives make **policy.** What this means is that the executive function is primarily to choose the directions in which an institution might proceed among the various alternatives that seem to be available at any time. This is called *policy making,* and it might be compared to the captain of a ship who has a powerful vessel with the ability to proceed to any number of destinations but the necessity to go to only one at a time. It is the captain who, by deciding on a particular compass heading, in effect guides the ship to the proper destination.

In the context of government, we might see the executive function in the following illustration. There is, in any community of any size, a multitude of traffic laws that have been generated either by the state, county, or municipal governments. It is generally impossible for the police, the traffic courts, or the city council to supervise the enforcement of all of these laws, all of the time. If one is honest with oneself, one will admit that many of these laws are broken on a rather regular basis, in various parts of the community, particularly with regard to such things as speed limits and stop signs. Suppose that one day, in a suburban neighborhood, a child is killed at an intersection where a stop sign is ordinarily not observed by the local traffic. The mayor of the town now decides to shift the direction of the law enforcement machinery under her command to that intersection. She may station a police officer nearby to discourage the further ignoring of that particular stop sign. This is changing the direction of government. The mayor makes the decision because she is the chief executive.

The mayor might have done something further. She might have gone to the city council, which is the legislative branch, and suggested that the stop sign be replaced by a stoplight. People are generally more observant of stoplights than stop signs for reasons that are difficult to explain. In this case, the executive would be giving direction, not by focusing attention on one law as opposed to others that she feels free to ignore for the present, but rather by initiating *new* law, by recommending a new approach to a problem now felt to be of greater seriousness than originally perceived. Thus, we see the executive function as one of directing the attention of government to areas of concern, as seen by the executive, and of recommending new legislation to move the government into entirely new directions.

How does an executive manage to move a government? What power does he or she have that causes the various agencies of government under his or her control to respond to changes of direction or to generate new concepts of legislation? The fundamental power of most executives is the power to hire and fire subordinates, particularly the power to fire them. In this way, an executive may choose individuals in whom he or she has confidence, with regard to their willingness to proceed along the direction the executive has outlined. Further, if a subordinate should decide not to remain loyal to the executive or to agree with that executive's basic policy, then the executive may remove that individual. Strong executive leadership is necessary for efficient government, because someone has to decide where the legislature is to locate its basic attention and where the agencies of government are to operate. This also includes where the judiciary needs to take action in the enforcement of laws.

This fact was recognized by our founding fathers when they chose to give to a single president the power to appoint key officers of the government, the major diplomats who would carry out policy abroad, and the military leadership that would on certain occasions lend military force either in foreign or domestic policy areas, and even the power to recommend those officials of the judiciary who can help the executive enforce the laws. The president of the United States can fire a Cabinet official, a general, or a diplomat who does not carry out policy directives. In the case of parliamentary governments, the collegial cabinets also possess this same basic authority within themselves and over the judiciary.

One of our government's basic problems on the local level is the dilution of the executive authority of state governors and of some **municipal** mayors by electing officials who would ordinarily be thought of as subordinates to the executive, such as state treasurers, superintendents of education, agricultural commission heads, and in one case[1] even the adjutant general, who is the head of the state's national guard. In county government, where such offices as superintendent of public safety, county treasurer, or sheriff are elective, we see again separate pockets of authority removed from the control of the executive to hire and fire. One does not fire an elected official for insubordination. A better understanding of the executive function on the part of the American people might go a long way toward remedying this particular defect.

POLICY-MAKING POWERS

Regarding the national government, in what areas do executives normally make policy? In general, there are six, although there might be others at any given time:

1. Foreign affairs
2. National security
3. The national economy
4. Keeping the peace
5. Leading the majority party
6. Speaking for the people in times of crisis

Foreign Affairs
The executive of a national government must make foreign policy. A national government must speak to other governments with a single voice, and we find it convenient to locate that voice within the executive wing of the government. Thus, the foreign office or state department is generally

---

[1] South Carolina.

under the close supervision of the chief executive. In the case of parliamentary governments, consultation among senior party leaders often precedes changes in foreign policy. It is, nevertheless, an executive function to make those changes.

National Security

The national security policy of a nation-state rests primarily in the hands of the executive. Thus, the makeup and size of the military forces, their deployment, and other questions regarding alliances and the use of force are left to presidents or the senior Cabinet ministers in the parliamentary system. The policies that ensue are generally subject to legislative approval, but the making of the policy is exclusively in the hands of the executive. In the nuclear age, this particular area of policy making is not one that is very attractive to the executive leaders of the nuclear powers, but it is a burden that they alone must bear. I shall discuss this subject more fully in chapter 12.

The National Economy

A third area of executive policy making is a more recent one. Executives now make something called economic policy. We hold the executive wing of our governments responsible for the state of the economy of the nation. We demand from them certain actions to control inflation, to control the level of employment, and to see that the currency stays valuable abroad. Since the Employment Act of 1946, in the United States the chief executive is free, and indeed bound, to use fiscal (budgetary) power and, through interaction with the Federal Reserve Board, monetary power (the power to distribute currency) in such a way as to achieve low levels of inflation and high levels of employment. It hasn't always been so. We did not speak of the executive responsibility for the economy prior to the Depression of the 1930s. Instead, people in general felt that calamities, such as the Depression of 1873, were merely the result of natural forces within the marketplace. However, since the New Deal, the executive has been looked to for remedial action when things go wrong and a kind of overseeing action in times of stability, in order to ensure a sound national economy. Whether or not this is the proper place to look for economic guidance is debatable, but whether a government is presidential or parliamentary, one of its major concerns is to convince the people that the executive leadership is in control of economic forces and has in its structure the wisdom and capacity to deal with economic distress.

Keeping the Peace

A fourth area of executive policy making has to do with keeping the peace. Ordinarily, this might be understood simply as enforcing the law, and in general this is what occurs to some extent in the exercise of executive authority. It must be remembered that law enforcement is a function that is shared by both the executive and the judicial wings of a government. The executive's function is to take note of the breach of the law and to remedy this by the investigation and apprehension of criminals. Once this is achieved, it is up to the judiciary to ascertain the facts and to mete out the punishment.

There is a great deal more to keeping the peace than simply enforcing the law. Keeping the peace might also mean exercising a particular kind of leadership in times of natural disasters, when the peace, which is to say the ordinary flow of life, is interrupted by a flood, a hurricane, or something else. People whose lives are suddenly put into disorder by such calamities have come in modern times to look to the executives for some direction and help in getting out of the particular situation in which they find themselves. Thus, when a long period of drought or sudden flood attacks a wide area, the political leadership within the stricken area asks the president of the United States to declare that place a national disaster area. By doing so, the executive turns over to that area certain resources such as the army, the national treasury, or any emergency supplies such as temporary housing. The purpose is to meet the immediate food, clothing, and shelter needs of the disrupted population and to advance money (at a very low rate of interest) for the rebuilding of businesses and public institutions.

This has become an increasingly important function in all kinds of governments, primarily because of three factors. First, in earlier times such disasters were easier to overcome, because the expense of rebuilding a business, a house, or a barn or even replanting a crop did not involve amounts of money that were beyond the ability of individuals to obtain for themselves. Second, there used to be a stronger sense of community cooperation, in which one could depend upon the friendship and help of one's neighbors to get through a period of disaster. Finally, there was a stronger set of religious and charitable institutions capable of supplying the level of aid thought necessary for disaster relief.

Today, not only has the cost of businesses and houses gone up substantially, but this has been accompanied by a breakdown in community solidarity and an inability of traditional religious and charitable organizations to meet the need. Thus, we look to government, and to the executive branch in particular, for the keeping of the peace in times of natural disaster.

Leading the Majority Party

The chief executive in modern democracies must make policy, not only for the nation, but for his or her political party as well. This is particularly important in parliamentary governments, where the party platform is so important and where there is party responsibility. Executive leadership is necessary in order for there to be understanding of the meaning of the party platform and in order to ensure adherence to it. Any change in a party's position, especially the position of a party in power, must be carefully sold, first to the members of the party itself, and then to the nation. Many a prime minister has run into serious trouble by making policy changes without close consultation with the party membership, only to discover disintegration within the party and an ultimate collapse of the government.

In the United States, where party responsibility is minimal at best and party platforms are essentially symbolic, party leadership often translates into the responsibility to see that the party fields proper candidates and that the president and other executives support and help campaign for these candidates in the hope that, when elected, they will support those executives. The role of the party leader in the United States is essentially optional for our chief executive, and it depends on his or her credibility with other party leaders and with the public in general.

Speaking for All in a Crisis

Finally, there is the ultimate executive policy-making responsibility—speaking for the people in times of crisis. When things begin to go wrong, people begin to get confused, and the danger of civil breakdown begins to manifest itself. During these times, the executive is in a particularly strong position to so define the problem and offer sensible solutions to it that the result will be to calm the forces of civil disintegration. This is not only the ultimate policy-making power but the ultimate responsibility within the government. It is a power not often seen because crisis is not an everyday phenomenon. When properly used, it provides the opportunity for an executive to become a great historical figure. One need only to think of Franklin Roosevelt during the Depression and World War II. He had such an enormous settling effect upon a very nervous population that he wrote his story into the history of this nation. Winston Churchill's role in World War II is a similar example. On other occasions, when there is concern rather than crisis, the office of chief executive can become, in Theodore Roosevelt's words, "a bully pulpit" from which to preach wisdom and restraint to an anxious public. In other words, when the president speaks, the public generally listens.

These, then, are the essential areas in which executives function and, in general, they sum up the modern executive in the government.

THE JUDICIARY

As I have already discussed, the essential purpose of the judiciary is to apply the law where there is some question about its meaning or applicability to certain situations. When a person is said to have committed a crime, what he or she has really done is to suggest that a particular law does not apply to him or her. Should that person go unpunished for the act, he or she will be proved right. On the other hand, if the law is enforced, then it will be the court system that will provide the criminal with the conclusion that the law did indeed apply to him or her, and now the person must pay the appropriate penalty.

Court systems settle these kinds of disputes by applying criminal, civil, and equity law. Courts also apply constitutional law, administrative law, and, on occasions, international law, such as it is. Further, in the Anglo-Saxon system of common law, courts can interpret the meaning of the law during the process of applying it. Also, in the American system of judicial review, the national court system has an additional duty of checking the executive and legislative branches and state governments in order to see that their activities conform to the Constitution. If they do not, then they can be declared null and void.

It sometimes comes as a surprise for people to discover the things that court systems do beyond the application of the law. Courts are also actively engaged in what we might call the **administration** of justice. Here we find judges engaged in activities that go beyond the seemingly short periods of time in which they are observed sitting on a bench and presiding over some piece of litigation. Indeed, much of a judge's work takes place behind closed doors or in quiet circumstances that generally escape public notice.

To begin with, it is a judicial function to set bail when an accused has been arrested. This may require a hearing or an investigation by the officers of the court and a serious determination by the judge as to whether to grant bail or not, and at what level to set it. Further, in some instances, appeals are made to judges to lower the amount of bail previously set.

Second, a judge must preside over the admission of an attorney to the bar. It is the role of a panel of judges to grade bar exams and to certify the suitability of an attorney to practice law in a given state.

Third, judges administer estates, especially when there is no will left by the deceased person. This is generally done by a special kind of judge, called a *probate judge,* but it may be done by other judges in a variety of situations.

Fourth, judges also have to receive bankruptcies. This means that the assets of a business or corporation that has failed are taken over by a judge, who must determine how they will be distributed among creditors, bondholders, and stockholders. This can be a very lengthy and difficult process.

Fifth, judges issue licenses, such as business licenses involving the sale of alcoholic beverages, marriage licenses, and, in some states, gambling licenses.

Sixth, judges also perform marriages, and, even when a marriage is performed by clergy, the authority still rests with the judges. The clergy merely acts as a substitute for the judge, and the clergy must present to a judge a signed document, including the signatures of witnesses, showing that the marriage has occurred. That document must be certified before the marriage is legal. Judges also do such exotic things as deporting undesirable foreigners and naturalizing aliens. When a non-American applies for U.S. citizenship, the final process of naturalization is presided over by a U.S. district court judge in the national court system.

These and other administrative duties of judges do not catch the public eye to the extent that they might, and most of us generally have a false impression of the judge's role if we don't consider the fact that these kinds of duties are inescapable to some extent for most of our judges. This, in turn, seems to suggest the necessity for an even higher degree of qualification to be a judge than those for the mere application of the law in a trial.

THE REGULATORS

Beginning in the late nineteenth century and continuing with great acceleration in the twentieth century, a fourth element of government has evolved that is considered by many to be equal in importance to the aforementioned functions of the executive, legislative, and the judiciary. This fourth branch of government, in the eyes of many, is the amalgamation of regulatory agencies that have grown up not only within the American government but to some extent in all political democracies. In this section, we will deal with essentially American examples, but it should be remembered that the same sort of regulatory activity also exists in parliamentary forms of government within the expanded executive bureaucracy or through special commissions such as the Indian Planning Commission.

The regulatory function is, to some extent, a departure from what one normally expects in the way of governmental purpose. The regulatory role, in effect, is an attempt by government to limit the activities of particular citizens in order to restrain them from certain practices that are thought to interfere with the rights of others or to take unfair advantage of other citizens. There is also, within the regulatory purpose, an attempt by government to promote certain other activities deemed to be within the public interest, such as in the case of the Tennessee Valley Authority (TVA), which is a national agency whose purposes are to control flooding, to generate electrical power, and to engage in other public works and conservation activities for a multistate area in the "impoverished" South. The major thrust of the regulators, however, lies in the first area mentioned, which has begun to include requiring that certain operating standards and safety requirements be met.

HISTORY OF THE REGULATORY FUNCTION

The power to regulate interstate commerce was given to Congress under Article I, Section 8, of the U.S. Constitution, yet, for a century, the responsibility fell primarily to the states. With the rise of industrialism in the latter part of the nineteenth century, however, state agencies found that they could not deal effectively with complex national economic structures and increasingly technical issues, so they looked back to Congress for help. Congress soon found that it, too, lacked the time and technical expertise required to establish detailed rules for a modern economy. Even if members of Congress *had* the necessary skills, such a large decision-making body as Congress lacked the flexibility needed to adjust existing rules and regulations to ever-changing conditions. Thus, the *regulatory commission* was born to meet both of these requirements.

Our modern experience, then, began in the late 1880s, when certain economic trusts and industrial combinations headed by the Morgans, the Rockefellers, and the Carnegies had, through monopoly structures, gained control over such vital industries as oil, railroads, and finance. The precursor of all of the regulatory activity that was to follow was the Interstate Commerce Commission, created in 1887 in order to allow some governmental management of the railroads, which were being used by their owners to exact punishing rates from dependent farmers. This action established a clear change from the older idea that government should operate to punish unlawful acts after they had occurred. Now the ICC would attempt to *prevent* such acts by laying down rules that were to be applied to only one class of industries and, further, to attack abuses in general rather than on a case-by-case basis in the courts.

Soon thereafter, in response to the danger to the public in general through unrestrained monopoly, the United States Congress in 1890 passed the Sherman Anti-Trust Act. This legislation was designed to eliminate monopolies altogether and to foster free competition in industry.

In 1914, the simplicities of the Sherman Anti-Trust Act, which proved to be somewhat inadequate to deal effectively with certain of the monopolistic combines, were enhanced through the passage of the Clayton Act. This legislation outlawed specific abuses affecting interstate commerce (such as price discrimination) in a more detailed and enforceable way. Throughout the administrations of William Howard Taft and Woodrow Wilson, a serious attempt by government to enter into the economic interrelationship between producers and consumers continued on a relatively even pace.

In 1914, the Federal Trade Commission was established to assist anti-trust efforts by interpreting and enforcing provisions of the Clayton Act. Then, in 1920, the Federal Power Commission was created to regulate the interstate sale of electricity and the transportation and sale of natural gas.

During the 1920s, there was a reaction against the regulatory motive, and a proliferation of business abuses characterized the economy of the country. This led, ultimately, to the Great Depression, which began in 1929. In order to deal with the Depression, in 1933 Franklin Roosevelt induced Congress to pass the National Industry Recovery Act. From this evolved the National Recovery Administration, which was an attempt to suspend antitrust activities by the government and to join producing corporations in a cooperative agreement wherein codes of fair competition, wages, hours, and prices were to be coordinated by a vast governmental bureaucracy. The Supreme Court, however, invalidated much of the structure in 1935, and the New Deal had to find other ways in which to address economic problems.

However, the idea of a governmental regulatory bureaucracy and its close association with the major producers of the American economy remained in the forefront of considerations with regard not only to dealing with the Depression but, after World War II, to dealing with the economy and nation in peacetime. New regulatory agencies had been created, including the Food and Drug Administration (1930), the Securities and Exchange Commission (1934), the Federal Communications Commission (1934), the National Labor Relations Board (1935), and the Civil Aeronautics Board (1938). More recent times have seen the creation of the Equal Employment Opportunity Commission (1964), the Environmental Protection Agency (1970), the Occupational Safety and Health Administration (1970), the Consumer Product Safety Commission (1972), and the Nuclear Regulatory Commission (1975).

A feeling has arisen that government on all levels, but especially at the national level, may be doing and requiring too much. Regulators seem to touch virtually every part of our lives including transportation, food, medicine, ordinary household chemicals, clothing, housing, and so forth. The list is quite long. Nearly sixty major agencies, employing over 90,000 people, spend around $10 billion a year to oversee our economy, health, and safety. Further, during the 1960s and 1970s, regulatory agencies were used to pursue social goals such as the establishment of income minimums, achieving school desegregation, and creating equal opportunity in employment.

All of this regulation has produced two basic points of view about its legitimacy in a free society. Those who oppose regulation argue that free enterprise is best regulated by competition and that regulatory agencies interfere with market mechanisms and thus work to the disadvantage of both consumers and producers. Those who favor regulation respond that a completely unrestrained market would lead to monopoly practices and a lower quality of goods and services. In fact, the thrust of both arguments has led to a general philosophy of regulation in the United States in which the agencies have attempted to strike a balance among regulating producers, encouraging competition, pursuing standards of safety and effectiveness, and enabling producers to make a decent profit. It is not an easy task, and it will no doubt remain a controversial one for some time.

REGULATORY STRUCTURE AND PROCEDURE

The key to the structure and practices of regulatory agencies is independence from those industries and businesses being regulated, from the president, and, less so, from the Congress that created them. Five principles seem to apply to agency structures: (1) plural leadership; (2) fixed, and quite long, terms of office (up to fourteen years); (3) staggered terms of office for the members; (4) an odd number of members; and (5) as near even a partisan balance (as between Democrats and Republicans) as possible. These provisions were designed to provide some separation from those who would attempt to manipulate the members, and thus, it is hoped, the public interest is protected. Whether this really works is debatable, as we shall see.

Regulation procedure falls into two categories: *rule making* and *adjudicatory actions*. In pursuit of these objectives, regulatory agencies have a special kind of power, which is defined as *quasi-legislative* and *quasi-judicial power*. This kind of power is difficult to describe in exact terms, but the essential meaning of the concept is that agencies at various times can act as if they were legislatures in making regulations that have the effect of law. Further, they can, at other times, look like judicial bodies in making judgments with regard to the proper conduct of public activities, including the issuance of administrative fines on occasion.

These powers are somewhat less than full legislative or judicial powers, however, even though they may look as if they were. The difference between actual legislative or judicial power and the **quasi** version is that when Congress establishes these regulatory agencies, it applies limits to the areas in which regulations may be passed and to the extent to which those regulations may affect the particular area of concern. The judicial aspect of a regulatory agency is similarly restricted by the act that establishes its existence as an agency. The agency's power to judge certain aspects of an industry and the degree to which administrative fines may be levied are curbed by that act. Therefore, the basic controller of the regulators is the legislative body that established them in the first place. The limits imposed on the regulatory agencies may be changed at any time by the legislative body from whence they sprang.[2]

In rule making, the agency first issues a notice of a proposed rule in the *Federal Register* (a publication used by the government to inform the public on the implementation of statutes). The public (usually clientele groups and other interested groups) then has thirty days to respond by written or oral comment. Oral comment occurs when agency hearings are conducted on the matter. Then, at the specified time, the rule goes into effect as amended during the process of consideration. Of course, the deadline can be extended if necessary, and the agency can also be talked out of the regulation altogether.

Adjudicatory proceedings are usually done on a case-by-case basis and resemble both courtroom proceedings and congressional hearings (i.e., they involve the use of attorneys, the giving of testimony, the examination of witnesses, etc.). More and more, instead of conducting these proceedings themselves, members of agencies will assign the task to an *administrative law judge* appointed by Congress for the task. This individual then recommends to the regulatory commission whatever punishment or action he or she deems appropriate. Such recommendations are generally accepted. Formal decisions by the commission can, of course, be appealed to the U.S. Circuit Court of Appeals in the District of Columbia.

---

[2]It is surprising how many people fail to grasp the power of Congress to limit the scope and power of the regulatory agencies that they have created. This has enabled some of them to take on a life of their own, intimidating the very Congress that set them up. One example is the Federal Reserve Board, whose chairman, Alan Greenspan, set in motion a monetary policy (raising interest rates to combat inflation) in 1994 that the Congress didn't like. Despite the public outcry, the Congress took the view that it was powerless to change the policy. It was not. It just didn't want the responsibility for such an action. Further, Congress, with the assent of the president, showed its power over regulatory agencies in a fundamental way by abolishing the Interstate Commerce Commission in 1995.

Apart from the basic rule-making and judicatory activities of regulatory agencies, they also try to achieve informal cooperation by industry toward the goals of the agency. This is done through the issuance of *advisory opinions* suggesting that industries might want to adjust their practices lest a rule be written or a case be brought against them; by convening *trade practices conferences*, in which members of the commissions and industry can come together to air their differences and promote mutual understanding; and through *consent orders*, wherein, before an adjudicatory action is brought, an industry may be asked to promise to stop doing something that it has not admitted doing in the first place. These three devices seem to be very effective in keeping down the caseload of regulatory bodies and are quite popular with industry in general.

REGULATORY INDEPENDENCE

Regulatory independence from the president has proven to be somewhat difficult to sustain despite that, legally, the president cannot fire commissioners whose staggered terms tend to exceed his or her own four years, yet two-term presidents have had an impact. For instance, former President Nixon managed to appoint the *full* membership of eight regulatory agencies and a majority of most of the others during his five-and-one-half years in office. Presidents also try to involve themselves directly in agency activities. Former President Carter sought direct control over the Federal Reserve Board, and he intervened in the making of regulations in several agencies during his four years. Ronald Reagan pursued two approaches to regulatory agencies. First, he attempted to suspend or postpone regulations or to have new ones cancelled before they could be finally acted upon. In 1985, he issued an executive order that directed most regulatory agencies to submit to the presidentially controlled Office of Management and Budget (OMB) an overview of their regulatory policies, goals, and objectives for the following year. The OMB then determined whether the proposed rules are in line with administrative policy. Any disagreements between OMB and an agency were resolved by the president. Under succeeding presidents, the order has remained in place and its future is undecided.

Regulatory independence from Congress was never supposed to be all that great. Congress, after all, reviews the activities of regulatory agencies and votes on their budgets every year. Congress can also modify their authority at any time. While it seldom *does*, the threat to do so has been known to restrain the regulatory impulse on several occasions. The major problem is that of individual members of Congress who involve themselves with regulatory activities on behalf of their constituents. Subtle hints are often enough to cause an agency head to lose his or her interest in a particularly controversial proposal. This has contributed to the disasters in the banking and savings and loan industries.

The greatest problem of regulatory independence comes from the charge that the agencies are unduly influenced by the industries that they are supposed to regulate. Some critics, such as Ralph Nader, have gone so far as to charge that certain agencies are owned or at least have been co-opted by their relevant industry. Here the issue is complex. Members of commissions tend to come out of the industries they regulate. This is because they are the people most knowledgeable about such things as nuclear power, civil aviation, banking, and medicine. They could easily be seen as favoring that industry over the public interest by failing to enforce existing regulations, watering down new ones, and failing to prevent monopoly practices because of their previous attachments, friends in the industry, and value orientation.

How can the agencies isolate themselves from their clients? Some interaction is absolutely necessary if they are to do a realistic job. The test is whether the commissioners can maintain their objectivity and respond to their sense of public responsibility. In general, it is apparent that industries do not own most of these bodies, and yet they seem to be sympathetic to the industries much of the time. Whereas direct pressure on a regulator seems rare, the existence of such phenomena as the revolving door pattern, wherein agency members rotate back into their industries at the end of their terms, does tend to create a picture of undue influence. Nevertheless, the public and Congress have influence as well. Indeed, an increasingly consumer-conscious public through its consumer organizations can and does go to federal court over abuses and also involves itself in open hearings on many proposed rule changes. The many victories of consumer groups testify to the degree of independence maintained by most of these agencies. In spite of this, the problem remains and seems endemic to the function of regulatory agencies.

DEREGULATION

With regard to the aforementioned concern that regulatory agencies are too powerful and too intrusive into the lives of the average citizen, we have seen, since 1971, a consistent attack on the spread of federal regulation. Whereas President Nixon proved ineffective in this regard, President Carter managed to achieve significant deregulation of airlines and the trucking industry (with mixed results). The airlines now have a crazy quilt fare system, there has been a loss of service to small communities, and many have gone bankrupt. The industry seems to be unsure about the blessings of deregulation. In the trucking industry, we have seen the appearance of double and triple trailers, which threaten safety on the highways. On the other hand, smaller operators have been able to gain entry into the industry through deregulation.

The Reagan administration moved into railroad deregulation by selling Conrail and attempting to abolish AMTRAK, among other things. Rates went up and the industry entered a period of great uncertainty. This was followed by significant reductions in the regulation of activities affecting the environment, health and safety, banking, and the savings and loan industry. A stock market crash in 1987, the collapse of hundreds of savings and loan associations in 1988, and new fears about banks and the environment raised serious questions about the wisdom of too much deregulation for the Clinton administration, but the impetus toward deregulation has continued, nevertheless.

What do these facts portend? What can we say about the future of government regulation? Perhaps the future is being intimated by the curious rise in the sentiment among some businesses that they *remain* regulated. Some airline companies have even requested re-regulation. At the same time, some agencies, such as OSHA, have made a concerted effort to ease the regulatory burden by voluntarily reducing the number of their rules. Thus, the future of regulation is probably secure, but the politics of regulation will no doubt continue to ebb and flow.

POINTS TO PONDER

Why do Americans seem more distrustful and unsupportive of governmental bureaucracies than people in Canada or Germany?

Does federalism make American bureaucracy less efficient or more efficient? Why?

Evaluate federal block grants as they would affect such areas as education, crime control, and environmental concerns. Would they be better or worse than categorical grants?

6 | The Nature of Law

Law is a subject that is only superficially understood by most people. The American legal system, in particular, is plagued by a simplistic understanding on many levels. We must, as a nation, improve our level of understanding of law. Indeed, it seems that before long we might want to alter our legal structure and processes in some fundamental ways. This chapter is concerned with both the basic principles of legal systems in general and how these principles affect our current legal structure.

NORMATIVE AND POSITIVE LAW

≥ natural

To begin with, there are two separate schools of legal thought: **normative** and **positive.** These can be and often are subdivided into many others, but those will not concern us here. The oldest school of law is called the *normative school.* According to this point of view, law is either the result of divine revelation or is found in the common, natural reason of all humanity. It is sometimes referred to as **natural law.** It is a set of principles that are immutable and contain the same basic truths throughout time and from place to place. Such famous legal documents as the Ten Commandments and the Law of Koran and precepts of law found in such ancient writings as those of the Samarians seem to reflect in most cases similar ideas about what basic rules should govern the conduct of human beings. These precepts generally include the following or similar ideas: killing a human being is wrong; taking a person's property is not to be condoned; lying in an official or unofficial capacity is repugnant to the proper conduct of humanity. In the normative context, law takes on a rather high order of value in the scheme of things, and those who participate in the law tend to be elevated to some extent above everyone else. There is a sort of sacredness to this kind of law and a comfort to be found in its order, predictability, and therefore security. If kept within simple enough boundaries, such law can and has ordered many societies, although sometimes producing rather harsh enforcement practices and rather severe limits on certain varieties of human conduct.

People still like to think of law as normative, immutable, orderly, and predictable. However, a close examination of history reveals many flaws in the normative concept. Different societies seem to have evolved different kinds of rights and wrongs. Taking a human life may be proper under certain circumstances and not under others. Governments may condemn and seize property, and amounts of property may be taken in civil suit that are far beyond what reasonable people might expect. In certain instances, the telling of an untruth may serve a social end, and so it goes. These difficulties in reducing law to simple, normative proscriptions have produced in more modern times a second school of law, the *positivist view of law* or *positive law*.

According to the positivist view, law is little more than what a society decides, at any given time, is necessary to regulate itself and to achieve some degree of security and order under a variety of conditions. Positive law is changeable not only from time to time but from society to society. Whatever rules and regulations seem to fit the needs of a society at any given time are proper, and whenever a society no longer seems to be content with these rules they may be changed.

WHAT IS LAW?

What follows is essentially a description of law in western society that is predicated on the thesis that law is basically positive and not normative. This does not, however, preclude certain normative *attitudes* about law or even normative *goals* on certain occasions. Societies may actually think in normative legal terms while applying the law in positive ways. The positivist point of view might be summarized in the humorous retort given to a young child by a distinguished lawyer when the lawyer was asked, "What is law?" His response was, "Law is what lawyers do." Whether humor was intended or not, there is a great truth here. The positivist concept of law says, in effect, that the combined actions of a group of people, whom we shall define as lawyers, in dealing with the rules and regulations of a society is what law ultimately amounts to. The word *lawyer* in this context includes far more than attorneys. It includes all people who interact in some official context with the law. This would include the legislators who write the laws, the police who initially enforce the laws, judges, jurors, witnesses, and even people on the periphery of the law such as prison wardens and parole board members. To the extent that it actually exists in any real-world context, law is the collection of what these people do when confronted by a problem concerning the obedience to a law, the application of a regulation of a society, or a disorderly situation of some other kind.

The striking fact, and the basic difference between positive law and normative law, is this: There is not nearly as much order and predictability under the law as seen from the positivist point of view as one might be conditioned to expect, especially if one thinks of law in normative terms. Let's take a typical case to illustrate the principles of the positivist point of view. First, let's assume that a robbery has occurred. What will be the outcome of this breach of a clearly established legal norm that says that a person cannot take money or property from another person without his or her consent?

We begin the analysis of this case of law with the lawyers who first deal with the problem. These would include the police and witnesses. If the investigating police officer is good, he or she may, through witnesses and investigatory techniques, develop sufficient evidence to determine the perpetrator. On the other hand, if he or she is incompetent, overworked, or uncaring, sufficient evidence may not be collected to discover the culprit. As a result, the culprit goes free. In this instance, despite all that has been written in the statutes and despite society's desire to see the law enforced, there is no law. Law is entirely dependent in this and in all cases on what the lawyers do. In New York City, the chances of being arrested for an armed robbery are less than fifty-fifty, and the chance of serving a day in jail are somewhere in the neighborhood of 1 out of 100. So much for order and predictability.

Let's assume, instead, that the culprit is caught. The culprit now engages a defense attorney, who will be opposed by a prosecuting attorney. The prosecuting attorney may have 150 cases to try during the next week, and he or she may decide that this particular robbery does not warrant the time and expense necessary to prosecute it. Since there may be some doubt as to the exact nature of the crime (for instance, was it an armed robbery or a simple robbery?), the prosecutor may go to the defense attorney and suggest that, if his or her client pleads guilty to simple robbery, the prosecutor will ask the judge to mete out the minimum penalty, which may be two years in prison. On the other hand, should the accused decide not to plead guilty to simple robbery, then the prosecutor may tell the defense attorney that he or she will try to get a conviction on armed robbery, which carries a twenty-year penalty. It is up to the defendant, then, to decide whether or not to gamble on a lengthy term through a trial or to accept a much less severe term by pleading guilty to a much lesser offense (provided, of course, that the judge and, in some instances, the "victim" will accept the deal, which must happen if this process is to work). This is called **plea bargaining,** and it is as unpredictable in its outcome as any other part of the judicial proceeding.

A corollary to this particular situation is the question of what to charge a perpetrator with in the first place. There is a process called **arraignment,** in which a judge or **magistrate** has to decide, initially at least, what specific crime has been committed or which law has been broken. This, in turn, often depends on the amount of evidence that has been produced by the prosecuting attorney, the police, and others. Again, the unpredictability of the situation stands out.

Let's take our case a step further and assume that our culprit decides to gamble on a trial in which he has been charged with armed robbery. Now other lawyers enter the picture: a judge and a jury plus a set of rules of procedure. These concern not only the evidence, but also the sequence and manner of its presentation. Is the prosecuting attorney as smart and as able as the defense attorney? Is the jury susceptible to a variety of psychological maneuvers by either adversary? What will the outcome be when the jury is placed in the backroom, where they must decide the question of innocence or guilt? Nobody can predict the outcome of this contest, and this particular situation has been the source of many an interesting drama. The 1995 murder trial of O. J. Simpson, the former football star, may be considered an extreme, if not grotesque example of this.

Let's suppose that the jury has found the culprit guilty. Here, under the Anglo-Saxon Common Law system under which the United States operates, the judge takes on a particular importance. She must decide on the sentence. Will she go for a maximum sentence or find mitigating circumstances that seem to require a minimum sentence? Is she prejudiced against the defendant's race or ethnic background? Has there been a lot of crime in the general area, which seems to call for some demonstration of governmental authority? Many factors go into the judge's decision as to the nature of the punishment. Unpredictability reigns again.

We could carry this illustration further to the point of the attitude taken by a prison warden toward a convicted prisoner, which, in turn, affects that warden's recommendation for parole. The actions and attitudes of a parole board will decide whether a parole is granted or refused. The attentiveness and the attitude of a parole officer will decide whether or not a prisoner is recommitted. And so it goes.

Law is what lawyers do. This truth is found in a thousand illustrations that occur daily across our land.

Having suggested that law is essentially positivist as we practice it, an important *caveat* is necessary. Our law is not *exclusively* positive, nor should it be. Law must be rooted in normative principles. It cannot be so changeable that anything is possible. Lawmakers must be guided, in all cases, by the basic principles of their system and its moral values when making and applying the law, however positivist the dynamic. Although the precise relationship between normative (natural) law and positive application is a source of rich debate in America, a normative element remains to some extent. Further, as we shall see, law should also be applied in a spirit of justice.

CLASSIFICATION OF LAWS

Law is generally divided into two categories. There is public law, which we often refer to as **criminal law**, and there is private law, which often bears the title **civil law.** These two kinds of law are, in certain respects, mirror images of each other. Public law is defined as rules that describe the conduct between individuals and the state. Here we are concerned with such things as the protection of life and property and the general rules of conduct that relate to the operation of a good society. Public law is also punitive in its intent. That is to say, the state's purpose is to punish offenders under the criminal law. This raises the interesting question of just what punishment is.

In basic legal theory, punishment is what is done by the state to prevent the recurrence of the crime. The simplest way to prevent the recurrence of a crime by an individual is to hang the individual. That certainly seems to take care of the problem of recurrence. Perhaps punishment can be achieved by other means—incarceration, fine, community service, or even a warning accompanied by public embarrassment. The point is that criminal law, in demanding punishment, is mainly seeking to prevent the recurrence of the crime by the person who did it. Most people have some serious misunderstandings in this regard.

Let's assume that John kills David. We might ask, "Who is the victim of the crime?" If you answer that David is, you are incorrect. David is dead. The law is not concerned with dead people. Law is concerned with the living within a society. A more astute answer might be that society is the victim of the crime. David is the subject of the crime, but society is the ultimate victim. Why is this so? Perhaps David needed killing. Perhaps David had nothing to contribute to society, anyway. Perhaps society is better off without David. How, then, was society victimized by David's demise? The answer is that David's death could be repeated; John could kill again; and society must be protected from this threat. Thus, the punishment meted out to John must be done in such a way as to prevent, within tolerable predictability, the recurrence of the crime by John. Many people confuse punishment with vindictiveness or vengeance, with rehabilitation (a doubtful proposition), and even, unfortunately, with the deterrence of others who might commit a similar crime.

Punishment *may* deter if it is swift, and if it is *seen* to be effective. However, that is not the purpose of punishment. Indeed, if one thinks about the subject logically, one can see the flaw in the goal of deterrence through punishment. Man A has committed a crime involving Man B. The purpose of punishing Man A is to see that he does not commit a crime against any other person. If, in seeking the punishment for Man A, one seeks to deter Man X from committing a similar crime against Man Y or Man Z, why must Man A be made to suffer to such an extent that an unknown person (Man X) under unknown circumstances involving unknown people (Y and Z) may be deterred from a similar act? This places an intolerable and unjust burden upon Man A, and it might not work, anyway. After all, what guarantee is there that Man X is rational to begin with? In addition, does Man X know about Man A's punishment? The unfortunate fact is that punishment works better for some than for others. Deterrence is ultimately an individual, not a collective, matter. Man A's punishment should relate to the real world of his action and the conditions under which it occurred. His punishment cannot be justly determined in order to serve as a warning to an unknown person under unknown circumstances against unknown individuals. Again, deterrence may result through swift and just punishment of Man A, but this must be an incidental result of Man A's punishment and not the purpose of Man A's punishment. As far as vengeance and vindictiveness are concerned, one need only apply the proscription in the Bible, "Vengeance is mine sayeth the Lord; I will repay." To understand that there is great danger of injustice any time punishment is meted out of wrath and anger rather than out of logic and justice is to understand that proper punishment is anything done by the state to *reasonably* and humanely prevent the recurrence of the crime—and nothing more. However, if Man A's punishment is too weak to be considered a reasonable response to his crime, then that punishment is equally inappropriate, in that society is now put at some risk.

Another misunderstanding involves compensating victims. Criminal law is noncompensatory. If John kills David, the state will take no notice of David's death, its effect on David's family, or society's loss of David's worth. The law's purpose is only to punish John. Perhaps the illustration can be seen better if, instead of murder, we discuss robbery. If I steal $100 from you, and I spend it before I'm caught, I may be tried and convicted of robbery and go to jail. However, you will not get your $100 back, because criminal law is noncompensatory. It looks to the future rather than to the past. In some states in the United States, and in some other countries, this particular characteristic of criminal law is undergoing some subtle changes. Many states have set up funds to partially compensate the victims of certain kinds of violent crime. These funds tend to come from confiscated property or from fines. In other states, criminals with assets are ordered to directly compensate their victims to whatever extent possible. Someday we may define criminal law as being semicompensatory, but there are problems with this. Why should law-abiding taxpayers have to compensate those people who have suffered because of the actions of those who have broken the laws of the society? How much compensation should be paid? Who is responsible for the criminal act? Is it society itself or is some psychological deviation found in the nature of the criminal? Who shall decide? Although some countries and some U.S. states are wrestling with these questions, the answer is not yet clear as to whether or not criminal law will forever remain noncompensatory.

The other category of law is civil law or private law. As already noted, it is the mirror image of public law. Civil law is law covering conduct between individuals. It is nonpunitive, and it is compensatory. Here we see problems relating to the loaning of money, a marriage or divorce, a contract, or an accidental or inadvertent harm caused by one person to another. Society is not threatened by any of these occurrences. If a bank lends money to an individual who does not pay it back, it is within the power of the bank to prevent the recurrence of the problem, and the bank may go to court and be compensated for its loss by the seizure of the assets of the individual involved. A marriage between two people is an agreement concerning the sharing of property and the custody of children, which, though indirectly affecting society, does not necessarily endanger it should the marriage fail and should there be some argument about the division of mutual property or who should have the custody of the children. Civil law is less dramatic. It is law that seeks through the power of the state to do something to make right a situation that is deemed to have been wrong in its basic dimensions. The civil law, then, looks to the past and present, but not necessarily to the future.

LAW ENFORCEMENT

The enforcement of civil law is generally rather undramatic and easily achieved. What of the enforcement of criminal law? As most of us know, this is a problem in American society. Why is this so and what is the problem with American law enforcement?

To begin with, law enforcement, especially in the criminal context, can almost be considered a contradiction of terms. If there is law, if there is *good* law, there should be little enforcement, and if there is enforcement, then there must be little law. What is meant by this conundrum? It is that laws that *properly* regulate a society, especially a political democracy, should be the result of a consensus among the vast majority of that society as to their rightness and proper relationship to the characteristics of that society. If the law is broken so often that vast numbers of police and vast numbers of courts and prisons are necessary in order to "make the law stick," then one of two things is true: either the society is too primitive and uncivilized to have a government of law, or the laws are not reflecting the needs and aspirations of large groups within the society. In either case, enforcement is only a symptom of the problem rather than an answer to the problem. The answer to a society with a large law enforcement problem is either to change the society or to change the law. Critics of the American system of justice have suggested that we might need to do both. They point out that there are numerous laws on the books that a significant fraction of people are simply not going to obey. These include low speed limits on interstate highways, laws forbidding the drinking of alcohol by those under twenty-one years of age, laws against drug use, and laws forbidding certain kinds of sexual conduct even among consenting adults. There are others. The problem is that because most of these "laws," however well intended, are regularly broken by large numbers of people, there is a resultant tendency to depreciate all laws to some extent. In other words, a habitual breakage of some laws sometimes leads to a disrespect for all laws and for those who would enforce them.

In addition to this problem, many note that another significant fraction of the American population seems to be alienated from any law at all. There are growing inner-city areas throughout the country in which there is little positive manifestation of government (e.g., building codes enforced, trash picked up, schools properly funded, parks maintained). There is, instead, a strong negative attempt by police to disrupt many inhabitants' major sources of income (drugs, theft, gambling, and prostitution). This situation often breeds a profound distaste among the inhabitants for any law and order and even for government itself. Such areas become places "outside the law," which is to say that they are also outside the society. One is forced to ponder in all of this the efficacy of continuing to try to change certain kinds of public behavior through tougher laws and of ignoring the growing ghettos in many of our cities while bemoaning the growing problem of "crime in America."

THE RULE OF LAW

An accompanying problem in America is our application of the rule of law. This is a basic rule of democratic governments. It says that the law must be known to all, that no person is above the law, that all public acts must be done in accordance with the law, and that all changes in law and policy must be sanctified by the legal principles of the society. Though we have had a few lapses of these precepts in our history (as in the Watergate affair of the 1970s), by and large the United States adheres to these aspects of the rule of law. There is another part of the rule of law concept: all people should be treated equally by the law. The law should be applied equally and even-handedly, no matter who is before the bar of justice. Here is where the American justice system has often come up short.

Most Americans are well aware that the rich, the well-born, and the otherwise successful people of our society frequently receive a higher quality of justice than do the poor or members of ethnic minorities. One of the basic reasons for this phenomenon has to do with some rather deep-seated ideas within the American political ethos. The Protestant ethic (which has been a major element in the American belief system since the days of the Pilgrims in the seventeenth century) assures us that some people are blessed by God and are predestined to prosper and be "saved" for heaven. Wealth and position may be considered evidences of this propensity under the grace of God. Others within the Protestant ethic concept are, for whatever reasons, doomed to damnation, both in this life and in the hereafter. As a result, they will remain poor and unsuccessful. It is an easy step from this early American religious philosophy to the subtle implication that some people are indeed better than others and that the law in its application should take this into account. Indeed, this mental process takes place almost without conscious thought.

A police officer in a small town apprehends a banker's son, who is drunk and speeding in his automobile. The officer scolds the young man and returns him home. The police officer then goes out and arrests a young black teenager equally drunk and equally misbehaving in his automobile and takes him to jail. Here is an event that happens in variation almost every day somewhere in our society. The remarkable thing is that in most instances the police officer is doing what he or she honestly thinks "ought" to be done, if he or she thinks about it at all. The officer is responding to a subtle social-ization process that has been drummed into his or her consciousness by the attitudes of others in real life or in stories and common practice. Beyond this sort of thing, on a higher level, the rich literally have the best justice money can buy (as in the aforementioned O. J. Simpson case), whereas the poor have only the public defender, who is overworked and more often than not inclined to persuade a defendant to plea bargain and get it over with.

Other countries have somewhat better records in this regard, and even government and party leaders have found themselves against the bar of jus-tice with essentially the same procedures and the same substance of the law applied to them as applies to anyone else in their country. We ought to take a hard look at their approach to the rule of law.

LEGAL CONCEPTS

Before we leave the general discussion of law, let's raise the question of what relationship there might be between law and other concepts normally asso-ciated with it if law is merely what lawyers do. In particular, what is the rela-tionship between law and justice, law and morality, law and truth, and law and ethics? Surely there is more to law than simply what a group of lawyers does in some kind of social or moral vacuum. Surely they are guided by morality, justice, truth, and ethics. Thus, enforcing the law is surely an attempt to achieve justice, protect morality, discover the truth, and ensure ethical conduct among men and women. Our legal system must bear *some* relation to these issues. While this is true to a point, there is great misunder-standing here as well as in other areas concerning law.

Justice

Let's first raise the question of justice. Should not the law be just? Of course. The question really ought to be, what is the relationship between justice and the law? The answer is there is *no necessary* relationship between justice and the law. To begin with, what is justice? This is a question that has been answered in many ways, by many people, and for which no single answer has served to satisfy everyone. In effect, Plato defined **justice** in his great work *The Republic* as essentially anything that is done in the public realm that leaves individuals and the state in the best possible relationship with each other. Other relevant ideas concerning the meaning of justice assert that, however it may be defined from society to society, the end result should be the achievement of social happiness in a context of social order. This goal should guide a society in defining its particular standards of justice, espe-cially when making and applying laws.

Does the law or, more to the point, do the lawyers work in their various activities with the laws and their applications in such a way as to leave everyone concerned—criminal, subject, and society—in the best possible relationship with each other? Do the lawyers apply their best efforts to this goal? This requires that police officers be conscientious in their jobs, not only to collect evidence but also not to abuse their authority. The judges must be impartial and effective in their punishments. The prosecutors must avoid plea bargaining when it is unnecessary or it will obviously result in society's endangerment, as when a serious offense is reduced to a misdemeanor and a vicious criminal is returned to society. The defense attorneys must give their best efforts to the defense of their clients rather than simply yielding to work load and deciding to let one go because the accused is probably guilty anyway. The jury must avoid any competing ideas beyond those developed during the trial in ascertaining guilt or innocence. The prison wardens must be conscientious in giving their prisoners a fair chance to show their worthiness for parole. And so it goes. In these acts, we will find the answer to the question of the role of justice in the law.

No matter how the law is written, justice is not written into it. Justice is found in the society; if the law is just, it is because the lawyers are just. There ought to be a direct relationship between law and justice, but if any relationship exists at all it is because of the lawyers and not the law. Indeed, law can be completely unjust. It can be prejudicial, arbitrary, severe, and debilitating to the society. If, however, it is enforced by a government and understood and observed by a people, it remains law, whether just or unjust.

Morality

What of morality? Surely here is a relationship with the law. Let's begin again by defining the concept of morality. In this case, our task is simpler. It is generally agreed that morality is society's definition of those things that are right and those things that are wrong. Although different societies may evolve different codes of morality, each society still has rather definite ideas on the subject. When a society is fairly clear in terms of its concept of right and wrong, laws will generally be written in such a way as to reflect this moral consensus, and the law will indeed be moral. The lawyers will also tend to uphold the moral code in the enforcement of the law. Remember that law reflects the moral code; it does not create it. If there is confusion in a society with regard to certain moral principles such as cohabitation between the sexes, abortion, euthanasia, or genetic research; if there is confusion as to what is obscene or pornographic; if there is confusion concerning such things as sexual activities of an unusual nature, where does the law come in? It comes in where it has always come in. That is as a reflection of society's moral code. If society has no clear-cut consensus of a code of morality, the law will reflect the confusion of that society.

In the United States, we have been wrestling for some years with a legal definition of obscenity. Why look to the law if the people do not understand the concept or are confused about its dimensions? How can we enforce laws with regard to sexual conduct when society cannot agree what forms of conduct are permissible and what forms are not? Americans, in particular, have been confused in this regard since at least World War II. A hundred years of moral consensus has begun to erode. To deal with the situation, Americans have erroneously looked to the courts for answers to questions that really lie within the society itself. However, when a society is unsure about morality, then, as the old saying goes, you cannot legislate it. Indeed, it is impossible for law to bear this burden. We are placing on an already burdened institution, the American court system, the burden of our own moral confusion, to the detriment of both.

Truth

What of truth? Of course the law should be based on what legislatures, executives, specialists, and other concerned citizens regard as the truth of some situation they are trying to address. Indeed, there usually is not much of a problem in the creation of laws. However, when laws are broken, when it is time for the law to be applied by courts, then "the truth" may be seen to be of secondary importance to arriving at a solution that both satisfies the court and protects individual rights. Although this situation may anger and confuse some citizens, it is, nevertheless, a reality of contemporary law.

Consider the following examples. Evidence that is crucial to proving the reality of a crime may not be allowed to be presented to a jury if the judge rules that it has been seized illegally under the exclusionary rule, which comes out of the Fourth Amendment to the U.S. Constitution; a witness who knows the truth may decline to testify because he or she is married to the defendant; the defendant (who knows the truth) may also decline to testify under the Fifth Amendment; certain kinds of testimony or photographs that might explain more fully the circumstances surrounding an act may be declared by a judge to be inflammatory and kept from the jury lest they allow emotion to distract them from reason; a defense attorney will not willingly bring up any evidence that may hurt the client's case; and, in some rare instances, evidence that might clear a defendant may be purposefully withheld by the prosecution.

Ironically, most of these rules were originally designed to "get at the truth." The problem is that they can also be used for the opposite purpose. Thus, a contemporary trial is not always an activity aimed solely at truth. Rather, it is an exercise designed to reach a solution to a problem under clearly (and sometimes not so clearly) defined rules of procedure, which we have come to call *due process*. The outcome may be due (which is to say, reasonably fair), but it may not be completely in accordance with the truth. Courts can conduct no independent investigations and must rely solely on the facts brought out by opposing attorneys.

Lest one be too put off by this grim reality, consider an analogy. A baseball umpire must make a judgment call on a disputed play. The outcome may affect a player's career; the team's position in the standings; and the incomes of all concerned, especially if it is a crucial play-off or a world series game. Shouldn't the players, fans, and owners know the truth? Must they accept the solution (decision) offered by the umpire solely on the basis of his field of vision, his knowledge of the rules, and his judgment? The truth could be discovered if a videotaped replay was studied to see what really happened, but major league baseball does not do it. Why?

Simply put, the costs are too high. It takes a lot of time; it requires expensive equipment; it distracts from the game; and most of all, it undermines the authority of the umpires. You must go with the umpires most of the time. They are the professionals. It is better to suffer an occasional missed call than to undermine the nature of the game for the sake of the truth.

Of course, the law must approach its issues with a much higher degree of seriousness, but, even here, in many cases the costs of the truth may also be considered too high. These costs may include the trampling of people's rights to privacy or their protection against self-incrimination. Insisting on the whole truth could delay a case indefinitely. It could make our courtrooms fearful places where people's lives are stripped bare and issues extraneous to the problem before them are bandied about in public. If we can settle the issue in ways that produce some degree of justice, then maybe we can ignore some attendant truths along the way. In the final analysis, the truth can sometimes hurt more than the solution.

A major difficulty in this concept, particularly as it affects American jurisprudence, arises in the temptation by many lawyers to see the process as essentially a game wherein the idea is to avoid losing rather than to seek justice for all concerned. A trial can thus become a contest between your facts versus mine (neither of which may have much to do with the other) before a jury, which is not supposed to know anything more than those "facts" submitted to it. This tends to place salesmanship and showmanship above both truth and justice, as in the infamous O. J. Simpson trial already mentioned. A solution might be found if the courts and other bodies of legal oversight of our land would require that lawyers take more seriously their role as officers of the court and, thereby, agents of the state's pursuit of justice, rather than focusing on their private pursuit of wealth and fame. In other words, it is, at heart, a question of ethics.

Ethics

Finally, what of ethics? Here again the definition should precede the discussion. **Ethics** is a form of morality that is different in degree. Morality is a society's definition of right and wrong, and it generally prevails throughout the society. Ethics, on the other hand, is an individual code of right and wrong that is relevant to who a person is and where he or she is. It is a code of right and wrong for one person that may be quite different from a code of right and wrong for another person. An illustration here would be helpful. Suppose you are walking down the street, thinking about purchasing a bicycle to improve your health and to get you to school more cheaply. As you cut across a used car lot, a very effective salesman seizes upon you and in a few minutes persuades you to buy an automobile instead. The automobile is a good one, but you do not need it. You cannot afford it, and it is not what you came to town to purchase, but you buy it. The question is, did the car salesman behave unethically? The answer is no. He is a car salesman. As long as he did not lie to you, as long as he did not cheat you, as long as the car was indeed what he represented it to be, then whether or not you wound up where you wanted to be is immaterial to the ethics of the salesman. He behaved correctly. You reacted foolishly.

On the other hand, suppose you go to see your physician and you complain of a stomachache. The physician knows that you need some form of antacid pill to break up the particular cause of your stomach distress, but she wishes to sell you an operation so that she can make a little money. The physician tells you that you should have your appendix removed. You proceed, then, to buy her operation and have your appendix removed. Did the physician behave unethically in selling you an unnecessary operation by convincing you that you needed it? Here the answer is clearly yes. The physician was unethical. She is not entitled to sell operations when her main function is to protect health. By selling you an operation that you didn't need, she undermined your health even though she "delivered the goods"— she removed your appendix.

What was clearly unethical for one person was ethical for another, but it depended on who the individual was and where the individual was. This leads us to the law. What are legal ethics? Prior to the Watergate scandals of the early 1970s, many law schools did not even necessarily encourage a course in the subject of legal ethics. This left many lawyers unsure as to just what kind of conduct under certain circumstances was ethical and what was not. Actually, schools should have required such a course. Any attorney with an ounce of imagination should have already realized that the ethics of the law concern the concept of justice. When a lawyer does anything that undermines the possibility of a better relationship between the people he or she is dealing with and the society as a whole, he or she is behaving unethically. If a lawyer charges too high a fee, fails to represent a client to the fullest ability, too easily accepts plea bargaining, or allows prejudice or other factors to intervene in punishment, that individual is not only being unjust, but he or she is also being unethical.

These, then, are some of the basic elements of what is called law. We are dealing here with law as it relates to government. We are not, of course, discussing scientific law, economic law, or even social law. What we are discussing is law as it appears in our statutes, in our constitutions, in something called International Law, and also in custom and precedent. It is even found in something we call *equity*, which will be discussed later in this chapter. In order for a nation to have a good legal system, the leaders of the nation, but better the society as a whole, should understand these principles so that they can make more intelligent decisions with regard to the concept and operation of law.

LEGAL SYSTEMS OF THE WESTERN WORLD

Law generally exists on two levels: (1) the law of general principles, which is often found today in constitutions and referred to as **organic law** or basic law, and (2) the specific rules and regulations that evolve from basic law and are more often considered to be the laws of the land. One of the major characteristics of a sound legal system is that the rules reflect correctly the principles of the legal system. When rules do not reflect these principles, they are often difficult to enforce and are ultimately rejected by the society. For example, two of the basic principles of our legal system are freedom of speech and freedom to organize politically for change. When the Smith Act of 1940 effectually outlawed the Communist party *as an organization*, these principles were violated. Two decades later, after many people were made to suffer unjustly, the Supreme Court rejected the law as unconstitutional. In a similar manner, the controversial 1988 decision by the U.S. Supreme Court that negated state (and national) laws against flag burning was based on the required agreement between such statutes and the First Amendment's assertion of the freedom of (symbolic) speech.

There are, in the western world, two sets of principles of law, which differ somewhat from each other. This results in two different systems of law, which are called Roman Law and Anglo-Saxon Common Law. Each evolved at different times and under different circumstances. Thus, although they affirm similar standards of justice, they differ in terms of procedures and structure. How did they (and other systems of law) evolve?

THE EVOLUTION OF LEGAL SYSTEMS

There have been many theories suggested with regard to how legal systems evolved, but one of the more popular suggestions stresses four stages that can be marked in the recorded history of several groups of people:

1. Tribal stage
2. Religious stage
3. Political stage
4. Codification stage

TRIBAL STAGE

The first stage is generally that of tribal law itself. This is the legal system briefly described in chapter 3 with regard to neotribalism. Tribal law, or the tribal stage of development, is law in which totems (do's) and taboos (don'ts) make up the bulk of the legal code. The totems and taboos tend to reflect a desire for economic division of labor, survival, health, and the protection of children. Tribal law is a self-help system. There are no judges, courts, or prisons. The general punishment for breach of tribal law is ostracism. The legal system is, therefore, of minimal significance in terms of governance of the tribe itself.

RELIGIOUS STAGE

From tribal levels of evolution, legal systems then tend to proceed to what may be defined as the religious level or religious stage. In the religious stage, totem and taboo give way to right and wrong or to religious and moral principles. Here, conduct relating to sex, marriage, and religious ritual enter into the legal system as new types of principles and statutes. In the books of Deuteronomy and Leviticus in the Bible, we see the tribe of Abraham evolving into a religious stage of the law, accompanied by a vast increase in new kinds of rules for daily living. The religious stage is also essentially a self-help stage in terms of its enforcement, but it takes on a new source of authority in the form of a priestly class. Stonings and other forms of punishment accompany ostracism as the means of enforcement in the religious period.

POLITICAL STAGE

A third stage might be called the *political stage.* This occurs when a secular rule of some continuous effect is established over the society. Again, using Israeli history as an example, this occurred at the time of the crowning of King Saul, which ended the period of the rule of the judges. In whatever form, when monarchs or other secular leaders evolve a system that can be passed on in its essential form to future monarchs or leaders, the entire legal structure also begins to evolve further in terms of secular decrees. New kinds of law concerning property, new kinds of crimes, and new kinds of economic organization and administrative regulation begin to enter the picture. There are also, for the first time, institutions of law enforcement: armies and police; prisons; formal means of punishment; and courts, judges, and trials.

[handwritten margin note: not clerical! any more]

CODIFICATION STAGE

The final stage in the evolution of a legal system follows soon after the political stage. It is called the **codification** stage. At this point, some writer or group of scholars puts into a single code all law known to that society. Some of these laws may date back to the primitive stage, as in the case of laws against incest; some may include religious proscriptions, as in the so-called Blue Laws in some American states. Mostly this code is a compilation of decrees and statutes in effect at that time.

The code itself is divided into criminal and civil portions; classifications of crimes or civil disorders are noted; and there is a catalog of degrees of offense. When the code is finally written, the law becomes available not only to the government but also to the people, and it can be known and obeyed far more easily. The law formerly under the political stage has now become less arbitrary and more predictable in its enforcement.

ROMAN LAW

One of the oldest known codes of law is that of the Babylonian kingdom in the days of Hammurabi (2123–2081 B.C.). It is called the Code of Hammurabi. One of the first western codes of law was written by the arcon, Draco, in an ancient Greek city-state during the seventh century B.C. Draco's code was a very severe code in which punishment very often took the form of death or severe injury to the accused.[1] Later, as the Greek city-states evolved into more civilized forms, the famous Code of Solon (640–558 B.C.), was written.[2] Solon's code was a more refined code accompanied by less severe penalties and more diversity within the law. In fact, Solon's Code was so popular that it was adapted by the Romans upon their conquest of Greece. It evolved to some extent into the famous Twelve Tablets of the Roman Law, which used to be displayed in the Roman Forum.

The greatest of the Roman codes was the Code of Justinian, written in the year A.D. 553. It was a combination of three previous Roman codes: the *Jus Gentium*, which was the law of all the people of the Roman Empire; the *Jus Civilis*, which was the law of Roman citizens; and the *Jus Natural*, which contained for the most part the basic principles of Roman Law. The Justinian Code compiled all of these codes into a single body of Roman Law. It comprised the last classic statement of Roman Law. When the Roman Empire began to shrink, with it shrank the Justinian Code or, at least, those who could apply it and those who would therefore be responsible for its enforcement. Throughout the bulk of the medieval period, the Justinian Code remained. Then the law of Europe was mostly in the hands of the clergy. They still had the old records of the Justinian Code. They advised the emerging dukes and kings as to the proper application of the law.

During the evolution of the feudal state, the Justinian Code was augmented by at least two other kinds of law. First there was Canon Law, or laws made by the church hierarchy in its attempts to normalize the relationships between people and the church during that rather unorganized period of history. Second came those rules that related to the relationships among the political individuals of the feudal system. These were rules known as Fealty Law, in which mutual obligations and responsibilities were written down in the form of laws. Thus, by the late medieval period, the law of Europe was, in effect, a combination of the old Justinian Code, Canon Law, and Fealty

---

[1]This gave rise to the word, draconian, meaning severe measures taken by any individual or group.
[2]This gave rise to the word, *solon*, meaning legislator in modern English.

Law. Together, all three of these were referred to under the general title of the *Corpus Juris Civilis,* which translates from the Latin as the "body of the Civil Law." There was no single code called the *Corpus Juris Civilis;* rather, the term alluded to all three forms of law as applied either in the secular courts of the monarchs or in the ecclesiastical courts of the church.

After the rise of the nation-state and during the age of Napoleon, a great change occurred in the legal system of Western Europe. In his attempt to unify Europe under a single form of government, language, and culture, Napoleon sought to unify and modernize the laws of Europe. To this end, he gathered the greatest legal scholars of his age, and in 1804 they produced what has come to us as the Napoleonic Code. This particular refinement of the *Corpus Juris Civilis* was so excellent that it remains the basis in most continental European states for what is referred to either as *Roman Law* or *Civil Law.* Even though Napoleon was cast out of the various countries he conquered, his legal code was preserved and modified by the governments that continued after his reign had ended. Even today one finds the Napoleonic Code in the basic principles of law applied to the state of Louisiana, which was, of course, once under the control of the French government. This, then, is the evolution of one of the great western systems of law—the Roman Law or Civil Law of the continent of Europe.

This system is characterized by a sort of rigidity in which the code encompasses the bulk of the law. A judge in a Roman Law system goes to a separate kind of legal school from that of trial lawyers and is taught the code, its history, its meaning, and its procedures. The judge's role is to apply the code with as much uniformity as possible. On the other hand, attorneys go to another law school in which they learn essentially the substance of the law, leaving to the judge the actual conduct of trials and the rules of evidence. A Roman Law trial is a rather clear-cut action in which appeal is rare and justice is relatively swift, certainly by American standards. The principles of humanity and civil rights contained within the code, however, do not differ greatly from those in the American experience. Despite its tendency toward rigidity, there is some flexibility in the Roman Law. Legislatures may add to it as new conditions arise, and the professors who teach the judges in the law schools may introduce new philosophical interpretations of the legal statutes that already exist. However, there is no concept of precedent in the Roman Law system, nor is there the right for a judge to find law where there is none. The law is what is in the code and its meaning—nothing more and nothing less—and the judges must find the proper law within the code in every case they try.

ANGLO-SAXON COMMON LAW

The Roman Law system may be contrasted quite markedly with the Anglo-Saxon system of the British world. *Anglo-Saxon Common Law,* as it is called, is found in the British empire and in those areas that were at one time colonies of Great Britain. This not only includes the United States but also such nation-states as Australia, New Zealand, Canada, South Africa, several African states, and to some extent India and Malaysia. The Anglo-Saxon Common Law differs from the Roman Law primarily because of different historical events.

Let's briefly review our history of Europe. The Roman Empire, which brought the Roman Law to the continent of Europe, came late to Britain. Even though Julius Caesar had occupied Britain earlier, there had been no permanent colonization until the latter part of the Roman Empire period. Even during this period, only the eastern and southern portions of Britain fell under any great administrative control of the Roman government. As the empire began to shrink, Britain was one of the first places to be abandoned. Therefore, what was left behind was no great institution of Roman Law but rather a confused collection of Roman principles and ancient tribal, religious, and political precedents that were different among themselves in terms of their sources and application. There were Danish Laws and the laws of the Saxons. There were also the laws of the Jutes and some of the Norsemen who had occupied some of the northern parts of the area. Finally, there were ancient traditions of the original populations found mostly in the area of Wales. Therefore, there was no true uniform system of law in Britain until the late medieval period.

The Saxons ultimately prevailed in southern Britain and, in a political stage of development, applied a form of Saxon Law. This system was still in effect at the time of the Battle of Hastings in 1066. It was, of course, the famous Norman conquest of Britain in 1066 that was the turning point of British legal history. William the Conqueror, who defeated and killed Saxon King Harold, was a Norman from France who had a rather difficult task before him after his defeat of the Saxon army. His job was to find some way to create legitimacy and a new order over a foreign people working through his own Norman subordinates who had helped him conquer Britain.

King William established in his government the post later called the *Lord Chancellor*, whose purpose was to provide the king's justice over the entire realm. One of the first things William did was to begin a census whereby he could determine the total population of his new realm and its political subdivisions and their characteristics. Having collected this information in what is known as the *Domesday Book*, King William then sent to each county, borough, and shire a judge to carry out the king's law in those subdivisions of the realm. The judges had two instructions: (1) make sure the basic king's law was observed and (2) apply whatever local customs prevailed in their localities. The first instruction included the protection of the king's property, the protection of the king's highway, and the protection of the church, among other things. The second instruction was to be applied without upsetting the existing order any more than necessary. The judges were to make sure it was known that King William and his successors were the source of law and justice but not necessarily the *substance* of law and justice.

Thus, these judges were given rather free reign to decide how to resolve the conflicts that occurred in their particular areas. Each judge was required in all serious cases to write down the nature of the offense, the name of the accused, the evidence, and the result of the trial. These records, in turn, were sent to London. Over the years, then, an enormous amount of legal material began to accumulate. When judges visited the court in London, they had access to what their fellow judges were doing. Over a period of centuries, certain ideas seemed to be more popular than others, and a certain commonality began to enter into the actions of judges. To this extent, a common law began to evolve in which the precedent set by a certain judge would be followed by a subsequent judge when it seemed to meet the needs of a similar case.

A system of case law based on judicial precedent began to evolve. The old Roman Law dictum of *stare decisis,* "let the decision stand," began to enter the British system. Under Roman Law, this principle in effect decreed that a decision reached in a court of law concerning any particular case stood as law for that particular case regardless of what might happen in the future. Under the evolution of the Anglo-Saxon Common Law, *stare decisis* took on a second meaning. Henceforth, a decision made in a courtroom by a judge not only would be law for that case but could also become law for a future case if a judge so desired. Thus, precedent and the opinion of future judges as to the relevance of that precedent to their own particular case became the basis for the common law.

Over the years, an enormous amount of precedents had been accumulated, but still the judge was left pretty much on his own with regard to their use. There was also the possibility that a judge, upon rejecting existing precedent, might establish a new precedent, which then presented a subsequent judge with two conflicting precedents. Here again one sees the importance of the judge in selecting not only a precedent but *which* precedent to use.

Over the centuries, certain precedents began to be used more often than any others, and several legal scholars attempted to combine these into some kind of orderly collection to advise judges from a single source what all of the popular precedents were like. Early writers such as Sir John Fortescue and Edward Coke selected prominent precedents, put them in their logical relationship (that is to say, the criminal and civil precedents), and subdivided them into the various categories of those two kinds of law. They not only cited the precedent in terms of when and how often it occurred and exactly what it meant, but they also commented further on its particular logic, its relationship to other legal ideas, and its possible utility. These early books about the Common Law were called *commentaries.* In the eighteenth century, the greatest of the commentaries was written by Sir William Blackstone. Blackstone's *Commentaries on the Laws of England* is a valuable source of legal thought during the most highly developed period of the pure Common Law. Blackstone was studied by early American lawyers and is still cited. It is said that Abraham Lincoln learned the bulk of his law from reading Blackstone.

Thus, the commentaries on the English Common Law became a focusing point and a handy tool for judges throughout the British realm. Indeed, it might be said that the commentaries became the functional equivalent of a law code for the British people. Here two distinctions must be kept in mind between the commentaries and a formal code of laws. First, they were not the result of kingly decrees or legislative enactment; they were only suggestions as to what had been done by judges heretofore. Second, and more important, no one was bound to follow the precedents found in the commentaries as a Roman Law judge would be bound by the code. Nevertheless, for at least 100 years or more, the commentaries did produce a higher level of commonality to a judge-centered system.

In the nineteenth century, with the coming of popularly elected parliaments and the increase in the role of government and its functions, statutory law began to be passed in rather large quantities. This law was entered into law codes for the British people, and the codes coexisted with the commentaries and with the Common Law itself. Judges were then free to apply the statutes as written if they chose, but again, under the Common Law system, the judge could decide the meaning of the statute, its relevance to the particular case, and how to apply the statute (within loose limits). Today, in most Common Law systems, the statutes generally take precedence, and judges generally apply them out of common sense. The basic Common Law comes to the fore only when judges feel that the statutes are inadequate.

JUDICIAL SELECTION

All of this notwithstanding, the judge remains the center of the Common Law system. It is he or she who may be the central agent in fitting the particular law to the particular situation, using whatever means he or she feels are proper. It is, however, safer to follow statutes than not.

IN GREAT BRITAIN

All of this suggests that British judges must have been of a highly extraordinary caliber, and indeed they were from the beginning. Usually judges were the sons of the nobility. If born into a royal family, the oldest son could inherit the royal title and act as political agent over the royal land. A second son might enter the clergy and become a part of the spiritual nobility; another son might enter the military and become a naval or army leader or enter the law and become a judge. Only the wealthy could attend the universities, which were only beginning to emerge at places such as Oxford and Cambridge, or be tutored in the law by eminent jurists. These were the people of the higher levels of education and political experience. To this day, in most Common Law countries, there are special requirements for being a judge.

In the law schools of Great Britain, one is taught the law in a general way. One studies the basic meaning, procedures, and applications of the law and learns to do rather low-level legal functions such as writing a will, drafting a contract, advising a person of his or her legal rights, and preparing a case for trial by researching the precedents. Such an attorney is called a **solicitor.**

There is another kind of attorney called a **barrister.** A barrister learns all that the solicitor has learned, but in addition he or she also learns such things as trial procedure, the precedents and how they are to be applied, forensic decorum, and the rules of evidence. These things can be learned from a higher level of university study or through apprenticeship in a Chambers of barristers. Afterwards, he or she is considered qualified to try a case. For many years only barristers could become judges in Great Britain and only the best of the barristers. The general rule was that one must have been distinguished in one's studies and must have had several years of successful experience in the courtroom as a barrister before being considered worthy to be a judge. To become a judge, one was recommended by other judges and then appointed by the Lord Chancellor for a life tenure.

However, since 1990, the old barrister system seems to be coming to an end. Outstanding solicitors began to become judges as early as 1989, and some of them began to participate in serious trials even before. This has distressed many devotees of British justice. This suggests three criteria for becoming a judge in a Common Law system: qualifications, method of selection, and tenure of office. First, in almost all Common Law countries, the qualifications are high, similar in general to those of the old British empire. Second, appointment is made on the recommendations of a competent authority. Third, the term of office is life so that the judge will be nonpolitical in decisions and able to apply the law in a consistent way despite transitory popular ideas.

IN THE UNITED STATES

The United States is the one major exception to the normal application of the aforementioned criteria, and our being the exception goes a long way toward explaining a weakness of our own legal system. Let's first consider how we deviate from the Common Law norm and then why this is so. Let's begin with the national judiciary. The national judiciary, which coexists in parallel with fifty state judiciaries, consists essentially of three levels: the federal district courts of original jurisdiction, the circuit courts of appeal, and the United States Supreme Court.[3] Taking the first criterion, qualifications, we discover that there are none save that the appointee be a U.S. citizen and be breathing at the point of his or her investiture. Generally, one would

---

[3]There are, of course, several summary federal courts such as the tax court, the court of patent appeals, and military courts. These will be discussed later.

expect a judicial appointee to have a law degree, and generally this is true. However, when one considers the wide variety of law schools in America, one senses that it is one thing to have a degree from Harvard Law School and another to hold a similar degree from Hog Wash University. In any case, the law degree is not a formal requirement.[4] Further, many a federal district or circuit judge is appointed for reasons having little to do with superior legal background or expertise. Indeed, the proper political ideology has become a major prerequisite, especially since the Reagan administration. President Bush's appointment of Clarence Thomas to the U.S. Supreme Court in 1991 was particularly controversial in view of his having had only three years of relatively undistinguished experience on the U.S. Court of Appeals.

With regard to the second criterion, the method of selection, we find that in a formal sense a federal judge is appointed by the president of the United States on the advice and consent of the Senate, through the examination of the Senate Judiciary Committee. However, for Federal District judges, which are the most numerous, this is for the most part a perfunctory operation. In actuality, when a vacancy occurs in the federal judiciary, especially at the district court level, the senior senator from the state in which the vacancy exists is asked to recommend the appointee. The Senate Judiciary Committee automatically approves that appointee because the other senators who do the voting wish to have their appointees approved with equal dispatch. The qualifications of the chosen individual may have more to do with the candidate's relationship with the senator than with his or her judicial experience compared with other possible choices. Thus, the apparent process of appointment is not necessarily one in which the highest qualifications are paramount and a serious search is attempted, but rather it is the result of a political process of mutual convenience among the candidate, the senator, and the president.

The third criterion, tenure of office, finds the national judiciary at least equal to the rest of the world's Common Law systems. American national judges serve life terms, and this seems to be as it should. Unfortunately, because the other two criteria may not have been met the life tenure may be less than beneficial should the appointee turn out to be as incompetent as some national judges have been on occasion. Therefore, even life tenure in the American system is blighted by the fact that the first two criteria were not applied as rigorously as they should have been. Nevertheless, most of our national judges have proven to be competent, and the problem has been manageable for the most part.

When we examine the state court systems, we find *none* of the three criteria uniformly applied. Qualifications for state judges are sometimes specified, at least to the extent that a law degree is required, but, again, what kind of law degree and what kind of performance is attached to it? These

---

[4]The last justice of the U.S. Supreme Court who did not have a law degree was Justice Reed, appointed by Franklin Roosevelt in 1940.

questions are seldom examined at any length.[5] Some states do not even require the law degree. Further, there is no specification in some states for a long record of distinguished service before the bar.

Several illustrations will help make the point. In Vermont, in addition to elected superior court judges, there are lay judges (ordinary citizens with no legal training whatsoever) who are also elected to sit beside the regular judges and share much of their judicial power, including the power to overrule the regular judge on questions of fact and sentencing. In North Carolina there was a former grocer and auctioneer with no legal training serving as a district court judge (one of seven nonlawyers among that state's 135 district court judges in 1980). He had been reelected despite having served time in jail, being censured by the State Supreme Court, and having sentenced some defendants in criminal cases to attend church for specified periods of time. As late as 1980, a study by the Institute of Judicial Administration found that there were 14,000 nonlawyer judges of various types serving in forty-four states.

With regard to the method of selection, the record is even worse. Many states elect their judges, subjecting them to popular opinion, which is inadequate to discern who would be a good judge and who would not. A "beauty contest" is not a way to place a man or woman in a position to become the center of the legal system of any jurisdiction. Other states have modified-appointive systems such as the Missouri Plan. Under the Missouri Plan, a judicial vacancy is filled by the governor, who chooses from a list of five nominees made by the state bar association. After two years in office, the selected judge must seek election on his or her record. If he or she is successful, the term of office is now life. Again the idea of the popular selection of a judge leaves one in some doubt as to the ability of the population to perceive the necessary prerequisites for adequate judicial performance within such a judge-centered system. Some states look to the legislature as the electorate for judges, with the result that they often elect a judge from their own membership. This in turn can create an enormous conflict-of-interest problem when a lawyer/legislator appears as an attorney before a judge whom the same lawyer/legislator has helped elect and will be involved in his or her reelection when the term is up. The South Carolina legal system is notorious in this regard.

Finally, most states restrict judges to specific terms of office. They not only fail to enhance their experience should they not be reappointed or reelected, but they must face the voters or the legislature, making them sensitive to political winds of change whether or not these political winds are supported by legal doctrine. The result of having too many weak judges in too many

---

[5]Some improvement is being seen in this area. New Jersey requires an applicant for the bar to complete a basic skills test. Montana, New Hampshire, and Rhode Island have instituted special training programs as a prerequisite to admission to the bar. In addition, Colorado, Iowa, and Minnesota now require practicing attorneys to complete ten to fifteen hours of continuing legal education each year they practice.

states for too many years has been an accumulation of judicial errors throughout the first half of this century, especially as they relate to the due process of law.

The long succession of judicial error in the history of our country has not only led to an excessive amount of appeal and delay in our legal system, but it has also led to the attempt to clearly define the rights and procedures of the law through civil rights acts and court interpretations of the Bill of Rights. This has produced, in turn, a situation in which American justice has become hostage to words on paper that have become substitutes for the wisdom that was supposed to reside in the judicial brain. These words have become quite extensive over the past three decades. In particular, three Supreme Court cases have produced some basic changes in the way people are to be treated in courts and have generally complicated court procedures:

Mapp v. Ohio
(1961) ruled that, under the Fourth Amendment to the U.S. Constitution, a state court may not consider illegally seized evidence in criminal trials, leaving open many arguments about what constitutes an illegal search. Since the early 1990s, the Supreme Court has gradually narrowed the definition of illegal evidence and will probably continue to do so.

Gideon v. Wainright
(1963) ruled that, under the Sixth and Fourteenth Amendments, state courts are required to provide counsel to indigent defendants in criminal cases as a protection of due process of law.

Miranda v. Arizona
(1966) ruled that, prior to any questioning by police, a person must be warned that, under the Fifth and Sixth Amendments, he or she has a right to remain silent, that any statement made may be used against him or her, and that the person has a right to the presence of an attorney.

Many Americans are upset over such rules, feeling that they unnecessarily encumber the police and the courts and tilt the scales of justice in favor of the defendant. However, others claim that these rules had to be written because judges, out of ignorance or worse, had been violating the basic civil rights of some citizens for decades. The British have not had to write such rules nearly as much (and thus they have less to argue about) because the judges in general are better trained to know the law and to avoid such errors.

We must now face the question of *why* this situation exists in America, and the answer is rather simple, if very seldom understood. Our founding fathers were very resentful of the monarchy of King George III and of the nobility that served it. They resolved to do away with not only monarchy but also "government by nobility," wherein Royal Governors and judges had plagued Americans for years. Instead, they created state governors, who would be responsible, through various checks and balances, to two other branches of government. They also created legislatures, whose lower house would be directly elected by those who had the power to vote. This was not at all unexpected, and it seemed to logically address the problem of monarchy and royal government. However, in the zeal for democratization, they also turned to the judiciary with equal enthusiasm. The result was to reduce the judiciary to the same level of popular control as the other two branches of state government.

One should consider that to make policy and to draw up laws are active phenomena in which great issues of the moment are at stake. On the other hand, the judicial role, the application of the law and its enforcement, is more passive. It only comes into play when there is disagreement or breach of the law. One has to go to a court for the judiciary to begin to act. The judiciary does not initiate actions of its own. Since the courts are the last stop in the governmental process, the last voice of the public debate, it is logical, to the rest of the Anglo-Saxon world at least, that this voice should be the wisest voice—the best voice. If you democratize the judiciary, you make no great distinction among this voice, the voice that makes the policy, and the voice that writes the laws, and you place the judiciary on the same level of commonality as the other two branches.

The result has been that in a system of law where wisdom, restraint, and experience are so terribly important, we have placed, through our democratic zeal, a wide variety of qualified and not so qualified individuals. This has not been a wise choice. To some extent, a degree of care *has* been made, in most cases, in the selection of our judges despite the methods, the qualifications, and the tenure. However, care has not *always* been used, and the result has been too many incompetent judges, too many terms of office, and too many bad decisions.

CHANGES IN BRITISH LAW

A major difference in America's application of the common law from that of Britain's is that Britain has no specific Bill of Rights and no equivalent of our Supreme Court with the power to strike down acts of its Parliament. Thus British standards of civil rights have tended to vary, historically, from our own. For instance, the rights of the press to report on trials in progress have always differed from those in America, and the public's access to government documents is much less than is ours. Whereas we have a Freedom of Information Act, which can force all but the most sensitive information into the public domain, under the British National Secrets Act, almost any embarrassing official papers can be kept from public scrutiny. In 1995, under the Criminal Justice and Public Order Act, the government of Great Britain dramatically reshaped the criminal justice system, curtailing some traditional rights, increasing police powers and imposing stricter penalties for a broad variety of major and minor offenses. The changes were aimed at violent crime and other forms of disruptive behavior, especially by young people. Primarily affected were ancient British rights to refuse to answer questions when accused of a crime, the right to free assembly and restrictions on searches and seizures by police. Whereas there was a great hue and cry over this by British civil libertarians, a Conservative Party majority in the Parliament made these new standards stick. It is unlikely that many of them could survive judicial review by the U.S. Supreme Court.

EQUITY LAW

One of the most beneficial results of the Common Law system has been the evolution of a separate kind of law similar to civil or private law called **equity** or *cases in equity*. First, Equity Law is not so much based on what is right or wrong or on who is guilty or innocent, but rather it is a system of preventive law. Second, it seeks fairness above guilt or innocence. The word *equity* suggests the concept of fairness. What is Equity Law? How did it develop?

To begin with, it could only have evolved in a system of law where an individual, the judge, sits at the center of the process and can sway the events of the law as it approaches his or her court. Equity Law can be illustrated by the following example. Suppose I have a neighbor whom I dislike, and I wish to encourage him to move from my neighborhood. One day I go over to the edge of my property line and proceed to stack bricks one on top of the other. About twenty feet from the property line on his side is a large picture window in front of which his children often play. As the stack of bricks grows higher and higher, my neighbor notices the wind blowing his way and becomes concerned lest the bricks eventually become so high and the wind so strong that they will tip over and come crashing through his picture window. Suppose I continue doing this day after day, causing him great anxiety, thereby hoping to drive him away. What I am doing is not an illegal act since there is no crime that has yet been committed. What I am doing may eventually become a crime, malicious destruction of property or whatever, but at this point I am committing no legal offense. I am, however, behaving unfairly. Under the system of Equity Law worked out centuries ago, my neighbor can go to a judge, the center of the legal system, and describe the situation. The judge may dispatch a police officer to investigate and verify the particular aspects described by the complainer. Upon being convinced that the situation is indeed as described, the judge may apply Equity Law by issuing a **writ.** A writ is an order. In this case, the judge might issue a writ of **mandamus.** A writ of mandamus takes its root from the Latin word for command. The writ would tell me to take down the bricks. I am commanded by the court to do so and to do so immediately, thus ceasing my unfair behavior. If I do so, that is the end of it. Nothing further is required by the state, and I am not declared to be guilty of anything or further at fault.

Should I disobey the writ, which will probably be delivered to me by a police officer, I will have then committed a crime. The crime is contempt of court, and this is a criminal offense punishable in minor cases without even a formal trial. I could be given thirty days in jail and a fine by the judge simply upon the judge's own determination that I have disobeyed the order.

The result of the issuance of the writ would probably be my removal of the bricks. Failing that, and my subsequent conviction of contempt of court, the police might come and carry out the order by removing the bricks. I might also have been issued another writ, called an **injunction.** An injunction is an order to stop something that is unfair. It is used in unfair labor strikes, unfair management lockouts, or any other activity whose continuation would result in an unfair advantage of one party over another. This is what Equity Law is all about—*preventing* an unfair, if not illegal, act.

Three other writs used in Equity Law are quite famous and help to illustrate further its impact on our daily lives. One of the most famous of the equity writs is **habeas corpus.** It is designed to prevent an unfair arrest or an arrest without charge. Under the writ, a person who has been arrested without an adequate charge must be released to his or her attorney or else formally charged, and that charge must be backed up by sufficient evidence. The result of this writ is the prevention of police harassment of individuals.

Another writ in Equity Law is known as **certiorari.** This is the writ that prevents an unfair trial. If a judge has erred dramatically in the procedure or in the substance of a trial, a person who feels aggrieved may suggest this to an appellate judge and describe how it came about. If the judge agrees on the possibility of an unfair trial, he or she issues a writ of certiorari to a lower court judge, instructing the lower court judge to turn over the records of the trial. These records will include all major procedural steps, all statements made, and the identities of all parties involved in the case. The appellate judge can then, under certiorari, declare the trial void and order a new trial.

A final writ is not quite so well known, but it is often used nevertheless. This is a writ of **quo warrento.** This writ asks the question, by what warrant, or by what authority, do you do what you do? It is directed at public officials, and it suggests to them that they must not exceed the powers given to them under their offices. If an administrator of a particular program goes beyond the commission he or she has to administer that program and proceeds to act in new and different areas, that individual may be stopped from this unfair use of his or her delegated power through a writ of quo warrento.

All of these writs have in common the definition of Equity Law and some of its major aspects, which are preventive justice and the seeking of fairness among public officials, including judges. The judge must in all cases ultimately decide whether the unfairness exists and to what extent remedy may be found in some form of judicial order. It is a kind of law that gives to those within the Common Law system a greater degree of protection than is found in many other systems of law.

THE STRUCTURE OF LEGAL SYSTEMS

Almost all legal systems share a similar basic structure. It is generally referred to as the *three-tier structure*. Figure 6.1 illustrates this structure. The first tier is that of original jurisdiction—where cases begin. Whether a case is civil or criminal, there is an original court where it is heard and where a record is kept of the proceedings. In some countries, separate courts exist for criminal cases as opposed to civil cases. In American courts, in general, the same court can hear both kinds of cases, sitting either as a criminal court or as a civil court.

A secondary level of **adjudication** is the **appellate** level. In most countries, this level is not frequently used. In general, there are two reasons to appeal the decision of a lower court. The first reason is that some new and highly significant evidence has come forward, which, if presented in the original trial, would have substantially changed the outcome. As one can imagine, this is a fairly rare occurrence. The second reason for an appeal is judicial error, either in terms of procedure (which is the more frequent case) or in terms of the substance of the law adjudicated. As noted earlier, the specialized training of Roman Law judges and the very high qualifications of

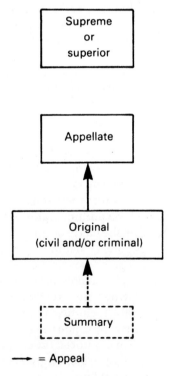

FIGURE 6.1 The Three-Tiered Legal System of Most Countries

Common Law judges outside of the United States would seem to make judicial errors also extremely rare. Indeed, this is usually the case outside of this country. However, as we have seen, because of our own lack of attention to the qualitative aspects of the judiciary, our system has been replete with judicial error, especially with regard to violations of the Fourth Amendment to the U.S. Constitution, which deals with the rules of evidence, and the Fifth Amendment as it relates to the prohibition of a witness testifying against himself or herself, confession, and other areas defined as due process of law. As a result, the American appellate level is a frequently used avenue of adjudication.

The third level of courts found in most countries is the supreme or superior level. If you look carefully at figure 6.1, you won't see a connection between the appellate level and the supreme level. This is because, in most countries, there is only one appeal, if that. The purpose of the supreme or superior level is for special kinds of cases under original jurisdiction. These would be questions of constitutional importance, cases involving foreign ambassadors, cases involving admiralty law or the law of the high seas, or perhaps international law cases in general. These courts meet infrequently and are of great significance in terms of the decisions they make.[6]

In figure 6.1 there is, of course, a fourth level as yet undiscussed. It is shown in the dotted square, and it is referred to by the word *summary*. **Summary jurisdiction** exists in most court systems in a variety of forms. All forms have the following characteristics in common: (1) summary jurisdiction is for very minor offenses such as speeding tickets, breach of the peace, violation of fish and game laws, and things of that nature; (2) the punishments are minor, generally in the form of fines of less than $100 or prison sentences of less than thirty days; and (3) no complete records are kept—the proceedings are informal and done in quick fashion. It is possible in many countries to reject a summary court hearing of a case and to appeal from the summary court directly to a court of record or to a court of original jurisdiction. Thus, the arrow connecting Summary to "Original" in figure 6.1 is not so much to indicate an appeal of a decision made by the summary court, but rather to reject that court in favor of one of original jurisdiction.

Another problem with the American court system is overcomplexity as found in figure 6.2. Once again, in reality there are fifty-one court systems in the United States. There is one national system and at least one system in every state.

The national court system is made up of some summary courts (such as military tribunals, low-level tax courts, and federal customs or patents courts) and the court of **original jurisdiction,** which is the most often used court of the federal system, the federal district court. One may appeal a case

---

[6]In those extraordinary cases when a secondary appeal is deemed necessary or appropriate, the superior level can be used or special appellate courts may be established for that purpose. Throughout the world, there are many variations of this basic pattern.

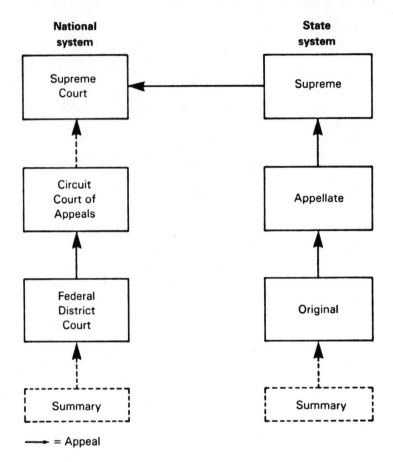

FIGURE 6.2   The United States Dual Court System

from the federal district court to a circuit court of appeals, a circuit being made up of several states in most cases. Again, the reason for the appeal is most often judicial error at the district level, and the reasons for this have already been discussed.

The top tier of the national system is the Supreme Court. It is possible for a case to go from the circuit court of appeals to the U.S. Supreme Court. This may happen when constitutional questions are involved. In general, however, our national court system was established on the same basic design as other world systems, at least insofar as it was envisioned under the Judiciary Act of 1789.

Most of the problems appear at the state court level. State courts vary widely in terms of the names given to the three basic levels and to a variety of summary courts. In the latter case, these may be called *magistrates courts, municipal court, traffic court, justice of the peace court,* and so on. Courts of original jurisdiction are sometimes called *county courts, district courts, recorders courts,* or even in some instances *circuit courts.* Most states allow the same kind of appeal from a summary court to an original court as previously described. The use of appellate court is a frequent occurrence in many state systems, and an appeal from that court to the state supreme court is generally a prerequisite for further appeal to the national court system, a subject that will be discussed later.

The supreme court of most states exists primarily for special constitutional questions. However, it does act, as just noted, as a secondary court of appeals when questions of judicial error occur. Given the propensity of lawyers to find error in procedural developments within a trial, and particularly under the *Mapp, Gideon,* and *Miranda* decisions (among others), appeals to the state supreme court are even more frequent now than they used to be. It is because one must "exhaust local remedies," to quote the language of the federal judiciary, before one can appeal to the national judiciary for national civil rights standards to be upheld, that supreme courts in the states are used so frequently as appellate courts.

Having appealed to the state supreme court, and having the same error uncorrected, an individual within a state system may appeal directly to the national Supreme Court under some civil rights clause. The Supreme Court then instructs the state courts as to what the national standard of civil rights is and how it relates to the particular case. The result of the dual court system combined with the potential for judicial error among the American judiciary is a system in which a defense attorney, who either seeks to increase his or her fee or else to prolong as much as possible the time his or her client spends outside of jail, has a tremendous advantage in being able to confidently appeal, in many instances, the same case at least three times. This has resulted in crowded dockets and a lack of swift punishment of criminals. The answer to the problem of the overcomplexity of our court system is far too complex for this study.

A final note on the American court system as described in figure 6.2 is called for. Our national Supreme Court also serves the purpose of judicial review. That is to say, the nine justices of the U.S. Supreme Court may, by their own decision, declare an act of the president, Congress, state governor, state legislature, or state court to be unconstitutional and thus void. Judicial review is an American invention, along with federalism and the modern political party. However, as other nations have imitated our political parties and our federalism to some extent, no serious comparison of the tremendous equality and power of the American Supreme Court in the exercise of its judicial review functions can be made to any other country. Indeed, most countries would not even consider the possibility that a judiciary could frustrate the will of the executive leadership or the legislative representatives of the nation.

Judicial review was first applied with great controversy in 1803 by John Marshall, but it so served the interests of those presidential theorists of separate functions within the government that it has prevailed over time to become a permanent concept of the American political establishment. When the United States played a leading role in the writing of the constitution of Japan and a contributing role in the writing of the constitution of the former West Germany, the countries included in those documents some provision for judicial review. The people of India, in writing their own constitution, also alluded to the concept. However, in none of these countries has judicial review taken root to the extent that it has in the United States. In Japan it has never been applied at all. In the other two countries it has been used sparingly and with great caution.

By now you should begin to sense the complexities involved in the establishment, structuring, and operation of a legal system. At some point, we all must decide on our own approach to law (normative or positive). We must keep in mind what kind of law we are dealing with (public or private) in order to understand the possibilities within the legal system. A clear-headed attitude toward punishment and law enforcement also helps to keep the subject in perspective.

It is incumbent upon all who would make political government to assess the state of their legal system with respect to its quality of justice and the application of judicial ethics to its operation. The problem of morality and truth in the law is probably less acute. It is also helpful to understand the nature of one's own legal system and its origins. Whatever the system, it seems obvious that citizens should insist upon a high degree of quality in the judiciary. Furthermore, in our own system, we should ask serious questions about the procedural aspects. Are they necessary in order to preserve justice or do they obstruct the search for it? Finally, we should be realistic in our references to law and not see in it more than is there. The key to effective understanding seems to be to see law for what it is and to place on the judiciaries of the world no more burdens than they are designed to carry.

POINTS TO PONDER

Assuming that you were innocent, would you prefer to be tried in an American court or a French court? What if you were guilty?

What factors seem to affect the rather low level of qualifications for judges in America as compared to either Roman Law judges or those of other Common Law countries?

Why do Americans have so many more appeals of judicial proceedings than one finds in other countries?

The legal system of Iran has become more normative while that of China has become more positivist. What does this suggest about America's approach to law?

7 | The Nature of Ideology

The nation-state system is primarily affected by sovereignty, nationalism, and ideology. The most recent of these phenomena is **ideology.** In the twentieth century, especially, it has emerged as the most confusing and difficult to understand of the three major characteristics of the world order. An ideology consists of a set of ideas about government and economics that often varies from individual to individual and yet seems to require some uniform method of labeling and classifying. This sometimes results in a babble of incoherent irrelevancies uttered by people who claim to know the "by-God truth" but who actually only succeed in defining not so much their ideology as themselves. Having placed a label upon themselves, they then proceed to use the position *it* defines as a measure by which to label others. In order to try to avoid some of these problems, I will attempt to go back to the emergence of ideological terms and to try to see what they originally meant so that we might have at least some anchor on which to tie our own ideological discourse. Thus, if we speak of liberals, conservatives, communists, and socialists, and other ideological forms, we might at least know where the terms began, if not where they end.

IDEOLOGICAL TERMS AND THEIR ORIGINS

ORIGINS

To begin with, let's note a historical event that occurred in France during the period from 1789 to 1791. Much of the basic language of ideology derives its origin from this particular event. During the first three years of the French Revolution, an attempt was made to reinstate the old and seldom used French parliament, the Estates General, in order to work out a common approach to what had evolved as a rather chaotic government. The delegates to that conclave met in a semicircular room. This was probably unfortunate because the relative position of one group to another resulted in the relativity of the ideological terms we know today. See figure 7.1.

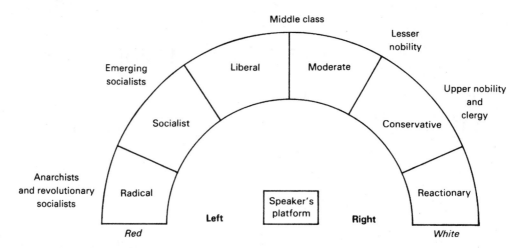

FIGURE 7.1   The Seating of the 1791 Meeting of the French Estates General

Arrayed around the central speaker's platform, beginning on the extreme right of the speaker, was a small group of people who wished to restore the authoritarian rule of King Louis XVI. Next to them, as the semicircle progressed, sat some of the members of the nobility and the clergy, who supported a new monarchy based essentially on the old order. Next to them sat some of the lesser nobility, who were wise enough to realize that some change was needed in the government of France if any kind of normalcy was to be restored after the havoc of the early French Revolution. Toward the middle of the semicircle sat a group of middle-class people who were new to the political order but whose voice was important primarily due to their improved economic position over the past few decades and their reputation for sensibility and moderation. These people tended to favor the creation within France of some form of liberal democracy similar to what had been recently established in the United States. To the left of these people sat a group of emerging socialists. They were not generally labeled as such, but what they sought was a basic program involving the seizure of all land and productive economic capital by the state to be used for the good of all people. Finally, at the extreme left of the semicircle sat a group of revolutionary socialists and anarchists who might be considered the philosophical descendants of Rousseau. They sought essentially to destroy the whole concept of the nation-state and reduce government to the level of the small city-states of ancient Greece.

Political commentators gave labels to the points of view and groups thus arrayed. Those who wished to go back to the days of Louis XVI were, in effect, attempting to react, which is to say, go back prior to the political conditions that now prevailed. Thus, the extreme "right" position became known as **reactionary.** Those members of the nobility and clergy who were attempting to preserve what remnants of the feudal regime were still left were referred to as *conservatives,* or people who wished to conserve the existing political viewpoint and its economic and legal structure. The lesser nobles seeking change were given the label **moderates.** It is rather difficult to say what they really wanted, but their major characteristics seemed to be that of approaching change in a deliberate way. The middle class knew what they wanted. They wanted the liberal ideology of America applied to France. They called themselves *liberals.* The socialists as a whole were not as sure what they wanted, but the term *socialist* had begun to be applied to any group that wished the state to seize formerly private property and convert it to public ends in a context of political equality and social responsibility. Finally, the revolutionary socialists and anarchists were simply referred to as **radicals** who wished to change the governmental structure in such a sudden and dramatic manner as to make whatever resulted completely unpredictable and unrecognizable.

Thus, being *conservative* came to be "to the right" under today's terminology; to be *liberal* came to be either toward the center overlapping some of the moderates or toward the left, depending on some more modern shifts. A *socialist* was clearly labeled a "leftist," and a *radical* was seen to be "extremely leftist." After 1932, the original American concept of liberal was somewhat amended by the New Deal, and it shifted slightly to the left on the diagram as the relationships are depicted for 1791. The nonideological moderates have claimed the middle ground. This does not make all modern liberals leftists, but it does make them more than just simple moderates.

To further add to the ideological distinctions during the debates, the supporters of Louis XVI brought into the meeting the official flag of the Bourbon family. It was a white flag with gold fleurs-de-lis embroidered on it, and it was often referred to as the "Lily Banner." In response to this, the socialists brought a flag of their own, which they placed on the left side of the meeting hall. It was simply a red square cloth cut from a piece of drapery that happened to be available. Since that day, the color white has been identified with the right and the color red with the left.

One of the amusing ironies of this particular subject has been that the liberals who occupied the middle position might presumably have tried to mix the red and the white, emerging with a combination of pink. Indeed, the word *pinko* was used in the 1950s and 1960s by those of the more extreme right to refer to liberals. In any case, this is the origin of the relationship between the modern words *conservative, moderate, liberal, socialist,* and *radical.* From these relationships, the ideological language of contemporary society is derived.

IDEOLOGIES TODAY

We must take this a step further. What divides the left from the right? The members of the contemporary right are seen to share certain *tendencies* that are almost mirror opposites of the tendencies shared by those of the left. To the degree that one shares these tendencies, an individual is more or less to the right or more or less to the left. To the extent that one adopts a combination of these tendencies, he or she becomes less defined as a rightist or leftist and more as a moderate. The description that follows is inexact at best, but it at least holds true in most cases and is faithful to the origin of the basic terminology just discussed.

Today, if one is on the right, one shares those tendencies indicated in figure 7.2. That is to say, he or she tends to prefer a class and/or a race structure to a society in which everyone has a place and knows where that place is. He or she tends to approach problems of public order, either domestically or in the world at large, with a military or police orientation, believing in strong law enforcement and strict laws, with frequent application of force whenever the government is challenged. He or she affirms private property as the only logical way to determine the ownership of capital goods, and so his or her economic system is capitalistic. Although change is admittedly a necessity, a "rightist" prefers that change be highly structured and approached with extreme caution. When a choice must be made between public order and the rights of people, the rightist would invariably choose order over public rights for fear that too much affirmation of rights might undermine the prerequisites of order from whence all government comes. Finally, there is within the rightist tradition a tendency toward **monism,** or singleness. This emerges as a tendency to affirm one church or one religion, one lifestyle, one language, or one economic system. There is a tendency to cluster about a single major idea in order not to have to change or to bring into question too many of the basic concepts on which life is based.

These tendencies of the right are just that—tendencies. They are held or felt in varying degrees and not necessarily altogether. In placing oneself or another on the right, one should ask how many of these tendencies are shared and how strongly they are shared in order to find one's proper place somewhere between the center of ideological terminology and its extreme right position.

In a similar way, there are tendencies to the left. The leftist is essentially an egalitarian. He or she seeks not class or race structures but equality for all

Tendencies of the left	Tendencies of the right
Egalitarianism	Class/race structure
Bureaucratic administration	Militaristic administration
Public property	Private property
Socialism	Capitalism
Dynamic change	Structured change
Rights over order	Order over rights
Pluralism	Monism

FIGURE 7.2   The Ideological Left and Right

people regardless of race, economic position, bloodline, or any form of classification. In approaching government, he or she prefers to see its fiats carried out through a bureaucratic and civilian kind of administration that minimizes police, military, and other uses of force in favor of laws and diplomacy. The leftist is a believer in public property for certain purposes basic to public life. The leftist would believe, for instance, in public ownership of transportation, some basic industries, and major communications. He or she tends toward a socialistic form of economy, although, as we shall see, there is much more to this than first meets the eye. He or she does not fear change. The leftist prefers a flexible and dynamic government that can respond rather quickly to shifts in public opinion and public values. If the question is one of public rights over public order, the choice tends to be made in favor of the rights of people. The idea here is that order will be restored at some point because humanity requires it, but human rights are too valuable to sacrifice on the altar of stability. Finally, the leftist is a pluralist. He or she accepts many forms of religion, many churches, many economic ideas or programs, and many and varied lifestyles. He or she seeks the richness of humanity in a variety of its manifestations.

When confronted with these traditional right or left tendencies, most Americans discover to their surprise that their own political thinking pattern is made up of certain tendencies of both the left and the right. This should not be surprising. One of the ironies of the American political ethos is that, although we developed the first of the great ideologies, liberalism, we so compromised it with an enormous strain of conservative pragmatism that we have never really been an ideological society. We are a mixture of left and right. The words *liberal* and *conservative* may be tossed about in our political rhetoric, but for the most part we are moderates, some shifting slightly to the left and others shifting slightly to the right. American presidents in the twentieth century are seldom elected on a strictly leftist or rightist platform. Indeed, some of our greatest political disasters have occurred when too much of a shift in either direction has been attempted. The presidential campaigns of Goldwater in 1964 and McGovern in 1972 are often seen as classic examples.

The elections of 1994 gave some a reason to doubt whether that would remain the case, however. It is perhaps too early to tell, but a new tone has seemed to enter the American political milieu. After the Reagan era (1980–1988) when the right seemed to dominate the American political agenda through "trickle-down" economic theories, a major expansion of military spending accompanied by more militant foreign policies, and a less vigorous pursuit of civil rights in favor of class and race preferences, the Bush and Clinton administrations appeared to demonstrate a return to more traditional patterns of moderation (despite the frequent use of the term "liberalism" by the right as an epithet with which to excoriate Clinton). Nevertheless, the Republican sweep in the Congressional races in 1994, which gave them control of both houses, was a clear victory of the more hard-line right wing of the party. At the same time, many state governments were also undergoing a similar ideological realignment.

Post-1994 policies aimed at the abandonment of affirmative action, more militant approaches to crime and punishment, expansions in defense spending, probusiness attitudes versus concerns about the condition of workers and the environment, a harder line on welfare and the poor, reevaluation of some civil rights laws of the 1960s, restrictions on abortion rights and an increasing tendency to see "Americanism" in the context of a monistic set of White-Anglo-Saxon-Christian "values" have become the new agenda for a growing number of leaders on both the national and state levels. Ideological positions in America continue to evolve in unexpected ways. Whereas the right remains somewhat ascendant in many areas, change remains the only consistent aspect of our ideological journey.

With that caveat in mind, it is still generally assumed that the average American does not believe in socialism; he or she prefers private property and some form of capitalism. However, he or she tends toward an egalitarian sensitivity, is not afraid of too much change, and tends to be pluralistic. Many Americans are also quite concerned about law and order and emphasize a strong police and strong military structure. Therefore, it is difficult to deal in ideological terms when discussing Americans. We simply are not very ideological. We are pragmatic. This makes it very difficult for Americans to discuss ideological concepts with any degree of clarity. We have borrowed ideas from both the left and the right, and so when you call me a *conservative* it simply tells me that you are more to the left than I am. If you call me a *liberal* it means that you are a little more to the right than I am. It really does not tell me exactly where you are, because you share some of the same ideas that I do, and furthermore the labels *liberal* and *conservative* are more often than not relevant only to a single issue. On some other issue, we might swap places.

There are very few radicals in our society, but, when we encounter them in the context of the Weathermen of the late 1960s or some other extreme group, the repugnance is rather general. Although we do have socialists in our society and have had an active Socialist party since the turn of the century, its ability to make inroads into the American system has been extremely limited. On the other hand, we also have the reactionaries in the form of the Ku Klux Klan, the American Nazi Party, and the New Order, who would take us back to racial segregation, pre-Depression economic systems, preincome tax policies, or perhaps even to the "robber-baron" era of the 1890s. These reactionaries have not held much political importance in our society, either.

One final word should be written about the American approach to ideological terminology. In the 1960s, a new phrase crept into the political vocabulary. It is by proper definition a contradiction in terms. The term is the *radical right*. To be radical is to be to the left, indeed as far to the left as one can go. To be an extreme rightist, which the term implies, is to be a reactionary.

Thus, the so-called radical right is really our reactionary group. Throughout the world, especially during this century, democratic governments by their very nature have tended to slide among periods of liberal, conservative, and socialist dominance. This is in keeping with the democratic tendency to respond to the desires of people as those desires are known. What is "democracy" in the political context, anyway? We are faced with one of those terms that everyone knows but understands in different ways. The distinction that is made between political and egalitarian democracy in chapter 2 is not sufficient for our purposes here.

POLITICAL DEMOCRACY

In attempting to evaluate political democracy, H. L. Mencken observed, wryly, that under its dynamics, "one party always devotes its chief energies to trying to prove that the other party is unfit to rule—and both commonly succeed, and are right." So, we might ask, is it nothing more than "the crude leading the crud" as Florence King has suggested? Does political democracy consist of "choosing your dictators, after they've told you what you think it is that you want to hear" as argued by Alan Coren? Must we "abandon the prevalent belief in the superior wisdom of the ignorant" as suggested by Daniel Boorstin? Is it that "democracy is a device that ensures that we shall be governed no better than we deserve" as George Bernard Shaw would have it. Such well-known comments clearly demonstrate that the subject has been one in which there has always been some disagreement as well as no small degree of cynicism.

Nevertheless, it is vitally important for our future to grapple with the concept in as clear a manner as is possible.

Let's begin by asking what democracy is not. First, political democracy is not a form of government. It exists in many forms. We have already examined some of these various forms in chapter 3. Second, political democracy is not an ideology. There is no necessary clash between democracy and communism, *per se*. Democracy, in the political context, can exist in a variety of ideologies, especially in liberalism and democratic socialism. It is these ideologies that clash with communism. Finally, democracy is not an absolutely measurable phenomenon. It exists in degrees, with some countries achieving a higher level than others. The question for democracies is whether or not the society is dedicated to the concept or whether it rejects democracy in favor of some other approach to government.

What is democracy, then, if it is not a form of government, an ideology, or a quantifiable phenomenon? Political democracy might best be described as a philosophy. Like all philosophies, it has a certain structure of ideas. We shall now discuss the structure of ideas that a society indicates to attempt to achieve democracy on some level. We might be reminded that, to the extent that these ideas prevail in any society, the society is democratic.

THE PREREQUISITES FOR POLITICAL DEMOCRACY

In order to achieve political democracy, a set of rules must prevail in the general understanding of the society, and these rules provide the framework for the philosophy of democracy.[1]

GOVERNMENT EXISTS FOR PEOPLE

The basic rule is that people are what government is all about. Government exists for men and women, not vice versa. Therefore, any government that exists must be at our consent and that government must serve humanity. This further assumes that all people within that government are created equal in terms of their right to approach government. They have those inalienable rights referred to so majestically by Thomas Jefferson in the Declaration of Independence—the rights to the protection of life, liberty, and the pursuit of happiness.

PEOPLE CAN MANAGE THEIR OWN AFFAIRS

A second basic rule is more difficult for believers in democracy, and it's sometimes abandoned in times of crisis. That rule is that people are capable of managing their own affairs. The meaning here is profound. No one would seriously argue that people are always wise, rational, and honest. Indeed, most of us would admit that sometimes each of us is dishonest, is rather stupid, and behaves in an irrational manner under certain circumstances. Nevertheless, the true believer in democracy says that, ultimately, it is better that people manage their own affairs, even with their shortcomings, rather than turn over these affairs to an elite class or individual known for a consistently higher level of honesty, intelligence, and rationality than the average level of the society. Logic would seem to argue against this proposition. If we ordinary mortals are let loose to govern ourselves, won't we, on occasion, do things that are irrational or stupid? Won't some of our public servants fall into dishonesty? The answer is yes, of course. However, when these unhappy events occur, as they ultimately will, they can be corrected by other people and that is the strength of democracy. The ability to correct mistakes, to change course without undue loss of confidence in the authority and legitimacy of the institutions of government is what democracy is all about. The institutions remain; the people change.

On the other hand, to entrust the fortunes of the nation to an admittedly superior individual or elite aristocracy would be to foreclose the possibility

---

[1]The sequence of rules discussed here is taken from Dragnich, A. N. 1966. *Major European Governments.* 2nd ed. Homewood, Ill.: The Dorsey Press, Inc., pp. 2–4. The description and evaluation are my own.

for correction and change, for who would tell them that they were wrong, stupid, or dishonest? If a congressman or -woman or a senator behaves in a less than perfect way, we may replace him or her without calling into question our overall ability to govern. For a dictator or aristocrat to have to admit his or her mistakes is to admit *his* or *her* inability to govern. He or she will, therefore, attempt as much as possible to obscure mistakes. There is no perfect human being. Only the matter of the degree of rationality, intelligence, and honesty is debated. The assumption that people are capable of governing their own affairs is not an assumption that they will do so perfectly but, rather, the assumption that it is better to trust people in general, allowing for mistakes, rather than to surrender the power of government to a group who would not admit to any mistake.

THE GREATEST GOOD FOR THE GREATEST NUMBER

A third rule is better known: the purpose of government is to do the greatest good for the greatest number. This is the goal of democracy. It means that public decisions are not to be made for narrow or private ends, and, if a decision appears to benefit one group over another, the benefit derived must be shown to be for all people. If this cannot be demonstrated, the benefit must be canceled.

GOVERNMENT CAN CHANGE QUICKLY

Another rule is that the government can change quickly. It can change both in terms of its constitutional character and in terms of its procedures. It can change whenever the majority decides that it should change. This assumption ultimately means that forms and procedures of government, and even constitutions, should take second place to the desires of people. As long as the change is worked out in the spirit of compromise and in the context of temporary law, then it is not only acceptable but also a desirable aspect of government.

THE RIGHT TO PARTICIPATE IS AS BROAD AS POSSIBLE

A fifth rule is that there should be the widest possible distribution of the right to participate in the government. This not only includes voting (which may be defined as the lowest form of participation, since voting is nothing more than a choice among predigested variables), but it also means the right to petition; to demonstrate; to write a letter to a congressman or -woman or to a newspaper; to make a speech, to form a political party; to run for office; or to do anything that is necessary to make oneself a part of the government process, whether in or out of office.

With regard to voting, which is the most popular form of participation in government, albeit the weakest, the right to vote in a democracy should be limited by only four restrictions: (1) children should not vote, for they are yet unable to understand the issues (a child is now defined in some democracies as being less than eighteen years of age); (2) convicted felons should not vote, for they have broken major laws of the land and have lost the right to participate in the definition of those laws; (3) aliens should not vote because they are not citizens of the nation-state and should not have a voice in its political decisions; and (4) certain individuals classified as "wards of the state," whose entire livelihood depends upon the state and who are, in effect, legal children despite their age, should not vote for reasons analogous to children in general (these include people in state mental institutions or other dependent people whose level of civilization has not yet developed to the norm of the rest of society). Beyond these four restrictions, anyone should have the right to vote.

ELECTIONS ARE FREE, HONEST, AND FREQUENT

A sixth rule concerns voting itself. Elections for public office should be free, honest, and frequent. This means that one should have the secret ballot and thus be free from public exposure to vote the way one chooses. Elections should be honest in that the results should not be corrupted. Here a digression is in order.

As we have seen, in order for good government to exist, there must be a close psychological bond between the people and the government, through which comes the authority and legitimacy of that government. This psychological bond is first created through such institutions as the public school system, but as people enter into adulthood it is more and more dependent upon the election system itself. To cast one's vote in an election is a strongly symbolic and essentially psychological act in which an individual commits his or her psyche, ideas, and action to a political outcome. We have often heard stories and even jokes about how elections have been rigged. The horror stories of Cook County, Illinois, and certain counties in some southern states are even notorious. It must be clearly understood, however, that an honest election is a prerequisite for a strong and healthy psychological relationship between the government of a political democracy and its people. Should that relationship be damaged too severely, the authority and legitimacy of that government is seriously undermined. Therefore, tampering with an election or even creating the suspicion that an election is less than honest is to tamper with the most basic relationship between people and this kind of government.

Elections must also be frequent. How frequent depends on the office and the society. There is no general rule. We elect members of congress every two years, which is probably too frequent in that they spend at least half their time running for reelection. We elect our senators every six years, which may be too long, since they tend to ignore their constituents for five-sixths of the time they hold office. We elect our president every four years, which to most people seems about right.

THE MAJORITY RULES

The seventh rule is perhaps the best-known rule of democracy and usually the least understood. It is majority rule, which is to say that decisions within a democracy should be made in accordance with the rule of the majority. What is the majority? Most people would say that it is one more than half of the participants in a decision, yet the presidential electoral vote of a state, and indeed the election of a governor or senator, may be determined by *less* than 50 percent of the votes in that state. This is called a plurality election, and we often award elective office on this basis. On the other hand, we do require what is correctly referred to as *simple majority* (one more than half) in order to pass a law in Congress or in most state legislatures. In order to approve a treaty for ratification, the U.S. Senate requires a two-thirds vote of its members. Finally, as supporters of the Equal Rights Amendment in the 1970s were only too well aware, it requires three-quarters of the states to ratify an amendment to the Constitution. All of these decisions fit the concept of majority rule, however, leaving one to suspect that the meaning of majority rule must be related to something other than arithmetic, and that is indeed the case.

What all of these numbers and variations have in common is this: the decision in all cases is made by the dominant view. This, then, is the definition of majority rule in a democracy: *rule by the dominant point of view on a particular kind of issue at a particular point in time.* Let's see how this works in the illustrations just given.

Who should hold public office in the United States or any other democracy? Under the theory that people are capable of governing their own affairs, anyone could conceivably hold any office. Therefore, the decision of who should hold an office is a rather low-level decision. In making that kind of decision, we will accept a very low degree of dominant opinion. We call the lowest degree of dominant opinion a *plurality* (the highest number of votes, whether 50 percent or *less*); thus, we often elect people on the basis of a plurality.

On the other hand, the passage of a law is a very important decision. It affects the daily lives of many people. This issue is more important than the issue of who gets elected. Therefore, here we demand a simple majority before a law is entered into the code. A treaty is recognized under American law and under those of most other nation-states as a kind of law that is higher than normal statutory law because it not only binds together the people of the nation-state, but it also binds them to people of other states.

Therefore, we demand from the Senate a higher level of dominant view before we will consent to that kind of decision—a two-thirds vote. Finally, a constitutional amendment changes the basic, organic law of the land. Its ramifications are unpredictable and run far into the future. Therefore, we do not approach this kind of issue lightly. Instead, we demand perhaps the highest level of dominant consensus obtainable within a large democracy— three-fourths of the states must agree before we take such radical action. Thus, the concept of majority rule is summed up in relation to the issue and to the degree of dominance that is properly relevant to that issue.

What of the "point in time" mentioned in the definition of majority rule? This is where the temporary nature of democratic decisions comes in. Although a relevant majority is put together at a particular point in time, it need not remain a majority view. The dominance of public opinion may shift. The majority is only good for the moment for which it is expressed. A majority is not, therefore, judged to be necessarily right. A majority can be wrong. Majority rule does not require that a majority is always right. It means only that the majority thinks it is right at the particular time. Should events prove that the dominant view, the majority, is wrong, then the issue may be redefined by a new dominant view resulting from a subsequent majority decision. Even the three-fourths majority that ratified the Eighteenth Amendment to the U.S. Constitution later realized that it was wrong and repealed it under the Twenty-First Amendment. Summing up then, the rule of majority rule says that there is a proper way to make a decision, but we are not stuck with it. It says that certain decisions can be made in certain ways and other decisions in other ways. It says, finally, that we, the people, not some arbitrary mechanism, are in charge of decision making.

One of the corollaries to majority rule as a rule of political democracy is the toleration of the minority. This means that, not only should minority views be tolerated in terms of their expression, but they must also be respected. Furthermore, the possibility that a minority view could become a majority view in the future must be considered. Therefore, majority rule means rule by the majority, but only as long as it *is* the majority.

ANYONE CAN ORGANIZE FOR POLITICAL PURPOSES

Another rule has also caused some problems. This is that any group or party should be free to organize itself, to speak out as it sees fit on any issue, to assemble peacefully, and to attempt to persuade the government to its point of view, as long as the attempt is within the law. This inevitably includes some groups such as the Communist and Fascist parties.

This fact caused a great deal of harm and misunderstanding during the McCarthy period of the early 1950s, when, under the Smith Act of 1940, the Communist party was effectively declared illegal. Membership at that time placed people in a very difficult position. More recently, the right of the

American Nazi party to parade in Skokie, Illinois, was disallowed by the city council of that city. Both of these actions were later overturned by the U.S. Supreme Court. If a Communist or Fascist party can be banned by dominant groups within the government, so then might the Democratic party, or any other party.

Most people understand this particular aspect of the rule. The problem arises when a party such as the Communists or the Nazis or any other splinter group actually threatens to destroy the basic structure under which democracy rests. How can we justify the attempt by one group to use the rules of democracy to destroy democracy itself?[2] The answer is quite simple. Democracy exists only as long as there is a majority of the people devoted to its assumptions and willing to accept its rules. Should a party seeking to destroy democracy gain the majority, then the democracy is already dead.

PEOPLE MUST AGREE ON THE RULES

The final rule for democracy is that there must be an agreement on the rest of the rules by the majority of the society. There must be a commitment on the part of the people that this is the way to be governed and a faith that government under these rules is superior to any other kind. Democracy does not signify that any particular thing will be done, but it does demand that whatever is done will be done under these assumptions and in accordance with these rules. To the extent that a nation can achieve this, to that extent it deserves the title *democracy*. To the extent that it aspires to these standards of government, it can still be called a democracy, though we may judge it less democratic than it ought to be. To the extent that a society rejects these assumptions and rules, it is no democracy.

MAJORITARIANISM

As we saw earlier, majority rule is one of the more difficult concepts of political democracy to master. We noted that while a majority represents a dominant view, it is only good for the time it exists and must be relevant to a particular kind of issue. It must also respect the existence of the minority point of view which may become the majority view over time. Beyond all that, there is another problem with majority rule. Since the advent of the Populist Party of the 1880s, we have encountered, from time to time, the simplistic notion that a majority is absolute. That is to say, whenever a group is able to demonstrate a majority opinion on any issue at all, then that majority must

---

[2]Let it be clearly understood that any individual member of any group may be legitimately punished for acts of treason, sedition, or other felonies relating to the use of violence against the security of the state.

be allowed to do what it wishes with regard to the issue. This populist conceit suggests that any untested idea (say congressional term limits) that enjoys a momentary vogue can, presumably, override fundamental principles of law.

As we noted earlier in chapter 6, the Rule of Law (which may be included among the Prerequisites for Political Democracy just discussed) demands that all changes in law must be sanctified by the legal principles of a society. Law cannot be made willy-nilly! Therefore, it is a dangerous idea to allow unbridled power to be given to a group that claims legitimacy solely on the basis of its being a majority. That claim is sometimes referred to as *majoritarianism*, and, ironically, it is one of the most serious threats to democracy as we know it. Indeed, majoritarianism might better be labeled "mobocracy"—the rule of the mob.

The United States Supreme Court spoke to this issue in mid-1995 when it struck down an attempt by the state of Arkansas (based on a majority vote of its citizens) to impose term limits on its congressional delegation, saying that the constitution demands only age, citizenship, and residence as proper requirements for one to be qualified to serve. The court further noted that a majority alone cannot change the constitution. That can only be done through the cumbersome process of constitutional amendment. Thus, if the mob wants term limits, then it can only get them by changing the basic principles of law found in the constitution. A "mere majority" may not undermine organic law. Indeed, our principle of judicial review by the U.S. Supreme Court is designed primarily to safeguard our basic rights from a runaway majoritarianism.

DEMOCRACY OR GUARDIANSHIP?

In his book *Controlling Nuclear Weapons,*[3] Robert Dahl raised a singularly important question for the future of democracy as we know it. It has to do with the second assumption we examined (that people are capable of managing their own affairs). We know that some decisions that fundamentally affect our lives are arrived at outside the reach of our democratic processes. A case in point would be those decisions concerning nuclear weapons, their manufacture and potential use. Similar issues (which I will not consider here) would include such things as environmental pollution and genetic research.

What all these issues share is the fact that they are highly complex. The average citizen cannot know enough about them to reach a rational conclusion as to their treatment. Must we then abandon democratic procedure and

---

[3]Dahl, R., 1985. *Controlling Nuclear Weapons: Democracy Versus Guardianship.* Syracuse, N. Y.: Syracuse University Press. Most of the ideas in this section are taken from this book. The organization and comments are my own.

trust guardian-specialists to decide for us? Didn't we do that with regard to nuclear weapons? When was anybody, outside of a nonelected fraternity of "nuclear priests," able to have a say in the deployment of, targeting of, and operational program for these weapons of mass destruction? Indeed, who was asked whether or not to inaugurate the nuclear age itself by dropping the first atomic bomb on Japan? These are not idle questions; they strike at the heart of all assumptions about democracy.

According to Dahl, we have moved from the direct democracy of the citizen assemblies of ancient Greece, through the eighteenth-century concept of representative democracy, and on to the twentieth-century phenomenon of shadowy bureaucracies that operate largely outside of the established and traditional organs of clear accountability (a subject to be discussed at length in chapter 10). Even within these traditional governing organs, one finds, more and more, that legislation is written in congressional committees or in White House offices and then bargained in quiet rooms before it emerges, mostly preordained, into the light of day. The courts have always enjoyed the privilege of quiet consideration before announcing decisions, which are explained in unchallenged statements.

Beyond this, Dahl notes that, when voters do "have a say," they are not confronted with clearly distinguished alternatives and, thus, make choices that are marginal—more often about means to a predetermined end rather than about the end itself. Thus, policy tends to be made for us, incrementally, with public input largely confined to opinions about each increment, with little consideration for the whole. The Vietnam War stands as a monument to such an approach to decision making.

With regard to questions about nuclear weapons, Dahl notes that they are technical, political, and moral. Certainly, few among the electorate can master the technical questions. Only slightly more can deal with such political considerations as the intentions of the leadership of other nations. Where is the moral competence of a society (given more and more to self-gratification and egoism) that finds it difficult to take into account the good of others and to give equal weight to the interests of strangers?

Thus, the argument goes, we need a guardianship for these kinds of issues. Plato advocated this in *The Republic*. In China, Confucius inspired such a system, which we call **meritocracy.** Lenin argued for it with regard to the role of the party in a communist society. Were they correct? Is political democracy in the twenty-first century doomed to submit to their logic?

Certainly, this much is true in all such arguments, even those that plead for *some* degree of political democracy: All governments bind their people to collective decisions, and, although people are intrinsically equal, a better qualified few can generally protect the interests of all the people better than all the people could by themselves, and, finally, even political democracies proscribe certain people from full participation (children, some felons, aliens, and wards of the state). Rounding out the argument, then, a political democracy *can* encompass a guardian class chosen by merit to protect the society and its collective good through binding laws for that purpose. Such guardians should be tested as to their technical, political, and moral competence, and, if they pass the tests, they should be able to operate for the good of all within the context of political democracy. In such a way was Venice ruled in the fourteenth century, Florence under the Medici, and China during the "Golden Ages" of its history.

How then should we respond to this assertion? Dahl suggests that certain kinds of human questions (such as those relating to nuclear power, the environment, and science and health policy) are *so* complex that no one person can so master them as to provide singularly superior answers. Indeed, to be highly specialized in one's knowledge is often to be impervious to other relevant considerations that may be equally important to the best resolution of an issue. Furthermore, overspecialization can lead to moral insensitivity. This seems especially true of nuclear weapons specialists. If war is too important to be left to the generals, is not survival too important to be left to the specialists? Is virtue always to be expected from mere mortals who have been given exclusive power over others? Lord Acton's aphorism that "power corrupts and absolute power corrupts absolutely" is but the beginning of the problem. To such people who have it, exclusive power also *alienates* them from any consideration of public opinion, which will tend to be viewed as inherently flawed. Finally, in the real world, things go wrong. As we have observed previously, the corrective for this inevitable failure is best kept in the hands of the people.

However, the dilemma exists. As Dahl puts it, "Whereas instrumental elites lack the special moral competence that might entitle them to make decisions on complex matters of public policy, ordinary people often lack the instrumental knowledge to judge which policies would be in their best interests. On complex issues the interdependence of moral and instrumental judgments seems to leave us with a dilemma from which there is no escape: on complex matters, neither instrumental elites nor ordinary citizens are politically competent to rule."[4]

Is there a way out of this paradox? Dahl suggests that the answer may lie in creating new institutions of government, which will use special processes to achieve three ends: ensuring that the best available information can be obtained by the public, creating access by all citizens to political discussions, and providing a highly informed body of public opinion that is truly representative of the public. All of this could be achieved through the use of advanced telecommunications to disseminate, on call, information that is adapted to a variety of individual learning capabilities and that comes from such reputable organizations of scholars as the National Academy of Sciences and the American Philosophical Society. This information could be used by a representative group of citizens, chosen at random for limited and

---

[4]Ibid., p. 64.

nonrepeating terms of office, who would study complex questions for periods of approximately one year (for pay). They would then advise the government on public questions. There is much more to Dahl's suggestion than this, but it is not germane to this chapter to analyze it to any extent. Dahl does assert his strong belief that we *can*, through strenuous and enlightened efforts, retain the gift of political democracy if we wish to do so. The job will not be easy, but political democracy is not an easy enterprise. What is required, first and foremost, is that the *faith* in democracy remain strong, for if it is ever lost, then the field will be surrendered to authoritarianism of one kind or another.

A WARNING TO AMERICANS

It should come as no real news to Americans that this is not a particularly happy time for our democracy. Since the 1980s, it has become more and more acceptable for the elite in our society to be economically classist and neglectful of the poor and disadvantaged. Basic necessities such as health care and education have been slighted in favor of incentives for the more wealthy among us. Wages for average workers fall yearly in terms of their purchasing power while corporate downsizings throw ordinary people out of jobs in order to drive up profits and the value of stocks. Worldwide competition, weakened labor unions, and basic changes in the definition of labor and its rewards have taken away from ordinary workers any real power over their wages, benefits, or working conditions. Crime in the poor to lower middle class neighborhoods is rising, while those in power tend to pay more attention to the punishment of it than the causes of it.

Average citizens feel less and less a part of the country's government, which seems to be distant and remote from their concerns. They are not optimistic about the future and see government more often as the enemy than the place where society's problems can be solved. Politics, the source of governmental legitimacy in our society and supposedly bedrock of our democracy, has become, instead, a contest of divisiveness, character assassination, and struggle between conflicting social and economic views, which seemingly will not admit to compromise. That necessary psychic bond between the people and their government on which all effective government rests is eroding across a broad spectrum of our society. Resentment is becoming epidemic, and it is not a resentment that can be contained within any single, contemporary political movement.

What is necessary is not the victory of the right or the left. Either would likely destroy our democracy in a very short time. Rather, we need to wake up to the principles defined in the second chapter of this book—those of political democracy and good government. We need to reeducate ourselves about the requirements of political democracy. We need a leadership that can induce a serious reexamination of the purposes and meaning of this country as a whole. We need to rediscover the process of conciliation and to deny power to those who would divide us for their own purposes. Unless that happens soon, peaceful and humane government will become increasingly difficult, and authoritarianism could someday dance on the grave of our lost democracy.

AUTHORITARIAN GOVERNMENT

Among the so-called Third World nations, we often encounter another approach to government. It is generally referred to as **authoritarian** government. Those nations that do not *aspire* to democracy will either *accept* some form of authoritarian rule or perhaps *submit* to something worse—totalitarianism, a subject discussed in the next section. Authoritarian government is the oldest kind of government and the most widespread. It can exist in a tribal form; it can be found in a theocracy, wherein a priest or judging class exists to rule over people, as in the case of contemporary Iran; and it can be seen, and often is, in the government of a charismatic leader such as former Philippine president Ferdinand Marcos. Latin America has often seen authoritarian governments in one form or another. They vary from civilian dictatorships to military juntas and from one-person rule to a collegial oligarchy.

We can say some general things about authoritarian governments that might help us understand both their prevalence and their numbers. First, there is a limited purpose to authoritarian government. It has limited objectives. Its goals are rather simple and straightforward: it wishes first to control the treasury of the nation and with that the major economic resources that produce the wealth of the nation. Thus, it would control copper, sugar, precious metals, or whatever a nation-state is most apt to produce as a money-making crop or resource. Second, authoritarian government wishes to eliminate any possible opposition to its control. To that end, it devotes a powerful military, a police force within all major municipalities, and a secret police to warn it of impending political opposition. Third, it wishes to tax the citizens so that it has additional sources of income and reminds the citizens of its power and its presence. Finally, the authoritarian regime may even wish to engage in certain public services that are either essential to the running of a civilized society (sanitation, water, power, etc.) or even to do something for the people in the name of the government, such as building hospitals or schools or enshrining national monuments. There is, after all, the desire for ego satisfaction even among dictators.

Whatever else the government may do, the important point is that its impact on the daily lives of the people of the state is often rather slight. The people's responsibility, under an authoritarian government, is to pay their taxes, to obey the laws, and not to attempt to involve themselves in political decisions. Generally, they should not organize political parties or engage in too many demonstrations. A rigged election every now and then is sometimes used to help legitimize the regime.

It makes no difference to the authoritarian government where people live, where they travel, what they do for a living, whom they marry, or what they believe. There is a general area of activity wherein a man or woman may be born, raise a family, pursue an occupation (even get wealthy), enjoy leisure, or choose not to work at all, and the government will take no special note of any of these activities. Although the press is generally controlled, in order to make the government look good, what an individual thinks about the government, God, or anybody else is pretty much his or her own affair, as long as the individual keeps it to himself or herself.

In some instances, authoritarian governments can be seen in a positive light, especially in the case of relatively new nation-states that face the twin challenges of establishing new and alternative institutions of public order and pursuing economic development at the same time. Depending on the conditions that may have existed prior to the nation-states' independence, there might be relatively few individuals with the know-how and experience to rule. The nation-states might cast their regimes in such euphemisms as "guided democracy" (as was done in Pakistan in the 1960s) or "caretaker regimes" (as in Chile since 1973), but they don't seem to mind being seen for what they really are. In any case, a new state facing such problems as national identity, industrialization, population control, social mobilization, and internal disorders often cannot afford the luxury of a political democracy, much less contain within it a knowledge of and appreciation for the prerequisites of democracy that we have just examined. That alternative is simply not available for some time.

What of the traditional authoritarian regimes, such as those in Latin America, the Middle East, and parts of Africa? In many cases, they result from the failure of previous attempts at democratic government. Such failures may have been the result of the lack of a strong middle class, a low literacy rate, major economic failures, outside military threats, or other indigenous problems. The authoritarian figure or group comes forward to "reform the nation's finances," to "restore governmental stability," or to "save the nation from outside aggression." In some instances, they do. It is generally recognized that Kemal Ataturk was primarily responsible for the integration and modernization of Turkey in the 1920s through the use of an authoritarian government. However, the precedent of authoritarian oligarchy makes attempts at other approaches to government more difficult. Further, even when the "success" of the dictator is ephemeral, as in the case of Juan Peron in Argentina, the habit of authoritarian rule is still hard to break.

This leads us to the consideration of governmental transition in authoritarian regimes. This problem seems to be common to almost all types of authoritarianism. It stems from the fact that stability of the regime is so highly prized that the mere suggestion of an orderly transfer of power can be seen as a weakness of the present government. Major exceptions can be seen in the long, drawn-out transfer of power in Spain from the dictator, Franco, to King Juan Carlos and thence to a parliament in the early 1970s and in the military control of both Peru and Argentina giving way to civilian government in Peru during 1980 and in Argentina in 1984, but these kinds of changes are rare. More often than not, especially in military juntas, power simply passes from one group of military officers to another, accompanied by different degrees of instability, ranging from hardly noticeable transitions to bloody revolutions up to and including civil war.

To the inhabitants of many nation-states, that is what government is like. Government is similar to death, natural disasters, and other things of an unfortunate nature that are apt to come along during one's lifetime and about which one can expect to do very little. The infrequent rise of revolutionaries only serves one of two purposes: either to cause great local disturbance in which innocent people may be killed and property destroyed or simply to replace the current leaders with a new regime that will do little more than did the old. As a result, there is a great deal of apathy and a great deal of stability in these authoritarian regimes. Justice, morality, and ethical conduct are not to be expected in any great degree from the government, and authoritarian governments need not concern us in this study except to be seen as rather unfortunate alternatives to preserving our own form of political democracy.

TOTALITARIANISM

A more modern and sophisticated form of authoritarian government is **totalitarianism.** Probably the father of modern totalitarianism was Joseph Stalin, although the seeds were certainly planted by Lenin in the former Soviet Union. Other practitioners of the art include Mao Tse-tung of China; Kim Il Sung in North Korea; and Hitler to some extent, however briefly, in Germany. There was also a rather lame attempt by Mussolini in fascist Italy. Perhaps totalitarianism, in its full theoretical form, has only truly been approached in the former Soviet Union, in North Korea, and in Maoist China. Hitler's regime had totalitarian characteristics for only a brief period of time, and I am unsure as to its ultimate continuation beyond World War II even had Hitler been triumphant. Mussolini attempted totalitarianism, but the Italian population could never quite adjust to it or fully accept its purposes. A bizarre form of religious totalitarianism appears to exist in contemporary Iran under its Koranic-based fundamentalist government. Its continuation since the death of the Ayatollah Khomeini in 1990 remains problematical. Totalitarianism has become an integral part of the ideologies of communism and fascism, as we shall see.

What is totalitarianism, and why did it come about in this century? Both questions can be answered somewhat by noting the basic characteristics of a totalitarian dictatorship:[5]

1. Official ideology
2. Single-party dictatorship
3. Remaking of individuals
4. Total distrust of the people
5. Mass organization to demonstrate the oneness of the population

OFFICIAL IDEOLOGY

First, in the beginning there has to be an official ideology. The ideologies of totalitarian governments have been fascism and communism (and, perhaps, the ideas of Shiite Islam in Iran), with communism by far the more successful of these. We will discuss these ideologies in a later section. At this point, it is important only to note that the ideology constitutes a great master plan for the present and the future. This organizes the economy and the government of a nation-state for the purpose of solving modern problems of economic and political control that have existed since the Industrial Revolution. The ideology is a complex set of ideas that involves an understanding of political and economic theory far beyond the capacity of most individuals in the society. The purpose of the totalitarian regime is to remake the society as a whole, from top to bottom, to conform to the characteristics defined by the ideology. Therefore, the ideology defines the nature of the totalitarian regime in terms of its goals and procedures.

SINGLE-PARTY DICTATORSHIP

The second characteristic of a totalitarian regime is the single-party dictatorship. A party, consisting of an elite group of individuals who presume to understand the ideology, rules the entire nation in a pyramidal fashion, with the very highest leaders understanding the ideology the most. These leaders, in the People's Republic of China and the former Soviet Union, are supported by a Politburo, a central committee, and a party congress. Each layer plays a lesser role and presumably possesses a lesser level of understanding of the ideology, always conforming to the interpretations of the top leadership of the pyramid. The elite party is also the government, despite other formal institutions that may be written into an essentially meaningless constitution. The government exists primarily for administrative coherency. It is

[5]The following list of characteristics is adapted from a similar list by Dragnich, A. N., 1966. *Major European Governments*. 2nd ed. Homewood, Il.: The Dorsey Press, Inc., pp. 10–11.

the party overlapping the governmental structure that makes the decisions, creates the laws, and provides for the enforcement of those laws. Indeed, it may be concluded that the ultimate purpose of totalitarian government is the preservation of the party, even at the expense of the society, as George Orwell asserted so magnificently in his novel, *1984.*

REMAKING OF INDIVIDUALS

The third characteristic of the totalitarian regime truly separates it from other authoritarian regimes. The totalitarian regime seeks to remake individuals into new people, suitable for its ideological goals and its utopian vision of the society. This is often referred to as "the use of force and terror to reshape humankind." The purpose of the government is to enter into every possible aspect of human life within the nation-state. Nothing is to be left to the individual's discretion that cannot be controlled by the government. It is important to the government where you live, what you do for a living, how much education you receive, and how many children you have. Your moving about is of concern, and even your thoughts are of greater concern insofar as they might be expressed to others.

Totalitarian government means the total governing of men and women. It means that the government must find some way to bend its citizens into the new shape described by the ideology. Force and terror are indeed a part of the process, but here we must remember something from the second chapter of the book. People do not govern others through force alone. Indeed, men and women can be brought to such levels of terror and fear as to resolve not to live at all rather than continue to become fearful and miserable individuals.

In the beginning, insofar as the regimes of Stalin, Hitler, Kim, and Mao Tse-tung were concerned, we did indeed see an enormous use of force and terror. The purpose was two-fold: (1) to get rid of any possible opposition and (2) to impress the people with the enormous power of the new regime so as to stifle initial discontent. Many people were shot, imprisoned, or otherwise dealt with in a horrible fashion, with the result that the survivors had little inclination to challenge the rule of the Soviet Red Army, Hitler's SA and SS, Kim's party, or Mao Tse-tung's People's Liberation Army. However, as previously stated, one can only apply direct force and terror for so long. Then something else must be added.

What is usually added is a payoff. Something good must happen to the people to provide a positive incentive for them to continue to submit to the totalitarian rule and to begin a substantial change in their lifestyle. After Hitler's takeover, it was not long before unemployment ceased, inflation came to an end, and German industry and self-confidence began to improve. This had more to do with Hitler's ability to make some Germans into fascist fanatics than anything else. Stalin had a more difficult time of it and had to reinvoke selective force and terror and even methodical mass starvation on occasion, but by the mid-1930s he, too, had improved the lifestyle of the average Russian in terms of food, clothing, and shelter far beyond what had been done in the past under the feudal czarist regime. Mao's success in China in eradicating starvation and the social exploitation of the peasants by other people is well known. His ability to impose upon the Chinese a new concept of who they were in the scheme of history has seldom been duplicated. Thus, with the stick goes the carrot.

Of course, there will always tend to be some group that will find something to complain about, especially since the government is so deeply involved with the individual from the time of his or her birth until the time of his or her death. There will be complaints about educational opportunities that were not correctly parceled out and complaints about bureaucrats who do not do their jobs efficiently even though they are members of the party. There will be complaints about food shortages, about favoritism, and about other things that affect the working and leisure activities of a society that is supposed to be uniform in its construction and characteristics. What do you do about these dissidents?

Of course, you could shoot them, but, to the totalitarian leaders, that would amount to admitting that the ideology and the government that operates it are inadequate for the dissentor. The suggestion follows that it might be inadequate for others. That sort of admission is out of the question. Therefore, the regime must find some way to convert the dissident into a supporter of the regime (active or passive), or else it must find some public reason for dismissing his or her complaints.

In the former Soviet Union, sudden selective arrests followed by the use of prolonged, sterile imprisonment in concentration camps produced success. This technique plays on basic human desires for interpersonal coexistence. Most dissidents are eventually forced to submit to the regime and to admit that their deviance was wrong in order to return to society and to continue to participate in the payoffs of the regime. George Orwell gives us a graphic example of these techniques in *1984*, which was essentially written about Stalinist totalitarianism. More recently, Soviet dissidents who did not give up their individual integrity (which is the great enemy of totalitarianism) have been dealt with by being committed to insane asylums to suggest to the rest of the citizens that these people are really insane and, therefore, that their dissent is meaningless babble. Others were exiled, as was Alexander Solzhenitsyn, with the excuse that they were unworthy of the great goals and the great mission of the regime. Thus, whether a person is returned from a concentration camp repentant, left in an insane asylum, or exiled from the nation, the leadership can always explain away the dissident's voice and commend to the rest of the people the joys of strict adherence to the ideological leadership of the regime.

Force and terror may exist throughout the history of a totalitarian regime, but, after the first few years, it does so on a very subtle level, and it must be accompanied by a material payoff. Until recently, these techniques have worked in Russia, North Korea, and the People's Republic of China. However, the hope that human integrity and the instinct for individuality can reassert themselves is a real one. This was certainly the case within the former Soviet Union in the early 1990s. Whether or not this can happen in China and North Korea remains to be seen. Perhaps it could occur in North Korea should the two Koreas be ultimately reunited and in China when the eight to ten elderly leaders who exercise ultimate control die.

Indeed, studies of the Soviet Union and China seem to suggest that the degree of control by a totalitarian regime may have been overstated by traditional theorists and that the classic description of totalitarianism outlined thus far may not be accurate. That is, it is more of an ideal than a reality. For instance, the Russian people have managed to rebel against the government in a variety of ways: drunkenness, black marketing, theft, absenteeism, protests through state-sanctioned trade unions, and a general corruption of the system that led to its downfall. In China, the instinct toward individualism is being reasserted through some new economic policies in agriculture and business that encourage profits and personal management. Variety is returning to the monistic world of Mao. Perhaps the best description of North Korea and China would be that they are severe and highly centralized single-party authoritarianisms using modern means of popular control.

TOTAL DISTRUST OF THE PEOPLE

A fourth characteristic of totalitarian government is total distrust of the people. This is expressed by a totally controlled press and broadcast media, secret police, and governmental control over the shaping of the minds of the youth almost from the cradle to adulthood. The latter is achieved through children's organizations for every age group, which are sponsored by the ruling party. The manipulation of public opinion and the infiltration by party members or informants of any group in which organized activity takes place are continuing devices to ensure uniformity of public views. Nothing is left to chance within the modern totalitarian regime. Again, more contemporary observation of China makes one suspect that, in the latest generation, the control is vastly weaker than it used to be.

MASS ORGANIZATION TO DEMONSTRATE
THE ONENESS OF THE POPULATION

A final characteristic of totalitarianism is the attempt to organize the population periodically for demonstrations of its oneness and singleness of purpose. Mass demonstration serves the purpose of assaulting the integrity of the individual. On a designated day, citizens must get up early in the morning in order to take their place with their co-workers at a designated point along the parade route, where the might of the army, along with athletic and cultural groups that represent the best of the regime, pass in review before the assembled leadership. They must stand there with a flag in their hands and wave and cheer the symbols of the regime that dominates them. If that is not bad enough, they see thousands of other people waving the same flags, saying the same cheers, being little cogs in the state wheel. Where is their integrity now? Where is their individuality? The demonstration has served to undermine and destroy it.

Z. B. Brzezinski, national security advisor to former President Jimmy Carter, proposed the following definition of the aspects of totalitarianism just discussed. It is, he says, "a system in which technologically advanced instruments of public power are wielded without restraint by centralized leadership of an elite movement, for the purpose of effecting a total social revolution, including the conditioning of man, on the basis of certain arbitrary ideological assumptions proclaimed by the leadership, in an atmosphere of coerced unanimity of the entire population."[6]

This, then, is totalitarianism in its ideal form. As already suggested, the *reality* is probably much less than this. Perhaps recent trends will ultimately show that, even in North Korea and China, humankind will ultimately resist such attempts to reduce society to the level of bees or ants. This already seems to be occurring in China. Indeed, it could be that what we now call totalitarianism has really become nothing more than communist technique, and we know that all techniques are changeable.

THE EVOLUTION OF IDEOLOGY

Whether a government is democratic, authoritarian, or totalitarian, it can be affected by ideology. A totalitarian government is, of course, practically defined by ideology, but a political democracy or an authoritarian regime may choose whether or not to accept a particular ideological view. The point remains that political discourse and much of international relations are affected, or have been affected, by five ideologies. In historical sequence, they are liberalism, conservatism, socialism, communism, and fascism. The only ideology not fully in effect is fascism. However, its seeds are forever being planted, awaiting an opportunity to fall on the fertile ground of circumstance and charismatic leadership. Thus, if only for historical purposes, but more for understanding political discourse, it is helpful to examine how these five ideologies evolved.

In order to do this, it is necessary to go back to the eighteenth century. One author, Frederick W. Watkins, has chosen the date 1750 as the beginning of

---

[6]Brzezinski, Z. B., 1962. *Ideology and Power in Soviet Politics*. New York: Frederick A. Praeger, pp. 19–20.

the "age of ideology."[7] This choice is not without reason. In Europe before the eighteenth century, there were not too many things a person could do in order to earn a living and ensure economic security. The word **economics** comes from the Greek word for home, and it implies the management of the home in terms of the shelter itself, the food eaten within it, and the clothing worn by the inhabitants. The economy was what a family did to meet its basic needs for food, clothing, and shelter. One could farm, which was the major occupation of those years; one could be a shepherd; or one could enter the very few professions of the day—the law, or the clergy, or perhaps one could even become a "doctor of physic" and practice a rudimentary form of medicine. One could also hunt, fish, or engage in such handicrafts as carpentry or metalsmithing.

The occupation of an individual of the early eighteenth century was characterized by two things. First, it was easily learned through apprenticeship or by observation. It did not change much over a period of time. A weaver who sat at a loom in 1700 sat at the same kind of loom that Penelope might have used waiting for the return of Ulysses. The spinning wheel was the same as it had been in ancient Egypt. Carpenter's tools were similar to those used by Jesus of Nazareth. The farmer used a plow that was little changed from those used in primitive times. Although the blade might now be steel instead of stone, its basic configuration was the same, and it was pulled by the same yoke of oxen, horses, or mules. With regard to agriculture, little improvement could be noted between the methods of antiquity and those of the day.

The second basic aspect of an individual's occupation was that, having acquired sufficient skills, a person could with reason be expected to prosper through his or her own labors. With the exception of natural disaster, such as flood, fire, or pestilence, people were truly responsible for their own economic security. Government served the needs of princes. It provided law enforcement and a few meager services such as record keeping, communication, the operation of roads, and the defense of the state. There was no thought among the leaders of government to minister to the needs of people. Should some unfortunate occurrence befall a nation, one looked to either the church or one's neighbors for help.

Europe had existed under these basic conditions for well over a thousand years when James Watt invented the steam engine. That changed the course of history. To take the textile industry as an example, this is the sort of thing that took place during the middle part of the eighteenth century: A machine had been developed that could provide more power than a horse or any other known source of energy. It could be harnessed to a gigantic loom that could weave cloth, not in yards but in bolts of thirty to fifty yards in length. Not only could the cloth be woven more efficiently,

[7]Watkins, F. W., *The Age of Ideology*. 1964. Englewood Cliffs, N. J.: Prentice-Hall, Inc.

but the thread could also be spun by other machines, which replaced the old spinning wheel and the simplicity that surrounded it.

From where would the vast quantities of wool and other fiber come with which to feed these new and gigantic machines, which promised an enormous increase in productivity and improvement in people's material welfare? In Great Britain, the answer came in the form of the Enclosure Movement. A peasant family who occupied some of the land owned by a local lord, usually farming it and perhaps raising a few sheep, would be told one day that they must move. Their house was destroyed, their gardens were replaced by pasture land, and thousands of sheep became the occupants of their farm and the other farms of the region. This, then, provided the wool for the vast new machines that were being established in the new industrial towns of Manchester and Leeds. What would happen to the peasant family? They would go into the cities and take up residence in apartment buildings and become the operators of the new machines. Instead of growing their own crops, spinning their own thread, and weaving their own clothes, they would now be paid wages. They would go to the local store and purchase their groceries and their clothes.

The peasants flowed into the new cities. As did the new businessmen, who sought the profits to be made from the enormous expansion of industrial capability. All went well for a while, but eventually the owner of the factory would have to tell the workers that the factory had overproduced; there was too much wool cloth on the market; the price had fallen; the factory must be shut down. That was fine for the owner of the factory, but what of the worker, whose economy was now entirely dependent upon wages? He or she had no farm to return to, no skill to sell in an industrial society except that of running a loom, which was now closed down. Must he or she and the family now starve?

The worker could turn to neighbors, but they were hard up, too, or turn to the church, but it lacked the resources to help all the poor. To whom, then, did he or she ultimately turn, and with what argument? For the first time in the life of Europe since the fall of Rome, a person could *not*, through his or her own sweat, provide for his or her family. An enormous intellectual, moral, and psychological crisis slowly began to grip the working classes and the intelligentsia of Europe. The only other institution to which the working classes could turn was the government. There was, however, as yet no consideration of a possible link between what had evolved as a national economy and the national government's responsibility for it.

In turning to the government for a solution to the economic crisis that was slowly developing, new ideas began to emerge. We call these ideas *ideology*. Ideologies are ideas that constitute an overall thinking pattern concerned with the best way to structure the government and the economy for dealing with the Industrial Revolution. These sets of ideas began to take root in the 1740s and 1750s, and many of them continue with variations to the present day.

POINTS TO PONDER

Are Americans today beginning to move more fully to the right? What evidence can you give for or against that proposition?

With regard to the first question, do you see similar tendencies in other countries?

Why do you think there are more authoritarian governments in the world today than there are democracies?

Is true totalitarianism possible in the future? Why or why not?

Are we entering a postideological world? Why or why not?

8 | Liberalism, Conservatism, Socialism, Communism, and Fascism

In order to understand how ideologies evolved, three ingredients generally precede the coalescence of an ideology. First, there must be an individual or a group with some ideas. These ideas must somehow relate to people, the state, and property. Second, there must be some publication or dissemination of these ideas to the population as a whole such as a book, pamphlet, speech, or manifesto. Third, there must be a particular time in which the ideas seem to be relevant to a specific uncomfortable situation and seem to offer a solution to it. This time is seen in retrospect as a flashpoint of revolution or perhaps simply as a time for change. The people and their ideas, the dissemination of the ideas, and the point of relevance all combine to produce what we later recognize as ideology. We will see how these three elements are mixed into the formulation of all the contemporary ideologies.

LIBERALISM

JOHN CALVIN

There are at least four key individuals to consider with regard to **liberalism**. The first one precedes the flashpoint by many years. He is John Calvin, who gave us, to some extent, the ideas contained in the concept of the Protestant ethic. Calvin's Protestantism was somewhat dissimilar to that of Martin Luther and of some of the earlier Catholic dissidents. He had a lot to say about the human-God relationship, but he also had some things to say that were of a political nature. First, if one were to carry out one's predetermined destiny, in the human-God context, one had to be allowed a maximum capacity to develop one's individuality. After all, salvation is an individual act and not a group effort. Government-supported churches should not interfere in a person's attempt to work out his or her salvation, which included, as noted in chapter 6, the right to prosper economically.

2.   Second, John Calvin suggested that an individual should also have no priestly class between him or her and God. This meant, in turn, that people should have a freedom to think as they wish and worship as they wish. It is a very small step from the freedom to think in terms of worship to the freedom to think politically as one sees fit. The ability to define an individual's relationship to God is similar to an individual's propensity to define his or her relationship with the state. Thus, the early Calvinists, our pilgrim forebears if you wish, and those who settled in New England and passed their ideas down the Atlantic seaboard, instilled very early in the American colonists a concept of individualism and the freedom of one's conscience.

JOHN LOCKE

The second man in the evolution of liberalism was a British subject, John Locke. I discussed him previously in the context of his *Second Treatise of Government*, where he defined his social contract theory. Central to Locke's theory is the right of an individual to own property and to have it protected, along with the right of the same individual to revolt against an unjust monarch and to create a new government should government be oppressive to his or her life, liberty, and property. The ideas of Locke were so compelling that they emerged in several places within the wording of the Declaration of Independence. This document was published in 1776, the flashpoint year in the ideology of liberalism.

ADAM SMITH

The third man in the liberal ideological history was a Scotsman by the name of Adam Smith. Smith was particularly concerned with the control of the British economy through the British Board of Trade and the prevailing philosophy under which that control operated. Great Britain had followed France and Spain in an economic philosophy known as **mercantilism.** Mercantilism had four basic tenets:

1. The healthiest national economy was one that had accumulated within its treasury the maximum amount of gold. Therefore, all economic activity within and without the nation should be devoted to that end.
2. A nation should export more goods than it imports. Thereby, gold would flow into the nation rather than out of it.
3. A nation should import raw materials that could be purchased cheaply and export finished goods that could be sold for higher prices. This again would maximize the gold inflow.

4. Colonies should be established outside of Europe, so that the nation might have a source of gold but, more to the point, so it would have a source of raw materials that would be obtainable under prices cheaper than those obtained by trading with other countries. The problem with the colony idea was that colonies should not develop their own economy, lest those economies compete with the economy of the home country.

Most of our American colonies were founded as economic investments by mercantilistic individuals intent on a ready supply of raw materials such as tobacco, naval stores, tar, pitch, wood, agricultural products, and, later, cotton. The idea was that the colonists would pay back the British economy for the expense of establishing the colony through the export of these materials at controlled prices. If there was any gold in the economy of the colony, it should be taxed so as to return it to the mother country. No trade between the colonies and other countries, and only minimum trade among the colonies themselves, should be allowed.

All of these mercantilistic restrictions assaulted not only the sensibilities of the American colonists, who rebelled against the suppression of their own trade and manufacture, but also the sensibilities of Adam Smith, the classic economist. Smith wrote a book that was published, ironically, in the year 1776. It was entitled *The Wealth of Nations.* The title is significant because he argued in the book that the wealth of nations was not gold. One could not eat it, wear it for warmth, build a house out of it, or use it for any purpose other than as a means for the exchange of goods. It was an artificial symbol of value. The real wealth of nations, he argued, was what they produced in terms of goods and services. What a nation should do, he said, was to maximize conditions under which productivity occurred. The best way to do that was for the government to stay out of the economic picture altogether. Borrowing a phrase from the French "physiocrats"—**laissez-faire,** meaning "leave us alone"—Smith argued that the government of Great Britain should not only leave Britain's economy alone, but it should leave the American colonists alone as well and allow the triangular trade in which such people as John Hancock were engaged to continue, allow Paul Revere and others to engage in manufacturing, and allow those colonists who were beginning to establish intercolonial markets to continue to do so.

How would the economy be controlled if the government stayed out of it? Smith argued that there was an invisible hand that would perform all the necessary control functions. This invisible hand was the "law of supply and demand" as it related to prices. If the supply of a good was too low, its price would be high because there would not be enough to meet the demand. Therefore, human greed being what it is, that particular good would be produced in more and more quantity. The price would then begin to fall. If, on the other hand, a good was overproduced, its price would be low because there would be too much of it to be consumed, and its value would be less dear. When that point occurred, those who produced that particular good would cease production until the market was ready for new production, as indicated by a rise in the price. At some point, supply and demand would equalize, producing stability in pricing as well as production.

These were rather simple theories, although the arguments for them were far more complex than need be recounted here. Their very simplicity made them attractive to those American colonists who saw in Adam Smith a rationale for changing their own unhappy economic situation. Adam Smith's capitalism entered the mix of John Calvin's individualism and freedom of conscience and John Locke's advocacy of private property and the right to change an oppressive government. Together, these ideas constituted a very thorough argument for change. However, that's all they constituted in 1776, and the argument might have been resolved by a wiser British Parliament under the leadership of the Whig faction. The Tory faction was in power though. Nevertheless, many prominent members of Parliament sought to induce the king to conciliate the colonies by lessening taxation, allowing more trade and manufacturing, and giving the colonists a freer rein in expanding not only their trade with each other but with other nations as well. The compromise, however, did not occur. The result was that the Americans took up arms and by revolution welded their ideas into an ideology.

THOMAS PAINE

The impetus for this came from the fourth man in our liberal evolution. He is often the forgotten man because he was not exactly the most attractive of the group. His name was Thomas Paine, and he is best known for his pamphlet *Common Sense.* It was Paine who made the ideas into ideology. It was Paine who told us something about ourselves that we have continued to believe, whether correctly or incorrectly, to the point that it has become a definition of who and what we are.

Thomas Paine wrote that, although government was necessary, it was a necessary *evil* and should be reduced to its absolute minimum. Paine argued further that, although people were fairly reasonable, they had often been deceived and that one of the greatest deceptions in history was that of hereditary monarchy. This kind of government was not only evil, it was stupid. The mere fact that one is the offspring of a king in no rational way entitles one to govern, absolutely, a nation.

He argued further that the American colonial experience was a unique experience in that, for the first time in human history, a large group of fairly intelligent people had been placed in a wilderness, a state of nature, with the ability, being over 4,000 miles distant from the king, to repudiate not only that king, but the system of European monarchy. Why should we do that? According to Paine, we would be fulfilling humanity's destiny and achieving something that men and women had never before been able to achieve and would probably never again have a chance to achieve. We were, in Paine's view, the "New Jerusalem." This was a potent, symbolic term implying a grant by God of a chance to reform the way men and women governed their fellows and the way the economy of the world, or at least the state, could be constructed. Further, Paine argued that we were "man's last, best hope" for achieving this new way of life.

He said, in effect, that it was not simply an argument with Great Britain that was at issue but, rather, the real purpose of the struggle was to remake the entire political and economic order of humanity. Now, there was to be a common purpose for all who had been aggrieved by the actions of the British government—to those whose land had been taken, to those whose homes had been used to quarter British troops, to those who had been taxed unfairly (at least in their opinion), and to those whose economic interest had been frustrated. There was a significant number of these people (approximately one-third of the population of the colonies), whose minds were literally set aflame by the audacity of the argument of Thomas Paine.

A SYMBOL OF THE NEW LIBERAL IDEOLOGY

We have forgotten much of the revolutionary nature of our ideology because our revolution, though itself quite bloody and prolonged, is so distant in our past. Furthermore, the triumph of liberalism has been so complete as to appear normal. Let's not forget, however, that what happened in this country from 1775 until 1783 was the beginning of something new in the history of government.

Our founding fathers knew this better than we. It fell to some of them, early in the revolution, to design a symbol of just what it was that we were about. In March 1780, the Continental Congress decided to produce a seal for the new nation with which to authenticate documents. The idea for such a seal had gone all the way back to 1776, but it was now imperative to have the seal prepared so as to begin to attest to the existence of the new nation. Three committee members submitted a design that is quite significant in what it contains. (See figure 8.1.)

On the right of the figure appears the well-known obverse side of the great American seal. The eagle, the mighty symbol of a fiercely independent people, has within its beak a scroll with the phrase *e pluribus unum*, "out of many, one," or "out of many colonies comes one nation." It further contains the symbolic representation of the colonies as thirteen stars above the eagle's head. The shield on the eagle's breast contains thirteen stripes, again symbolizing the thirteen colonies. In one claw is clutched

FIGURE 8.1 The Great Seal of the United States

arrows, indicating a willingness to fight, and in the other claw is an olive branch, indicating the willingness to live in peace with all nations.

Most people have seen this obverse side of the seal, and this is the side that is imprinted in wax upon official United States documents. However, seals have a reverse side as well. This side of the seal is usually seen by people only on the one dollar bill, where both sides of the seal are displayed. It is often dismissed as the spiritual side of the seal, and yet, if one studies it and remembers that it was drawn by people close to the revolution and its ideological underpinnings, then what the designers of the seal wished to say to themselves and to posterity might be glimpsed.

What we see at first glance is a pyramid. The pyramid is a symbol of permanence, so something permanent is being portrayed. The pyramid itself sits in a wilderness where there is little vegetation and vast open spaces. It is a state of nature. A pyramid begins with the lowest level—the lowest stack of bricks or blocks—and on this lowest stack of blocks is chiseled, in Roman numerals, a date—1776. Something permanent in a state of nature began in 1776. The pyramid is not yet complete. It must be completed by those who will come after the builders or the founders of the pyramid. Instead, above the uncompleted portion there stands an eye. The eye is physically separated above the pyramid and has a halo around it. The symbolic height of the eye and the halo around it tells us that this is the eye of God, or as originally expressed by the designers, the eye of Providence.

God, then, is sitting above the unfinished portion of the pyramid. Why is he sitting there? A Latin inscription tells us. It is found at the top of the picture, and it says *Annuit Coeptis*. Roughly translated, this means "He (God) has blessed our undertaking." God stands above this permanent thing, which began in 1776, blessing not only its creation but its continued evolution. What is this pyramid built in the wilderness under the watchful eye of God, and why was it built? The answer to the final question is found in the scroll beneath the pyramid, which reads *Novus Ordo Seclorum*—"the new order of the ages." This is Paine's new order, and Locke's, and Smith's, and Calvin's new order. Here is a new order of government under liberal precepts, a new order of the economy under Smith's ideas of capitalism and the free market. God would continue to bless this special people, who would serve as an example to all other nations.

We believed that then, and we believed that for a long time thereafter. Although we pay it less credence today than we might, we still believe it at various times and in various ways. This is how our ideology began, and this is what it was. The solution it seemed to offer to the emerging Industrial Revolution was that all people should be left free to find their own way out of its difficulties. The faith of liberalism was that, left to their own devices, people can better solve their economic problems through self-reliance and hard work rather than trust government to solve them.

NEOLIBERALISM

Of course, this is what might be called *classic liberalism*—the original vision of the American people. As time wore on and life became more complex within our growing nation, certain modifications of the more classic design began to occur. Government's role in the economy began to expand with the need for regulation of the railroads, the currency, and new inventions such as the airplane and telephone. By the time of the Great Depression in the 1930s, a whole new concept of government had emerged within the old liberal order. This is generally referred to as **neoliberalism.** It allows for more governmental activity than was anticipated by our forebears. In response to the Great Depression of the 1930s, President Franklin D. Roosevelt proposed the New Deal in America, which forever changed the concept of liberalism as defined in America. The New Deal liberals saw government in a more positive light and as an active force for good. They created Social Security, public work programs, new regulatory agencies, and set minium wages and hours for workers. Today's neoliberals support programs aimed essentially at the economy and the social structure of the state. They would expand the use of governmental regulations in the economy in order to protect the public interest. They seek an economic floor for all people that would ameliorate the worse aspects of poverty. (This has resulted in numerous welfare programs.) They are also concerned about the civil rights of the poor and also those of ethnic and racial minorities and would legislate both for a broader definition of those civil rights and for remedial programs to address historic abuses in that regard. Critics of such an expanded role for government often refer to much of this as social engineering and suggest that it goes far beyond what the original concept of the general welfare was all about.

The word *liberal* has been preempted by the New Deal neoliberals of the post-Depression era. Many people whose values are still rooted, for the most part, in the classic definition of liberalism have taken on the label of *conservatives* since the 1930s. As we shall see in the next section, these people do not so much reflect the classic conservative views of Edmund Burke as they have asserted something altogether new.

Another point should be made here that will also be developed later. The original liberals and makers of the revolution were people such as Thomas Jefferson, Sam Adams, and Thomas Paine. They made their revolution from 1775 at Lexington Bridge until peace was obtained through military effort at Yorktown in 1781. The peace was enshrined in 1783 in the Treaty of Paris, and the nation attempted to organize a confederal government. As noted earlier, the government of the confederacy did not work very well. By 1787, it was thought necessary to make certain changes. These changes were made by a slightly different group of men. They were younger men, easterners, businessmen, and lawyers; men who were somewhat more cautious now that the guns had fallen silent. They tended to be more intent on preserving rather than creating. They were the makers of the U.S. Constitution, a document whose acceptance and promulgation came thirteen years after the Declaration of Independence, reflecting a slightly altered view of the "new order of the ages."

The result is that, although the liberal ideology is often referred to in its substance, it has worked itself out within the framework of a somewhat conservative constitution. The political history of the United States, until recently at least, was the story of the progression from the Declaration of Independence, through the Constitution of 1789, and back to the ideals of the Declaration of Independence. One reads in the Declaration that all men are created equal, and yet slavery affects five different parts of the U.S. Constitution. We read in the writings of Thomas Paine that participation in government should be for all people, and yet we find under the U.S. Constitution only 6 percent of the population in 1789 had the right to vote, and they, in turn, could determine the makeup of only one-sixth of the government.[1]

A further example of the conservative provisions of the Constitution is the way the power of the legislative branches was defined. The Senate was to have more power than the popularly elected branch. It would approve appointments to the judiciary; it would approve all Cabinet, diplomatic, and military appointments; it alone would certify treaties for ratification; and it would sit in judgment upon the impeachment of a president. Further, its members served terms of six years rather than two. Even today, the United States is practically alone among the world's political democracies in having more power in the upper legislative house than in the lower house, which is closer to the people.

The electoral college and geographic representation in the U.S. Senate are other provisions of the Constitution that were equally conservative, but this is not the time to discuss them. With the beginning of the Jackson administration in the 1830s, a long struggle to overcome the conservative qualifications and to reaffirm the liberal ideas began. Property qualifications to vote began to dissolve; black men received the right to vote under the Fifteenth Amendment. The Senate became popularly elected after the turn of the century. The determination of the electors for president fell under popular control during the latter half of the nineteenth century. Women got the right to vote in 1920. Other affirmations of civil rights relating to equal justice for all have followed at various times. These were highlighted by the period of the Warren Supreme Court of the 1950s and 1960s.

It has been a long journey from the Constitution back to the Declaration of Independence, and the journey has not yet ended. One should keep in

---

[1]The presidency, which is one-third of the government, was to be elected by the electoral college. The judiciary, which is another one-third, was to be appointed by the president. The Senate, which is one-sixth (one-half of the legislative third) of the government, was to be chosen by the state legislatures. In Alexander Hamilton's words, each of these was to be selected by certain groups of people who were the "rich, the able and the well born." This left only the House of Representatives to be elected by the general voters.

mind the words of Abraham Lincoln, who once responded to the jibe that Thomas Jefferson was surely a hypocrite when he wrote that all men were created equal while he owned slaves. Lincoln said of Jefferson and the Declaration:

> *I think the authors of that notable instrument intended to include all men, but they did not mean to declare all men equal in all respects. They did not mean to say all men were equal in color, size, intellect, moral development or social capacity. They defined with tolerable distinctness in what they did consider all men created equal—equal in certain inalienable rights, among which are life, liberty and the pursuit of happiness. This they said, and this they meant. They did not mean to assert the obvious untruth, that all were then actually enjoying that equality, nor yet, that they were about to confer it immediately upon them. In fact they had no power to confer such a boon. They meant simply to declare the right so that the enforcement of it might follow as fast as circumstances should permit. They meant to set up a standard maxim for a free society which should be familiar to all: constantly looked to, constantly labored for, and even though never perfectly attained, constantly approximated and thereby constantly spreading and deepening its influence and augmenting the happiness and value of life to all people, of all colors, everywhere.*[2]

Indeed, Lincoln furthered this 1857 projection of America's purpose by suggesting (successfully) in his Gettysburg Address of 1863 that the Civil War was fought, in the final analysis, for the purpose of achieving the goals of a nation "conceived in liberty and dedicated to the proposition that all men are created equal," thus effectively defining the war as one fought to fulfill the Declaration of Independence.

CONSERVATISM

Conservatism is the least developed of the great ideologies. In its classic or traditional forms, it offers little specific guidance as to the proper economic order. Its main thrust is political. It is the ideology of authoritarian governments, and because of its less than clear dimension it has served the purposes of a variety of governments. It can and does exist within truly politically democratic societies, but only with great difficulty and some modifications of the concept of democracy.

In order to understand conservatism, one must realize that its origins lie within Great Britain in particular and later throughout Europe in general, in a reaction to the American experience with liberalism. Actually, the reaction

---

[2]From the Lincoln-Douglas Debates, 1857.

was more to the French experience with liberalism because that is where the problem began. As many Americans know, the American Revolution was not solely a war between American colonists and the British government. Rather, we had a very important ally, the government of France under the autocratic rule of Louis XVI. He had felt that his foreign policy objectives, which always included the reduction of British power, might be achieved through establishment of an independent America, thereby reducing British territory and hoping to create a puppet state in the new world that would ally itself with France in future colonial wars. For those purposes, and hardly for the purposes of achieving liberal goals, Louis was persuaded by Benjamin Franklin and others to send to this country not only large amounts of money, arms, uniforms, and ammunition, but also a French army and a French navy. At the decisive battle of Yorktown, which for all purposes ended the American Revolutionary War, the French army was significant to the fight, and the coast was blockaded by the French navy. The British, indeed, were more inclined to surrender their sword to the French rather than to the American colonists.

The French soldiers, who participated in our revolution for liberal ideals, took those ideas back with them to France, which was suffering under the increasingly oppressive and still feudal regime of King Louis. Paris, although ripe for revolution, had not yet found a rationale. America gave it one, and in the same year that we wrote the Constitution, which *qualified* our liberalism, that same ideology sprang up in France. The French Revolution began with the storming of the Bastille (a political prison) under the cry of "liberty, equality, and fraternity."

However, there are two major differences between the American Revolution and the French Revolution. First, our revolution was a limited one in which we sought to change only the political and economic structure of our society. We kept intact the legal system, the basic social order, the concept of private property, the religious ideals of the Anglican church, and the basic ideas of human rights that were common to British subjects long before there was an American Revolution. The French, on the other hand, sought to destroy much more of society than its government and its economy. They attacked not only the monarchy but the noble class, the entire governing intelligentsia. They also attacked the Catholic Church, abolishing it for a brief time. They rejected the law and the concept of private property. They destroyed the entire social order of the day. In sum, they went too far. Second, many of the leaders of the American Revolution were people who had been trained in government and economics and who had shared, in many cases, government experience on the colonial level. They understood what government was and what it was not. They understood the limits of government. They were, therefore, careful in what they did and how they did it. The people who seized power in France had no experience; furthermore, their education was less formal and less prevalent than among the American revolutionaries.

The result of all this was not the establishment of a new liberal republic in France, but rather the terror of the French revolutionary period from
1789 until the advent of Napoleon. France ran amuck in violence, murder,
seizure of property, and general chaos. Governments came and went and
contradicted each other. Leaders were assassinated. The story is an oft-
told one, perhaps depicted most graphically in Dickens' book *A Tale of Two
Cities*.

It was the early excesses of the French Revolution that prompted Englishman Edmund Burke, in 1790, to write a classic piece of political literature
entitled *Reflections on the French Revolution*. In that essay, which took the form
of a letter to a friend in France, Burke outlined the basic principles that we
now know as conservatism. He did this as a critique of liberalism and as an
antidote for it. Burke argued that human beings were by nature a mixture of
reason and passion. However, most people, because of original sin or human
nature, were more often moved by their passions than by their reason. The
result was that most people were incapable of participating in a government
that must keep order through self-sacrifice, duty, and a certain forbearance
of license. Only a few people were capable of rational dominance within
their psyches, and these people were generally those of the wealthier families, born of good bloodlines and well educated. To these people should go
the reins of government. The problem with liberalism was that eventually
the majority of passionate inhabitants of the state would submit to their
baser instincts and cause the downfall of the government and the society.
One had only to look to France to see the proof.

What should govern a society, according to Burke, were two things: (1) a
strong authoritarian government, made up of "the rich, the able, and the
well born," who would keep people and their passions in check through vigorous enforcement of laws against passionate excess; and (2) a strong, state-
supported church, which would instruct people in their moral development
so as to better contain their passions without the need of too much government. Thus ran the argument of conservatism, both in Burke's essay and to
this day.

One of the best contemporary statements of the principles of classic conservatism was given by a true American conservative, Russell Kirk. Those
principles are (1) a "belief that a divine intent rules society as well as conscience" in opposition to liberalism's premise of the rationality of human
reason; (2) an "affection for the proliferating variety and mystery of traditional life, as distinguished from the narrowing uniformity and equalitari-
anism" of liberal systems; (3) a "conviction that civilized society requires
orders and classes; the only true equality is moral equality; all other
attempts at leveling lead to despair"; (4) the "persuasion that property and
freedom are inseparably connected, and that economic leveling is not economic progress"; (5) a "faith in prescription" and a belief that people are
governed "more by emotion than by reason" such that "tradition and
sound prejudice provide checks upon man's anarchistic impulse"; and (6) a

"recognition that change and reform are not identical, and that innovation is a devouring conflagration more often than it is a torch of progress."[3]

As practicing liberals, to some extent, Americans have tended to reject this dreary formula for government and the dire predictions of those who saw eventual ruin in our system. First, Burke overestimated the extent of the damage done to the social fabric of France. Society is more resilient than Burke judged. Within fifty years of the French Revolution, France had enjoyed both the creation of a constitutional republic and the restoration of the church, the law, and private property. Further, the average French citizen was far better off after the revolution than he or she had been prior to it.

Second, Burke put too much hope for stability in government by aristocracy. He seemed to feel that aristocrats would control change and thus allow for a balanced evolution of society. In most cases, autocracies tend to resist change—even necessary change—lest they lose some power or prerogative through that change. The result is often that pressures for change build to a breaking point and ultimately become manifest in the chaos of revolution, which Burke most feared.

Although Burke could not grasp the more idealistic aspect of liberalism's hope for humanity, he might have judged more accurately the cautious manner with which we carried out those dreams. Instead, Burke's conservatism offered a bleak answer to the problems of the Industrial Revolution. In effect, the conservative answer to the people who were beginning to suffer greatly under the emerging Industrial Revolution of Great Britain was that *there is no utopia.* Life is hard. Economic disasters are a part of life; they must be borne as part of our unhappy stay on earth. Some people are luckier than others, and this fact must be accepted. A person is free to pursue his or her own solutions but only under the control of a strong government lest society as a whole be damaged by the solutions. Thus, the conservative answer to the Industrial Revolution was not nearly as hopeful as that offered by liberalism.

CONSERVATISM AFTER BURKE

As I have indicated earlier, what has been described thus far might be referred to as **classic** conservatism. However, if one analyzes most of the conservative parties and organizations of Western Europe over the past 100 years, one might be surprised to discover that they demonstrate an approximation of *Classic Liberalism* with a particular emphasis on minimal government and laissez-faire capitalism rather than the fundamental ideas of Burke. They also seem to share a concern for the underprivileged, albeit directed more often at the moral, physical, and intellectual aspects

[3]Kirk, R., 1969. *The Conservative Mind: From Burke to Santayana.* New York: G. P. Putnam's Sons, p. 2.

of their lives rather than the economic part. There is, to be sure, a tendency to assert a kind of "natural order of things" that resists too much change, but one also notes that government, though small, is seen as a positive element in creating the conditions necessary for a good and balanced society. Thus the conservative governments of Great Britain, especially during the Victorian Era, demonstrated a political ethos not uncommon to the contemporary American experience. This continued to be the case even through the postwar governments of Churchill and Macmillan. At the same time, one can see the same basic value system at work in the Gaullist governments of France up to the 1970s and in many other European nations of the period.

In America, the Eisenhower and Nixon presidencies are sometimes referred to as being more conservative than the neoliberal administrations of FDR, Truman, and Lyndon Johnson, and in view of the brand of so-called "conservatism" in Europe previously described, a good case can be made for that assertion. Eisenhower accepted many of the New Deal policies of his predecessors, but he did not push the concept much further. In addition, he attempted to hold down the size of governmental budgets and only reluctantly pursued the improvement in civil rights espoused by some Democrats and progressive Republicans. Nixon even accepted the Great Society concepts of Johnson, but he pursued them primarily through programs of block grants to the states and a minimum income for the poor to be derived through a negative income tax (which did not come to pass). Certainly one looks in vain for what could be described as the "conservatism" of today in the first two post-New Deal Republican presidencies. Rather one sees the same classic liberalism, parading as conservatism, as one also sees in Europe during the same period. The birth of an authentic American conservatism is to be found in later responses to the New Deal and its progeny, neoliberalism.

This is not to suggest that traditional liberalism was a universal ideological pattern of American government until the 1930s. Movements such as Populism and Progressivism, in particular, challenged classic liberal ideas, especially in the latter part of the 19th century. While acknowledging the concepts of limited government, political equality, capitalism and the like, Populists such as William Jennings Bryan sought to free the money supply; tax the rich through a graduated income tax; have the people, and not state legislatures, elect U.S. Senators; and use the government to protect the savings of ordinary people in the nation's banks. Whereas all of these things were eventually accomplished, more radical ideas of the Populists such as nationalizing the railroads, dismantling large and monopolistic industries, and the enforcement of a more equal sharing of the nation's wealth for all of the people scared the daylights out of a majority of the population. The more benign Progressivism of Theodore Roosevelt and Senator Robert LaFollette, which advocated more political rights for the poor and minorities; direct democracy through initiatives and referenda; and more regulation of the economy, though less virulent than the Populism of the "great unwashed," did not seriously undermine the basic philosophy of liberalism either. Rather, as previously noted, it was the New Deal that brought the basic American liberal consensus to an end.

MODERN CONSERVATISM

What has emerged since the 1940s is the evolution of a new conservatism vehemently opposing the bedrock assumptions of neoliberalism with regard to government's central role in managing the economy and seeking social justice. This movement, which begins in the late 1940s, has taken several forms since then. These are generally referred to as **Libertarianism,** the **New Right,** and **Neoconservatism.**

LIBERTARIANISM

Libertarian conservatives, at least those associated with the Libertarian Party, are first and foremost concerned with the liberty of the individual in an increasingly complex and interdependent society. One is tempted to say that they elevate the concept of individualism to the level of a neurosis. Their model citizen is self-reliant and needs little assistance from government on any level. Its proper role in the lives of citizens is to protect the country from outside attack and from crime or internal strife, to provide for a stable currency, and to provide only essential services to the people. (Exactly what is essential is often disputed, even by Libertarians.) Everyday living for most people should be the product of one's unfettered use of private property and the market. Government should not coerce citizens in their personal lives and in their pursuit of economic gain. Taxes should be minimal and related only to those basic services mentioned above.

To the Libertarian mind, government regulations, policies aimed at the redistribution of wealth, and any government welfare programs, are an anathema. Even such things as health, education, and morality are seen as the exclusive business of individuals, and government should stay out of them. In fact, it is generally asserted that when government does involve itself in such activities, it undermines the level of achievement that would occur without such interference. Rather than true conservatism, this is, in many ways, classic liberalism for the Cro-Magnon era! It is a reactionary form of conservatism based on a kind of Social Darwinism suggesting the survival of the fittest as a rule for modern life. Exactly where orphans, the elderly, the weak, and the unlucky fit in is never made all that clear. Probably as a result of all of this, Libertarianism has never made great inroads into the American political system. Its major influence is seen in a less stringent approach to conservatism generally labeled as the New Right.

THE NEW RIGHT

The "old right" is variously described as an upper-class intellectual group of traditional conservatives like the aforementioned Russell Kirk and others such as William F. Buckley, Peter Verick, and perhaps George Will. Until recently, they have tended to lurk on the peripheries of our political discourse making curmudgeonly attacks on neoliberal programs and government in general. The New Right is something altogether different. This is a middle-class movement of workers and small businessmen and women. It is anti-intellectual and suspicious of complex realities and generally rejects analytical attempts to deal with them. In its simplism, there is a strong strain of the old Populism except this time, the enemy is not Big Business, but Big Government! Nevertheless, there is the old populist theme of us against them along with the concept of majoritarianism, which, as we have seen, assumes that the majority is always right and its demands must be met no matter what the long term result may be. A major characteristic of this movement is its emphasis on moral values, especially those of Christianity (as defined by the New Right). Their concern is for the family, the church, and the neighborhood. They oppose abortion, sex education, homosexuality, pornography, drugs (except tobacco and alcohol, about which they seem to be ambivalent), "progressive education," and internationalism. They are nationalistic and fiscally conservative. They oppose government welfare, especially on the national level, and would replace it with private charity. Some oppose gambling as a source of state revenue, but when it is proposed as a substitute for such hated taxes as those on property, ambiguity sets in again. Indeed the New Right opposes all but the most minimal taxes, especially on the wealthy. Also on their hit list is affirmative action programs for women and minorities and government aid to arts and culture. Public education has become a prominent battle ground for the New Right. They would put mandatory prayer (presumably Christian) back into the school day, teach "creation science" along with or in lieu of evolution, deny homosexuals the right to teach in public schools, reduce school lunch programs and the like, return to a concentration on basic subjects in the curriculum, allow for public neighborhood schools whether they be effectively segregated or not, and control the kinds of books students read.

The New Right is dedicated to the concept that a strong military is essential to a free society. Despite their distaste for taxes, they tend to evaluate military strength primarily in terms of the amount of money spent on it and seldom concern themselves with the waste such simplicities inevitably produce. Further, whereas traditional conservatism resists change, the New Right embraces it so long as the change is directed against the dismantling of neoliberal programs and policies. One can't have enough of that, and the sooner, the better! Another major concept in the "get the government off our backs" character of the New Right is that of states' rights. What government there is should emanate primarily from the states where the "little people" have a bigger say. If that means less money to spend on social programs, then that is good too. Getting tough on crime is a more recent theme of the New Right. "Three (and sometimes two) strikes and you're out" is the new slogan for placing habitual criminals in prison for life, assuming that they haven't been executed first under the companion policy of streamlining the death penalty process. Meanwhile, private ownership of guns of a wide variety, along with the ability to pack them in public, is seen as the constitutional, if not moral, right of every citizen who is not crazed, a felon, or too feeble to use them. All in all, one senses that the New Right seems to be interested in making human life as exciting as it can possibly be.

The first success of the New Right was the election of Ronald Reagan to the presidency in 1980. He seemed to combine within his basic political ethos a combination of the New Right and Libertarianism. While his eight years in the White House produced more rhetoric than reality, the goals of the New Right, nevertheless, attained a legitimacy hither-to unknown in the American political experience. Reagan did manage to privatize some government operations and increase the defense budget by a factor of three. This, along with a major cut in taxes (especially for the upper classes) managed to triple the national debt before he left office. That, in turn, seemed to put a damper on the public's enthusiasm for the politics of the New Right.

This was seen both in the rather fuzzy Bush administration following Reagan and the election of the moderate-to-liberal Bill Clinton in 1992. Clinton's political ineptitude in pushing a neoliberal agenda with regard to health care, abortion rights, gays in the military, and multiculturalism in the appointment process generated a resurgence of the New Right agenda, first on the state and local level, where it had been slowly gathering steam for the past decade, and then in the congressional elections of 1994. Those elections brought to the forefront the New Right personality of Newt Gingrich as Speaker of the House of Representatives. He was able to push many New Right issues before the Congress and either get them passed or made a permanent part of the future Republican agenda. The New Right's effects on America's political agenda will, no doubt, continue to color the ideological transition of the country well into the next century.

What can be said for purposes of ideological clarity is that the New Right has succeeded in appropriating for itself the older term of conservative. In Great Britain, the Conservative Party leadership of both Margaret Thatcher and John Major (which has manifested many of the American New Right characteristics) did essentially the same thing. At the same time, at least in America, the New Rightists have managed to convert the term, liberal to a strongly negative, if not evil connotation by pointing out shortcomings in various neoliberal programs, accusing liberals of supporting things that they do not, and blaming them for problems having little to do with neoliberal programs at all. What has been so curious about all of this is the seeming inability or unwillingness of neoliberals to publicly challenge these New Right positions. As a result, one sometimes gets the feeling that neoliberalism as we have known it is already passing from the political stage.

In promoting its own agenda, the New Right has also managed to create a political climate of exclusiveness and division within the society that is opposed to the more traditional American inclination toward inclusion, compromise, and pragmatism with regard to major publical issues. There seems to be a tendency toward divisive demagoguery presenting itself as political leadership. That aspect of the phenomenon will either decline as the movement matures, or it will be a major factor in its decline. Time will tell.

NEOCONSERVATISM

There is a third strain of conservatism that seems to be the source of much confusion with regard to its actual place in the political spectrum. That is largely because many of its major proponents have shifted from the far left to a moderate rightist position since the 1960s. It is generally referred to as neoconservatism, and its central purpose is one of opposing anything that seems to be essentially leftist in governmental activities. Its major proponents are writers such as Norman Podhoretz and Irving Kristol. The movement shares with the older conservatism an essentially intellectual and upper-class character, but it makes common cause with the New Right with regard to its defense of capitalism, its sense of nationalism, and its dedication to moral values. However neoconservatives also seem to want America to play a more vigorous role in the world as the champion of democracy. Like traditional conservatives, they also see a paternalistic government taking care of the less fortunate but doing so primarily through encouraging private approaches to social and economic problems. The major problem with neoconservatism as an ideological movement is that, beyond its basic loathing of the political left, there is no absolute agreement among its supporters on the rest of its goals and values. Its effect on the actual governance of America seems minimal.

SOCIALISM

As an ideology, **socialism** took shape approximately at the same time that liberalism did. However, socialism evolved through several stages before emerging in its classic form. Rather than simply noting the classic form here, it is important to see the progression of ideas that led to it. To do so is to understand why there are so many varieties of socialism and why the word *socialism* does not convey to all people the same ideological position.

THE UTOPIANS

The first people who might be called socialists were simply labeled **utopians.** These included Frenchman Charles Fourier and Englishman Robert Owens. During the eighteenth century, both envisioned an escape from the horrors of the Industrial Revolution by a social retreat into small communities, where the traditions of agriculture and handicrafts would continue. The main difference between these utopian communities and the old society would be that the inhabitants of these communities would share the productivity of the group. They would work for the common good. Farmers would not own their farms; they would farm for the community. Spinners would spin, not for the sale of excess thread but to supply clothing for all. These utopians were never quite successful in these early attempts, and, at one point in Scotland, a utopian community even attempted to establish its own factory system and failed.

Indeed, history shows that most communes fail. Perhaps this is because of the unhappy fact that, however lofty are the ideals of utopians, eventually, as these societies progress and become more complicated, idealism gives way to more consistently human vices such as greed, sloth, and envy. This results in a loss of zeal and a descent into selfish and antisocial habits, which, unchecked by sufficient "government," wreck the fragile fabric of the utopian state. However, the utopian idea lives on, finding its latest expression in the various "drop-out" communes of the 1960s and in some contemporary religious communes.

SYNDICALISTS

A second part of socialist evolution was the **syndicalist** movement, a mostly intellectual revolution led by another Frenchman, Pierre-Joseph Proudhon. His idea was that each manufacturing group should be organized in terms of its own industry, such as shoe making, textiles, or iron, and the workers should seize the factories and their raw materials. The workers, upon owning the means of production in each craft or each manufacturing area, would then set their own wages and prices and share the produce or profit of the enterprise. Again, the idea of sharing and public ownership reflected a desire to get away from private property and the profit motive for private gain. Under this system, the state would be abolished and replaced by a loose federation of manufacturing units. Proudhon was essentially an anarchist, and in his great work, *What Is Property?* (1840), he expressed the belief that the state was really unnecessary and that order would become the moral responsibility of individuals.

The syndicalist movement hardly got off the ground and disappeared by 1920. Its contributions to contemporary society are several. The first, yet minor, contribution is found in the attempt by syndicalists in France to strike through the sabotage of machinery. The method used to undermine the machinery was to take off the wooden shoes worn by the workers and to throw these shoes into the machinery. A French word for shoe is *sabot,* and the action of intentionally destroying machinery gives us the word *sabotage.* The second contribution of the syndicalists is more important. This is the idea of organizing workers in the context of a particular craft. It was a major contributory idea to the modern labor movement, which eventually abandoned socialist ideas and sought improvement of the economy in a free-market, private-ownership relationship between the workers and the owners. One should not confuse organized labor with any attempt to involve the workers in the ownership of the means of production except perhaps through the purchase of stock in a corporation. Syndicalism also influenced the fascist conception of the corporate state, which will be discussed later.

CLASSIC SOCIALISM

Eventually, socialist ideas achieved what might be described as the classic stage. This is best seen in the writings of Saint-Simon. Saint-Simon had a greater vision than the others. The workers of the entire nation in all crafts and in all other economic activities would unite and overthrow the owners of the means of production. They would then take over factories and fields and all other means of economic production and operate them for the good of society. This might require some violence, but not necessarily. A democratic government was even thought possible. This government would provide for the sharing of the entire national production by some formula that would be related to the needs of individuals. This translates into free education; free health care; extra income for larger families; controlled prices; and the basic feeding, clothing, and shelter required for a decent life, with a general minimum level of economic security for all.

Classic socialism was of great attraction to Europeans who had no frontier to escape to, who had never owned their own land but who had become displaced and disorganized by the impact of the Industrial Revolution, and who seemed to seek solutions to problems in group activity and group effort. The American ethos of individualism and the American frontier that presented countless opportunities for highly individualistic enterprises were lacking in the rather cluttered world of Europe. Whereas the liberal possibility did not seem to be relevant to the urban masses of Europe and the conservative alternative was totally unacceptable, the socialist idea took root rather rapidly and still exists as a major ideological point of view and dream for socialist parties in many European countries. Its answer to the Industrial Revolution was that government should minimize economic differences among people by seeing to it that basic economic goods were distributed evenly to all people.

SOCIALISM IN WESTERN COUNTRIES

As an operational ideology, socialism flowered to some extent in Denmark, Great Britain, the Netherlands, Norway, and Sweden on the European continent and in Australia and New Zealand. However, its hold on several of these countries has been tenuous and sporadic. Even in Sweden it seems to be more of a waning phenomenon than a waxing one.

The major problems seem to stem from the fact that most of the Socialist parties that have come to power since 1945 have been, traditionally, opposition parties. Therefore, when *in* power, they first have to work with a basically nonsocialist bureaucracy, and they also must move cautiously lest the new opposition groups gang up on them at the first appearance of radicalism. As a result, none of these countries has created a completely socialist country of which Saint-Simon would have approved.[4] Sweden came the closest and maintained a socialist parliamentary majority the longest, although it was lost in the elections of 1990.

The socialist program usually involves, in varying degrees, state ownership of the following: mass transit, the major communications facilities (radio, TV, telephone, and telegraph systems), heavy industries (iron, coal, steel, and construction companies), energy sources (electricity, gas, and oil), major retail outlets, and any major economic activity not listed but of particular significance to a particular country. Often the banking and finance institutions are also state owned or controlled. The government, which presumably receives income from some of these activities directly (or indirectly through taxation), then provides for free education, health care, social insurance, and other vital needs such as transportation. Personal income taxes are usually quite high (up to 90 percent in some cases) for those in the upper-income brackets.

The assumption seems to be that, by reducing unreasonable levels of personal wealth, by taxing or owning the major industries of the state, and by then guaranteeing to all citizens a "safety net" against poverty, ignorance, or disease, the country will work together as a whole to achieve a high level of productive activity in which all will have a fair share.

Not every socialist government adheres exactly to this general design. Sometimes socialist governments are less than successful in their attempts to achieve their overall goals, and, at other times, opposition groups regain the majority and dismantle part of the Socialist program. In some states, such as Sweden, the Socialist party itself may have second thoughts about a program

---

[4]When Francois Mitterrand came to power in France in 1981, as the leader of a socialist majority in the parliament and as president of France, many French citizens sent their money out of the country, sold businesses, and made other panic adjustments to what they feared would be a social revolution. By the end of his first year in office, however, and after some initial and drastic changes in the economy under the rubric of "The Socialist Way" his administration began to beat a steady retreat from his original program. His nationalization of some industries and banks will probably hold for some time, and other changes (such as those in the welfare system) will no doubt survive, but most observers agree by now that a socialist government in France does not necessarily mean a socialist country, and, in France, change is always the rule, anyway.

and cancel it or modify it. In addition, although many of the teachings of Karl Marx are respected by socialists of all kinds, pure Marxism is still considered somewhat extreme to most Socialist parties, which operate in the mainstream of democratic politics rather than through the creation of revolutionary movements. (Marx and Marxism will be discussed in the next section.)

British socialism seems to be the most erratic. The Labor party (which is the party of socialism in Britain) grew out of earlier attempts by more traditional socialists to gain power in the nineteenth century and was influenced by the more successful trade union movement, the teachings of Christianity, some disaffected leftists in the declining Liberal party, and a healthy dose of typical British pragmatism. It lacks the general inclination toward centralized economic planning found in other socialist programs and seems to proceed in fits and starts toward its goal of a total socialist state.

Nevertheless, in Great Britain, when the Labor party was in power, the government was sometimes described as socialist. However, it was far less socialist than the regimes in Sweden and Denmark. The best way to describe British socialism is to adopt the label given by some of the earlier British socialists, including George Bernard Shaw. This label is *Fabian*. The word *Fabian* goes back to a Roman general whose name was Fabius Maximus. He was a very successful general, though not a particularly heroic or colorful one. His approach to battle was to reconnoiter the enemy, amass a force of at least three or four times the strength of the enemy, and then slowly march upon the enemy, grinding them down to ultimate defeat. This was hardly the kind of military prowess that would rate a great triumph through the streets of Rome. However, it was eminently successful.

To the British socialists, the basic tenets of democratic socialism are proper and workable within society, but they require a gradual change in the mentality of individuals who are wedded intuitively to the capitalist system. The program of the British Labor party and of other British socialists is to experiment with socialism, applying it in bits and pieces, and sometimes retreating from particular techniques that don't seem to work. The feeling among the Fabians is We will get there by and by, but we're in no hurry. We will march on capitalism as we gain strength, and we will overcome it piece by piece until socialism has become a reality.

In other countries, socialists use the label "social democrats" to describe their parties. However, there seems to be at least two distinct versions of social democratic parties. The more moderate social democrats see socialism as essentially a moral principle based on egalitarianism and government-run welfare programs, however structured. They tend to shun complex and dogmatic attempts at achieving public ownership of the means of production. The more leftist social democrats would push on beyond the welfare state to *some* government ownership of and centralized planning in the major sectors of the economy.

Thus, socialist programs vary from state to state, from time to time, and in the degree of social change they envision. The term *socialism* ranks with democracy in the category of inexactitude in both meaning and usage. To truly master all the nuances of socialism, one should study the actual structure and operation of several of the more or less socialist states, an undertaking too broad for this book.

Finally, a brief word about militant socialism (the socialism operated in authoritarian states through primarily military regimes). Such states as Iraq, Libya, and Syria do not follow any single pattern in their economic policies any more than do the democratic socialists. Rather, they seem to reflect the particular predispositions of their military leaders and the particular needs of their countries. In most such cases, socialism is less an ideology than an excuse for a dictatorial regime. Further, the collapse of the USSR and the economic reforms in China have led to a decreasing enthusiasm for socialism in such varied places as Eastern Europe, Myanmar (Burma), and Algeria. Again, while predicting the future is hazardous, it could be that the world is witnessing the beginning of the end of all forms of state socialism.

COMMUNISM

Although classic socialism became the ideological point of view for some European countries, it still lacked a definitive political structure. There was to be a fourth and more important evolutionary stage in the story of socialism. This was communism. Some might wonder why we should concern ourselves with what seems clearly to be a repudiated ideology. Indeed, there are those who would argue that none of the aforementioned ideological theory has any relevance to what is described as our current "postideological world." With regard to the latter idea, I would suggest that the contemporary debate among conservatives, neoliberals, and neoconservatives seems as ideological as ever, and that many Europeans still look at socialism, in whatever form, as a possible alternative to the rest. It must be granted, however, that communism as we have experienced during the 20th century is a thing of the past (with the possible exception of North Korea where it is claimed to continue unabated).

I would suggest that there are at least two things we can and should learn through a brief review of communism's unhappy effect on the modern world. First we need to understand what it was that motivated so many serious, if misguided, people who sincerely thought that communism was the best answer to the world's social and economic problems and that it would ultimately produce a better world. Second, we can see what happened to communist theory in the two examples we shall study. For these and other reasons, I would ask the reader's indulgence for what follows.

In its original form was often referred to as *scientific socialism*. It is with the word *scientific* that we must begin in order to understand both the certainty and the dedication of communist believers.

HEGEL

The man who first formulated the theory of communism and ultimately gave it its name was Karl Marx (1818–83). Before we come to grips with him, we must take a step backward and consider the theories of another German philosopher, Georg Hegel (1770–1831). Hegel had wrestled with the problem of how humans progressed through time. He pondered the ancient and Oriental idea of cyclical progression, which is, in effect, no progression at all. Rather, it is a view that humanity goes through several stages of evolution only to find society collapsing and returning to its lowest levels of development. He also reflected on the view of the Renaissance and the "rationalists" of the eighteenth century. This view saw human progress as essentially linear. Humanity moved from stage to stage in evolution, ever improving technology, lifestyle, institutions of government, and the whole social structure.

Hegel took a new and different view. To him, there was truth, to some extent, in both the cyclical aspect of humanity's progress and in its linear evolution. The way humankind really progressed, Hegel suggested, was through a process he called the **dialectic.** Using political evolution as an example, Hegel pointed out that the first political organization was nomadic. This tribal existence under a chieftain was soon the "thesis" or basic belief about how men and women should live. Before long, however, an "antithesis" evolved that suggested that the farming community that stayed in the same place might be a better idea. Hegel suggested that there was an inevitable clash between thesis and antithesis, out of which came a "synthesis." This process is illustrated in figure 8.2. It took the crisis and struggle between the tribespeople and the agrarians to produce a synthesis in the form of the rural village, which became a new thesis or new method of political organization.

This rural village, however, was soon challenged by the idea of local commerce or trading as between villages, requiring the connection between these villages by roads and the establishment of markets. This produced another clash between thesis and antithesis, which produced the city as the new synthesis. The city-state then became the next thesis on how the world should be organized, but city-states began to venture out and discover world commerce. This, in turn, produced rivalry among the city-states, war and further crisis, resulting in a new synthesis—the empire. The Roman Empire serves as the obvious example. Challenging the Roman Empire was another antithesis, the warlord states of Europe and the Near East. Although the Roman Empire existed as a thesis of government for centuries, eventually the clash came, and out of that clash evolved the feudal state. The feudal state became the thesis for a few centuries until it was challenged by religious authority. Again, a clash between thesis and antithesis resulted during the Thirty Years' War. It produced, after 1648, what Hegel considered to be the highest form of political organization, the nation-state.

Thus, Hegel suggested several things. First, there is linear progression in human history. The nation-state was certainly an improvement over the

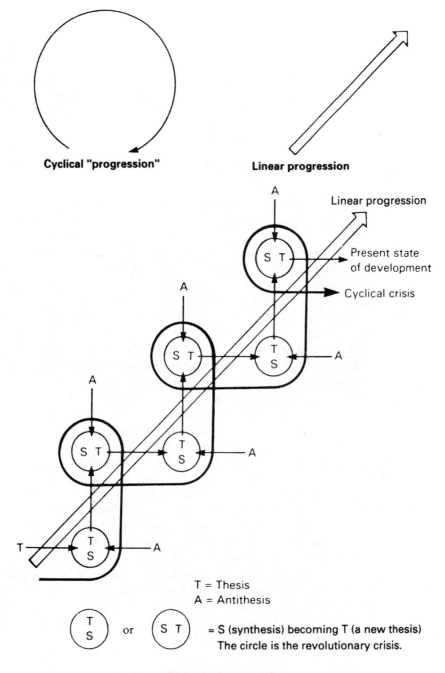

Cyclical "progression"

Linear progression

T = Thesis
A = Antithesis

= S (synthesis) becoming T (a new thesis)
The circle is the revolutionary crisis.

Dialectical progression

FIGURE 8.2 Humanity's Progress through Time

tribe, the rural village, the city, the empire, and the feudal state. However, in order to achieve that linear progress, one had to go through a cycle of clashes between thesis and antithesis or between basic ideas about human society that were inevitably in conflict. Thus, second, there is a cycle in human progress, a cycle of crisis. After each crisis, there is a linear improvement in society. As just stated, Hegel felt that the *dialectical* progress had pretty much come to an end in the creation of the modern nation-state, which he saw as humanity's highest achievement in government.

MARX

Karl Marx was a student of Hegel's thought, and it impressed him deeply. Due to his socialist inclinations, Marx sought to apply it not to the political realm, as Hegel had done, but to the economic realm. Marx became convinced that it was the economic structures and not the political structures that had produced the dialectical clashes of history. In other words, Marx was convinced that the economic side of life, the economic goals of a society, determined all other aspects of that society, including not only its form of government but also its choice of religion, family structure, and community structure.

As a result, Marx restated the dialectic as an economic evolutionary process in which the first dialectical clash involved hunting versus farming. This produced a kind of balance between the two in the rural village. It was commerce that challenged the balance and produced the modern city, which was a structure that allowed for the development of handicrafts and luxury goods. The desire for luxury goods resulted in world commerce, and that, in turn, led to the struggle for empires, which was not so much a desire for political expansion as it was a desire for economic expansion. With the achievement of a world economy, the next challenge came in the form of the looting and exploitive economy of the Goths, the Vikings, the Vandals, the Visigoths, and other Germanic tribes. They destroyed the world economy that was the Roman Empire and ushered in the feudal economy.

However, this secular economic norm was challenged by the Catholic Church, which had evolved in the latter states of feudalism into a parasitical economy in which tithing, the paying of indulgences, and the accumulation of wealth by the church challenged the accumulation of wealth by the secular nobility. That produced the Thirty Years' War, which was far more than simply an argument about theology. That great clash between secular wealth and religious wealth produced the nation-state, the triumph of private property and private wealth among a property-owning class.

The economic system of the nation-state **(capitalism)** was far more important than the concepts of sovereignty and nationalism, merely by-products of that system. The capitalistic system, said Marx, also contained within it two opposing forces, thesis and antithesis, and Marx believed that there was one more clash to come. Just as the clashes between economic ideas supported by differing groups had always occurred in history, it would occur exactly as it had in the past, inevitably, within the near future. The clash would come between the owners of capital, which he called by the French word for middle class, the *bourgeoisie,* and the workers of the factories, who were dependent upon wages for their livelihood, which he called by the French word for worker, the *proletariat.* The next, inevitable, and final clash between thesis and antithesis would be between these two groups, or more to the point, between the thesis of capitalism and its antithesis, socialism. This clash would produce, as its synthesis, first a socialist state more or less in the context of Saint-Simon's ideal. That state would, in turn, further evolve into its ultimate synthesis—the communist society. Figure 8.3 shows both Hegel's criteria for

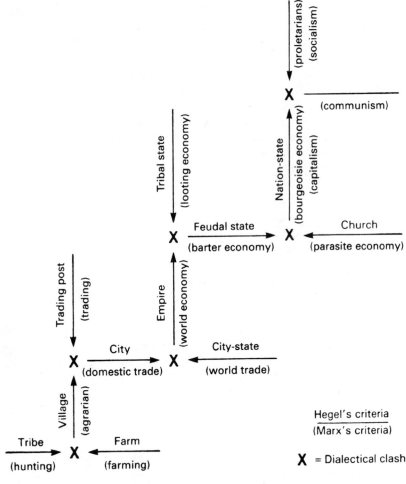

FIGURE 8.3 The Dialectical Process as Seen by Hegel and Marx

change (political choices ending in the nation-state) and Marx's criteria (economic choices ending in communism). Marx was convinced that the triumph of the proletariat was inevitable because they were right and there was more of them. This victory would end all historical economic class struggles, because, under the socialist formula of "from each according to his ability to give and to each according to his need," there would be no more argument about the economic structure.

The state had always supported the strongest of the economic groups within it. The tribal leaders, the farmers, the builders of cities, the creators of empires, the feudal nobilities, and now, the emerging middle class, had all ruled their respective political systems. Now the proletarians would control the new state. The workers would be in a state of peaceful solidarity, one with the other. Therefore, once the socialist society was established, the state itself would wither away. Just how the state would wither away is somewhat unclear in the writings of Marx. He was much more interested in analyzing why the bourgeoisie capitalist state would collapse and how this would come about. Some of Marx's ideas, developed in his tedious book *Das Kapital* and in numerous essays, were that the socialist revolution was an inevitable revolution and that his predictions were scientific because of this inevitability. The workers would rise up spontaneously once they figured out what was going on.

What was going on? Something called "the theory of surplus value" was going on, and it was important for the workers to know about it. In order to address this Marxist idea, one must back up to an earlier idea. This is an idea by a British economist, David Ricardo (1772–1823), who had formulated what he called "the labor theory of value."

To Ricardo, the value of anything was contained in the labor that it took to produce the thing. A wooden desk was worth only the labor that went into producing it. The wood came from a tree that was made by God and thus cost nothing. The stain was also a product of natural resources, as were the wooden pegs that held it together and the glue used where pegs were inappropriate. Thus, to Ricardo the value of a desk was found in the work of the individual who sawed down the tree, cut it into boards, stained the boards, and glued and pegged the desk together.

What was the desk then worth? It was worth what it would take to sustain the worker and his or her family at a decent level of economic existence. This was all right until the Industrial Revolution came along, and workers did not make desks anymore but spent all day sawing boards, making glue, shaping pegs, or assembling the desks themselves. Marx noted that the workers were paid a wage determined not by the market value of the desk but rather by whatever the manufacturer saw fit to pay them. This, in turn, was influenced by how many workers were available and what level of income would spur the workers on to greater effort in order to improve their economic condition.

Marx called this distortion of economic justice "the theory of surplus value." The problem with the Industrial Revolution and the capitalist economy, said Marx, was that the owners of the means of production, the capitalists, placed artificially high prices on their goods, paid only a fraction of the price back to the workers who produced the value, and kept the remainder for themselves. As a result, they got richer and richer while the workers got poorer and poorer. The worker never received full value for his or her labor, while the capitalist, who contributed nothing, received the bulk of the economic prosperity of the nation.

When workers began to realize that they were being had, all they needed to hear further would be an explanation of the theory of surplus value, accompanied by the program of socialism, and then they would revolt in order to achieve the utopian dream of a stateless, communist society in which all would be equal and share equally in the resources of the state. In fact, as the state withered away, the entire world would unite into a vast world economy wherein all people would benefit.

There is much more to **Marxism** than this, but these are the points that Marx expounded during the bulk of his attempt to organize a communist revolution. In 1848, when the government of France suffered one of its periodic breakdowns, Marx, along with his collaborator, Friedrich Engels, issued the *Communist Manifesto*, containing the famous language: "The proletarians have nothing to lose but their chains. They have a world to win. Working men of all countries, unite." Marx thought at that point that the workers would get the message and overthrow the French government. Instead, although the government changed, it prevailed in its essential form, and the workers continued in their somewhat miserable plight. Afterwards, Marx set out to organize an international movement, which we call the *First International*.[5] That movement was designed to spread the word of communism to the workers through pamphlets, newspapers, and organized political discussion.

A second chance came in 1871 when the government of France was completely defeated and demoralized in the Franco-Prussian War. At this point, sufficient instruction in the communist philosophy had been achieved to allow for the formation, within Paris, of "the commune," a group of communists who seized several blocks of downtown Paris, barricaded themselves behind the walls, and announced the formation of a communist society. They sent word to other Parisians, other French citizens, and others throughout the world to join them in the overthrow of the capitalist society. So great was the fear of these communist radicals who were holed up inside Paris that the German army, victorious over the French army, rearmed that army, and together they assaulted the Paris commune. It was a bloody battle fought with no quarter given, and thousands of communists were killed, many shot in the act of surrendering. The

---

[5]This later evolved into the *Comintern* or "Communist International," founded by Lenin in 1919.

attempt to crush the Paris commune was absolute and completely successful. Thus ended the attempt in France to form a communist state.

Marx died in 1883, a rather disillusioned man. His writings were all that
he had left behind, and no communist revolution had occurred. That might
have been the end of the story insofar as the concept of communism is concerned, and we might dismiss it, much as we do the syndicalists, as a very
sophisticated but rather bizarre set of ideas. However, an accident of history
brought about a combination of Marx's scientific socialism and the comple-
mentary ideas of Lenin. It is Marx's and Lenin's ideas together that we recognize as the modern form of communism.

MARXIST-LENINISM

Vladimir Ilyich Lenin was a Russian social revolutionary who wished to see
the end of the last of the European feudal monarchies in the person of Czar
Nicholas II of Russia, who still ruled in the early 1900s. Lenin had chosen
socialism as the basis for his revolutionary program and was particularly
impressed by the communist vision of Karl Marx. However, he was convinced that Marx had made at least three major mistakes in the formulation
of his program. Lenin sought to correct these and to create a more sophisticated program of **communism.**

First, Lenin realized that the average working man and woman of Europe
were far too uneducated and far too simplistic in thought to grasp the intri-
cacies of Marxist theory. They could not be organized effectively in a spon-
taneous manner for a successful revolution. What was necessary was some
structure between the few intellectuals of the international movement and
the actual workers who would revolt and take over the state. His solution
was an elite party—a tight, pyramidal organization of those people who
could be taught, to some degree, the tenets of communist thought and who
could translate these in simple terms to workers. Also, the members of the
party would organize the workers, know who they were, and provide targets for their action. Finally, after the revolution, the party would provide
the structure for the "dictatorship of the proletariat" or, more properly
speaking, the government. Thus, the Communist Party, as we know it, is the
creation of Lenin and not of Marx.

Second, Lenin saw a possible contradiction between the Marxist assertion,
on the one hand, that the economic forces of society control the state (which
Lenin believed to be true) and the assertion, on the other, that the proletariat
in an industrial society would win in the inevitable class struggle because it
outnumbered the bourgeoisie. After all, although the bourgeoisie were outnumbered, they controlled the means of force and could continue to exist
despite dissatisfaction among the majority proletarians. Therefore, Lenin
proposed that the Communist Revolution should take place in a relatively
undeveloped society, a society on the threshold of the Industrial Revolution.

To use Lenin's terms, he would "telescope" two revolutions into one, much as a telescope can be compressed from two cylinders into one. The Industrial Revolution and the Communist Revolution would take place within a developing country simultaneously, or, put another way, the successful communist country would industrialize as it communized itself. Not only would workers rise up in revolt against the emerging capitalist regime, but peasants, simple farmers, craftsmen, and shepherds would also rise up together to create a new government and society.

Lenin's symbol for the Communist Revolution became the hammer, representing the proletariat, and the sickle, representing the peasants. Together they would build an industrial society without the problem of a governing, managerial class, who owned capital. They would seize the government and then, together, build industrial machinery and communalize agriculture. They would first produce a socialist economy under "the dictatorship of the proletariat," which would be the government, and then the state would wither away.

The dictatorship of the proletariat, including representatives of workers and peasants, would rule during the socialist period of the Communist Revolution. Once that stage had been achieved, a combination of workers and peasants would rule themselves without the state. Thus, the telescoping revolution concept of Lenin suggested that the Communist Revolution would not begin in France, Germany, Great Britain, or any other industrialized country but was more likely to occur in a marginally developed country such as Czarist Russia.

Third, Lenin explained why the communist revolutions of 1848 and 1871 in France had failed, and why the clash between the bourgeoisie and the proletariat, which Marx had believed to be inevitable, had not yet taken place. The answer, according to Lenin, was found in the concept of "imperialism as the last stage of capitalism." In this context, Lenin noted some historical events of the late nineteenth century and correctly predicted some events of the early twentieth century. To begin with, he noted that, although the capitalist classes were getting richer and decreasing in number throughout the latter part of the nineteenth century and the working class was increasing and getting poorer, there were still ways for the bourgeoisie to relieve the pressure. The chief method was colonialization. The European and American capitalist economies, Lenin noted, had succeeded in taking over large portions of Asia and Africa.

These colonies had served at least three purposes. First, they provided a way to get rid of excess labor by sending over to these colonies armies, civil servants, and workers for the plantations. Second, they provided additional cheap resources so that the surplus value of the capitalist could continue. Third, they provided a national mystique, a national pride that could be sold to the suffering proletarians as something to be a part of that was greater than themselves, a reason to labor for an otherwise insensitive government. Therefore, as a result of colonialization, the inevitable dialectical clash had been postponed through the successes of the imperialist period of the late nineteenth century.

Writing at the turn of the century, Lenin predicted that eventually the area for colonialization would be exhausted. The capitalist countries would then turn upon each other, in order to take each other's colonies away. As a result of this competitive effort in the colonial world, there would be a great world cataclysm, an outbreak of world war. It would be during this time that the proletarians would finally see the light, led by a well-structured Communist Party, and seize the governments that were intent upon sending them into the slaughterhouse. Then they would establish a state socialism such as Saint-Simon had described. After the socialist system was perfected, in the future, the state would begin to wither away and pure communism would be the result.

SOVIET COMMUNISM

Although he had accurately predicted World War I, Lenin had to overthrow a democratic government in Russia instead of the czar he hated. He succeeded in establishing a communist regime by November 1917. The impetus to his revolution was World War I, which he had predicted. As a result of the war, the Russians first overthrew the czar and ultimately attempted a parliament under Aleksandr Kerenski. It was this government that Lenin and his party overthrew.

Lenin worked tirelessly to create a brave new communist order. He was largely unsuccessful, and, by the time of his death, he had abandoned many of the early experiments and replaced them with more traditional economic institutions in an attempt to regroup and proceed in a more evolutionary way. His rule was followed, in 1925, by the twenty-eight-year reign of Joseph Stalin. As discussed earlier, he developed, in a most brutal fashion, not only the classic form of communism (to be imitated to some extent by all future such regimes) but also the totalitarian model of government. He led the USSR through World War II and the Cold War that followed. He justified his brutal state by asserting that communism itself had not yet arrived and that the totalitarian state was in the "socialist stage" of development. It would eventually disappear with the advent of true communism.

His successor, Nikita Khrushchev, who ruled from 1956 to 1964, sought to lessen the impact of totalitarianism, restrain the Cold War as much as possible, and introduce some changes in the economic policies of the Soviet Union, but he was deposed by hard-liners who objected to these reforms and to his flamboyant ruling style. He, in turn, was followed by Leonid Brezhnev, who, from 1964 to 1982, presided over an ever-increasing decay in the economy and a burgeoning bureaucracy. Public cynicism over an increasingly affluent party membership, which was not improving the lives of the rest of the people, began to manifest itself in various ways throughout the fifteen republics of the Soviet empire.

With Brezhnev's death came a succession of leaders and a hiatus in the evolution of the communist state. Yuri Andropov was followed by Konstantin Chernenko, both within a three-year period. Finally, in 1985, Mikhail Gorbachev took over as party secretary and, later, president of the USSR (in 1988). He launched a period of unprecedented reforms calculated to improve the ailing economy and the low morale of the people. This was accompanied by a major attempt at arms control between the superpowers and another attempt to attenuate the Cold War between them.

It was too late. As he introduced his policy of *glasnost* (openness), which was to lead to *perestroika* (restructuring), he found to his dismay that the people wanted an elimination of the entire communist system—government and all. By 1991, the entire Soviet system had collapsed, and all fifteen of the old Soviet Socialistic Republics had broken away to form a loose confederation whose future is still in doubt.

CHINESE COMMUNISM

A second and equally important strain of communism evolved within the boundaries of China. It, too, began with the ideas of Marx and Lenin, but there a deviation occurred in the person of Mao Tse-tung, who shaped and applied Marxist-Leninism to China. Mao is the key to Chinese communism **(maoism)** as we have come to know it, and Mao's death in 1976 raised questions as to the future of that system within China.

Who was Mao, and what did he hope to achieve through communism for his nation? Mao was a revolutionary who at one point joined the nationalist crusade of Sun Yat-sen to overthrow the western control of China, begun in the mid-nineteenth century. In the early 1920s, Mao and his colleagues relied upon Soviet Communist party advisors to create their party and to advise them on how to successfully overthrow not only western control but also the emerging nationalist government of Sun Yat-sen. However, Mao realized, after some difficulties and failures during the mid-1920s, that the Soviet model did not apply to the Oriental civilization that was China. His revolution would be based primarily upon peasants, and it would differ from Stalin's Russia, especially as that phenomenon evolved in the 1930s, on two basic points.

First, Mao saw in communism a device to redefine the Chinese as a people, to rediscover a Chinese concept of selfhood that had been thoroughly undermined by a hundred years of westernization and exploitation. In other words, Mao was more interested in the people of China than in its industrial development or its economic system. Although he accepted socialism as the proper economic order and looked to the ultimate creation of a stateless society, he was content to mold the people's minds toward that end before creating a modern industrial society on a socialist basis. Marx inspired Mao more in the area of **humanism** than in the area of economics. Stalin was more inclined to operate in Marx's political and economic areas.

Of course, Marx was essentially a humanist, although he loved humanity abstractly rather than on a personal basis. Marx was serious in saying that people should not be downtrodden under the wheels of industrial machinery. People were more than simply wage earners, participants in a **vocation.** Vocation itself was, to Marx, a western hypocrisy and an assault on basic humanity. Marx had hinted that, under the socialist and, ultimately, the communist regime, individuals could develop many talents and do many things without fear of the loss of their economic security should they wish to change their particular activity during the course of their lives. Communism would allow individuals to develop to their full potential. People could become artists or artisans, bureaucrats, or farmers. They could switch from education to manufacturing. They could do whatever their talents led them to do as long as they gave themselves to society. Thus, an individual would become more than simply a wage earner shackled to a single enterprise as envisioned by the capitalistic system.

Mao picked up on this idea to the extent that he foresaw in China the creation of a new kind of individual under the communist state. The large population of China led Mao to envision a new "mass-man," a twenty-first-century individual essentially selfless, giving, and loving and contributing to the welfare of all under the economic protection of the state. Thus, Mao cared less for production quotas and the advancement of the industrial society than for the changing of a man's or woman's outlook on who he or she was, why he or she lived, and what his or her goals were. Maoism looked first to the changing of the individual rather than to the industrial production that so dominated Soviet communist thought.

Second, Mao conceived of the dialectical process as a continuing process. To Mao, it was absurd to suggest that the socialist revolution would end all previous dialectical clashes. Even in the socialist period, and possibly in the communist period, there would inevitably develop new contradictions, new theses on how the state should be run, and new antitheses to challenge them. Therefore, the dialectical revolutionary process would be a continuous process, and Mao preached continuous revolution—constant turmoil with periods of consolidation, leading to higher and higher levels of communistic and human achievement.

Thus, Mao's original revolution (1946–49) against Chiang Kai-shek, who had succeeded Sun Yat-sen, was a classic socialist versus capitalist revolution. It was followed by a communist revolution (1950–52) within the society itself, in which the old order was abolished, with much bloodshed. This, in turn, was followed by another revolution (1958–1960) known as the "Great Leap Forward," in which the party was in conflict with the intelligentsia, and the urban workers were in conflict with the communal farmers. The result was a disaster for the economy, but out of it came an increase in awareness by all citizens of their common purpose in achieving a mass society. This, in turn, was followed by the cultural revolution (1964–69), a clash between pure communist ideas and any lingering ideas of humanity's particular relationship with fellow humans that might be left over from Confucian, Taoistic, or legalistic philosophies of the past. The purpose of the cultural revolution was to shake up the party, the bureaucracy, and the society as a whole to root out all old ideas and achieve an even higher degree of pure communist thought. Mao barely survived the cultural revolution. China was thoroughly exhausted after his series of catastrophic upheavals, and he began to lose prestige up until the time of his death in 1976.

A post-Mao regime in China headed by Deng Xiaoping approached communism less and less in the Maoist tradition of placing people ahead of industry, and it completely rejected a continuing revolutionary posture. However, during the tragic events of mid-1989, when government hardliners shot down thousands of student advocates of more "democracy," less corruption, and more modernization, one had to wonder just what the future of the Chinese economy will be like. The ghost of Mao still haunts that troubled land, and, although one can see little of the old communism there, the militant socialism of the past will continue to challenge efforts to privatize the economy. China's future will no doubt remain radical and volatile.

FASCISM

Fascism is a strange kind of twentieth-century ideology. Unlike socialism and communism, which prepare a program for action, fascism more often serves as an excuse for action already taken. To add to the difficulty of defining it, there are no truly fascist regimes operating in the world today. Therefore, if we must consider the fascist alternative, we have to deal with it in historic terms.

Fascism first came to Italy in 1922, during the depression that followed World War I. Its leader was Benito Mussolini, who spread the ideas of fascism through newspapers he edited. Later, during the Great Depression of the 1930s, fascism came to Germany under Adolph Hitler. His program was outlined in his autobiographical book, *Mein Kampf*, meaning "my struggle." Hitler's regime lasted from 1933 to 1945, while Mussolini ruled Italy from 1922 to 1943. Using both the Italian and German models, we can say several things about fascism and then form some conclusions.

First, as an ideology, it begins with a historic view of the state rather than a futurist view. Mussolini's fascism was an attempt to recreate the Roman Empire under modern economic and political structures. Hitler's fascism was an affirmation of the superiority of the Aryan races who had once ruled northern Europe in mythical times and again during the early period of the medieval world in the context of the Holy Roman Empire. Hitler called the Holy Roman Empire the "First Reich," or the First German rule over Europe. The "Second Reich" was the German Empire of 1871–1918. The "Third Reich" was the fascist regime that Hitler fashioned in 1933, and which, like the First Reich, was to last for 1,000 years.

Second, fascism seems to be an ideology that is imposed upon a people who are essentially inexperienced in the complexities of government. This certainly describes the Italians of the 1920s and the Germans of the 1930s. Government is carried on by a single, paternalistic party that eliminates all possible opposition through totalitarian methods. This is more acceptable to a people already used to authoritarian government.

Third, fascism seems to occur in a period of enormous economic distress, usually characterized by unemployment and inflation wherein the middle class is essentially wiped out. It occurs during a time when material concerns become more important than moral, philosophical, or religious concerns, when people's search for economic stability overrides their better judgment in the realm of spiritual and political values.

Furthermore, it is accompanied by moral decay, which not only includes religious concepts of right and wrong, but also public morality. It is characterized by the population's acceptance of sporadic violence, tendency not to get involved in public issues, and apathetic attitude toward corruption within the government. There is often a tendency to look the other way when police and others beat up individuals or otherwise abuse their rights.

Finally, fascism is brought on by an opportunistic and charismatic leader, like a Mussolini, who strutted about as if he were a Roman Emperor, or a Hitler, who had a spell-binding speaking voice given to facile explanations of history and the painting of purple dreams. Fascism, then, is a kind of adventuristic response to economic tribulation, encompassed within an anti-intellectual vacuum, involving the surrender of the spirit and the will of the people to a colorful leader and a dictatorial party. It is not a pretty sight.

CHARACTERISTICS

The characteristics of a fascist regime are several.

Corporate State

First, fascism's most basic and defining characteristic is the "corporate state." A corporate state might be compared to a modern conglomerate wherein many diverse industries are organized under a single managerial board. In the case of fascism, the state itself becomes the conglomerate corporation, and it controls, through interlocking boards of directors, all major sources of production. Although the major industries remain in private hands, their boards of directors are linked to the government. Production quotas, wages, and prices are set under government regulation, and compliance is expected with regard to rationalizing the national economy. In return for submitting to the rule of the government, the corporations receive a monopoly or near monopoly position within their industry. Even the labor unions are brought under the control of a central labor board, and working conditions, wages, and other aspects of employment are controlled by the government in exchange for a guarantee of employment for the workers.

Rejection of Individual Liberties

Second, there is an almost total rejection of individual liberties. The state defines the rights of individuals and what constitutes crimes against the state. There is a secret police, with secret trials and concentration camps for those who will not abide by the dictates of the state. There is no claim, under law, for any right not granted by the state.

Mystical View of the State

Next, there is an almost mystical view of the state itself. Italy was to become the "new Rome," a reincarnation of the days of the caesars. Germany was to achieve mastery over not only Europe but the rest of the world, fulfilling the old myths of the Nordic gods that the Aryan races would rule humanity. Individuals surrendered their personalities to this mystical state and became much more than mere persons. They were now a part of history. This was all accompanied by great pageantry and unrelenting propaganda.

Distinct Class Structure

Fourth, in a fascist state there is a distinct class structure. Each person has a place within the society and knows what that place is. There is no great mobility from place to place, although that is possible under certain circumstances. The point is that, at any given time, people are classified by their position within whatever economic, political, racial, or other organizational structure they are found.

Lust for Conquest

Finally, there is an inevitable lust for conquest, especially over peoples labeled inferior. There is a kind of Darwinistic attitude toward other nation-states that proclaims that only the strongest should survive.

I cannot say with finality what fascism might have produced in terms of a solution to the Industrial Revolution. Socialism sought to solve the Industrial Revolution by a sharing of most of the output of the society on an egalitarian basis. Communism would achieve this on a higher level without the state. What did fascism do for the depressed peoples of the chaotic industrial society of the 1920s and the 1930s? First of all, it gave them jobs and economic security, and it worked. (In Italy, even the trains ran on time, which by Italian standards is something short of miraculous.) In Germany, unemployment ceased primarily through the building up of the military; inflation was ended by rigid currency controls; and the confidence of the German people was restored, along with their national pride. Indeed, had Hitler died in the year 1937, he might still be acclaimed a national hero in Germany. However, in both Italy and Germany there was something about the mystical view of the state and the egocentric and highly nationalistic orientation of the people that ultimately led to war and brought about the downfall of the fascist experiment. Therefore, we are left to ponder the possibilities of fascism.

The fact that it worked under Mussolini in the 1920s was an inspiration to some Americans during our own depression. Under Franklin Roosevelt, we copied some of the fascist techniques. The National Recovery Administration's wage and price controls and government control over basic trade and manufacturing practices had to be declared unconstitutional by the Supreme Court lest they continue to grow in a fascist direction. There is a statue in Rome, Georgia, given to the people of that city by Mussolini in the 1920s in grateful appreciation for the support given to his regime by many Americans. The American-Nazi Bund and other fascist-type groups flourished during the 1930s under such leaders as Father Coughlin and Huey Long.

The problem with fascism seems to be not only that, under a mystical and highly exaggerated nationalism, it is apt to lead to war, but more basically that it seems to lead to a stagnant economy. Economic growth is achieved up to a point, and then the thrust of government is to stabilize growth at that point to ensure economic security at a minimal level for most of its citizens. Technological development is left to government planning commissions. Competition, which breeds new techniques, is stifled. Models of production goods that sell well are continued year after year under the momentum of a largely uninspired concept of success.

The German system, especially, demonstrated this weakness during World War II, when only toward the end of the war was it realized that the particular military technologies that had evolved by the late 1930s were no longer capable of competing with those of the Americans and British. Where there was an attempt at technological improvement, it was done under the heavy and complicated hand of governmental bureaucracy, and success came too late. The extent to which fascism ever flowered in Italy is debatable, and, therefore, we cannot draw many examples from that experience.

One final note about fascism is of particular interest to Americans. As stated before, the American political ethos is one of individualism, freedom of conscience, private property, and capitalistic initiative. We have a frontier image of the "macho" Americans, who do not need government to solve our problems, who will pursue our own solutions and go our own way. This is demonstrated in our love affair with the automobile rather than mass transit and in our great difficulty in controlling firearms, which are a symbol of our independence from the needs of governmental protection. We have not developed a very high degree of social responsibility or even social awareness. Should our communities, our churches, and indeed our families break down, we would be far less an integrated society than those of Europe. Therefore, we might conclude that the conservative, socialist, and communist ideologies would find it very difficult to find root in the intellectual part of the American mind.

On the other hand, there is always the temptation toward fascism. Should economic distress occur in our land, the temptation to flirt with fascism, even at the highest levels of government, should give us pause. True, the Supreme Court saw in the National Recovery Administration (NRA) a breach of the standard American liberal approach to government and economics. What would happen in another period of economic distress? What would happen if we found ourselves overly concerned with material things or if moral decay of a public nature became rampant, as it was in the early days of the Watergate scandal and, later, during the Reagan administration? What if a charismatic leader, such as Roosevelt, succeeded in attacking the intellectual basis of our liberalism or, worse, if we forgot to teach successfully the intellectual foundations of our ethos? Could some new and mystical view of the state within a highly nationalistic context be sold to the American people as a guarantee of economic security? Admittedly, this is an area of some controversy. However, because of both the nature of our political ethos and the experience of the 1930s, the issue is one Americans might fruitfully ponder. The hope remains, of course, that it will be our long experience with political democracy that will keep us from such a temptation. Thus, it is that a public knowledge of our government and its ideology remains necessary for the future of our way of life.

POINTS TO PONDER

In view of the transmogrification of the terms "liberal" and "conservative" during the past fifty years in America, do you think that they serve any useful purpose in the evaluation of political candidates or issues?

Compare the "New Right" to classic conservatism, traditional liberalism and fascism.

What do you feel was the most serious flaw in communism as it was applied in the old USSR?

Evaluate the dialectic as a theory of historical change devoid of any particular ideological uses.

Is Marx's theory of vocation valid in today's capitalism?

9 | Political Parties and Interest Groups

In the previous chapters, we have discussed the structure and functions of governments. What we have discussed in essence, might be considered the skeleton of a political government. The flesh and blood of such a government lies, for the most part, in such organizations as the political parties and special interest groups of a society and *their* interaction with the holders of power within the government structure. It is, therefore, also important to have some conceptual awareness of what political parties and interest groups are like and to come to grips with some of the problems connected with their use. We will begin by examining political parties.

THE ORIGIN OF POLITICAL PARTIES

DEFINITION OF A POLITICAL PARTY

A classic definition of a **political party** is a group of citizens within a nation-state who are united in their general agreement about certain basic ideas concerning how that society should function. This group organizes itself in order that it may run candidates for public office under its platform, which consists of a statement of the basic ideas of agreement. The hope is that these candidates might take over the control of the government and function in the interest of the majority under the basic outline of the party platform. In short, political parties seek to gain control of governments by using the political process of their nation-states.

A political party must have some form of organizational structure, some generally consistent membership who recognize themselves to be members of the party, and some kind of regular process of meeting and discussing so that ideas of consensus can remain consistent throughout the party structure. One might begin to suspect already that American political parties are somewhat less than this definition would seem to require. This is quite true, and it represents another problem for the American government.

THE UNITED STATES AS A ONE-PARTY-DOMINANT SYSTEM

If one were to properly define the pre-1980 American political process, one might call it a relatively nonpartisan, one-party-dominant system that, nevertheless, lacks political parties as they are generally defined. Let's begin by examining the one-party-dominant aspect.

After the defeat of the Federalists, who ruled from 1789 to 1800, there began a Democratic era, which lasted from 1800 until 1860. This era was characterized by a shift from Federalist centrality in government, elitism and a generally pro-business and industry economic policy to a program of Democratic decentralization, egalitarianism and a pro-agriculture policy. One might protest that during that period there *was* another major party, and indeed there was—the Whig party. This was organized in the 1830s as a protest against certain actions taken by the Democratic Party during the administration of Andrew Jackson and his successor, Martin Van Buren.

In 1840, the Whig Party, a small party consisting of some leftover Federalists and some deviant Democrats, succeeded in electing as president a military hero, William Henry Harrison, famed for his exploits in the Indian Wars, particularly at the Battle of Tippecanoe. Unfortunately, President Harrison died thirty days after his inaugural, giving way to the presidency of John Tyler, who was not popular and who was the first man to claim the right to be president upon the death of a president. Despite his unpopularity, the precedent of swearing in a vice president as president was established. However, Tyler (sometimes referred to as "his accidency") was thrown out of office four years later, and the country returned to the Democratic Party with the election of James Knox Polk.

President Polk embarrassed the Democrats and created dissension by engaging in the Mexican War. As a result, in 1848, the Whig Party again succeeded in electing a military hero, Zachary Taylor, to be president. In keeping with precedent, General Taylor also died in office, leading to the infamously weak presidency of Millard Fillmore. That did it for the Whigs. The country returned to the Democratic Party in 1852 and continued with the presidencies of Franklin Pierce and James Buchanan until 1860.

During the Whig presidencies, the basic policies of the nation, both foreign and domestic, remained relatively unchanged from those established by the Democrats. There was nothing like the basic shift in governmental direction that occurred in 1800 or that would occur again in 1860 and in 1932. Despite the successes of Harrison and Taylor as Whig presidential candidates, the Whig party succeeded in electing very few state governors, very few members of state legislatures, and very few members of the Congress. Most of these offices remained essentially in the hands of the Democratic Party throughout the sixty-year period.

What happened to the Democratic Party after 1860? It was the casualty of the issue of slavery and the ensuing Civil War. Unfortunately for the Democratic Party, it could not resolve within itself the issue of slavery. When the

Democratic South seceded from the Union, it left the country open to a new political party that would be organized around newer concepts of government and economics.

Actually, the new party began in 1854 with a meeting in Ripon, Wisconsin. It called itself the Republican Party. It was an amalgamation of small midwestern farmers who did not like the slave-farming economic system of the South, individuals who disliked slavery on moral grounds, and a group of eastern businessmen from the growing industrial sector of the economy who felt that the government, heretofore, had been too much in favor of the agrarian community in areas such as credit and the money supply. They wanted a new economic base for expanding the industrial potential of the nation. There were other groups as well.

As their first presidential candidate in 1856, the Republicans ran a military hero, just as the Whigs had done. However, John C. Fremont, famous as a military explorer of California, and infamous because of a later charge that he had engaged in cannibalism, was not elected president. However, as the clouds of Civil War began to gather in 1860 and with the inability of Democratic President James Buchanan to do much about it, the Republican Party suddenly found strength and a new candidate—Abraham Lincoln.

Although Lincoln campaigned on a platform of solving the schism between the North and the South, he was generally recognized as an antislavery candidate and as a new kind of political leader, who would restore some semblance of unity and direction to a government that had drifted under the last two Democratic presidencies. Therefore, in the heat of controversy surrounding the issue of slavery, and with a four-way split in the Democratic Party, Lincoln was elected, and the South seceded. Lincoln became a heroic figure during his five-year presidency, whereas his Democratic successor, Andrew Johnson, was unable to maintain a credible administration. The Republican Party again prevailed in 1868 under Ulysses Simpson Grant. In the final analysis, the Democratic Party had ruined itself over the issue of slavery and the Civil War. It was not to be heard from (outside of the South) as a dominant party again for the next seventy-two years.

The Republican Party elected all but two of the presidents from 1860 to 1932. The two exceptions were, again, explainable in terms of particular circumstances. The election of Grover Cleveland, a Democrat, in 1884 was primarily the result of the assassination of James Garfield and the somewhat mediocre performance of his successor, Chester A. Arthur. Although Cleveland was reelected in 1892, he could not prevail against William McKinley in 1896. Woodrow Wilson, also a Democrat, was elected in 1912 primarily because of the split in the Republican Party between the progressive Roosevelt wing and the traditional Taft wing. Wilson became a very successful domestic leader and ultimately a war leader. Due to his support of the League of Nations, his long illness, and a certain amount of weariness over his domestic program of reform, the Democratic Party was soundly repudiated in 1920.

Not party goods But
charismatic leaders

During the periods of the Cleveland and Wilson administrations, the Democratic Party did not hold many offices in the state legislatures or in the national Congress, except in the South, which remained defiantly Democratic, if irrelevant to national politics. It was rather clear that the Republican Party ideas about tight money, the expansion of our industrial base, and thrift and conservatism in government prevailed throughout the period. One might ask, then, what happened to the Republican Party?

The answer, of course, is the Great Depression. During the presidency of Herbert Hoover, who was elected in 1928 only to face the beginning of the Depression in 1929, the Republican Party proved unable to come up with a clearly defined program for dealing with this new national disaster. However, the Democratic Party found an attractive new leader of tremendous charismatic appeal and offered all kinds of solutions to the Depression. With the election of Franklin Delano Roosevelt to the presidency in 1932, the Democratic Party was able to some extent to "hang the Depression" on the Republicans.

So popular was Franklin Roosevelt that not only was he elected to the presidency four times, but he also presided over the political restoration of the Democratic Party throughout the nation. His particular achievement was the organization of the poor, the ethnic minorities, the working class, and the traditional governing class in the South into a new national coalition that redefined liberalism into what it is today. Liberalism in the new Democratic definition became a government-to-people partnership wherein the government would take a leading role in an egalitarian approach to the solution of economic difficulties. This became the basic approach to government by both Democrats and Republicans until 1980. The Roosevelt administration did not necessarily solve the Depression, but it presided over its evolution and over the successful conclusion of World War II. The Democratic Party emerged from the war under the leadership of Harry Truman still "the party of the people."

Despite the fact that after the election of Truman two Republicans (Eisenhower and Nixon) were elected to the presidency, each for two consecutive terms, the country remained essentially under the domination of the Democratic Party until quite recently. As of 1980, the Democratic Party had maintained most of the governorships since 1932, and the Democrats had been the majority party in Congress all but three times since 1932. Finally, the Democratic dominance was seen as late as 1980, when approximately half of the American voters considered themselves Democrats, while fewer than one-fourth considered themselves Republicans. It seemed to many that the Democratic Party would remain the dominant party in our two-party system for some time unless another crisis, such as the Civil War or the Great Depression, should arise.

At the time, some Republicans felt that the Vietnam War might have proven to be the crisis that would destroy the Democratic Party. Indeed, this might have been the case had not the Nixon administration taken the war under its own wing, so to speak, and continued essentially the same policy as the Democratic government that had preceded it. Furthermore, the Vietnam War got lost in the Watergate episode, and the voters returned to the Democratic fold in 1976.

What do we make of the post-1980 American party politics? At this writing, some things are clear and others are not. Ronald Reagan's large popular majorities in 1980 and 1984—coupled with his successful implementation of an essentially "conservative" program including tax cuts, a stronger defense, deemphasis of many federal programs, which shifted the initiative on education, social, and environmental issues to the states; his neglect of civil rights; and his appointments to the federal judiciary—along with the rise of the "religious right" in Republican Party politics, seemed to indicate a basic ideological/political realignment such as those that occurred in 1800, 1860, and 1932 (and perhaps in 1896 within the Democratic Party). Indeed, few of the governors or legislators—not even the Democrats—expect to see Washington reclaim its pre-Reagan leadership role in domestic politics for a long time.

As the Bush administration continued in the same general direction as Reagan's, other changes began to be noted in the American political party scene. The legitimacy of the traditional liberal agenda of the Democrats came into question because of a steadily weakening and fragmented leadership and a series of weak Democratic presidential candidates beginning in 1980. Indeed, Democrats began to sound like Republicans—a sure formula for defeat on the national level. In the states where one-party Democratic majorities had held sway since the 1930s, Republicans began to create credible two-party systems, especially in the South. Finally, the enormous popularity of Reagan and Bush (until late 1991) caused a significant shift in voter identification. By 1991, 30 percent of voters called themselves Republicans, while the Democratic bloc fell to 32 percent. Interestingly, a rising tide of Independents numbered 38 percent. A Republican dominance seems to have emerged on the presidential level (five victories out of the last six elections) and in the Congress, which the Democrats lost in 1994. Republicans have also gained a slim majority of state governments since 1994. The "experts" have offered many and varied (and sometimes contradictory) views of the current scene. For instance, while the election of Bill Clinton in 1992 reunited the White House and the Congress under the Democratic Party for the first time in twelve years, the party's program was never defined with precision. Should he, like Bush before him, become a one-term president, which is not clear at this writing, then the situation will be even murkier in 1996. Suffice it to say that nobody seems to have the foggiest idea where American political parties are heading.

Perhaps the ultimate reality in all of this is that, never having been all that strong to begin with, the American political parties as such have become largely irrelevant. The labels have become so meaningless that we focus almost exclusively on personalities and issues instead of on parties. What we are seeing is a possible *policy* realignment without a *party* realignment. If so, then the future becomes totally unpredictable.

After all, our parties have never functioned the way political parties have functioned in other countries. Let's retrace our steps somewhat and look at European parties and the way they have evolved. Then we'll refocus on the American political scene.

EUROPEAN POLITICAL PARTIES

The evolution of the Democratic Party in the United States, perhaps more than anything else, influenced the evolution of political parties in Europe. Certainly, after the Civil War, the operation of American political parties as organizations of like-minded people that were united in their attempt to capture a government became the norm for European politics. There was one major exception to Europe's imitation of our system, however. Let's recall that the Europeans have tended to be more ideological in their approach to politics than have Americans. Although we may have invented ideology in the form of American liberalism, we have abandoned an idealistic or ideological approach to our politics based on a consistent application of that ideology, at least until recently. On the other hand, conservatism, liberalism, and socialism became very pronounced and uniform ideologies on the European continent. They tended to emerge through political parties during the nineteenth century. This tendency produced Conservative parties under various labels such as the Conservative Party of Great Britain and the Christian Democratic Parties of other nations, Socialist Parties under the label *socialists,* and Liberal Parties under such labels as *liberal* or *liberal democrats.* There is a definite, ideological cleavage among them. One generally knows one is associating with fellow Conservatives or Socialists or Liberals within the political party, even when one speaks of the left or right wing of that party. One may also associate with the political party of choice at an early age, attend meetings of that party, help raise money, participate in the elections, and otherwise identify oneself on a regular basis with that party. In addition, there is a permanent party structure, with complex subdivisions throughout the country. Usually, each subordinate organizational unit is headed by a professional party person and an experienced staff.

In some European states, the tendency to operate under proportional representation schemes has strengthened the concept of ideological parties. This results in a situation where an individual votes for his or her party without paying great attention to who the candidates are. Therefore, political parties in Europe fit all the prerequisites for our definition of political parties. What of American political parties?

THE AMERICAN APPROACH TO POLITICAL PARTIES

The irony of American political parties is that, although we invented the concept, we did not fully develop a true political party system like that which evolved in Europe. The reason for this irony might be found in a propensity within the United States to seek general agreement on basic political ideas and values and to try to operate within the context of that area of agreement for as long as possible. This situation arises, in turn, from a general inclination of Americans to be pragmatic about public issues and to resist the simple orthodoxy of ideologies and ideological solutions. We prefer to compromise broad differences of opinion in a spirit of conciliation rather than to insist on a single point of view that must win over a conflicting point of view. At least, this was the case until recently. The ideological conservatism of the Reagan adminstration and the Republican victories in the Congressional elections of 1994 placed this thesis in some doubt.

Nevertheless, the general instinct toward pragmatism and general agreement is further supported by the high values we place upon the individuality of the voter. American voters are much more interested in choosing the individual who will represent them than in the overall set of ideas that individual might represent. Further, we want the ability to switch parties when we feel like making a general statement about either the ruling party or the separate candidates involved in an election. We demand not only that our representatives shift opinion along with us voters, but also, on occasion, that they resist the concerted pressure of party leaders to force them into conformity with party principles, such as they are.

Finally, Americans are not joiners when it comes to politics. We do not like to be in large political organizations. We do not like to attend political meetings or even discuss in any great detail political and economic issues. We prefer to get interested in politics when there is something that interests us. We prefer not to maintain an ongoing relationship with government. Indeed, we do not like to think about government at all unless we have to. Therefore, party membership in the United States requires no identifying cards, no regularly scheduled meetings, no mass involvement in fund raising, and no mass electorate. Rather, the political party is little more than an organization that takes on the characteristic of the legendary bird, the phoenix. Our "parties" appear every two to four years in glorious splendor during an election campaign, only to burn themselves up in the heat of that campaign and become little more than ashes after the election. They rise again two to four years hence in renewed splendor.

Actually, the political party organization in the United States is rather meager even during the periods of elections. Consider that the ordinary party organization consists of a national committee made up of representatives from each state, a state committee generally made up of county representatives, and a county committee supposedly made up of equal representation from the precincts or wards of the organizations that come under the county level. However, the national committees seldom meet, and, when they do, they cannot dictate any kind of policy to state committees. State committees, in turn, seldom meet, and they do not dictate policy to county committees. County committees meet generally only during election years and primarily for purposes of organizing the election, not the campaign. A related problem seems to be that, in a federal government such as America's, the party structure is also inherently federalized, with the result that parties may be stronger in one geographical area and weaker in another, dependent on a variety of circumstances. This undermines the attempt to arrive at a uniform leadership, with uniform policies. Then there is the problem of the nomination of candidates.

Political parties in most countries serve two important functions during an election period: they nominate the candidates for their party, and they contribute, both in money and effort, to the election campaign. In the United States, however, the nominations for office are often made in an open primary, wherein any individual qualified for the office can, by gaining a majority of the popular vote through a media campaign, become a party nominee, even though he or she has never before identified with the party. This is especially true in state elections. Also, in the United States, the candidate is generally responsible for running his or her own campaign and raising his or her own funding. Thus, federalism has fragmented the parties in terms of uniformity of leadership and policies, primaries have reduced the role of parties as nominators of candidates, and, as we saw earlier, vagueness on issues has undermined the significance of party labels. What does all of this leave for the party to do? Does it have any useful function? The answer to these questions is significant in that it defines the basic political party dynamic in America.

Essentially, the role of the major American political party, either Democratic or Republican, is

1. To provide a structure in which to rationalize some kind of link between people and government
2. To produce a vehicle through which to elect new representatives within the system
3. To create legitimacy for those representatives through the election process
4. To provide a method for organizing the national and state legislatures into minority and majority groups
   Unfortunately, there is little beyond that.

Perhaps there are better ways of conducting political contests than the rather wide open, loosely structured, and pragmatic American approach. However, given the general American political ethos of pragmatism, nonconformity, negativism toward government, and a certain absence of public philosophy, we should not expect much change in the American political party system. Nor should we place too many demands upon it.

We can continue to maintain a political, democratic society in this country without ideologically oriented parties. Perhaps our nonpartisan attitude is one of the reasons our system has lasted as long as it has. One is still left with the nagging question of the ability of people who have serious concerns about public policy to make these concerns known to government and to find some mechanism for change. The answer to that question is that the United States has evolved a different set of institutions for expressing particular points of view. Other nations have the same institutions, but they exist alongside strong ideological parties. In the United States, they usurp the role of political parties. These institutions are called *interest groups,* and we have elevated them to a high level of activity in our system. There is a wide variety of such groups because of their importance as communicators of values.

INTEREST GROUPS AND THEIR ROLE IN POLITICS

Whether one is discussing a European political party system or the American party system, the first characteristic of interest groups, and what sets them apart from political parties, is that their function is to organize for the purpose of expressing the interests of minority groups. The interest group is the vehicle whereby any minority with a separate and rather narrowly defined set of special interests may express its interests and participate in that political dialogue that leads to consensus. A second characteristic of interest groups is that they seek the passage, or more often the defeat, of specific laws rather than the achievement of the overall political program of a party. A third characteristic is that interest groups do not run candidates for public office. Rather, they attempt to influence those people who are already in office to appreciate and support the particular issues and positions they have taken.

Rather than *candidates,* the key individuals in interest group operations are called **lobbyists.** Lobbyists have taken on a rather unsavory reputation in some countries. This is unfortunate because lobbyists play a significant and important role in the political process. After all, the assumption of a political system is that all major and relevant points of view with regard to public issues will be heard. Lobbyists are invaluable sources of information to marginally informed legislators and administrators. The lobbyist has every right to be enthusiastic in the pursuit of a single point of view and in the insistence that the group he or she represents be given a piece of the action.

The problem comes when the lobbyist pursues his or her influence on an officeholder in illegal ways. Throughout our history, we in the United States have had some difficulty in defining what methods of influence are appropriate and what methods are illegal. Certainly, an out-and-out bribe of a public official to support a lobbyist's position is illegal. However, what about giving a small gift to the campaign committee of an elected representative or inviting that representative to participate in some recreational activity sponsored by the interest group the lobbyist represents? What about an offer of a job in the special interest area to a member of the legislator's family? These and similar activities have generally been condemned in principle but have occurred too often in practice, leading to a rather vague understanding of what is proper in the realm of influence peddling and what is not.

Apparently, the most successful kinds of lobbying groups or special interest groups are those that cluster around the business community. This should not be surprising when one considers that most state and national legislators come either out of the legal system, which is in itself a business, or out of the business community. These kinds of public officials are quite susceptible to the approach of people "like themselves." Labor special interest groups in general have had more success within the Democratic Party because of an affinity between the Democratic Party and labor that seldom exists, to the same extent, in the Republican Party. However, all interest groups can find some path of communication whereby a lobbyist can become an idea broker to government. The key is to organize a special interest lobbying effort properly and to try to conduct it legally, so as to enrich the political discourse.

Most Americans are involved in lobbying whether they realize it or not. Most belong to some association that lobbies for benefits relevant to it. For instance the American Automobile Association, American Association of Retired Persons, Girl Scouts, Boy Scouts, YMCA and 4H Clubs probably include a fourth of all Americans, and all of them lobby the Congress for something. Indeed, if you are employed, active in your community, belong to a church or participate in parent/teacher activities, you are represented by at least one or more lobbies. At last count there were over 7,400 national associations with headquarters in Washington, D.C. hard at work for their constituents.

Who should a lobbyist lobby? This question arises especially in the presidential form of government, for, when one approaches a government in which the executive or policy-making function is separate from the legislative function, a lobbyist can either attempt to change policy or attempt to change the law. In any case, in the presidential system, a lobbyist has the option of attacking his or her goals either in terms of policy implementation through the executive branch and the regulatory agencies or in terms of influencing law making through the legislative structure. In a parliamentary system, it is rather pointless to lobby the legislature because its members will vote, in most cases, in accordance with the policies of the party as laid down by the executive leadership. This has been previously referred to as party responsibility. Therefore, in a parliamentary system, the special interest groups are more likely to be found lobbying members of the Cabinet and the heads of other administrative agencies of the government. They are seldom, if ever, seen lobbying members of Parliament itself.

The lobbying effort of special interest groups in the United States has become so broad in modern times that, in political jargon, the special interests and their lobbyists are sometimes referred to as the "third house of Congress" or the "assistant government of the United States." One is left to ponder how individuals or the public in general can hope to influence government as successfully as the well-financed special interest groups with their carefully orchestrated activities. Perhaps it would be more relevant to think of the general interest or the public interest in terms of being, in the long run, little more than the amalgamation of all special interests and to recognize that any interest is special to those people who are interested in it.

Thus the National Association of Manufacturers; the United States Chamber of Commerce; the AFL-CIO and its Committee on Political Education; the American Farm Bureau Federation; the American Medical Association; the American Bar Association; the National Association for the Advancement of Colored People (NAACP); the National Organization for Women; the National Council of Churches and the B'nai B'rith; the American Legion and the Veterans of Foreign Wars; Common Cause and the Women's Christian Temperance Union; the Consumers Union; the National Rifle Association; and even those ubiquitous Political Action Committees (PACs), which raise large amounts of money to contribute not only to the advancement of their various causes but also to political candidates in the hope of influencing their votes after they are elected, are all at it in Washingtion trying to determine the outcome of the public agenda.

Finally, there are foreign countries that engage in special lobbying activities. Since World War II, many countries have attempted to tap the great resources of the United States in order to receive grants or loans for their development programs or to promote trade. These groups have special restrictions placed upon their lobbying activities with regard to requirements that the lobbyists be publicly registered and that they present a detailed financial accounting of their activities to the American government.

In Europe, a basic pattern of lobbying is seen in the close relationship of labor interest groups and Socialist Parties and an equally close relationship between business interest groups and the more conservative parties. Whereas in the United States the field is generally wide open for all kinds of lobbying efforts at any given time, in Europe the kinds of lobbyists that can expect success will often be determined by the kind of party that is currently in power within a parliamentary system. The American party system is really a "no-party" system, thus, lobbying in the United States is a far more extensive and politically meaningful activity than it is in countries with well-defined political party systems and parliamentary structures. Therefore, the American political party structure, or lack thereof, has created a different kind of mechanism for the interaction between citizens and their government than that of other countries. One wonders which option is the better one.

POINTS TO PONDER

How would you explain the decline of the Democratic Party as the dominant political party in America after 1932?

What different aspects of European government practices make their political parties differ from ours?

Would the European model of the political party work in America? Why or why not?

How does party leadership differ most dramatically between European political parties and those in America?

10 | Administration and the Bureaucracy

Anyone who engages in a serious study of executive, legislative, judicial, and regulatory functions must ultimately come to grips with the phenomenon of bureaucracy. Indeed, public administration (which is mostly a study of the bureaucracy and how it operates) is an entire subdiscipline of political science. At this level of study, however, a brief introduction to the subject must suffice. Although at present, the political winds are blowing against the national bureaucracy, and we, as citizens, tend to complain at all times about **bureaucratic** red tape, organizational redundancy, and the endless and time-consuming steps toward the accomplishment of some governmental end, we should at least begin our examination of the subject with some sense of charity, for it is a fact of modern life that complex social structures require bureaucrats and other "paper-pushers" so that complicated activities can take place with some sense of order.

Bureaucracies are designed to be authoritarian, impersonal, rule-bound, and specialized, for this is what gives order to government. The challenge is to get them moving toward the goals sought by the leadership. President Truman, contemplating the arrival of his successor, President Eisenhower, on the morning of the latter's inauguration, is supposed to have said, "Poor Ike. He will come in here (the Oval Office) and he will say, 'you do this, and 'you do that,' and not a damn thing will happen. It won't be at all like the army."[1] This is probably a more charitable view of the army than it deserves, but it does point to the problem—how to make policy and law operational. The problem is not new.

From ancient times, we have had bureaucracy. Without it, the pyramids would never have been built, nor the Great Wall of China. Nor could the Roman Empire have grown to its enormous size by the fourth century. All complex operations need direction from the top, a logical division of the labor, and a support system to provide the tools, plans, schedules, and resources to get the job done. Finally, someone has to account for the activity

[1]Neustadt, R.E. *Presidential Power.* New York: John Wiley & Sons, Inc., p. 9.

and measure its relationship to the original goal. Executives or quasi-executives must first master their bureaucracies before any significant action can take place. Those who don't may *preside* or *reign* over an agency, but they will never *direct* or *rule* it.

First things first. Most bureaucracies are divided in at least two ways: those who do the line function, that is, the job itself, and those who support the effort or staff the job by providing the plans, resources, and supervision (and do such things as hiring personnel and purchasing supplies). An illustration of the two activities that comes to mind is the U.S. Army. Line functions begin with the infantry, the tank drivers, and the artillery gun crews. Those who issue operational orders to these people are also in the line, all the way from the squadron leaders, company commanders, battalion, regiment, and division commanders up to the generals, who command the armies. *Staffing* these line forces are clerks, paymasters, recruiters, medical personnel, procurers of resources, and providers of other services that bring the line forces to bear on the enemy. Both groups are needed to win the war, but it is the staff bureaucrats who get most of the complaints and little of the glory.

Another aspect of bureaucracies is the degree of professionalism they exhibit. The Chinese were among the first to recognize the need for those who implement laws and policies to be highly trained and well suited to their jobs. This idea, called *merit selection*, has been imitated by many nations who desire an elite civil service, prominent among them being the west European states and the United States.

Unfortunately, there is another way to create a bureaucracy—through political patronage, family connections, friendships, or other biased methods wherein merit plays little or no role. Both European and American systems have fallen prey to this approach at various times, and still do at certain levels, particularly at the higher ones. This nagging problem constantly defies the best attempts at the use of merit examinations and other devices, such as the Hatch Act in the United States, which, since 1939, has sought to "depoliticize" the civil service. Thus, bureaucracies often vary in their effectiveness in direct proportion to the ratio between merit selected professionals and political appointees. In some developing countries, where there are few educated people to begin with and where there is a history of nepotism and corruption, this problem becomes especially acute, often leading to instability and civil disorder.

In America, during and after the Andrew Jackson administration, we also had a bout with what we unashamedly called the *spoils system*, as in "to the victors go the spoils." In this case, civil service jobs were transferred back and forth as the party in power changed.[2] This practice has

---

[2]Ironically, it was the Jefferson administration, in 1801, that began the spoils system by throwing out more bureaucrats than Jackson did, but Jackson got the rap for it. Such is the accuracy of our historical memory.

been reduced by the aforementioned Hatch Act and the advent of civil service examinations open to all on an equal and nonpartisan basis.

THE EVOLUTION OF AMERICAN BUREAUCRACY

Although Americans share the frustration found elsewhere in the Western world concerning the complexities of bureaucracy, we seem to have felt it more strongly in recent times. Therefore, it might be instructive to observe those attitudes as they evolved. Our government, on all levels, remained quite small until the 1930s, and those who served it were generally perceived as serving the people first. They were paid relatively low wages, enjoying instead the security of their positions and, generally, the esteem of the public. Government services and bureaucratic procedures were rather simple, and paperwork was mostly done by hand, rendering it both minimal and manageable. Above all, bureaucrats were seen as responsible and reliable people.

Thus it was that, when the Great Depression came, the public readily accepted the government giving greater responsibility to administrative officials, often with large discretionary power as well. The national recovery agencies (NRA, WPA, CCC, etc.) that Washington created, and similar ones in the states, began to expand in size and in the amount of power given to their employees to make day-to-day decisions concerning the way the new laws would be applied.

No national referendum was ever taken as to the public's desire for this new "branch" of government or its place in the constitutional order. It simply grew under its own momentum, accompanied by a general attitude of public acceptance and approval. Indeed, as this activity increased through the 1940s and 1950s, the general trend was for the public at large to demand *more* government services despite the new bureaucracies that they produced. These services included additional programs within the original Social Security concept, agricultural subsidy and price support programs, increased activity in public health and education, crime control, safety in the air and on the ground, housing, and stimulus to small business. The cost of the new bureaucracy was still relatively cheap.

By the late 1960s, however, things began to change dramatically. Public salaries began to increase as bureaucratic interest groups began to demand professional pay for professional work. The public perception of the increased cost was probably greater than the actual increase. More important was the rise of newer and more controversial government activities, particularly with regard to civil rights, foreign aid, and ultimately the Vietnam War. These things exacerbated the traditional American antipathy toward government and caused the public to focus their frustrations on the bureaucrats involved in the disputed activities. Then came the scandals—Watergate, defense "cost overruns," Korea-gate, and Iran-Contra—in which bureaucrats were perceived as corrupt, inefficient, and self-serving. Bureaucracy itself was perceived as out of control and too distant from the people.

This direct kind of negativism is compounded by a strange dichotomy of American thought wherein some people expect too much from government and yet feel that government is too intrusive into their lives. This irony rests on what has become a modern, if childish, faith that we Americans are all born with a guarantee that we will live forever in perfect bliss and that, if anything arises to threaten our well-being, we have the right to government intervention to set it right by a program or through a lawsuit. Then, when our childish expectations go awry, we blame it on the bureaucrats. Truly, "a bureaucrat's lot is not a happy one."

BUREAUCRATIC ORGANIZATION AND PROCEDURE

Beyond the simple line and staff distinction noted previously, most bureaucracies are characterized by the following: (1) an internal division of labor; (2) work is subdivided by specialty; (3) an established routine or "flow" to the work; (4) clear rules concerning how work is to be done; (5) greater reliance on precedent (i.e., how a thing has *always* been done); and (6) a clear chain of command linking the tasks both horizontally and, more important, vertically, focusing ultimately on the most visibly responsible bureaucrat in the agency.[3] That person is often called the director, head, chairperson, or perhaps cabinet secretary. All of this is usually illustrated by those ubiquitous organizational charts one sees when studying the operation of a unit of the government.

Bureaucracy has traditionally been perceived as being administratively neutral because it is designed to respond to laws rather than to create them. Indeed, we consider neutrality to be the first principle of bureaucracy. As a result, a certain image of bureaucracy has evolved that includes the assumption that bureaucrats only follow the intent of the law, are subject to legislative oversight to see that they do, are carefully directed by the executive part of government to their proper ends, and are professional and competent in their activities. However, image and reality are often at odds, especially when we examine bureaucratic practice in the American presidential system of government.

Remembering that parliaments fuse the executive and legislative functions into one organ of government (centered more and more on the cabinet) will help one understand that a coherent approach to legislative oversight and executive direction, which produces bureaucratic neutrality and competence, is more likely to occur in that setting than it is in our system of separated functions. We lack this centralized mechanism to control our

[3]Gordon, G. J. 1982. *Public Administration in America.* New York: St. Martin's Press, p. 8.

bureaucrats because ours is a presidential system. This results in three distinctive characteristics of modern American bureaucratic practice: polycentrism, power vacuums, and fragmentation of effort.

Polycentrism results directly from this lack of a singular control. Some agencies respond to executive direction, whereas others tend to follow congressional wishes. Others become relatively independent of both. Thus, power vacuums are created, wherein agency heads compete to grab control of a program for themselves. Further, as each agency develops a sense of administrative discretion over its own activities, lower-ranking executives become independent power centers and can decide for themselves how a law is to be administered. This in turn results in fragmentation of effort, wherein no single person is in a position to take overall responsibility for a single set of activities. The ultimate result is that presidents have a tremendously difficult time trying to command the bureaucrats, who in turn tend to operate toward the *status quo* for reasons of safety and convenience. This situation will be examined in more detail in the following section.

PUBLIC AND PRIVATE BUREAUCRACY

Out of the frustrations just described often comes the plaintive, if irrelevant cry to "make the government more businesslike." One can sympathize with that plea only to a point. Closer examination of the phenomenon of governmental bureaucracy reveals some basic differences between this activity and private business. First, we are dealing with *political* structures, and they must be as sensitive to *how* a thing is done as they are to *what* is done. Businesses usually are not so sensitive. Second, as we have seen, we intentionally cripple the government structure by separating its functions in ways that we would consider stupid if applied to corporate structures. Third, we allow citizen groups, other interest groups, specialists, government officials, and a wide variety of input organizations to suggest to bureaucrats what to do. No business would tolerate so much interference in its affairs. Fourth, bureaucrats generally must do what they are told to do, and only that; businesses do what they want to do and can change their agendas at will. Fifth, the bureaucratic manager operates in a glass house; he or she does everything openly and in public view. Business executives can hide their sins. Sixth, bureaucrats spend the public's money, and we don't trust them very much, so we set up numerous accountability procedures that rob them of their efficiency. Businesses spend their own money (or that of their stockholders) and can operate pretty much under their own supervision. Next, bureaucrats generally have a monopoly on providing their particular services, and competition does not stimulate them to improve their act. Businesses do not have security and must innovate and improve in order to survive. Finally, governmental agencies are not profit-oriented. There is no incentive to save money. There is no bottom line to be used to evaluate their activities. Business lives or dies on the bottom line. In short, governmental agencies are not, cannot be, and will never become like business.

BUREAUCRATIC GROWTH

Despite all of the negative statements expressed thus far, bureaucrats are here to stay. We simply cannot get along without them, and they will continue to grow at some level despite all attempts at "new federalism," reducing "big government," and the like. Why is this so?

As stated in chapter 5, one reason is the growing complexity of our society, which belies the attempts of legislative bodies to control its increasing variety of functions with any degree of immediacy. Further, it has become the norm for every conceivable group to demand some bureaucratic support mechanism to protect it. Beyond this tendency is the one wherein each period of bureaucratic growth caused by a war, a depression, or a social reform movement tends to level off where it is, never contracting after the situation that produced it has ended or become normalized. We just keep adding on. Each new unit takes on a life of its own, and no amount of legislative action seems adequate to eliminate it.

The contemporary mood in America is, however, one of overcoming this growth and reducing the size of government in general. Whereas some successes may be achieved at the national level, it is likely that the bureaucratic function will simply be reordered at the state and local level. Indeed, the figures show that this is the case already. During the past forty years, the national expenditures for government have risen by a factor of six, while the state and local budgets have increased by a factor of nine. The same ratios exist for the most part in the number of national government employees as opposed to state and local employees. These trends will likely continue.

INTERGOVERNMENTAL BUREAUCRACY

The modern American federal system has produced a new kind of political relationship totally unanticipated by our founding fathers, the intergovernmental bureaucracy. This label applies to a new set of activities among people on all levels of government within the complex American federal structure: national, regional, state, county, district, and municipal. It creates a new kind of public employee, who is often appointed because of his or her expertise in a single area of activity.

One should be aware of the dynamics of this new form of bureaucracy because of its relationship to traditional assumptions about representativeness and accountability within a political democracy. These new structures involve like-minded bureaucrats on many separate levels of government who know each other and who constantly cross over the normal federal jurisdictions in quest of common approaches to social problems. Their relationships can be described as

1. *Invisible:* Unless one is involved directly in the designated activity, one seldom sees these bureaucrats in action. There is even less control here than among regulatory agencies. The main constraint is usually budgetary.
2. *Personal:* It is not really governments that interact here as much as it is individuals. The relationships are more personal than structural. Decisions are more often negotiated than subjected to legal procedures.
3. *Professional:* The bureaucrats are mostly appointed or hired for their knowledge and experience. They are expected to be relatively self supervised and competent in what they do.
4. *Continuous:* Most programs are considered to be ongoing. There is a history of interaction over the same problems, wherein the people concerned share a long-range view of the activity. Goals are seldom finally met, and the assumption is that work will go on.
5. *Policy making:* Unlike most assumptions about federalism, wherein each layer of government has its own sphere of activity, the intergovernmental bureaucrat seeks to make a single policy or rule for all levels of government within the sphere of his or her particular concerns.[4]

The effectiveness of this kind of activity can be seen in the fact that, despite the assumption that state governments have primary responsibility for public health and safety, the nation used to have a single national speed limit for automobiles (55 MPH from 1974 to 1987) and still has a single drinking age for alcoholic beverages (twenty-one years old) and a single standard for evaluating environmental pollution of air and water. This has come about through the actions of intergovernmental bureaucrats, under the sanction of the Congress and the courts (thus far). No single or direct legislative act began the process. Rather, the relatively invisible professionals among the various levels of government, working in such continuous areas as highway funding, safety, and environmental control, hatched among themselves these provisions of law, which arose out of *their* ideas of public policy. Congress then made these standards obligatory on the states if they wished to continue in these large programs. This country is not exactly sure what has hit it yet!

All of this is not to say that the legal division of power in America has been changed or undermined. It *has* been superseded, but one can expect to see the states fighting back when the process goes too far, as they did with regard to the old national 55 MPH highway speed limit, which resulted in its increase in 1987 and its abandonment in 1995.

The points here are the effectiveness of intergovernmental bureaucracy in bringing about changes in public policy to begin with and the fact that

4Ibid., pp. 136–37.

more subtle activities go on constantly. The reasons are the same as those
for bureaucracy in general: complexity, specialization, and the need to
have ongoing expertise in the governing process. However, it is ultimately
still up to the people to accept or reject the concept of intergovernmental
administration.

GRANTS-IN-AID

Another source of problems for the American bureaucracy is in the area of
national grants-in-aid to the states, a subject briefly discussed in chapter 4.
The subject bears further attention. As of the early 1980s, there were close to
500 grant-in-aid programs, divided into thirty-one categories (such as higher
education, ground transportation, social services, health, etc.), calling for
expenditures of just under $90 billion annually. The Reagan administration
made some organizational changes in the 1980s and made significant cuts in
the expenditures but only minor changes in the number of programs. Why
is this so?

Part of that answer lies in the fact that these programs (which, as we have
seen, go back to the 1860s) have fulfilled to some extent at least eight major
purposes:

1. Establishing minimum national standards of public service (as in education, for instance)
2. Bringing resources from richer states to the poorer states
3. Improving local programs
4. Addressing regional problems regionally
5. Keeping the national government smaller by helping state governments
   expand
6. Teaching better administration techniques to state and local officials
7. Providing for experimentation by the states
8. Encouraging state acceptance of social programs (such as racial desegregation or welfare)[5]

Few would doubt the benefits of these achievements, especially over the
past fifty years. Problems such as pollution, public health, and transportation
could not have been addressed nearly as well without a national approach to
them. This was largely achieved through the singular focal point of grant-in-
aid programs. This , however, has not come without problems.

The controversy has come primarily from the structural approaches
taken by the national government in designing the programs themselves.
One issue has been that of **categorical grants** versus **block grants.** The
greatest number of grants have been categorical. These are narrowly

---

[5]Ibid., p. 143.

defined in terms of their purpose and give the granting agency a great deal of say about the precise use of the money. They also tend toward extreme specificity in such areas as quality control, matching formulas, and procedures for expenditures. This is where much of the complaining by state and local officials comes from. Many state and local governments have learned to operate in the resultant quagmire of red tape and bureaucratic minutia through the use of specialists, called grantsmen who search out grant programs, collect the relevant data for filling out the complicated forms, make the applications, and then track them through the interagency jungle from whence the funds will ultimately come. Such people are quite literally worth their weight in gold.

However, this practice has led to several problems: (1) richer states and cities get more grants than poorer ones because they can hire more and better grantsmen; (2) local priorities get distorted by what grants are available, in that unsupported activities, which may be equally valuable and necessary, are often neglected in favor of activities supported by a grant program (thus, the police may get new cars and radios while the emergency medical teams may languish with outdated equipment for lack of grant support); (3) policy initiatives are subtly shifted from the local level to the national level; (4) the paperwork saps local budgets and discourages small but needy communities; (5) many projects require more than one separate categorical grant but can never be sure that the community or state will get all of the grants needed, an eventuality that has undermined the coherency of many an overall project.

In the 1970s, such problems led to the concept of the block grant. These grants leave more discretion and flexibility to local governments with regard to how the money is to be used. Block grants also tend to cover broader areas than do the categoricals (for instance, crime control or urban housing programs instead of lesser ones in police training or the reconstruction of multifamily structures in federally impacted areas). They also tend to be heavily influenced by matching formulas and allow for more decisions to be made locally as to how programs can be adapted to local situations. Block grants tend to be popular with many state governments, but they have been less so with Congress, which fears that national funds might not be spent with the same degree of care that the categorical grants demand. Nevertheless, with the new Congress of 1994, block grants again became popular, primarily as a means to reduce federal expenditures in such areas as welfare.

Even more controversial was the idea of general **revenue sharing.** During the early Nixon administration, the president pushed for greater local discretion through this device. The idea was a rather simple one wherein federal funds would be returned directly to the states and to some kinds of local governments in accordance with a formula defined by Congress. That formula would compare the states' populations, per capita incomes, and other economic factors to determine which areas were more needy than others. A fraction of the whole amount of national funds earmarked for revenue sharing would then go to the states with no strings attached. Local governments could use the money any way they pleased. Nor would a state or local government have to apply for the funds. They could determine their own priorities and take their own initiatives. This device proved to be very popular among state and local governments and even among many in Congress who valued its efficiency over its seeming abandonment of national controls.

The Reagan administration did *not* support revenue sharing and ended the program by 1984. Reagan's reasons had to do with a philosophical concept of reducing the size of all government programs, shifting the burden of government back to the states as much as possible, and reducing national taxes. The resultant problem for state and local government seems to be how to raise enough money to meet its new responsibilities, many of which have been mandated by Congress but not funded from the national treasury. Since the end of most of the revenue sharing programs in the mid-1980s, many states have had to resort to increasing the sales tax, raising license fees, and, in some instances, introducing state lotteries. Whereas funding patterns may come and go, bureaucracy will probably be with us at *some* level forever.

THE BUREAUCRATIC PROBLEM

A major concern about bureaucracy in America and in most other modern states lies in the area of lethargy and inefficiency. As Franklin Roosevelt often said of his days as under-secretary of the navy when he would try to get that bureaucracy to do something new, "The thing is like a gigantic feather pillow; you beat it; you kick it and you pound it, but the damned thing just sits there—just like it was when you started." This aspect of bureaucracy requires a more lengthy attempt at analysis.

We should begin with two famous oddities of bureaucracy: **Parkinson's Law** and the **Peter Principle.** One will eventually encounter both in any serious study of public administration. C. Northcote Parkinson noted in the 1950s that bureaucratic work expands to fill the time available to it. In other words, a bureaucracy can expand without any appreciable increase in the work done. The work just gets subdivided and is made more complex, justifying, after the fact, the increase in the number of people doing it. Of more recent vintage is the *Peter Principle,* first observed by Laurence J. Peter in 1969. In complex bureaucracies (public and private) a career person is promoted gradually, until he or she reaches his or her level of incompetence. At that point, since demotion is considered to indicate the failure of the system and further promotion is out of the question, bureaucracies often wind up being managed by the incompetents. Although these rules are not absolute, they do tend to point out difficulties to which bureaucracies are prone.

The general ability of bureaucracies to defy change, innovation, and any other kind of leadership by the heads of the organizations they serve has become a focus of study by several prominent political analysts in the past three decades. Graham Allison, writing on presidential decision making in 1969, defined two problem areas as the *organizational process model* and the *bureaucratic politics model.* The essence of his remarks was that large bureaucracies tend to divide complex functions into a maze of small fragments, each surrounded by its own sub bureaucracy, and that what is often described as "decision" at the top is little more than the sum of many small decisions made in relative isolation to other, related decisions. In other words, executive decision is little more than bureaucratic output.

Allison went on to observe that these low-level decisions are often made in ways that, first and foremost, bring comfort to the sub bureaucracies and sometimes actually frustrate the goals sought by the overall leadership. Thus, the watchwords of small organizations within larger ones are "standard operational procedure" (SOP), the maintenance of existing programs, and a general and instinctive resistance to any change at all. He also argued that, even at the top levels of government, the heads of separate bureaucracies are often more intent on maintaining the importance of their particular activities than they are on arriving at some integrated policy *among* bureaucracies. In addition to such turf protection, there is also the instinct for agency heads to compromise on what, professionally, they know to be the best policy in order to maintain their links to other agencies and to the chief executive. Again, rational executive decision making is undermined by bureaucratic complexity.

Stephen D. Krasner countered Allison's argument in 1972 by contending that Allison was providing executives, particularly the president of the United States, with facile excuses that the executives may use to justify failure or inaction. He went on to argue that good leadership at the top should be able to slice through bureaucratic inertia by knowing where the levers of power are and who wields them, and by inculcating these smaller powerbrokers with an overall sense of the values and purposes of the leadership. This, coupled with careful supervision, should force lower-level bureaucrats to operate in such a way as to achieve the goals sought at the top.

Morton Halpern, in his many works on the problems of bureaucracy, has noted some of the weapons or techniques that frustrate even an executive who meets Krasner's criteria for leadership. They include such devices as giving one-sided information, presenting untenable options along with the one the bureaucracy really wants, creating a false sense of objectivity that is really biased toward that one outcome sought, leaking to the press information that is favorable to the sub bureaucracy's point of view and thereby putting public pressure on the key decision maker, and, finally, simply ignoring directives that would cause change or outcomes not favored by the smaller groups. These and other ploys support the natural inertia of bureaucratic organizations, some of whose members' attitudes are satirically summed up by James H. Boren, who, with apologies to Shakespeare's *Hamlet*, has them saying that

> . . . *the dread of something different,*
> *The undiscover'd country from whose bourn*
> *No bureaucrat returns, puzzles the will,*
> *And makes us rather hold to that which we have*
> *Than to fly to changes that we know not of.*
> *Thus status quo makes heroes of us all;*
> *And thus the sanctity of proper channels*
> *Avoids attack from the pale cast of thought,*
> *And enterprises of Great Change and danger*
> *With this regard their currents turn awry,*
> *And lose the name of action.*[6]

To return to an earlier theme, let us conclude our brief survey of the structure, habits, and problems of bureaucracies by looking on the positive side. Bureaucracy is still an indispensable part of the governing process, slow, complex, and frustrating as it may be. Most bureaucrats have sufficient self-esteem to enable them to attempt to get jobs done somehow, and many of them are more often victims of complexity rather than the cause of it.

Every now and then, take a bureaucrat to lunch; be kind to them; "some of my best friends are bureaucrats," and some of them are almost like people!

POINTS TO PONDER

Why do Americans seem more distrustful and unsupportive of governmental bureaucracies than people in Canada or Germany?

Does federalism make American bureaucracy less or more efficient? Why?

Evaluate federal block grants as they would affect such areas as education, crime control and environmental concerns. Would they be better or worse than categorical grants?

[6]Boren, J.H. 1972. "Bureaucrat's Soliloquy." *When in Doubt, Mumble*. New York: Litten Educational Publishing, Inc., & Van Nostrand Reinhold Company.

Think different.

Make no payments for 90 days!

Find out how you can finance computer purchases through the **AppleLoan** program.

Call 1(800) Apple-LN today

Loans are for a minimum of $ 1,000 to a maximum of $10,000. You may take out more than one loan, but the total of all loans cannot exceed $10,000 annually. Your loan amount will consist of the amount you requested, plus a 5.5 percent loan origination fee. If you are purchasing through an authorized Apple campus reseller and your products is not readily available, you may differ disbursement of the loan check for up to 90 days after loan approval.

For more information, call 1(800) Apple-LN

Monday-Friday	8 a.m.-10 p.m. E.S.T.
Saturday	8 a.m - 6p.m. E.S.T.
Sunday	10 a.m. - 6 p.m. E.S.T.

Before you call to apply, be sure to have the following information available:

> Name
> Social Security Number
> Address
> Date of Birth
> Annual Income
> Monthly Mortgage or Rent Payment (name of Mortgage co., account no., and home value).

 # 1 (800) Apple-LN

11 | Problems in Political Democracy

Despite all that has been said about the theory of political democracies, their structures, and their functions, we must face the fact that, no matter how well structured or well designed the government of a political democracy is, it will, nevertheless, continue to face certain problems in achieving its goals. These problems are inherent in the manner in which we try to achieve compromises and solutions to problems in an increasingly complex world.

WHO SHOULD VOTE AND HOW?

THE EXTENSION OF THE FRANCHISE

In the matter of voting, we have already observed that in most political democracies the widest possible distribution of the right to vote should be manifest. All persons, except for children, aliens, convicted felons, and wards of the state, should be able to have the **franchise,** the right to participate in elections. We also know that this has not always been the case, and it is within this century that most of the barriers to some persons other than those just described have fallen. In our own country, property qualifications were perhaps the first barriers to fall. This was followed by granting the franchise to former male slaves and, by implication, to men of any racial minority within the United States, through the passage of the Fifteenth Amendment. In 1920, women received the right to vote in the United States, and, in 1928, they received the right in Great Britain. Other countries among the western democracies followed suit by degrees. Switzerland was one of the last of the democracies to allow for women's suffrage. The most recent extension of the franchise has been the granting of the vote to eighteen-year-olds within the United States during the early 1970s. This places the American electorate among the youngest of the western democracies. Most countries still prefer voters to be at least twenty-one years of age.

Voting is a symbolic as well as a functional activity. When large numbers of people vote, they are not so much determining the outcome of elections or referenda as they are engaging in a symbolic relationship with the government from whence it draws its legitimacy. Therefore, the ballot should be secret, and voting should be an activity encouraged by the government as much as possible.

REGISTRATION

One of the problems connected with the encouragement of voting is found in the process of registration. In the United States, we have a philosophy with regard to registration that differs from many of the other western democracies. Here it is assumed that registering to vote is the responsibility of the citizen, who must earn the "right" to vote by taking the time and effort to seek out the registrar, give him or her the proper information, and do so within certain periods of time before an election so as to participate in that election legitimately. Thus, the responsibility to be registered falls upon the voter, and the vote itself is a right to be won partially through the process of registration.

In other parliamentary democracies, such as Great Britain, the government assumes the responsibility for registration, and voting is viewed as a "duty" rather than a right. The government uses all necessary means to see that citizens become registered and that they participate in the election process. The election commissions of these governments take it upon themselves to seek out people who have moved into new neighborhoods, or who have come of age, and see that they are registered and told where to report for the election. Lists of eligible electors are published prior to an election so that a person whose name is not on the list can see that it gets on, usually by simply dropping by the local election headquarters and requesting that it be done. This has resulted in a higher voter turnout among those eligible to vote in other countries than is seen in our own country.

There have been some improvements in the American registration system. The motor-voter concept of the 1990s allows voters to register at their Social Security office or at the nearest state motor vehicle office by filling out a postcard and mailing it to the appropriate election commission. This has brought the American practice nearer to that of other western democracies, but the difference in philosophy remains.

THE SECRET BALLOT

Perhaps the two most radical changes in voting patterns within political democracies were the advent of the secret ballot, which was first introduced in Australia and therefore bears the name **Australian ballot,** and the extending of the franchise to women. In the first instance, many may be surprised to learn that, in the early philosophy of popular democracy, it was thought that if a person wished to participate in the election of an officer of government, he should be unafraid to stand up in public and literally be counted. However, as the process of public elections evolved through the nineteenth century, people became aware that it was possible for persons in government to retaliate against people who had opposed them in an election. The secret ballot came into vogue in order to avoid this possibility. It has become a mainstay of the election system, to the point where voting may take place not only by a paper ballot, secretly marked and placed in a box to be counted later, but also by pressing a lever on a machine, causing a dial to record the accumulated votes automatically, bringing anonymity to its highest level. Few would debate the correctness of the secret ballot as an integral part of the political process of truly democratic societies.

WOMEN'S SUFFRAGE

The other breakthrough, women's **suffrage,** came in this century primarily for two reasons. Many people had expressed opinions, prior to this century, that women should not vote because they were intellectually unable to understand the issues, because "a woman's place is in the home," or some other equally obnoxious reason. Actually, there were two very fundamental reasons women did not vote until this century, which no amount of male chauvinism was necessary to justify. First, until the turn of the century, women in many countries could not own property in their own names. Since many governmental decisions involved the use of property or the taxation of property, it was not considered proper that those apparently "unaffected" by such decisions should participate in them. Second, until this century, women played little or no active role in the defense of the nation.

About the time of the First World War, the laws concerning property in many western countries began to change, allowing women to jointly own property with their husbands or, in some cases, in their own names. With the coming of World War I and its demand for the services of masses of people, women came to play a supportive role as auxiliary forces, first in Great Britain and then in the United States. In addition, the particular work of the Red Cross, which was staffed by many competent women, was recognized during that war. Women now played a role in the security of the state. As a result of these two changes, both barriers to women's participation in public decisions were removed. From the 1920s, women have played an increasing role in western governments, becoming heads of government in some cases.

DIRECT DEMOCRACY

Up to this point, I have discussed voting essentially as an exercise in choosing representatives or candidates for office. Popular voting can also be a method whereby the actual passage of legislation occurs, and, on other occasions, officeholders can be unelected by the popular vote.

With the coming of the populist movement in the United States in the 1880s, a trend toward "direct democracy" manifested itself in certain western states of the United States. The result was a whole new electoral technique called the **initiative and referendum.** This had the effect of allowing citizens' groups outside the legislature to propose legislation, in the form of initiative petitions, and then to vote on that same legislation through a referendum. Thus, citizens could take the reins of law making directly into their own hands.

The process of initiative and referendum generally works in the following manner. Under state law, a fraction of the number of voters who participated in the last major election is defined as the number of signatures necessary to begin an initiative petition. If that number of names can be affixed to a petition on which a proposed law is written, then that law must be presented to the voters at the next general election. Some officer of the state government, generally the secretary of state, authenticates the number of signatures and announces the inclusion of the initiative on the ballot in the next election. A simple majority will generally suffice to pass legislation itself. Thus, citizens who are dissatisfied with the normal legislative process have, in those American states where initiative and referendum law exists, a method to completely bypass the state legislature and achieve goals despite the wishes of the elected representatives.

A special form of initiative and referendum is called the **recall** election. In this situation, citizens may, by a petition governed by a similar formula to that of the initiative petition, request the recall of a public official from the office he or she holds, for any reason. Ordinarily, one would not expect a reason to be given in the petition itself. The causes of a recall election would generally relate to charges of incompetence on the part of the officeholder or a feeling by the public that certain expectations with regard to the officeholder have not been met. In any case, upon the certification of the sufficient number of signatures on a recall petition, an election to remove the officeholder is held, usually within a few weeks of the verification of the petition. If a majority of the voters decide that the official should be removed, he or she is, and a new election for that office is held.

The initiative and referendum and the recall are not in operation in all of the fifty states of the United States. They are found most often in the western and midwestern states, although some eastern states, such as Maine and Massachusetts, have begun to include certain versions of them in their own state constitutions. Initiatives and referenda are frequent in those states that allow them. For instance, California has often been the scene of dramatic initiatives and referenda that have changed such things as the method of taxation and environmental control. The recall election is used far less frequently. Attempts have been made in the recent past to recall both the mayor of Philadelphia and the governor of California. Both attempts failed for lack of required signatures on the recall petition. However, in 1988, a successful attempt to have a recall election concerning the governor of Arizona was made but the governor was impeached before the election took place. The national government in the United States has no initiative and referendum or recall laws. Direct democracy is not available in questions of national law making or policy making. In other countries among the Western democracies, the referendum is available, but one seldom finds the process of initiative. Most referenda in other countries concern constitutional amendments only, and statutory legislation remains in the hands of the elected representatives.

SECOND THOUGHTS ON THE INITIATIVE AND REFERENDUM

Some second thoughts have emerged with regard to the efficacy of direct democracy through the initiative and referendum process in our complex age. When citizens have tried their hand at lawmaking in this manner, the results have too often looked amateurish and have sometimes produced unexpected results. California's famous Proposition 13, which rolled back property taxes in 1976 not only undermined the state's excellent education system, but it has produced dozens of lawsuits and at least sixteen clarifying ballot amendments thus far. When Oregon voters passed a similar property tax limit in 1990, it led to teacher layoffs, crowded classrooms and the loss of bands and athletic programs. The 1992 Florida ban on gill nets in state waters put many people out of work and doubled the price of cheap fish on which many of the poor depended. Further, many citizen initiatives are eventually overturned by courts such as the Colorado prohibition against local laws discriminating against homosexuality.

Nevertheless, it is still argued that initiatives and referenda constitute an alternative way to do politics, a means to bring an issue before the public in a dramatic fashion. California's Proposition 187, which denied illegal immigrants most public services including schooling and required teachers to turn in suspects, is an example. It made the immigration issue a nationally debated topic in 1994. Similar results have been obtained through state ballot initiatives on such subjects as term limits, gay rights, and antismoking measures. The problem with all of this is that when the normal legislative process is usurped in this manner, the expertise, experience, caution, and thoroughness of that process is usurped as well. Great issues are thrown before the public as if they were reducible to the same kinds of either/or answers that elections are. A lot gets lost in translation. Compromise is eschewed in favor of choosing between one extreme position versus another. The propositions have to be worded in such a way as to be understood by the average voter, which tends toward a simplistic set of options. "Debate" is limited to the devices of campaigning wherein obfuscation, exaggeration, and deceit are frequently used. The public tends to be more confused than informed. Finally, all of this gets reduced to a decision made alongside other decisions, by people of varying degrees of intellignece, within the heat of a general election. All in all, it seems like a hell of a way to run a government.

VOTING BEHAVIOR

As noted in chapter 7, voting is the most popular form of political participation, but it is also the weakest. This is truer for American elections, in which one is never quite sure what a candidate will do after the election, since there is little or no platform consistency to the party label under which the candidate runs. In European and other parliamentary elections, a voter's effect can transcend the mere election of candidates for representative office. That same voter can affect national policy through elevating to power a party whose "mandate" to move the country in a certain direction is clearly defined in the party platform. In either system, because of its widely acknowledged ability to link a people to their government, however tenuously, voting is approached with some degree of seriousness by the people of all political democracies.

The questions about voting that intrigue political scientists most seem to be these:

1. Who votes?
2. Why do people vote?
3. For whom do people vote?
4. With what expectations do people vote?

The answers to these questions have varied over time, and the "science" of voting behavior is inexact at best. Despite the less-than-concrete nature of the subject, there are some areas of general principle that can be defined, as well as some problems that ought to be addressed.

WHO VOTES?

Most studies of nearly all the political democracies tend to show that, although the number of eligible voters is large, restricted only by those factors noted in chapter 7 (childhood, alien status, convicted felon status, being a ward of the state), not all who can vote do. The younger voters (eighteen to twenty-five years of age) vote the least, followed by the older voters (over sixty-five years of age). Most voters seem to be between thirty-five and sixty-five years of age. Men vote slightly more than women, but this tendency may be the result of the lingering effect of a traditional concept of the role of women, and this voting pattern may soon change. Voting by both sexes seems to be higher among the more educated portion of the population, except voting tends to increase when there is either a strong ethnic or racial relationship to current issues or when the contest has well-defined ideological connotations. These two factors cause a higher voter turnout regardless of the education level of the population. Finally, American practice seems to show a higher level of turnout by all segments of the voter population during a presidential election than during elections for state and local candidates alone. This is a factor most relevant to federal societies or to loose unitary systems like that of Great Britain, but non-American systems in those categories do not show quite the same degree of consistency in this area as the United States.

WHY DO PEOPLE VOTE?

The answer here seems to be the same one discussed in terms of political socialization in chapter 2. People vote because they have been taught to vote as a political or civic duty. The voting is done either in the context of an enthusiastic participation in one of the privileges of a political democracy or else it is a reluctantly performed obligation done in response to peer pressure. However approached, some sense of choice must provide the most basic motivation. The degree of choice is often directly proportional to the degree of voter turnout. This choice can be defined in terms of issues (in parliamentary societies), candidates (in presidential countries), or a mixture of both. The choices are seldom made (at least initially) without an enormous amount of influence from public opinions of various varieties. Public opinion and the shaping of it is a complex subject beyond the scope of this book. Let it suffice to say that media, money, opinion leaders, and the progress of events may interact with certain types of charismatic candidates to produce the drama and even the pageantry of an election campaign that is supposed to culminate in the ultimate distillation of public opinion into that authority necessary for ruling democratic societies.

The problems associated with elections will be discussed later, but one additional factor of motivation might be noted here: voting out of protest. Such voting may take the form of unexpected support for extremist candidates of the left or right as an indication of a disenchantment with the policies of more moderate governments. Indeed, it used to be a cliché in Italy that certain very religious voters would vote for the communist candidates and then go to church to pray that they didn't win.

FOR WHOM DO PEOPLE VOTE?

In the elections of the 1970s, a tendency "back to the center" was noted throughout the political democracies. The 1980s saw a shift more toward the right, as seen in the victories of Ronald Reagan, Margaret Thatcher in Great

Britain, and Helmut Kohl in West Germany. The precise nature and significance of such trends should be approached with caution, for they are tran-
sient, and many a general theory of such voting trends has been dashed on
the rocks of human unpredictability and the course of unforeseen events.
Nevertheless, the question of for whom people vote is a continuing preoccupation with a growing number of political scientists. The selling of candidates is a growing enterprise in this and other countries, and techniques
refined in the United States have emerged in such diverse places as
Venezuela and Japan. The general consensus is that most voters make up
their minds fairly early during an election campaign because of family reasons, regional or traditional influences, or idiosyncratic snap judgments. The
goal of most election campaigns is to influence only that margin of voters
necessary for victory. The nearer the major parties are in voter support, the
more fervor will be attached to the campaign. When all is said and done, the
issue of for whom the people vote must rightfully be an open one if the
health of political democracy is to remain sound.

WITH WHAT EXPECTATIONS DO PEOPLE VOTE?

Here is a question of prime importance to political democracies. It reflects a
theme discussed previously—namely, that the success of a political democracy depends upon a satisfactory degree of expectation that the voters' will
can make a difference in the policies and laws of their countries. It is a general assumption that, the higher the degree of expectation, the higher the
voter turnout. However true this may be, it does not necessarily follow that
low voter participation in an election means a lessening of expectations or
confidence in a government. It may connote a high degree of satisfaction
with things as they are. The essential problem is to accurately measure the
reasons for and the extent of a political malaise, especially when low voter
interest is accompanied by a sense of apathy and alienation between the government and the people. A negative situation such as this could signal real
troubles for a democratic society. This is the time for a positive expression of
leadership of the highest caliber. One should remember that, in the final
analysis, no political democracy can be better than the sum of the desires and
achievements of its people.

IMPROVING VOTING BEHAVIOR

Voting behavior can be encouraged and improved by a variety of factors.
Despite the admittedly controversial aspects of the subject, most political scientists would agree that in the United States we vote for too many candidates for too many offices, especially local offices. It is a part of the American political faith that the election method is the proper method with which
to determine the proper holders of power. It is therefore felt necessary to run

candidates for state and local positions as diverse as judges, comptrollers, and, in one state (South Carolina), even the adjutant general.[1] Most voters do not know all of the candidates in such elections, and many are even unsure of the nature of the office being contested. In such cases, where "bed-sheet ballots" serve only to confuse, one wonders if the philosophy of political democracy is not being mocked. The national government in the United States seems to survive quite well through the appointment of most executive department heads and other subordinates of the chief executive, who not only picks them but is held accountable for their conduct. Regulatory heads and national judges are jointly appointed by the president and Congress from lists of people that are theoretically scrutinized to assure quality appointees. This norm has not been easily transferred to the states and counties of our land, and the task of sorting out the candidates and offices has proved formidable enough to discourage a significant number of voters from participating in these elections. In most parliamentary elections, and in local elections elsewhere, the list of offices to be filled is rather small by American standards and is easily managed. Democracy survives.

Another essentially American problem is the primary election, wherein a political party's candidates are chosen for such important offices as the presidency, the U.S. Congress, and state governorships and legislatures. As we saw earlier, in a primary election, anybody can run. If elected (by whatever means—a costly media blitz, personality, charisma, previous exposure to the public in another endeavor, etc.), this person becomes a party candidate whether or not he or she has ever before served the party in any way. Indeed, he or she may never have been a member of the party under whose platform he or she now presumably runs. Furthermore, the leadership of that party may actually despise him or her.

The rise and spread of the primary system in the United States has all but destroyed the already shaky structure of our political parties, as was discussed in chapter 9. In other countries, candidates tend to be chosen by the organized party structure through conventions, caucuses, or other more informal means. One is relatively assured, thereby, that the candidates chosen will both understand the party's basic positions and demonstrate some loyalty to that party.

Finally, voting behavior, at least among that margin of undecideds to which the election campaigns are mostly directed, tends more and more to be influenced by money and the techniques of persuasion developed by the advertising community. At least this is generally assumed to be true. The result in the United States has been an attempt on the one hand to limit the amount of money that can be spent by a candidate or by those on his or her behalf and, on the other hand, a similar attempt to make the publicly regulated media treat serious candidates equally. The problems surrounding

---

[1]This is the military commander of the state's unit of the National Guard. It is the functional equivalent of electing the U.S. Chairman of the Joint Chiefs of Staff by popular vote.

both efforts are horrendous. The same kinds of problems are seen in other countries, such as Japan and Great Britain, where, for many years, serious attempts to control the local campaigns of members of Parliament have been successful, but efforts to control expenditures by the national party as a whole have not. This will be a continuing problem for all political democracies in the years to come. It has been exacerbated in the United States by our propensity to have lengthy political campaigns that radically increase the expense to the candidates and more greatly draw upon the imagination of the image makers. A presidential campaign of two years in length is not at all unusual. Even campaigns for state offices can run from six months to a year. Considering the primary method of selecting candidates to begin with, coupled with the expense and time involved in lengthy campaigns, one wonders if a person of ability but limited resources can ever get elected to an American office on his or her own. When this whole situation is contrasted with the typical parliamentary nominating process and campaign period of three to four weeks, one is left in some envy of that system.

BASES OF REPRESENTATION

The question faced in this section is, who or what shall a representative assembly represent? Most people would immediately reply that it should represent people, and this seems to be the case in the majority of legislatures that exist. However, analysis of past and present legislatures reveals other alternatives for **representation.** The British House of Lords, for instance, during the days of its power as a representative assembly, represented not people but *a class of people.* Only persons born with royal titles or persons given temporary titles (or life peerages) could sit in that body. Further, we saw in the former Soviet House of Nationalities a parliamentary body that represented several *ethnic groups.* Each of the Soviet Socialist Republics was dominated by a different national group, and each of these groups was given representation in the upper house of the Supreme Soviet. Mussolini, in setting up his limited representative assembly in Italy in the 1920s, advocated a system of *functional representation,* in which a person's professional or vocational position would entitle him or her to representation within the parliament. In other words, what a person did in life constituted his or her constituency, and this constituency would be represented in the government. In the Native-American parliament, there are seats set aside for "scheduled tribes," producing what might be called *tribal representation.* Finally, even our own American system deviates from simple, popular representation.

The U.S. Senate does not represent people, even though its members are chosen by the voters. Actually, in accordance with the Constitution, the U.S. Senate represents *geography,* that is to say, the land area of the states. The vast land area of Alaska entitles that state to two senators. The much smaller land area of Rhode Island also entitles that state to two senators because, in the words of the Constitution, "no state, without its consent, shall be deprived of its equal suffrage in the Senate." If the Senate represented population, a vast discrepancy would be present, in that California, with a population of over 20 million, has a representation in the U.S. Senate of two senators, while Alaska, with a population of four hundred thousand, also has two senators. The problem with geographical representation is that it seems to fly in the face of principles of equality before the law that underlie the concept of political democracy. How can one part of a coequal legislative body represent something other than people, or, worse, represent people unequally?

The answer, in the case of the U.S. Senate, is found in the fact that the U.S. Constitution could not have been written without this qualification to political democratic theory. The representatives of the thirteen states who met in Philadelphia in 1787 were sovereign. They did not wish to completely lose their identity in the new national, sovereign government. In order to induce them to give up their sovereignty, the Connecticut Compromise was made. This allowed for equal representation of the people in the House of Representatives, but it protected the identity, if not the sovereignty, of the states by guaranteeing to them equal representation as geographical entities in the U.S. Senate. This compromise was a pragmatic concession to reality. It is not in accordance with democratic theory, but it did produce a government in which political democracy was possible.

The major problem with this is that a theoretical group of twenty-six states can produce a simple majority in the U.S. Senate, while the combined populations of those states do not equal one-half of the nation's population. The result can be the frustration of the will of the majority of the people by a combination of geographically based opposition. Senators from rural, conservative states have often ganged up to prevent the passage of legislation favored by smaller groups of senators representing more populous, urban, and industrial states. This is a situation with which the American people must continue to cope unless we wish to change it by rejecting the Constitution. It is doubtful that we shall choose to do so.

However, if we have to live with geographical representation in the U.S. Senate out of constitutional necessity, we do not have to live with it in the states. Nevertheless, we did live with it for far too long. When our state governments were reestablished, after the promulgation of the U.S. Constitution, most of them chose to copy the basic structure of the national legislature when establishing their own new legislatures. They chose the bicameral model, and, in a predictable way, they established as the lower house a body based on representation of population. Aping the national Congress, they based their upper house on geographical representation, using the county as the base of representation. However, counties were never sovereign, and there was no compelling reason to dilute political democracy by the institution of geographical representation in the states.

The reasons for doing it were reflective of both the conservative tide of the period and a particularly American view of city life. There was in the minds of many people a kind of virtue that came from living in rural environments. The independent farmer, who worked hard and who worked with nature, tended to be viewed as a more trustworthy person and a person given to wise judgments, caution, and moral righteousness. He or she did not go into the sinful city to engage in those sorts of immoral practices as are condoned by the anonymous population of cities. Therefore, it seemed proper to some to check the rash impulses of the urban individual, which might emerge from a popularly elected legislative body, by linking this body to a coequal one dominated by the virtuous, rural people who lived out in the nonindustrialized counties. Therefore, in most of the states, a bicameral legislature was created that represented the people of the cities and large towns effectively in the lower house but represented the farmers and the other rural folk in the upper house in a way far disproportionate to their number. Thus, the senates of the states became the burying ground of popular legislation.

In states such as Alabama, Tennessee, and Georgia, by the 1960s, the situation had become somewhat desperate. Only a few counties were urbanized to any great extent, and the vast majority of the counties were rural and sparsely populated. For example, a bill in the Alabama legislature calling for increased taxation to support something like improvements in municipal sewer systems would pass the house, where the majority of the people speaking through their representatives would agree to its wisdom, only to be defeated in the senate, where rural people dominated and had little interest in the problems of the municipalities.

In the Supreme Court case of *Reynolds* v. *Sims* in 1964, a case that followed two previous cases on the subject, the U.S. Supreme Court declared that geographical representation was counter to the Fourteenth Amendment's provision for equal protection under the law. Since each county had one senator, the citizens of the rural counties with their small populations were much better represented than those who lived in urban counties with their large populations. Thus, a citizen in a rural county was more powerful in his or her ability to influence legislation than a person living in a city. Equal protection under the law meant equal approach to the law. The citizens of cities lacked the same effective approach to the law as citizens of the country. As a result of the *Reynolds* v. *Sims* decision, geographical representation was declared unconstitutional, and upper houses of state legislative assemblies were ordered to be redistricted on a basis of population.

The effect of this and previous decisions was to make the state senates little more than miniature state houses of representation. One would have thought at this time that the wisest move for the states would have been simply to abolish the upper houses, since they had no special group to represent. This did not happen, of course, and I will address the reason in the next section. However, despite an attempt to amend the Constitution to allow for geographical representation in the upper houses of state legislatures, the people of the country as a whole have understood the lack of necessity and the inherent injustice in geographical representation. It is a benchmark on our road to political democracy that the equality of all individuals before the law has now been ratified by both the Supreme Court action and the acceptance of the people in doing away with geographical representation.

Although we are left with the anomaly of geographical representation in the U.S. Senate, we should constantly remind our senators that they should strive somehow to create a national point of view in their deliberations and not act always as defenders of special, local interests. However, we should also always expect to have some difficulty in this regard.

BICAMERALISM AND UNICAMERALISM

Part of the problem with geographical representation in the states might have been avoided if they had adopted **unicameral,** or one-house, legislative assemblies. Instead, they consistently chose to construct two-house legislatures, and the **bicameral** approach to legislation has come to be thought of as an almost self-evidently proper methodology. Is the usefulness of that methodology self-evident? Is there an inevitable advantage in having two houses to write legislation instead of one? To begin with, unicameralism is not unknown to American political practice. Our first national legislature, the Continental Congress, and the second national legislature, the Congress of the Articles of Confederation, were both one-house legislatures. Little concern was noted over this reality at the time. Two of our state legislatures (Pennsylvania and Delaware) during the days preceding the Articles of Confederation were also essentially unicameral. Furthermore, almost all our municipal governments and most of our county governments are unicameral today. Finally, the state of Nebraska has had, since 1937, a unicameral state legislature. We have, therefore, a long and rich history of making laws within the confines of a single legislative chamber.

Apparently, the government of the state of Nebraska is as efficient and secure in its liberties as those of the states immediately surrounding Nebraska that have similar populations and similar problems. Certainly, they seem to produce the same kinds of laws in much less time and at less expense. One wonders, then, why other states do not adopt a unicameral approach to legislation.

The two reasons most often given in defense of bicameralism are:

1. Bicameralism allows for dual consideration of legislative acts, with the result that mistakes made in the first consideration might be resolved through a second. Caution is the watchword of this argument.
2. The existence of two separate, coequal legislative houses makes it more difficult for special interest groups to affect legislation against the popular will. The point here is that lobbyists would be more visible and would have to work twice as hard to achieve their nefarious results.

Let's first examine these reasons and then I'll suggest alternative views on legislative methodology.

With regard to the dual consideration argument, logic cannot be used to prove it. If a mistake can happen in the course of one legislative consideration, why is it not logical to assume that it could happen in the second consideration instead of the first, or perhaps be compounded by even worse folly in the second consideration? One of the assumptions of political democracy is that the people are not always right and that error is possible. It would seem as logical to suggest that a single house might reconsider a bill at any time it chooses within the confines of that one house. Further, if there *is* some logical potential for correcting a mistake during a second legislative hearing, why not have a third house that would give a third consideration, or a fourth house, or, to take it to its logical extreme, why pass legislation at all? The safety of democracy is seen in the ability of any legislature of any type to reconsider any bill at any time. Why burden the law-making process with two considerations of every bill? Logic neither proves nor disproves the advantage of dual consideration, but logic does tell us that dual consideration is more expensive and time-consuming than single consideration.

Turning to the argument of the supposed difficulty of lobbyists, the situation is not quite what it appears at first glance. Lobbyists seldom try to *pass* legislation. More often than not, they are attempting to prevent remedial legislation (which would affect what they are already doing) from being passed. If this is the case, then logic suggests that, in the minority of cases where lobbyists do attempt to pass special legislation, they will indeed find it more expensive and more visible to pursue their aims. However, in the majority of cases, where they are attempting to *prevent* bills from being passed, their job is made much simpler by the existence of bicameral legislatures. All they have to do is pick the smallest group, the Senate, and lobby for the defeat of bills already passed by the House. This is why state senates continue to be the burying ground of legislation, whether they are based on population or not.

In those cases where bribery and corruption are rampant, it is the Senate that is more often on the receiving end of bribes and other corruptive practices. Thus, logically speaking, the lobbyist's job is probably made easier with a bicameral legislature than with a unicameral legislature. Lobbyists play a legitimate role in legislation. They are the providers of important information. One should not assume automatically that there is an evil intent in lobbying. The previous argument is directed at the perversion of lobbying, and bicameralism does not always prove an effective countermeasure.

Finally, with regard to the question of bicameralism, within the United States especially, the federal balance becomes more and more difficult to maintain as government becomes more complex, and issues are seen more and more in the context of the general, rather than the particular, welfare. It would seem that any technique that could enhance the efficiency and lower the expense of state government would enable our federal balance to operate more in keeping with the original assumptions of federalism. It would enable the states to do more of the governing without national interaction. It would seem that a shift to unicameralism would be a very useful technique in this regard.

Unfortunately, the factors that work against the change to unicameralism are formidable. First, in order for a state to eliminate its upper house through constitutional amendment, the upper house itself must voluntarily vote itself out of office without some clear instruction from the people to do so. Second, the tradition of bicameralism is rather hard to shake from the public mind. The arguments for bicameralism, however weak, continue to be the arguments against change. Finally, there is a general reluctance to change *any* political structure as long as it seems to work fairly well. There is always a risk in reform. Until state governments do even worse than they are doing, it is unlikely that the will to change will be manifested. Thus, bicameralism will continue to be a major aspect of American national and state government.

SINGLE-MEMBER DISTRICTS VERSUS PROPORTIONAL REPRESENTATION

DEFINITIONS

The question to be considered here is the link between the people and their representatives. Let's assume, for purposes of illustration, that we are talking about congressional districts in the U.S. House of Representatives. Let's also assume that we are dealing with a state that has six representatives. The question is, how shall these six representatives be linked to the people? Looking at figure 11.1, we see two alternatives. In the first alternative, each of the six representatives could represent the entire state. We call this *at-large representation,* meaning each of the six represents the state at large.

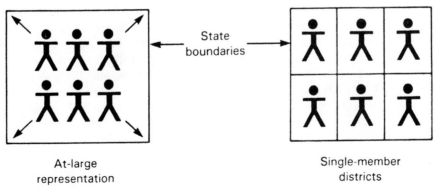

FIGURE 11.1 Two Methods of Electing Representatives

According to the second alternative, we could divide the state into six subdivisions of fairly equal population and call these *congressional districts.* Each district would elect one representative. We call these districts **single-member districts.**

The United States uses the single-member district method in selecting most kinds of representatives. We use it in the cities to elect city council members, electing each from a district called a *ward.* We use it for our county councils, dividing the county into council-seat districts. We divide our states into representative districts and elect one representative from each (or in some instances, multiple members from a single district in a combination of the single-member and at-large methods). Since 1967, we have elected our national representatives, in every case, from single congressional districts. Our executives, including mayors, governors, and the president, are also, in their own way, elected using the single-member district method. The president is elected by state electors, each of whom is chosen from a single district that consists of that person's state. In all of the situations described, there is a clear link between the single representative or the executive figure and a defined set of constituents to whom he or she is ultimately accountable.

The at-large option can be used within the single-member district method, as just noted. However, this device more often reflects an entirely different approach to linking legislators with their constituents. Here, instead of a single person being elected under majority rule, many members are elected from the same district under a different methodology. We call this alternative method **proportional representation.** The way a person gets elected under this system is related to the proportion of the votes in the entire district that went to that person's political party. For instance, if there are three parties wishing to offer candidates in an election involving six representatives in one district, the awarding of seats will be done in accordance with the proportion of votes gained by the three parties.

A ballot of proportional representation might look like the one in figure 11.2. Here Party A fields six candidates—one for each of the seats. Party B is less ambitious; it fields four candidates for the six seats. Party C, a rather weak party, puts up only two candidates. The voter in a proportional representative system does not vote for the candidates. Instead, he or she votes for the party. When the results are in, we find that Party A drew 52 percent of the votes. Party B got 31 percent of the votes, and Party C got only 17 percent of the votes. Therefore, Party A won 52 percent of the six seats. Fifty-two percent of six is three. Party A won three seats. Party B won 31 percent of the seats, and 31 percent of six is two. Therefore, Party B got two of the seats. Party C got only 17 percent of the votes, and 17 percent of six is one. Party C got one seat.

The question that then arises is, who gets the seats? If the ballot was "open," then each party is free to name from the list of candidates on the ballot the ones who will get the seats. If the ballot was "closed," then the

Columbia–6 seats		
Mark here ◯	Mark here ◯	Mark here ◯
Party A	Party B	Party C
1. J. T. Bray 2. B. D. Dulin 3. J. B. King 4. A. T. Harrill 5. B. L. Moon 6. R. W. Wheeler	1. H. D. Backus 2. T. M. Davis 3. R. T. Elliot 4. P. K. Miles	1. B. J. Jones 2. J. M. Smith

Results

Party A   52%
Party B   31%
Party C   17%

FIGURE 11.2   A Proportional Representation Ballot

seating will be done in accordance with the position held by the candidate on the ballot. This means that the first three names under Party A will be seated, and, likewise, the first two under Party B, and the first name under Party C.

Each of the six representatives now theoretically represents the entire population of the district, but in reality what each represents is his or her political party. The party's total strength will determine whether or not it will form the government in a parliamentary system. Proportional representation is most often used in parliamentary systems, and it serves a useful purpose in determining exactly the strength of political parties throughout the nation.[2]

ADVANTAGES AND DISADVANTAGES OF BOTH SYSTEMS

Which is the better system, single-member representation or proportional representation? The answer is not a simple choice between the two. The question is really one of priorities. The question should be, which system produces a mixture of results and conditions favored by a national group? Let's consider the results of choosing either by single-member districts or by proportional representation.

To begin with, the proportional representation system is much more democratic than the single-member district system. Consider a hypothetical case under the single-member system in which the winning party won all six of the seats in each district by a vote of approximately 55 to 45 percent.

[2]The British parliamentary system uses the single-member district method.

This would mean that the winning party has all six seats in the state despite the fact that 45 percent of the people did not vote for the winning candidates, and, therefore, their choice is not represented. Compare that to the situation under proportional representation, in which a party with only 17 percent of the vote was, nevertheless, represented. Under the single-member district system, it is also possible for each seat to be won by a plurality rather than a majority vote if there are more than two parties contesting. Although this is rare, for reasons to be discussed in a few pages, it is nevertheless conceivable that one party might claim all six seats in a state while gaining *less* than 50 percent of the vote, the rest of the vote being divided among two other parties. In this last case, a majority of the people are not represented. Therefore, in terms of accurately reflecting the political spectrum of opinion within the entire state, the single-member district is less adequate than proportional representation.

Second, the method of voting by party is a simpler method of election than trying to distinguish between candidates, with the result that proportional representative contests tend to produce a higher voter turnout than single-member district contests.

Third, there is, in the proportional representative method, a tendency toward party responsibility and political coherency, yielding a clear mandate, since the party must sell to the voters its ideological position rather than the candidates themselves.

On the negative side of proportional representation, this system tends to multiply the number of political parties. This is because the proportional system allows some party representation for even a fraction of public support for a party. In the example, Party C needed only 17 percent of the vote to gain official status in the parliament. The incentive for Party C to organize and to contest the election so as to have a platform from which to advertise its views is therefore quite high. As we saw earlier, parliamentary governments that have many parties tend to be unstable because, the more parties, the less likely for a single-party majority. This, too, is a negative aspect of proportional representation.

Finally, there is a tendency toward advocacy representation in the proportional representation system. Advocacy representation is one of two major role definitions of representation; the other is mirror representation. A representative can be a mirror of his or her constituency, voting in most cases the way he or she thinks they would like. This type is, therefore, more representative. Advocacy representation, on the other hand, involves the legislator's use of his or her own intelligence and imagination in deciding how to vote on an issue. An advocate-type representative assumes that he or she was selected because it was thought that he or she could decide issues better than the citizens themselves. In proportional representation, the representative really represents only the party. His or her name might not even be known to the constituents. Therefore, the individual votes the way he or she thinks the party should vote. Indeed, under party responsibility, he or she votes the way the leadership says to vote, taking little account, in the short run, of the particular wishes of the constituents.

If we compare both the positive and negative characteristics of proportional representation with the single-member district method, we begin to understand the kind of choice that must be made. As we have already seen, single-member districts are less democratic, but they are more stable. The reason for this is that they tend to produce two-party systems. How does this happen?

In a single-member district contest, there is going to be only one winner, not multiple winners as in proportional representation. Therefore, one of two methods must be used to determine the winner. The first method is to require a majority winner. If no candidate gains a simple majority, there will be a runoff election between the top two candidates, ensuring that in the runoff one candidate will have a simple majority. The other method is simply to allow the winner to be determined by a plurality vote, which is to say, the candidate with the highest number of votes gets the job. In either method, generally speaking, a candidate from one of two major parties is the most likely winner. A third party or small party simply does not have a chance because third parties do not win majorities or pluralities. In most countries where the single-member method dominates, as in the United States and Great Britain, small parties do not normally contest legislative races unless they are really the majority party in certain isolated districts. In the United States, third parties generally restrict themselves to presidential politics. The reason for this is found in the peculiar makeup of the American electoral college. This will be discussed in the next section.

Returning to our comparison, the single-member district election, while more complex than proportional representation in that one has to consider individual candidates rather than parties, is nevertheless easier to understand in terms of its results. One simply counts the votes and determines the winner. One need not speculate as to percentages and allocate seats where the percentages are marginal.

Furthermore, there is, in the single-member district method, a tendency toward mirror representation. The idea here is that, if only one candidate is going to be elected in each constituency and, thus, represent only one district, then the voters will know who he or she is and hold that person accountable for some measure of response to the public will, regardless of the political party. This will vary in terms of whether or not the system is presidential or parliamentary, but there is at least some pressure on single-member district representatives to be aware of the needs, if not the desires, of their constituents.

Finally, there is a negative aspect of single-member districting that is uniquely American. It is called gerrymandering, and it will be discussed later in this chapter.

SINGLE-MEMBER DISTRICTING
AND THE ELECTORAL COLLEGE

The reason we have third-party attempts in the American presidential race is found in a little noticed flaw in the structure of the electoral college machinery. First, it is doubtful that the electoral college machinery was ever well thought out, in view of the numerous complaints about it over the long period of its current manifestation in the Twelfth Amendment to the Constitution. Certainly, there have been many movements in our history to alter or abolish this complex and cumbersome system. What is not generally acknowledged in most attempts to debate this question is a logical fallacy contained within the structure itself.

That fallacy is seen in the fact that, in the event that a third party becomes dominant in a small geographical section of the nation and thereby wins a small number of the electoral votes, the third-party candidate can then cause neither of the major party candidates to win a clear majority of the electoral vote. Under the existing machinery, the election must then be transferred, for purposes of a runoff, to the House of Representatives. Remembering that single-member district methodology requires a runoff between the top two candidates, one would expect at this point that, even with the distortion of each state having one vote in the House of Representatives for the purposes of the runoff, a winner *would* nevertheless be chosen between the top two candidates. However, if one reads the Twelfth Amendment, it is found that, in the case of a runoff election in the House of Representatives, the members of the House shall choose from among the top *three* candidates. This means that the third-party candidate would also have to be considered in the voting by the members of the House of Representatives. Further, that candidate's electoral vote in a few states becomes magnified because those states are now coequal with the other states in the House vote. The result is that the small-party candidate is in an enormously powerful bargaining position vis-á-vis the other two candidates. He or she could conceivably extract concessions of enormous consequence. The temptation to do that has led to such third-party candidacies as those of George Wallace in 1968 (which almost succeeded) and of Strom Thurmond and Henry Wallace in 1948. It seems somewhat astonishing that in current times we would still not only suffer the complexity and unnecessary distortion of the electoral college system but that we would also continue the methodological error contained in the Twelfth Amendment.

Under the Twelfth Amendment, the U.S. Senate would choose the vice president in case of a failure of any major party to gain the majority vote in the electoral college. However, the Senate would choose from between the top *two* candidates for that office—the proper method. Perhaps instead of debating the issue of abolishing the electoral college in favor of a popular election, we might, as an interim measure, consider amending the Twelfth Amendment to read that the House of Representatives shall choose from between the top two candidates.

In this general milieu, a conceptual warning should also be registered. One popular proposal for modification of the electoral college is that the electoral votes in each state be apportioned to political parties in proportion to the vote that they get in each state. This, of course, would be an application of proportional representation methods rather than single-member district methods in the selection of the president. I have already noted how these methods tend to produce multiple parties. In short, if we adopted the folly of apportioning the electors from each state in proportion to the vote gained by parties, we would invite multiple-party contests in each state for the simple purpose of diluting the electoral vote and forcing an election in the House of Representatives. One need only consider that, in the case of California, a candidate would need to gain only one-fortieth of the vote in order to gain an electoral vote. This situation would be intolerable, and the American public should avoid this particular "remedial" method at all costs.

GERRYMANDERING

One of the more unfortunate by-products of the single-member district method of selecting representatives is **gerrymandering.** This is defined as the drawing of constituency boundaries so as to benefit one political party over another.[3] Constituency or district boundaries should be drawn in such a way as to make the population balance between the districts as similar as possible. Also the boundaries should be drawn with some reasonable geographical consistency so that geographically contiguous areas can be represented intact as much as possible. In the United States, with the concern for "one-person, one-vote" districting, the Justice Department has suggested that no electoral district should vary from a similar district by more than 5 percent of the population. However, it has long been an American tradition to ignore both equal population constraints and logical geographical contiguousness in drawing district lines. Rather, they have been drawn by the party in power after each ten-year census in order to promote the interests of that party.

Since the *Reynolds* v. *Sims* decision, many state senate districts have been redrawn, and the party in power has all too often applied the gerrymandering concept. The word *gerrymander* dates from early nineteenth-century Massachusetts, where then Governor Elbridge Gerry drew up a district plan that worked to the disadvantage of the Federalist Party and to the advantage of the Democratic Party. This design lumped most of the Federalists of Massachusetts within one district, thereby creating relatively Federalist-free areas

---

[3]The gerrymander has also been used to dilute the power of racial or ethnic minorities. The techniques for these purposes are essentially the same as those used for party reasons.

in other districts. The new Federalist district was very elongated and did not seem to fit any theory of population or geography. A cartoonist drew the district in a newspaper, added two eyes and a tongue, and announced that it looked like a salamander. The governor's name, Gerry, was incorporated into the word *salamander,* yielding *gerrymander,* and it entered into our political vocabulary.

What Governor Gerry did in Massachusetts might be called a *simple gerrymander,* defined as the grouping of all one's opponents into a single district. This can be seen in the diagram on the left in figure 11.3. Here, two pockets of Party B strength have been incorporated by Party A into a single district. This lets Party A claim five of the six districts, yielding only one to Party B.

However, we have become more sophisticated over the years, and now it is possible to use a *compound gerrymander.* This is also seen in figure 11.3 in the diagram on the right. Here, Party A has effectively eliminated *any* influence by Party B by spreading its strength, in small quantities, into all six of the election districts. This is achieved by blocking out on a map the geographical centers of opposition, based on recent election returns. The central point of each geographical pocket is then pinpointed. A line is drawn, linking the geographical central points, and that line becomes a boundary axis

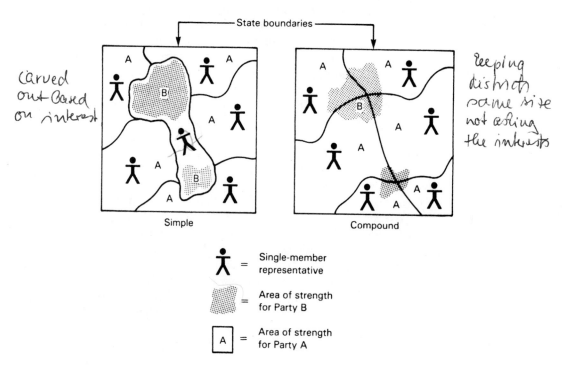

Carved out Based on interest

Keeping district same size not asking the interests

FIGURE 11.3 Two Types of Gerrymander

through which the remaining district lines are drawn. The result is to divide the opposition in each area into four districts, making it the obvious minority in each case. Whether gerrymandering is done by the simple or compound method, its purpose is blatantly political and devilishly effective.

One change in the American pattern of gerrymandering dates from the late 1980s. In order to get more black representation in the Congress, some states, such as Georgia, Louisiana, North Carolina and South Carolina, produced black majority districts that defy all geographical norms. This was referred to as remedial gerrymandering, and it became very controversial. In 1995, the U.S. Supreme Court declared that minority districts based solely on race were unconstitutional. The fall-out from that decision remains to be seen.

The remedy to gerrymandering is superficially simple. The legislature, which generally draws the gerrymandering lines, should be relieved of this responsibility. That responsibility should be given over to an objective, professional districting organization made up of representatives of the Census Bureau, the State Bar Association, or some other group that will not be immediately affected by the drawing of district lines. However, this seemingly simple solution becomes more difficult when one confronts two realities. First, legislatures are reluctant to give up power that tends to enable the majority group within the legislature to maintain itself in power. Second, it is rather difficult, in real terms, to define a purely nonpolitical and objective organization to do the job. Any organization in state government is ultimately politicized. Therefore, we must conclude that some form of gerrymandering, for some purpose or another, will always be a part of the single-member district system. The challenge is for the public to understand it and to try to minimize its effects as much as possible.

QUALIFICATIONS AND CHARACTERISTICS OF LEGISLATORS

There are very few formal qualifications for being a political representative. In theory, almost anyone should be able to represent his or her fellow citizens in a politically democratic legislature. Certainly, an analysis of the membership of most of the legislatures of most of the political democracies demonstrates a clear choice for a fairly ordinary, if not mediocre, group of individuals. Whereas age and citizenship qualifications are noted in the constitutions of political democracies, little else is mentioned. Ages for representation run from a low of twenty-one years for selection to the British House of Commons to a high of thirty-five years for election to the German Senate. In general, the age of qualification in most countries is the early twenties. Almost all countries demand that a representative be a citizen of that nation-state.

Legislators, however, tend more and more to come from two major sources within many countries: the law and business or finance. It should not be surprising that many legislators come from the profession of law.

Lawyers deal with the operation of the law and are, therefore, generally considered qualified to participate in writing the law itself. Furthermore, there is among lawyers an enormous interest in government that impels many of them to seek public office. The second major group, members of the business and financial community, is a growing group in many countries. Here, because business and government are more and more intertwined, there is a natural inclination for senior businessmen and -women to seek to affect the pattern of government in their societies. Also, senior businesspeople have more time to devote to a political career, and often they have, within their own resources, sufficient funds to finance a great portion of the effort involved. Therefore, in many western legislatures, the law and business communities are both very well represented.

In those countries that have a socialist government, there is often a third major source of representatives—organized labor. The British Labor party is a classic example. Labor leaders are very well represented among the members of the British House of Commons and in other legislatures among the European democracies.

What is perhaps more interesting is the question of who is *not* represented in legislative assemblies. In general, there are few engineers, scientists, physicians, and professional entertainers, as well as few blue-collar workers. The legislature is, thus, a semiprofessional organization with a heavy business and legal bias.

One wonders how a legislature can maintain its effectiveness in an era in which more and more questions of government involve very narrow specialties such as genetic research, space engineering, and medicine when most of its members are trained in law and business. The problem is perhaps greater than this. It is not logical to assume that people whose interests lie in the areas of law and business will tend to legislate in favor of legal and business interests, sometimes to the detriment of the general welfare? Will not business-oriented legislatures write business-oriented legislation to the detriment of the working population? Will not lawyers tend to make legislation more complex than it needs to be in order to assure a continuing role for the legal community? Who will write the legislation needed by scientists and engineers as they begin to play a greater role in our national life?

Some have suggested that it is time to rethink the question of who should run for office, and some public effort should be made to try to broaden the characteristics of national legislatures. However, this will be difficult because of the nature of government itself. Specialists in the areas just mentioned tend to be less than enthusiastic about the prerequisites for compromise and the often boring and fruitless mechanizations of a modern legislature. Finally, there is something basically political about lawyers and businesspeople. They are, by nature, agents of compromise and tend to relate to the job requirements of politicians more readily than do specialists with narrower interests. Perhaps in the long run, despite our best efforts to broaden the vocational basis of representation, we will continue to be served for the most part by the legal and business community.

REPRESENTATION AND POPULATION

One of the most subtle and yet important characteristics of popular government is population. This factor alone will have an enormous effect on the ability of a society to achieve political democracy. This is very relevant to the United States and yet often ignored when questions of representation arise. The problem is this: How many people can a representative assembly represent? If we begin by looking at the American system in terms of national legislature, we find that the average member of the House of Representatives represents, in some fashion, over 500,000 people. There are some variations, of course. There are not 500,000 people in Alaska, but they must have at least one representative. However, by and large, representatives are assigned districts with populations approximating 500,000 people.

Can one person represent 500,000 people? It is doubtful that any member of Congress has ever seen his or her entire constituency at any time. It is doubtful that the representative could seek out all the members of the district if he or she tried. It is nightmarish to think that all of them might one day write the representative a letter. If they did, he or she would spend the next two years (a full term in office) answering one day's mail. Should they all attempt to telephone, most of them would never get through. The fact is, one individual *cannot* effectively represent 500,000 persons.

The people who get represented are what we might term the *relevant minority*. This suggests that less than one-half the population of *any* constituency will truly be represented on any regular basis by the congressman or -woman. Probably the American figure is less than 50,000 per district or one-tenth of the total population of the district. Therefore, it seems that we face, in this country, a very difficult situation when we attempt to describe ourselves (and function) as a political democracy.

If we compare our situation to other well-known political democracies, an interesting conclusion may be reached. In Great Britain, each of the 650 members of the House of Commons represents approximately 90,000 people. In France, each member of the National Assembly represents fewer than 100,000 people.[4] General European standards suggest a ratio of 1 to 100,000 or less in assigning representatives to constituencies. In other words, the European political democracies are at least five times as representative as our own.

Is there something we can do to bring our representative factor closer in line with European standards? We could increase the size of the House of

---

[4]Actually, the figures are less significant when diluted by the fact that parliamentary representatives tend to represent parties rather than individuals.

Representatives by a factor of five, but that would leave us with a House of Representatives of over 2,000 members. That would not be a legislature. It would be a mad house. Little, if anything, could be accomplished with so many participants. The problem is that, whereas the average European political democracy has a population of between 20 and 75 million, the United States has a population of over 250 million. We are three to four times as large as our European counterparts. We face a unique problem in trying to achieve effective representation. If we compare ourselves with some non-European countries, we find another interesting situation. The population of India is somewhere in the neighborhood of 850 million. The average member of the Lok Sabha, their lower house, which represents the people, must represent at least one million people. Although democracy is attempted with great earnestness in India, one can quickly realize that it is impossible for the Indian national government to be truly representative in its deliberations. The population of China is well over 1 billion. Therefore, one would not expect any attempt at national political democracy to succeed in the sense of representation. There could be no effective single organ of government big enough to represent such a large population. Russia has a population just under 200 million, and it is now attempting to create a political democracy. Given the difficulties in our own country, with a similar range in population, one would expect that this will be very difficult for the Russians, who lack our experience and our aspirations toward making representation at least marginally meaningful.

HOW WE MAKE IT WORK

What have been our adaptations? How have we made representation possible within such a large and populous nation-state? By and large, it has been through an attempt to maintain open channels of communication between our representatives and anyone in their congressional districts who wishes to be heard. Fortunately, most people do not need to be heard specifically and individually at any given time. Every member of a constituency should know that he or she has access to the representative by way of letters, phone calls, or periodic meetings held at various places within the legislative district. All of these things are generally provided by an effective congressperson. In addition to this, our representatives conduct periodic polls through the mail to solicit information in a manageable form in terms of specific replies to selected questions. Fortunately, there is sufficient apathy among our population to allow even this technique to function with some degree of relevance. Only a small fraction of the population will respond to a poll, go to a periodic public meeting, write a letter, or make a phone call.

There are many congressmen and -women who would secretly like to change the national motto from *E Pluribus Unum* to "Thank God for Apathy." It is their fondest hope that apathy will continue as the basis of the relationship between them and most of their constituents. Nevertheless, we must face the fact that, if our population continues to expand, the job of representation will become increasingly more difficult. Perhaps the United States is already too large to be an effective political democracy on the national level. One hears the ghost of Jean-Jacques Rousseau laughing in the background at our attempts to maintain reasonable contact between our people and our national legislature. Here, again, is a challenge to maintain and strengthen the federal relationship and keep government in the states as much as possible. This will require greater efforts to improve the quality of state government. This challenge must be met if the United States is to continue to be a political democracy.

LEGISLATION BY COMMITTEE

Another subtle problem in achieving effective political democracy is the committee system of most legislatures. Legislative committees are an outgrowth of two phenomena of modern government. First, there is the enormous increase in the number of bills that must be considered by a legislature in the contemporary world. Many problems that, in the past, were not subject to legislative attention now are, and the workload of bodies such as the U.S. Congress can achieve enormous proportions. A second problem related to the first is the growing specialization of legislation. Legislators now face the task of drafting laws relating to medical, environmental, scientific, technical, and even psychological concerns. Not only is it difficult for the average legislator to deal with all of the bills he or she faces and make a judgment about them, but he or she must also be able to understand a variety of highly technical information.

The committee system addresses both of these problems. First, it divides the legislature into special committees in order to break up the workload of the entire body. Instead of each bill going before the entire membership for full consideration, the committees can consider fifteen to twenty-five different bills at the same time. Further, each committee can specialize in a certain kind of legislation. A labor committee specializes in labor legislation, while a banking and finance committee specializes in that area. Scientific legislation can go before a committee on science and technology, whereas questions such as welfare and taxation can go before a committee specializing in those areas.

A new member of the legislature who already possesses certain expertise can be placed on the appropriate functional committee and thereby enhance its ability to cope with that particular kind of bill. If a legislator has no relevant experience, he or she may be placed on a single committee and over the years acquire a special knowledge of its particular area of concern. In either case, not only is workload broken up through simultaneous committee attention to numerous bills, but functional expertise is also gained by the types of committees that are created. Thus, there seems to be a good reason to break up a legislature into special committees.

There is a price to be paid for this. In effect, a citizen is not so much represented in the national legislative body as he or she is in the particular committee on which his or her representative serves. If a person is a military veteran and his or her own representative serves on the Veterans Committee, that person will be well represented indeed, but only on those questions concerning veterans. If, at the same time, the same individual runs a small business and his or her representative is not on the Small Business Committee, then he or she is not as well represented.

THE STRONG-COMMITTEE SYSTEM

The strong-committee system in this country in national and state legislatures works in such a way that the real legislature for most bills is the special committee to which they are assigned for major consideration. This is true because the members of the special committee decide whether or not to consider a bill; whether, and in what way, to amend it; and whether to vote it out with a favorable recommendation or an unfavorable recommendation. If the committee decides to combine one bill with another, producing an entirely new bill, this will be done. If the committee decides to pigeonhole (not consider) a bill, then that bill is usually dead. If, on the other hand, a committee decides to strongly support a bill before the entire legislative body, then that bill will most likely pass. The members of the full legislative body will generally get a chance to vote on a bill that comes out of committee, but it must be understood that this opportunity will occur after second reading of the bill and after the legislative predisposition toward the bill has already been established. There is usually only a marginal chance to amend or defeat a bill after it has received strong support by its own committee. Therefore, representation is diluted by the existence of strong committees.

It does not seem possible to do away entirely with committees or their effect on legislation because of the aforementioned difficulties of workload and the need for functional expertise. Beyond this, the United States has a particular problem relating to committees that has been addressed somewhat but remains vexingly difficult for American government. This is often referred to as the seniority problem.

Actually, this problem is not one of seniority at all. This is a false issue if one analyzes it closely. Presumably, the seniority issue concerns the fact that the chairperson of a special committee has generally been the person with the most seniority on the committee if he or she is a member of the majority party. Therefore, it is said that the legislature becomes government by gerontocracy, which means government by the old. The committee chairperson often has the power to decide what bills should be heard, when they will be heard, whether amendments will be allowed, and who will be invited to attend hearings as the bill evolves. The committee chairperson sets the date for voting on the bill and has an enormous impact on the specifics of the bill. Therefore, when older members of the legislature, who sometimes are rather conservative, gain this power, it tends to frustrate the will for change that often exists among younger members of the committee.

The problem, however, is not the seniority of the chairperson. Indeed, there is a certain logic in suggesting that the most experienced individual ought to chair the committee, whether he or she is conservative or not. Nor are all senior people conservative in their attitudes. The basic problem is that the committee chairperson has had too much power. In an already diluted representative structure that has resulted from the necessary committee system, it seems less than necessary for the crucial decisions with regard to a bill to be placed in the hands of any one person, be that person the eldest or the youngest member of the committee. There is no reason to suppose that most of the decisions ordinarily made by the committee chairperson could not be made by a majority vote of the members of the committee.

During the early 1970s, a series of reforms were undertaken in the U.S. Congress to curtail some of the powers of committee chairpersons. As usual, the rhetoric was mostly directed at the issue of seniority. The Democratic Caucus, after 1975, began to elect the chairperson of the standing committees every two years from candidates not always limited to those members who were the most senior. Even though most of those elected proved to be the senior members, some younger members became chairpersons of a few committees. In addition, a long-term tendency to create more and more subcommittees was accelerated in order to "share the wealth" of committee chairs. One of the more significant effects of all of this has been some growing circumspection by some of the old-guard chairpersons toward the more flamboyant exercise of their traditional powers, lest they fall victim to a "caucus coup" when next the biennial chairperson elections occur.

Despite all of the effort at reform, the more things change, the more they stay the same. The chairpersons of the old committees and the new subcommittees still exercise enormous power over legislation falling under their jurisdiction. Power remains a magnet that repels reform while it attracts the ambitious.

Why, then, haven't the other members of the committees in such bodies as the U.S. Congress voted to alter the power of the chairperson? As we have seen, this can easily be done, since the organizational structure of a legislature is entirely up to its members. Perhaps the reason for the reluctance of the nonpowerful members to strip further the committee chairpersons of their powers can be seen in a completely different context. The answer can best be discussed by use of an example.

Suppose you were asked if, given adjustments for inflation, an income of $50,000 per year would be adequate for your needs. Most people would probably agree that it would be. If you were then asked if you would be willing to support legislation that would make it impossible for any person to make more than $50,000 per year, would you also support that? In all probability, you would not. Why, then, would you be reluctant to pass legislation limiting incomes to $50,000 when you have already decided that $50,000 is adequate? The answer is generally that you would like to have the opportunity to make more if that should become possible. In a sense, this is what happens in the U.S. Congress. The average member of the committee may still feel that the power of the chairperson is excessive, but he or she would not vote to completely abolish it because there is always the chance that, given enough reelections, the less powerful member might become the committee chairperson and inherit its great powers. Thus, we should not expect much to be done with the so-called seniority problem. At least we should recognize that the rhetoric is generally misplaced and that the problem is not seniority but the concentration of unnecessary power in the hands of a few key individuals.

OTHER TYPES OF COMMITTEE SYSTEMS

There are two types of legislative committee other than the strong-committee system that I have described. There is, in Great Britain, for instance, a weak-committee system characterized by having the special function committee receive a bill after it has been passed by Parliament as a whole. The purpose of this committee is simply to restate the bill so that it now reflects all amendments and ideas that evolved in parliamentary debate and so that it is in proper form for enrollment into the law code. This requires specialization, and it is helpful to have many committees doing this for different bills at the same time. The committee itself, however, plays little substantive role in the evolution of the legislation. In effect, the Cabinet is the committee for most bills insofar as their submission and their evolution before the parliamentary body.

In the Italian Senate there is another type of committee, the super committee. Here, a functional committee of the Senate becomes the entire legislature for bills submitted to it from the lower house. No plenary decision is required. If the committee approves the bill, that is the end of the Senate reconsideration. This is a much stronger committee than we find in the United States, but the main function of the Senate committee is simply to address a bill already passed by the lower house and to make only small changes, if any.

THE FUTURE OF REPRESENTATIVE DEMOCRACY

During the course of this chapter, I have discussed a number of problems relating to the nature and structure of representative democracy. In previous chapters, we looked at other problems. With regard to the judiciary, chapter 6 addressed the problems that are of particular concern to contemporary American government. With regard to the executive branch, chapter 4 pointed out some of the difficulties with the American single executive as opposed to the more numerous collegial executives of the world. Most of the problems, however, are to be found in the heart of the governing system—the legislature. Questions with regard to legislative districting, the comparison between proportional representation and single-member district methods, bicameral versus unicameral legislative structures, the qualification and vocational backgrounds of legislators, the size of the population of the country attempting political democracy, and even such apparently benign questions as the nature of committee structure and the basis of representation all combine to produce situations that, more and more, demand that all participants in a political democracy understand the inevitable difficulties in any contemporary attempt to make this system work the way it was designed to work.

The future of democratic government is a frequently debated subject. Former Representative to the United Nations and U.S. Senator Daniel Patrick Moynihan stated in the 1980s that the democracies of the world are on the decline insofar as numbers are concerned. Other people have expressed a similar fear that the world is too complex for representative government. Nevertheless, the 1990s have seen the greatest outpouring of democratic yearnings in this century. The collapse of the eastern European empire of the Soviet Union, the reunification of Germany, the break-up of Yugoslavia, and the rise of fifteen separate Soviet "republics" searching for new ways of government have all led to various attempts at achieving at least some level of democracy. In a similar but less dramatic fashion, countries in Latin America and Africa are also throwing off the yoke of authoritarianism and seeking representative government. While this is a thrilling sight to behold, one might ponder the tasks ahead with some trepidation. There is no guarantee that all will succeed. Truly, we live in interesting times.

The problems that will plague the new states and governments are the need for rapid economic development, a lack of unity of the people, old animosities held in check by old governments but now brought to the surface, a lack of a strong public philosophy among the people, cynicism, apathy, and corruption. These last three problems will affect even established democracies, especially in times of economic decline. The antidote is knowledge and faith. These are not easy things to impart to people, but it is time for all political democracies to begin to understand that a proper political education is not a luxury but a necessity and that care should be given to see that the necessary degree of nationalism that normally accompanies such education is supported by an objective and honest appraisal of the functioning of the system. Here is where the question of the future of political democracy will ultimately be answered.

POINTS TO PONDER

Do you see voting as a privilege or a duty? Why?

Europeans vote in greater proportion than Americans do. Is this good, bad, or irrelevant to the future of democracy in this country?

Why do you suppose that unicamerialism as a political dynamic is more popular in Europe than in America?

What do unicamerialism, parliamentary government, and strong political parties suggest about differences between European attitudes toward government and those in America?

12 | International Politics

This chapter will outline the principles of politics and what passes for government on the international level. With the exception of the material discussed in chapter 3, up to now I have largely limited the narrative to one of politics and government *within* the nation-state. (It might be useful for the reader to review that chapter before going into the material that follows.) Now we will examine political activities as they occur across the lines of sovereignty, and, as one might suspect, the problems of *achieving* political solutions to conflicts in this arena are difficult at best.

FOREIGN POLICY AND THE NATIONAL INTEREST

As of this writing, there are approximately 175 political entities that claim to be sovereign states, completely independent in their dealings with each other. On the surface, this appears to be a prescription for chaos. As we shall see, this is because each state has its own agenda of interests. The national interest of each state is nothing more than a collection of goals and values that each state seeks in the world. For example, the national interests of the United States have remained essentially the same over many decades: to prevent the domination of Europe by a single power, to maintain a balance of power in East Asia, to secure the Western hemisphere, to preserve access to Persian Gulf oil, to strengthen free trade, and to protect U.S. assets and citizens overseas.

Who decides what a nation's interests are? Unfortunately, for most nation-states, that decision is not made by the general public, even in political democracies. Such decisions are the prerogative of a policy elite, usually made up of the highest leaders of the government, the military high command, the major leaders of the business and financial community, and certain intellectuals from universities, think tanks, and journalism.[1] This is

---

[1] If you want to know precisely who most of them are in the United States, consult the current membership of the *Council on Foreign Relations,* which lists its members publicly in its annual report.

so because most people do not know very much about the world (or seem to care to), are not immediately involved (unless fighting in some war), have little experience in world affairs, and do not have the responsibility for these kinds of national decisions. The opposite is true for the afore-mentioned groups, and the fate of nations is, for good or ill, left to their machinations. Until publics take the trouble to truly inform themselves and to focus on world issues, this will remain the case, even among demo-cratic governments.

The problem is that the goals and values that make up the national inter-est of one state are not shared by other states. Indeed, some of them are directly antithetical to the interests of other states. Thus, there are potential and real disputes about such things as the nature of the world economy, who gets what raw materials, and who prevails in the various international conflicts of our time. A further complication, as we saw in chapter 3, is that some of these interests are considered *vital* to the security of the state and are, therefore, backed by force, while others are deemed *secondary* and sub-ject to negotiation. Which is which? The question that arises from all of this is, how does a state navigate through this ungoverned thicket of conflicts, desires, and ambitions—those of its own and those of other states? The answer is that each nation-state adopts a policy, a direction to take, referred to as its foreign policy.

Foreign policy is not only the choice of directions to take toward one's national goals, but also the amount of power one wishes to commit *to* those goals. It may also involve a decision to abandon certain goals whose attain-ment is judged to be too costly. Perhaps, on occasion, a nation's foreign pol-icy will require a decision to fight for an interest deemed vital to the state. After all, there are over twenty wars going on in the world as of this writing. However, a major consideration is that no one nation-state, even a super-power such as the United States, has power superior to that of any possible combination of states that might oppose it. One can never be sure that the power committed toward the attainment of a foreign policy goal will be suf-ficient to achieve that goal. Thus, foreign policy is far from an exact science, and decisions of this nature are extremely difficult.

Sources of power for a nation to use in this quest include obvious things, such as its population, geographical area and natural resources, military armaments, and industrial strength. It also includes such subtle elements as the quality of education and training of the public, the food supply, the morale of the people, the cohesion of the government, the reputation of the nation-state in world affairs, and the diplomatic skills of the nation's lead-ers. The central idea is to apply only as much power as is necessary to achieve the end sought and to match the cost of the power used with the presumed value of the goal. From these elements of power, one senses the same three *types* of power that we saw in chapter 2: military, economic, and psychological power. Again, one can argue that the best type of power for achieving one's goals peacefully would be psychological power, but, in a world of sovereign nation-states without a government to control them, force and economic power (such as trade sanctions) are often used.

NATIONAL SECURITY

The preoccupation of a nation state's military (and their central function) is generally referred to as national security. That being the case, what does the concept of security mean, especially on the national level? Webster defines security as, "the state of feeling free from fear, danger and doubt." One can quickly perceive, then, that security is essentially a psychological phenomenon; it begins in the mind of the perceiver. Whereas a state's national security is often based on tangible realities (soldiers, guns, ships, missiles, planes, etc.), except for the case of an actual war, the end product is essentially mental, and the question that arises is this: what fears, dangers and doubts must be addressed in the national mind, and through what means, in order for a general sense of security to occur?

Let us shift the focus to a personal level. What makes an individual feel secure or insecure? What can be done about it? Are his or her fears and doubts based on real dangers, or are the dangers merely imagined? If the fears are imagined or irrational, does it follow that the response to them will also be irrational? Can complete security be achieved? If not, and if, therefore, security exists only in degrees, what degree of security is necessary for a healthy person? Can security be diminished or increased by certain actions? If so, does not the search for security involve a rational assessment of real dangers followed by a rational degree of activity to address them? These questions highlight several aspects of the security dilemma for people as individuals or in groups (nations).

Certainly individuals fear many things. There are real dangers in our world. Some degree of doubt about one's well-being is ever present. Consider three common dangers—physical assault, serious illness, and auto accidents—as applied to the questions raised previously. In seeking security in the face of these possibilities, a rational person would avoid placing himself or herself in a position where people are inclined to be physically assaulted such as in a bad neighborhood; take care of one's health through exercise, proper diet, immunizations, and the avoidance of dangerous activities such as smoking; and wear safety belts while driving ones car sensibly and defensively. These cautionary steps should produce a reasonable degree of security through diminished fear and doubt. Nevertheless, one could still be shot while in a bank that is being robbed; get Legionnaire's disease while on a cruise ship; or be hit head-on in one's car by a drunk driver coming over a hill in one's own lane of traffic. In short, there is no absolute security. It can only be achieved in degrees. Sadly, at some point, we will all die of something! The key to a normal level of security is in properly assessing the likelihood of perceived dangers and taking rational measures to address them. Thus, the best that a rational person can hope for is to live with relative security in a world of uncertainty.

However, some people might seek to maximize their degree of security. When addressing the three dangers listed they might barricade themselves in their houses and never leave; reduce their contact with people and any other conceivable carrier of disease (like Howard Hughes did in his latter days); and never ride in a vehicle of any kind. Whereas these actions might actually increase the degree of one's security, a rational person might find them peculiar to say the least. By overreacting to the dangers they face, they have seriously diminished the quality of their lives.

What of nation states? What do they fear? What dangers are out there to be addressed? What is necessary for their security, and to what degree should they pursue it? War is usually the major preoccupation as it has been for centuries. It has been said for many decades that those who would prevent war should prepare for it. No rational person looking at the world would dismiss the possibility that a war could come at some time. (I will have more to say on that subject later in this chapter.) A rational nation, like a rational individual, must accurately assess the danger of war and then respond with rational measures to prevent it or deal with it when it comes. War is a collection of dangers including nuclear attack, conventional mass destruction, lesser levels of the loss of lives and territory, loss of markets and raw materials, subversion of the government or that of one's allies, and even state-sponsored terrorism. How likely are these eventualities? How much must be done to address them and at what cost? Can a nation be as irrational as some individuals in both assessing dangers and attempting to counter them?

The sad fact is that, for a period of over forty years, we Americans have greatly exaggerated the overall threat of nuclear war and have overreacted to other threats as well. We have constructed, over the past four decades, a large and enormously expensive military machine (with its inherent waste and inefficiency) in order to make us feel better about the possibility of attacks from a variety of sometimes questionable sources. The quality of our lives has been diminished to a significant extent, and, ironically, our sense of security has itself often been diminished.

During an actual war, a nation can erect a large and complex military organization and rationalize its waste and inefficiency because of the single, unifying objective of preserving the state itself. The military's inevitable negatives are usually balanced by a high state of morale, self-sacrifice, and dedication among a tolerant public willing to support the enterprise no matter what it costs. However, in peacetime, a military organization, undirected toward a singular task, inevitably falls prey to a darker side wherein ambition, greed, waste, and cynicism take root. Knowing that a rational and intelligent nation will reduce its military to a level that balances the public's concept of threat with a reasonable ability to respond to it, the American military, supported by its industrial suppliers, seized the initiative in defining what the threats to American national security actually were throughout the period of the Cold War, and it continues to do that. In many ways, the Cold War, especially after 1955, became the military's substitute for an actual war that would justify their existence on a high level. The military's "vision" of threats, (a vision shared with those who support its activities for whatever purposes) has become the nation's view as well.

Unfortunately, in our preoccupation with military threats, we have tended to downplay other dangers more immediate and more fearful than unlikely military confrontations. Nation-states can also be destroyed from within through economic collapse, social breakdown, disease, environmental disaster, and a loss of public commitment to national goals. The United States is in some danger from all of these. What do we do about these realities? How much fear and doubt are we prepared to endure in proportion to the amount of remedial action we are prepared to take?

It would appear, judging from the public policies of the past five administrations, that we are inclined to live with these internal threats and suffer the consequences of domestic violence, growing economic deprivation, sickness, environmental entropy, and declining morale. What we are apparently not prepared to do is to tolerate perceived military threats, real or imagined.

Apparently, we are prepared to expend vast resources rather than run any risk of a military attack. Sometimes we have even been prepared to start wars in order to reduce the outside possibility that one might be started against us. Thus, scarce public resources that might go toward better schools, job creation, the rebuilding and modernizing of our industrial infrastructure, research for new economic products or the control of disease are committed to the military without a great deal of regard to efficiency or effectiveness. Is this rational? If not, why do we do it?

SOCIALIZATION TO THE MILITARY VIEW OF NATIONAL SECURITY

The answer is that we have been carefully taught. We have been conditioned to this view of the world by a long line of opinion leaders since World War II who have had their own agendas and reasons. The decisions to focus on the military aspect of security have mostly been made for us, and we have accepted this without a great deal of complaint. The American people have essentially conceded to the military "experts" and their supporters all decisions about such things as missiles, armed force levels, deployments, equipment, and levels of defense expenditure. The citizenry has accepted, with little debate, their statements of our military vulnerability to a wide array of foreign nations, some large and others, ridiculously small. How did we come to be conditioned to this? The answer begins at the end of World War II.

We, as a nation, emerged from that vast conflict strong, full of energy and standing on the threshold of a full and rewarding national life. When it came to a deep understanding of this brave new world, the majority of Americans were mired in a traditional ignorance of world politics. They were ready to accept the views of a political, economic, and military leadership that had just piloted the country through a great war and had brought the ship of state safely home. There seemed to be no need for the public to ask hard questions or to seek to understand for themselves the complex truths about the emerging Cold War. An emerging class of geopolitical "experts" provided the answers—obvious "truths," many of which were passionately believed by those who described them. Alas, not all of those "truths" reflected the greater realities of world politics. Others knew this. They were doubtful of the simplistic answers of the day and the necessity for turning this nation away from its previous practice of limited, though adequate, military power and an initial reliance on political, economic, and moral suasion in our dealings with other nations. They seriously doubted the necessity to convert this nation into a garrison state with a permanent wartime economy and its resultant social structure in order to deal successfully with the Soviet Union and other threats perceived by the "experts." In their view, we were scaring ourselves silly out of both ignorance and the ambitions of some who saw their own future and fulfillment in a world order controlled by America and in which they would play a major role. Unfortunately for those who would keep the military element of our government in check, the United States confronted a series of events that soon robbed them of their effectiveness. A series of actual (but ultimately manageable) threats by the Soviet Union toward Turkey, Greece, and Berlin during 1947 and 1948, and a communist take-over of Czechoslovakia during the latter year provided the impetus for the establishment of the **North American Treaty Organization** (NATO), a peacetime draft, the **Central Intelligence Agency** (CIA), a separate Air Force, a new version of the wartime **Joint Chiefs of Staff,** and the **National Security Council**—in other words a basic re-creation of the old World War II fighting organization. The "Truman Doctrine," proclaimed in 1947, all but declared a global Cold War, which ensued for the next forty-five years and was aimed at the "containment" of a "worldwide" Soviet threat. The fact that little or no military action was required to address the contemporary threats to Greece, Turkey or Berlin (or Iran in 1946) seemed to escape the "experts" somehow.

By 1950, we began a military build-up that, in many ways, continues despite some marginal cut-backs in spending and the closing of some obsolete bases. The "fall of China" in 1949; the Korean war of 1950–53; and a few spy cases led to the era of **McCarthyism** (a fit of national panic and paranoia), which from 1950–54 further foreclosed any rational debate about the true dimensions of any actual threats the country faced.

By 1955, the military was firmly established as a permanent part of our social structure, ever ready to protect us from any conceivable enemy. The actual fighting forces were buttressed by an industrial and intellectual structure with deep roots into the government, including the Congress, and the society as a whole. A kind of Cold War Catechism evolved wherein the Soviet Union and its communist ideology was described as a singular, monolithic, militant, expansive, and ubiquitous worldwide threat requiring massive military power to contain it. It was as if Hitler had become Stalin, the USSR had become Germany, and communism was the same as Fascism. Thus the catechism declared that the Soviet communists would take advantage of any weakness on our part either by force or through the use of traitors and spies, and pursue, mindlessly, their territorial expansion all over the world. This vision pushed by those in government, the media, and the defense industries was so powerful that it made serious debate fruitless if the debater valued his or her job or reputation. However, except for the problematic Cuban Missile Crisis of 1962, one searches in vain for an actual set of circumstances that seriously threatened the basic security of our country from 1955 to the present (a period of over forty years!). Nevertheless, we continued to repeat the Cold War Catechism whenever any set of circumstances occurred that even looked like a Soviet threat. Thus began our collective failure, through today, to reverse the tide of ignorance, fear, greed, and ambition leading us to stalemate in Korea, disaster in Vietnam, and incredible levels of material and intellectual waste.

It is time for a serious reassessment of the proper role for the military to play within the broader context of actual threats to our country. We also need to reexamine those internal weaknesses that threaten us more than our so-called adversaries ever could. Not to do so could invite the same economic and social collapse in America that we saw in the Soviet Union during the 1990s, for if we do not soon learn to better perceive what really threatens us as a nation, the internal collapse of America as we have known it becomes a possibility.

NATIONAL SECURITY STRUCTURES

Turning from the contemporary American military ethos (an approach not currently shared by the rest of the world's major powers with the possible exception of China) let us examine how nation-states organize for their military security. One is tempted to introduce various organizational charts from the world's great powers to illustrate how the national security policies are made among them. I shall not do so. It has been said (and rightly so) that organization charts show how things would work if it were not for the personalities involved. In the national security area, the situation is infinitely worse. There are enormous sums of money at stake, and, as we have already seen, there is also a tendency to overstate threats so as to safeguard not only the state itself but also the power of those who are involved in the financial end. Indeed, whatever the formal organization of a nation-state's defense structure, one can be fairly certain of this universal key to military power within the state: that, *outside of an actual war, those who do the military planning, set its various programs and budget the resources are the ones who are actually in control of the enterprise no matter what the formal structures might imply.*

ORGANIZATIONAL PRINCIPLES

Beyond this, there seem to be five major organizational principles at work in the national defense structures of most of the larger powers. They are:

1. Executive Leadership
2. Combined Services
3. Interservice Rivalry
4. Interdepartmental Coordination
5. Civilian Control

Executive Leadership

The first and most striking similarity in all the major nations' military structure is its relationship to the executive function of government. Whether this leadership emanates from a single president, as in the United States and France (insofar as defense is concerned), or from a prime minister and his or her innercabinet, one does not usually see much by way of initiative coming from either the legislature or the courts, and when those bodies do attempt to interject their views, the executive structures invariably resist and do so with general success for the most part. Military policies need to be clear, consistent, and long term, and there must be a singular chain of command and communication. The executive is therefore the logical place to locate this kind of authority. Legislative action can take place with regard to certain aspects of the budget and general foreign policy topics related to the military, but intrusions into such issues as weaponry, doctrine, strategy, and the like are generally unwelcome outside of the United States. Our separation of powers structure invites the Congress to go much farther than the legislative role within most parliamentary governments. The ability of Congress to have effect here waxes and wanes from time to time depending on the capabilities of the executive and the issues of the day. It is an area of much controversy given the ambiguities of the Constitution in this regard.

Combined Services

Prior to World War II, armies and navies were generally ruled separately by different executive departments. For instance, in America, the War Department ran the army while the Navy Department ran that service. In Great Britain, the Admiralty ran the navy while the War Office oversaw the army. The British added an Air Ministry during the 1920s while the United States allowed the army and navy to develop their own air capabilities separately. A similar pattern to that of Britain prevailed in most countries. In the earliest years of World War II, the British created the Combined Staffs as a coordinating body through which to prosecute the war. In 1942, the United States followed suit by creating the Joint Chiefs of Staff, which though abandoned in 1946, was resurrected in 1947 with the Air Force as a separate entity within it. In 1964, the British formed a centralized Ministry of Defense to control their three service organizations. By the 1950s the Soviet Union had combined its five services (ground forces, navy, air forces, strategic rocket forces and air defense forces) within a single Military Council. Likewise, the French have a Committee of Chiefs of Staff, and most other major nations combine their forces either directly in a joint body or indirectly through a ministry of defense. The central idea is that modern war requires coordination of all major elements of the military so that missions are carried out efficiently and without undue duplication of effort or cross purposes.

Interservice Rivalry

"The best laid plans of mice and men go oft astray" said one poet. Despite the efforts of coordination of the separate army, naval and air services noted previously, all major military organizations manage to succumb to interservice rivalries of various kinds. Two areas of dispute generally arise. The first, and greatest, is money. Who gets what portion of the budget? The battles are usually played out within the various coordinating committees noted previously, but the politics can be vicious, leading to a lack of cooperation in other areas of concern to national security. Although these decisions should be made with a view toward maximizing the national capabilities through rational balances among forces, many times compromises have to be made that lessen the overall effectiveness of the military. The second problem is missions. Which service controls transportation? How can you coordinate military intelligence gathering and distribution? Does the army and the navy need their own separate air capability? And so it goes.

In 1961, under Secretary of Defense Robert McNamara, the United States attempted to address both problems through the Planning, Programming, Budgeting System, which placed these functions in the hands of the Joint Chiefs of Staff who would, presumably, cause the services to work together in planning their priorities, programming their resources, and budgeting accordingly. It has seldom worked out that way. After over thirty years of trying, interservice rivalry continues both here and in other countries.

Interdepartmental Coordination

Gone are the days when the leadership of a nation decided to go to war and then turned the enterprise over to the army and navy to fight it. In the twentieth century, especially after World War II, national security policy has become an ongoing concern in which military capability is combined with diplomatic activity, economic policy, and intelligence gathering and dissemination. This requires the same kind of coordination as that between the services. Realizing this, the United States created the National Security Council (NSC) in 1947 to bring together the Joint Chiefs of Staff, the Secretary of

Defense, the Secretary of State, the Secretary of the Treasury, the Director of the Central Intelligence Agency, and the vice president to assess threats, coordinate security activities, and to evaluate the effectiveness of current policies. Other nations have done the same. Smaller countries do this within the innercabinets of their executive organizations. Germany has a Federal Security Council similar to our NSC. The French, British, and Russians do it within their ministries of defense. How this is organized is of lesser importance than the requirement that it be done in some fashion.

Civilian Control

From the days of the American Constitutional Convention of 1787 to the coming of democracy to the Western world, the principle of civilian control of the military has been a consistent measure of the quality of that democracy. Indeed, it is almost axiomatic that when military leaders control the civilian government, a state ceases to be a democracy. Civilian control is usually exercised through a bureaucracy headed by a civilian minister or secretary of defense who is, in turn, subordinate to the civilian executive, either singular or plural. Further, military budgets are essentially dependent upon a civilian legislature.

In the United States, civilian control is buttressed by placing civilian secretaries of the army, navy, and air force parallel to the services' various chiefs of staff. In addition, since 1958, the Joint Chiefs of Staff have been taken out of the direct chain of command of their services and replaced by unified and specified commanders, organized on a geographical or functional basis, under the direct command of the Secretary of Defense, a civilian. These same basic principles apply to today's Russia, but there is growing concern among close observers that military ambition to rule that unhappy land may yet undermine the emerging forces of democratic rule there. Time will tell.

BASIC PROBLEMS IN NATIONAL SECURITY

A major difficulty in the pursuit of national security is that it takes place within the context of what is called the threat system. That system is seen as the inevitable by-product of the nation-state system wherein sovereignty and nationalism lead to a competitive and conflict-prone world assumed to be unstable. Further complicating the situation is the assumption that, despite alliances with other nation-states and organizations such as the United Nations (which will be discussed later) each player (state) in the game of national security is essentially on its own; it is a self-help system. The world is seen in Hobbesian terms of inevitable conflict requiring the maximization of one's military options lest the life of the state become "nasty, brutish and short." At least this is the military view.

However, as citizens of a nation-state based on Lockeian views of the social contract and the possibilities for human cooperation within a milieu of compromise, we will at least attempt to challenge the dismal view of the militarists. Indeed, I would argue that the threat system as we have come to know it is beset by inadequate models and impaired assumptions about the world we actually live in and are likely to remain in for some time. Let us examine some of its flaws.

The threat model assumes that when states find themselves in conflict, violence is a predictable outcome. At some point, there will likely be an aggressor and a victim. If your state does not wish to become the victim, then it had better be able to deter the aggressive intent of its adversary or overcome it in battle. This kind of mind set finds it difficult, if not dangerous, to ask some simple questions we often ask when internal conflicts arise within the nation-state itself: "What do they want? Why do they want it? What will it cost us to grant it? What can we get in return?" and so on. And yet, more and more international conflicts are actually dealt with in this manner than through violence. Otherwise, the world would be constantly at war.

Another assumption is that a nation's military capabilities are synonymous with its intent to use them. This is the best explanation for the nuclear arms race between the United States and the former USSR (1961–91) as one is apt to find. When we decided to produce 1,000 solid fuel intercontinental ballistic missiles (ICBMs) in 1961–63 when the Soviets had less than fifty missiles, which were liquid fueled and thus slower to fire and less reliable, they assumed that we meant to attack them. Thus began, in 1964, an enormous Soviet arms build up reaching a level of about 1,500 missiles, convincing us by 1979 that a window of vulnerability existed wherein we were subject to an imminent attack from them. History will show that neither country had the slightest intent of attacking the other with nuclear weapons. Nation-states increase or decrease their military capability from time to time. To assume that these changes imply some specific intent is to go back to the late 1930s when Hitler's arms build up was specifically directed at his aggressive megalomania. Hitler is dead, yet, as we have already seen, his ghost still haunts the military mind.

A more basic flaw in the threat system view is that it overlooks the many forces of interdependency among nations including trade and monetary stability; technical cooperation in communications, transportation, health, science, and meteorology; mutual fears of annihilation; and concern for the environment. Whereas these things have not yet produced a functional world community, they do indicate a strong and increasing preference for the integrative aspects of human life over those things that divide us. Perhaps instead of spending so much time studying the wars that have happened during the past two centuries, we should study those that didn't in order to discover how cooperative dynamics overcame those of competition and violence.

Finally, the threat system paradigm omits any deep thought on the reciprocal relationship between the leaders and the system itself. Does the threat system determine the way national political leaders think, or does the way they think determine the way the system works?

Certainly the leaders of nations must be careful to safeguard their countries in a less than perfect world. If the second question is more correct than the first, shouldn't some chances for peace be taken despite the appearance of potential conflict? Despite the usual rhetoric, this happens more often than not. Creative leadership can and often does slice through the Gordian Knot of war, at least when it tries.

Regrettably, the threat system manages to reflect a significant portion of the reality of our age when Bosnian Serbs slaughter their neighbors or when Middle East dictators covet the resources of another state. National security and war will share the same arena for the foreseeable future. The trick for all countries is to make the quest for that security more balanced and less costly. It is in this pursuit that the threat system concept creates problems. Nonetheless, we should take some hope in the fact that more conflicts manage to get solved today through diplomacy than through war.

DIPLOMACY

Diplomacy has been described as "the sending of an honest man abroad to lie for his country" (Benjamin Franklin) and "one-upmanship" (John Foster Dulles). These ideas get at the two principal operations involved in the concept: communication and negotiation. Actually, diplomats do *five* basic things: (1) They represent their nation's views to relevant people in the host country, often explaining why a policy has been decided upon. (2) They report back to their own country the views, conditions, and events within the host country. (3) They provide a symbolic link between their country and the host country. (4) They aid the citizens of their country while they are in the host country (though on a more limited basis than some might expect). (5) They serve the interests of business and commerce across international boundaries, arranging for the necessary contacts and paperwork attendant to modern international trade. In addition, they occasionally serve as crisis managers, trying to keep open the channels of communication and lower the level of tension when conflicts appear to be getting out of hand.

In earlier times, diplomats in residence in foreign countries also negotiated agreements between their country and the host country, but, more recently, this function has largely been given over to particular diplomats who specialize in arms control, trade, and cultural or technical activities and who attempt to reach agreements in these areas for transmittal back to their countries. Having done so, they return home. In any case, the central functions of diplomacy remain the same: communication and negotiation.

Certain customs have evolved over the centuries to enable diplomats to achieve their ends. These customs have often been misunderstood by those not experienced in world affairs, but they are essential to the diplomatic function. The first is **immunity.** A diplomat in a foreign country is immune from prosecution for *any* offense under the laws of that country. The diplomat represents the sovereignty of his or her country, and that sovereignty cannot be subject to the laws of any other country. One can sense the opportunities for abuse, but one should remember that diplomats are not sent abroad to commit crimes. On the other hand, they must feel free to travel about, speak to whomever they wish, and say whatever they like (or are told to say) without fear of being arrested by the host government. This makes for effective communications. Should criminal acts *be* committed by a diplomat (or more likely by members of his or her immediate family, who share the immunity), then that person may be declared *persona non grata* by the host government and expelled (but not prosecuted). It is a small price to pay for the essential function of communication among sovereign states.[2]

A second custom concerns rank. Diplomats in a host country are divided into ranks from *ambassador;* followed by *chargé d'affaires,* or deputy chief of mission (the number two person) in the American foreign service; down through *first, second, and third secretaries.* These ranks parallel the executive structure of most national governments: prime minister, cabinet secretary, deputy secretary, assistant secretary, and director of some office within that ministry. The purpose is to place each diplomat at the level of government within the host country at which he or she can communicate with a person of similar responsibility and experience. This, too, makes for effective communication and negotiation.[3]

Finally, there is **protocol.** Each nation-state has a variety of relationships with other countries. Some countries are more important or more powerful than others. It is important to demonstrate this in subtle ways without openly suggesting that one sovereign government is not as favored as another. Thus, elaborate rules and rituals are established for such things as the seating arrangements at public functions and who gets invited to what event. Again, the purpose is to enable communication to be as free and easy as possible without hurt feelings.

Diplomacy takes place in a variety of structures. Most of it is direct and bilateral (one country's diplomats talking to another's). Sometimes it takes place in multilateral conferences, where complicated issues are studied, debated, and resolved through public decisions, agreements, or both. The United Nations General Assembly (which will be discussed later) is a continuous diplomatic conference. Conducting a successful diplomatic conference is a complicated and difficult operation and worthy of a separate chapter by itself. That is beyond the scope of this study.

---

[2]In the case of spying, the same holds true. If a spy has diplomatic immunity, he or she is simply kicked out of the country. If the spy does not have immunity, he or she is arrested. Most diplomats avoid spying because it undermines their credibility as communicators.

[3]There are other ranks and titles, such as consul general and various *attachés* for special functions such as military, agriculture, or cultural liaison with the host country. They, too, have their proper level of contact with that government. Such complexities of modern diplomacy are beyond the scope of this study.

Another form of diplomacy occurs when leaders of governments meet face-to-face at a **summit conference.** This can be both dramatic and dangerous, and for these reasons professional diplomats generally do not like the practice. The major problems are that leaders of nation-states are generally too busy to concentrate sufficiently on the complex issues before them at the summit and, in some cases, are just uninformed. They also tend to be egotists, used to getting their own way within their governments, and, therefore, lack the instinct for compromise. Further, they must do their work at the summit in the glare of public opinion, under great pressure to agree to *something* because of raised expectations that they will. Finally, there is no chance for second thoughts by higher authority. When a head of government commits to something, the nation is committed. Thus, when a summit meeting is deemed to be useful, it is usually best for the participants to meet over a predigested agenda of mostly settled points. Then, perhaps, summitry can become the symbolic celebration of the achievements of professional diplomats, who actually did the work.

THIRD PARTY DIPLOMACY AND THE SETTLEMENT OF DISPUTES

Another kind of diplomacy is called *third party diplomacy.* Its major goal is to achieve a peaceful settlement of a dispute, usually between two states, that threatens the peace and security of their neighbors. When bilateral diplomacy has failed, a third party or parties may feel it necessary to intervene in order to help the parties find a solution to their dispute. There are five levels of third party intervention. Three of them are purely diplomatic and political in nature, and two are mostly legal.

The first method is called *good offices.* In this case, the third party simply offers some pleasant place in its country to the two disputants as a neutral ground on which to discuss their differences. The third party is doing two things—showing concern about the dispute (thus creating some degree of moral suasion toward settling it) and providing the physical facilities for negotiation. President Theodore Roosevelt offered good offices to Russia and Japan to settle their war of 1905 and, of all people, he was awarded the Nobel Peace Prize for his efforts.

A second and more complex method of third party diplomacy is called *mediation.* The third party offers to discuss the dispute independently with each party. After hearing both sides, the third party then suggests a fair solution. The point is that the solution comes from neither disputant and is, therefore, more likely to be acceptable to both without a loss of face by either. President Carter used both mediation and good offices in achieving the Camp David Accords between Egypt and Israel in 1978.

Third, there is *conciliation.* Here, the third party is really a number of states that are jointly concerned about a dispute. This produces a mediation on a higher level. In addition to listening to the two disputants, a group of diplomats from the conciliatory states conduct an independent inquiry into the dispute and jointly recommend a solution based on what they heard from the parties and what they discovered for themselves. Not only is the degree of concern over the dispute much higher, but the moral suasion toward accepting the proposed solution is also much stronger. An example of conciliation would be the Contadora group of Central American states, which proposed a solution to the dispute between the United States and Nicaragua in the late 1980s.

The next method of third party intervention, **arbitration,** moves from the political realm to what might be described as the quasi-legal approach. A political solution is usually achieved through some degree of compromise wherein nobody wins it all; a legal solution is one in which one side can and often does win it all, while the other side loses totally. That is why legal solutions are so rare and difficult to achieve in a world of sovereign nation-states. After all, the *sovereign* should not lose, at least not without a fight. Properly speaking, an arbitration falls between political and legal methods. If the parties agree to accept an arbitration (and they must do so without coercion), a **comprom'is** is first negotiated. This is a document that establishes the number of judges that will decide the issue, the fraction of judges required for a decision (two-thirds, three-fifths, etc.), the precise question to be decided, and the basic rules of procedure. This ends the political phase. After that, the court of judges chosen by the disputants, hears the case and makes a legal decision that is binding on the parties. The United States arbitrated with Great Britain over the location of the northern boundary of Maine in 1831 and with Mexico over El Chamizal (the swamp) near El Paso, Texas, in 1910. Unfortunately, neither judgment was accepted due to violations of the comprom'is. The United States did successfully arbitrate the *Alabama* claims (1872) and both fishery questions and boundary issues (1893 and 1903) with regard to Alaska. All of these arbitrations were with Great Britain. Arbitration, however, has never been a major tool of American diplomacy.

The last of these methods is *adjudication,* which involves going to an established international court for a solution to a dispute. The major court is the International Court of Justice, a part of the United Nations system that will be described later, as will the process of adjudication in the section on international law.

It must be kept in mind that no method of settling an international dispute can be successful unless certain preconditions exist, and it is pointless to try until they do. First, the dispute must not concern a vital interest. Such disputes are nonnegotiable and best avoided altogether. Second, there must be a possible compromise solution wherein reasonable people can see mutual advantage. Otherwise, negotiation will result only in raising the level of hostility. Third, there must be a desire to negotiate on the part of both disputants. This desire will most likely exist in the early stages of a dispute (before positions have become too rigid and national prestige has been attached to them) or when the dispute has dragged on so long that every-body is thoroughly sick of it. Fourth, negotiators should have flexible positions they can maneuver around and not go into a discussion with only one outcome in mind. Fifth, there must be a feeling of good faith and reciprocity on behalf of both parties. In other words, they must be able to trust each other. Sixth, there must be good negotiators on both sides. Prima donnas, egotists, and ultranationalists need not apply. Negotiation is a slow and painstaking process requiring the use of patience and expertise by self-effac-ing people who are earnestly trying to achieve a true compromise. Seventh, the issues must be clearly defined and fully understood. This is not always as easy as it would appear. Ideological blinders, ethnic or cultural differ-ences, and differing interpretations of events often get in the way. Finally, some degree of secrecy is absolutely necessary. Diplomats must not be required to bargain back and forth, giving up this for that (quid pro quo) under the watchful eye of nationalistic publics who would give up nothing. The public is entitled to know the results of a diplomatic negotiation but not the manner in which they were reached.

Thus it is that nation-states converse with each other through their diplo-mats and try, thereby, to avoid unnecessary disputes or to resolve the ones that inevitably occur. It is not a perfect system, and it breaks down periodi-cally, but it is the best we have come up with so far. There is a better way, perhaps, and that is through a true system of international law, which is our next subject.

INTERNATIONAL LAW

Despite the fact that many volumes are written on the subject of interna-tional law and many courses are taught in the field, one cannot help con-clude, upon thorough study, that international law is not really law. It is, at best, an evolving system of law that is still somewhat in its primitive stage. That is to say, any enforcement is essentially a self-help action. Perhaps one could say that it is at the political stage in terms of its specific statutes, there being several bodies capable of issuing some sort of treaty or administrative regulation. However, international law lacks any standard method of enforcement, a complete codification, and even a general recognition as to its legitimacy or even its meaning by those over whom it presumes to act.

International Law might better be referred to as *international business* because it is within the business world that we see the closest parallel to the realities of international law. People do business on a reciprocal basis. One acts in a certain way in the expectation of a similar and equal action by the other. Goods are sold at prices agreed upon. Obligations to deliver are based on the hope of future contracts. Fairness will also ensure the continuation of business. Admission of responsibility is sometimes necessary in order to continue a business relationship beyond an unfortunate act. And so it goes.

If a contract is broken, suing in court is a possibility, but this can be time consuming, very expensive, and draining on precious resources. Therefore, in most cases, one simply refrains from doing further business with the rule breaker and advises others to do the same. If one observes it closely, this is what happens in the context of what we call international law. If its rules or understandings are broken, then the usual practice is to cease doing business with the rule breaker until that nation-state begins to behave properly.

If we lived in a more orderly society, perhaps international law would be the highest form of law. There have been many political thinkers, since the evolution of the nation-state, who have sought to create such a higher law that would make sovereignty less than what it is now. The greatest of the early thinkers along this line was Hugo Grotius, a Dutchman of the seventeenth century, who proposed that something like the old Roman *Jus Natural* (or "laws of nature") be applied among princes so that there might be a law for all monarchs, under which they would be bound. It would cover such areas as war, the internal administration of their states, and the protection of their citizens. Although he wrote voluminously on how this might be accomplished and what the substance of international law should be, the princes of the world were loathe to abandon their new toy of sovereignty. Indeed, to this day, nation-states still cling zealously to the theory that no higher law can exist, except by consent, beyond the law of the nation-state itself.

With the coming of modern warfare, however—especially near the end of the nineteenth century, when war's destruction appeared to approach the destruction of civilization through such modern inventions as long-range cannons, the machine gun, and even the possibility of aerial warfare—a new attempt was made to create some kind of international legal order, at least as it related to the laws of war.

In studying the modern history of international law, we must go back to the Hague Conference of 1899, which was conducted in the Netherlands. The purposes of the conference were to argue against the wisdom of war and, if it wasn't possible to prevent war altogether, then at least to agree on some rules for war. The major accomplishment of that international conference, which was attended by most of the major nations, including the United States, was not so much the few rules they did agree upon with regard to the use of poisonous gas, the protection of nonbelligerents, the laws of neutrality, and a few things relating to weaponry, as it was the creation of the Hague Court of Arbitration.

Arbitration has been defined previously. This Court of Arbitration was established as a specific court building, and a list of judges was made available to nations, on call, for purposes of resolving their disputes peacefully under international law. The Court of Arbitration had quite a few successes during the period of the Hague conferences, which were to continue every eight years. A second Hague conference was held in 1907. It produced some further rules for war, and it also further encouraged the use of the Hague Court. The third meeting was to be held in 1915, but *World War I* ended the series. At the end of that disastrous conflict, in which many of the more dire predictions of the horrors of war came true, it was decided to have a permanent court to apply international law under some kind of enforcement provisions. In other words, this would be a court of *adjudication*, not *arbitration*. It was called the Permanent Court of International Justice (PCIJ), and it would have fifteen judges chosen by the Council of the League of Nations, with which it would be associated.

In drawing up the statute for the PCIJ, the substance of international law was defined as emanating from five sources, set down in their order of importance. The first and foremost source of international law would be *treaties*, as between two or more states. In effect, all signatories to a treaty bound themselves to its provisions and accepted those provisions as law adjudicable by a permanent court of fifteen eminent international jurists. The second source of law would be *custom* long accepted among nations. Such customs as the three-mile limit of sovereignty over territorial waters would be respected by all members of the court. If treaties or customs could not be found to resolve a case between nations, then a third source might be *general principles* that exist among civilized states. Such principles included the fact that one state should not send a uniformed army across the boundaries of another state without that state's permission. This did not happen frequently enough to become a custom, but it certainly was a principle shared by most states. If great principles were not available, then **precedent** from earlier cases of a similar nature might be applied by the court as international law for the resolution of a dispute. There were cases of individual arbitrations going back to the eighteenth century that might produce some idea of how to resolve an international dispute, and in the heyday of the PCIJ, which lasted about eight years, many of these precedents were dug up and used by the judges. Finally, if no treaty, custom, principle, or precedent were available and an international dispute was still to be resolved under the court's jurisdiction, the court would apply *equity* or, to quote the Latin expression within the charter, *"Ex aequo et bono"*—"from those things that are fair and good."

Thus was established a court in which nation-states agreed to participate to preserve peace through international law. The PCIJ was a successful experiment to the extent that, as long as the remembrance of the horror of World War I remained among the major nations of the world, the court was able to begin the establishment of a fairly respectable tradition of international law. This led to serious study of international law and to the writing of many volumes to describe and explain it. From 1920 to 1930, there arose an enormous number of legal precedents and commentaries. Serious problems came, however, with the breakdown of the international community, caused by the worldwide depression of the 1930s and the cynicism that accompanied the rise of the dictatorships of Hitler, Mussolini, Stalin, Franco, and others.

Further, the United States never joined the court, although we had a judge on the court and our government officially encouraged the court in principle. With the end of World War II, during which the horror of war had once again manifested itself, an attempt was made to revive the PCIJ. Instead of having the court be simply an adjunct to the new world organization, the United Nations, the court would be an integral part of the new world system. Thus, when a nation-state joined the United Nations, it also joined the new ICJ, or International Court of Justice. The ICJ, was the PCIJ made over. It differed very little from the previous court except that it was an integral part of the United Nations.

When a nation joined the United Nations, it had to write an official statement of allegiance to the ICJ. The United States, although always in favor of international law in theory, was somewhat **xenophobic** about its relations with other nations and its possible dependence upon them. We wrote into our acceptance of the ICJ's jurisdiction a disclaimer saying, in effect, that the United States would accept the jurisdiction of the ICJ (and, thus, international law) in all cases except those that were essentially within the domestic jurisdiction of the United States. What the word *essentially* meant was somewhat vague. It is quite possible to interpret almost any aspect of any international dispute involving a nation-state as affecting its domestic affairs. If that weren't bad enough, to that language was added the famous Connelly Amendment. This was drawn up by Senator Tom Connelly of Texas. It added eight significant words to our document of allegiance to the court. The words were "as defined by the United States of America." Now it read that the United States would accept the court's jurisdiction except for cases that essentially involved the domestic jurisdiction of the United States as defined by the United States of America, meaning in effect that we were willing to go to court under any circumstances except when we didn't want to go.

So cynical was this particular document perceived to be by other countries that many of them in turn followed suit, and the allegiance of many nations to the ICJ from the very beginning became more symbolic than real. In point of fact, though several nations have asked the United States to take an issue with them to the ICJ, the United States generally refuses to do so.[4] The Soviet Union had its own particular reservations about international law, and particularly the ICJ, and it was more than the Cold War that prevented the court's use between major nations, particularly the superpowers.

Even though neither the United States nor the Soviet Union did much to advance the cause of international law throughout the postwar period, when they did feel the need to do business, especially with regard to arms control, both were quite ready to go the treaty route and did so with a remarkable

---

[4]This was seen in the refusal of the United States to accept ICJ jurisdiction over a case brought by Nicaragua concerning the United States' mining of its harbors in 1984. Nevertheless, the "trial" was held, and the United States was "convicted" and ordered to pay reparations. The United States then refused to accept the decision or to pay reparations, declaring that international law did not apply to its actions in Nicaragua.

degree of success. Beginning with the Test Ban Treaty and the Hot Line agreements of 1963, and continuing through treaties concerning nuclear weapons on the sea bed and in Latin America, nuclear nonproliferation, and bacteriological weapons and the ABM and SALT II treaties, there was an enormous amount of general agreement and compliance (despite an occasional disagreement over the fringe areas of some later pacts). Although never ratified by the United States, the SALT II treaty of 1978 was the subject of solemn promises from both parties to adhere to it, and they did.

With the end of the Cold War and the advent of the new regimes in the former Soviet Union, one might hope for a new interest in international law. Whatever ultimately emerges in Russia, it is generally assumed that, unlike the state that preceded it, a genuine desire for an orderly and predictable comity among nations will assert itself. Will that be enough to breathe life into institutions of international law such as the ICJ, insofar as the rest of the world is concerned? Perhaps not for some time to come. In fact, the International Court of Justice has become moribund since about 1965, when, in a case involving South Africa, in effect it decided not to decide at all. Although smaller issues have arisen periodically since that time, the ICJ has become a vestigial organ of the United Nations. Whatever international law there is exists more in terms of reciprocal relationships of mutual benefit worked out on a businesslike basis between nations that are observed as long as they serve mutual interest.

No one calls this *law* in the context of something higher than national sovereignty, but periodic observations about international law are made and formal relationships between nations do exist, but these hardly deserve the label *law*. Law tends to reflect a common perception of reality, the strength of governments and the strength and coherency of societies, the desire for order, and agreement on mutual principles under which governed order should take place. To achieve international law, these conditions imply some form of world government. In summary, international law must await international government before it can be called *law* at all.

THE BALANCE OF POWER

In the absence of effective international law or consistently successful diplomacy, one other device has been used in the attempt to keep order in the modern world, that is the **balance of power.** The central idea is an ancient one whose usefulness and relevance may be seriously questioned today. Nevertheless, a large body of literature exists as to its effect on world politics, and we should try to come to grips with it.

The theory holds that, if a nation-state faces an adversary, it should take into account the power relationship that exists between the two and try somehow to maximize its power vis-á-vis the adversary, gaining, if possible, a position of superiority. If this is not possible, then at least some discernable balance of power should be reached between the two states. Either situation, then, should dissuade the adversary from taking some drastic action against your state. These two possible situations are often referred to as a favorable balance of power, in the first instance, or a balance of equilibrium, in the latter. Both concepts are subjective, deceptive, and potentially dangerous ideas. After all, what do we really mean by the balance of power? Is it a goal to be sought? Is it merely a description of the current situation? Is it a major framework for the analysis of policy? In fact, it has been all of these things and more, depending on who is doing the talking.

What most describers of the balance of power seem to agree on are the following principles gleaned from the history of the past 200 years: first, the existence of some kind of mutual balance among the world's powers has generally been conducive to world peace; second, static or confrontational-type balances, such as that between the United States led coalition and the USSR and its allies, are inherently dangerous and should be avoided if possible; and third, flexible balance of power structures are apparently the safest.

This isn't much to go on, but, then, the balance of power is a pretty ephemeral concept to begin with, and there are some basic problems when nation-states make too much of it, as they tend to do from time to time. Indeed, the notion of power in international relations is inexact at best, as we have already seen. National power is made up of various elements, and each is hard to measure in relation to some other element. The only definitive way to test the power relationship that is *thought* to exist is through war. Further, the power relationship is constantly changing and is unpredictable, as we have also seen. Then, when alliances are involved, balance of power structures can cause local conflicts to become bigger than they might otherwise be, drawing unaffected states into them in order to support the alliance. Finally, the balance of power concept assumes that world leaders all see it the same way and will act rationally about it. These are dubious assumptions, indeed.

INTERNATIONAL ORGANIZATIONS

Perhaps the best chance for world peace, short of world government, lies in the realm of international organizations. This is an old idea, older than the nation-state itself. The United Nations, which is the premier international organization today, has many ancestors. Indeed, one might say that the UN represents the latest attempt, going back to the Medieval period, to re-create the universality of the old Roman Empire (see chapter 3). Among its theoretical ancestors are Dante's call in 1300 for a "collective security" arrangement among the feudal leaders of his day; Pierre Dubois' idea in 1305 for a "temporal union of princes," with a council and a court; Henry IV of France and his "grand design" of 1610, which would have divided Europe into fifteen equal states under a council, an assembly, and a court; Emeric Cruce's idea in 1623 of a worldwide union of states, including China, Persia, and India; William Penn's plan in 1693 for a "world parliament"; and other similar ideas from such well-known people as Victor Hugo, Jean-Jacques Rousseau, and Jeremy Bentham.

By the nineteenth century, even poets got into the act. Thus, Alfred Lord Tennyson, in *Locksley Hall*, provided the following vision in 1842:

> *For I dipped into the future, far as human eye could see,*
> *Saw the Vision of the world and all the wonder that would be;*
> *Saw the heavens fill with commerce, argosies of magic sails,*
> *Pilots of the purple twilight, dropping down with costly bales;*
> *Heard the heavens fill with shouting, and there rained a ghastly dew*
> *From the nations' airy navies grappling in the central blue;*
> *Far along the world-wide whisper of the south-wind rushing warm,*
> *With the standards of the peoples plunging through the thunderstorm;*
> *Till the war-drum throbbed no longer, and the battle flags were furled*
> *In the Parliament of man, the Federation of the world.*

There were real ancestors as well. These include the Hanseatic League (a trading association of northern European towns in the thirteenth and fourteenth centuries), the interstate sanitation councils of the 1700s, the Rhine and Danube River Commissions of the early 1800s, technical organizations such as the Postal and Telegraph Unions of the late 1800s, and regional organizations such as the Pan American Union founded in 1899. The most significant of these predecessor organizations, and the grandfather of the United Nations, was the group of Hague Peace Conferences of 1899, 1907, and the one scheduled for 1915. These were referred to in the previous section on international law, but the Hague system was a regularly meeting (every eight years) international conference designed to stabilize an increasingly dangerous world of nation-states through the creation of some mutually agreed upon standards of conduct and that its membership was practically universal. Then, after World War I came the League of Nations, which had a **Secretariat,** a Council of leading nations, an Assembly of all of its members, and the aforementioned PCIJ. The League was officially superceded by the United Nations in 1945, during the last days of World War II.

Thus, the United Nations is the third universal, continuously meeting, multipurpose international organization. Its purpose, as stated in Article I of its Charter, is, first and foremost, to prevent a general war (such as World Wars I and II) from occurring. This purpose is fulfilled by providing structures for third party diplomacy aimed at settling disputes peacefully, serving as a safety valve for pent-up tensions, wherein nations may make their complaints public and seek sympathy for themselves and against their adversaries or, if necessary, applying political, economic, or military sanctions against an aggressor nation (as in Korea in 1950). This purpose has also been served by placing small quasi-military forces between warring states, as in the cases of the United Nations Commission on India and Pakistan (UNCIP) along the Indo-Pakistani border since 1947, the United Nations Emergency Force (UNEF) in the Middle East from 1956 to 1967 and from 1973 to 1979, the United Nations Operations in the Congo (ONUC) in the Congo from 1960 to 1964, and others in Cyprus, Lebanon, and elsewhere. The results of all these activities have been uneven, to say the least.

The second purpose of the United Nations has seen more success. It is to become a "center for harmonizing the actions of Nations" toward achieving joint cooperation in dealing with economic, social, humanitarian, and cultural areas, including the feeding of the hungry, the treatment of disease, the settling of the homeless, and the coordination of communications and technology across national boundaries. It is in these areas that the United Nations has more often lived up to its promises. The structure of the UN will help demonstrate this. Basically, the organization looks like figure 12.1.

The Secretariat provides both administrative support for UN activities and executive leadership through the person of the secretary general. The General Assembly is the heart of the organization. All members of the UN are represented in this body. It may discuss any issue not currently before the

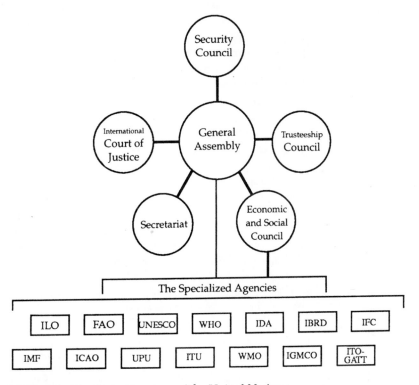

FIGURE 12.1   The Basic Structure of the United Nations

Security Council, and, by a majority vote, it may pass resolutions that are binding on the members to the extent that members wish to be bound. The Security Council, which has fifteen members, may be viewed as a permanent conciliation commission, always on call, that can deal with disputes that threaten peace. It takes action by way of resolutions passed by a vote of at least nine members, including the affirmative votes of the five permanent members (the United States, Russia, Great Britain, France, and China). Should any of these states vote no, the resolution does not pass. Among the options the Security Council may take to restore the peace are political, economic, and military sanctions against nations deemed to be the aggressors, but, for reasons beyond the scope of this study, it seldom does. (The ICJ was described in the section on international law.) The Trusteeship Council was designed to deal with leftover trust territories (former colonies) lost as a result of World Wars I and II and other small territories turned over to it for its administration. Most of these colonies and territories have either become independent or have otherwise changed their former status, leaving the Trusteeship Council with little to do.

That leaves the Economic and Social Council (ECOSOC) and the specialized agencies it coordinates and that report to it and to the General Assembly.[5] The ECOSOC has fifty-four members, representing the broad spectrum of rich, poor, powerful, weak, eastern, western, and nonaligned nations. It can create new agencies as it sees fit in order to promote the general welfare of the world. It is in these specialized agencies that we see the UN's best and most consistent contributions to UN's world order.

It is often startling to observe the degree to which otherwise sovereign nations submit to the directives from such organizations as the World Health Organization when it issues guidance for the purpose of controlling an outbreak of disease, the International Telecommunication Union in its instructions on satellite communications, or the World Meteorological Organization and its requests for climatic data. We see international cooperation over a wide range of activities that has become almost routine. Can this be the wave of the future? Perhaps, but many see the UN itself as declining in influence primarily because its organizational structure is fifty years old and considerably out of date.

This can be illustrated by a 1995 report to the Secretary General by a committee headed by a former president of Germany and a former prime minister of Pakistan. The report called for the UN to be reorganized as an

---

[5]The specialized agencies are indicated in figure 12.1 by their initials. In order of their appearance on the diagram, they are The International Labour Organization; The Food and Agriculture Organization; United Nations Educational, Scientific and Cultural Organization; World Health Organization; International Development Association; International Bank for Reconstruction and Development (World Bank); International Finance Corporation; International Monetary Fund; International Civil Aviation Organization; Universal Postal Union; International Telecommunication Union; World Meteorological Organization; Inter-Governmental Maritime Consultative Organization; and the International Trade Organization, which oversees the General Agreement on Tariffs and Trade.

"international civil service" to be financed by "taxes and fees derived from use of the global commons." The Security Council would be expanded from fifteen to twenty-three members selected for their willingness to contribute not only to UN peacekeeping but also peace enforcement and peace building operations sponsored by regional organizations. Replacing the current Economic and Social Council, would be an Economic Council to coordinate trade, monetary and development policies, and a Social Council to oversee human rights and "help societies in distress." While many believe that these reforms would be very helpful, they would only come to pass as the result of an even broader commitment by the major world powers to the concept of a world order based on international cooperation.

Alas, as an effective force for world order, the UN is surely lacking. It is not a government in any sense. It is not a functioning confederation, which it sometimes looks like. It is, however, more than a mere debating society. Like a great *magnifying glass*, it can focus the opinion of the world on a dangerous situation and thereby induce a degree of caution concerning it. Using the aforementioned metaphor of the *safety valve*, we can see the UN allowing disputant nations to "let off steam" before they take drastic action against each other. The UN can also be seen as simply a *group of buildings*. Inside, when nations want to agree about something, they can come together to do it and much good can result. If they can't agree, nothing much has been lost. Thus, the United Nations is neither strong nor weak. It simply *is*. It is the membership, at any given time, that determines the strength or weakness of the UN. Finally, the UN can be seen as the great *tap root* of the tree of human hope, reaching back in time to the beginning of humanity's search for world peace and cooperation. Chop down the tree (The Hague System, the League of Nations, and the UN itself) if you will; the tap root will inevitably produce another such organization for peace.

As noted previously, the United Nations has waxed and waned as an effective peacekeeping institution. In the earliest years, it was fairly successful in bringing about peaceful settlements among small states with low-level concerns. However, with the advent of the Korean War, two factors decreased the role of the UN. One was that the United States took over the war, for all practical purposes, casting doubt on the legitimacy of UN peacekeeping insofar as the communist bloc and many Third World nations were concerned. The other was that the first secretary general, Trygve Lie of Norway, was perceived as too prowest to be depended upon by those same nations. The next secretary general, Dag Hammarskjold of Sweden, was more successful. Being scrupulously neutral, he was able to create the previously mentioned UNEF peacekeeping force in the Middle East War of 1956, and the somewhat less successful ONUC force in the Congo War of 1960, where he lost his life overseeing it.

From 1961 until recent times, the UN went into a great decline as an effective peacekeeper. Its attention was directed more toward the problems of Third World countries and international economic issues. This reorientation was encouraged by its Third World secretary general, U Thant of Burma who served from 1960–74. He felt that the UN had to abandon its central role in keeping the peace because of the intensification of the Cold War after 1960 and the the Vietnam War (1965–75) in particular. The latter proved to be beyond the capabilities of successful UN intervention because it involved the superpowers. Indeed, the United States and the other great powers became rather disenchanted with the UN during these years, and they failed to adequately support it financially and otherwise. With the winding down of the Cold War and the appearance of the fifth secretary general, Javier Perez de Cuellar of Peru, things began to change. He played a major role in the politics of the Gulf War of 1990–91 and he also played the central role in the ending of the various hostage crises in the Middle East. During the last three years of his tenure as secretary general (1988–91), no less than eight peacekeeping operations (in the Middle East, Africa, Cambodia, and Yugoslavia) were mounted by the UN. That compares with thirteen in the previous forty-three years of the existence of the UN. Thus, he left to his successor, Boutros Boutros-Ghali of Egypt, a set of precedents whereby the new leader had the opportunity to bring the UN back to the central peacekeeping role envisioned by its creators.

Those expectations were dashed when the UN attempted to insert a larger peacekeeping force into the war that broke out in 1991 in the former state of Yugoslavia, among the Serbs, Bosnians and Croats. It was an extremely bloody affair full of ethnic and religious fury and a desire to settle ancient feuds and treacheries. The leadership of Boutros Boutros-Ghali proved to be weak and confused. Leadership from the French and British (who were the powers closest to the problem) was also poor. The United States refused to play a dominant role at the outset, seeing it as a European problem, while the Russian government vacillated between its desire to stay out of the mess and its traditional support for the Serbs. The result was that the "peacekeepers" had no peace to keep and became, themselves, the hostages of the most aggressive participants in the fighting, especially the Serbs. The whole enterprise became a debacle, and the UN's new reputation for peacekeeping, already weakened by a failed attempt to stabilize the civil war in Somalia in 1992–93, was now seriously undermined.

Whether the UN will be able to do much about anything in the future is a serious issue. Many observers question not only the effectiveness of the secretariate for the past two decades, but they also disdain the growing bureaucracy of that organ. Too many highly paid dilettantes, connivers, and mediocrity's from small western and Third World countries have infiltrated the various offices of the UN since the advent of U Thant's tenure as secretary general. Boutros Boutros-Ghali has demonstrated little interest in changing the situation with the result that the major contributors, including the United States are demonstrating a lowering of both their contributions and their expectations. The future of the UN as we have known it is certainly in some doubt as it enters its second fifty years.

WAR AND TERRORISM

Not all international relationships take place through institutions of international politics. As we have seen, there is also war. As long as the state system allows for this possibility, one can be sure that some government at some time will avail itself of this technique at some level, whether it makes sense or not. Such is humanity and its follies. Although nuclear war and large-scale conventional war are the images that usually spring to mind, the likelihood of either is much less than one might suppose. Actually, an all-out nuclear war is impossible. The term is an oxymoron. War is an activity with a purpose. Nuclear exchanges on a large scale would so destroy the earth's fragile ecosystem that they would really be acts of suicide. At some point in the future, humankind may experience a nuclear disaster or a nuclear holocaust, but not a nuclear war. Nuclear weapons may work as deterrents to war, but their utility as a rational means of state violence is greatly limited.

In a similar way, World War II levels of conventional war are almost as unlikely as nuclear wars. They are simply too expensive. In today's world, the economies and social structures of nations with the capacity to launch such wars are too fragile and complex to allow for the long-term mass mobilization, industrial conversion, and singleness of purpose required by such a war. Both Iran and Iraq have discovered this. Conventional wars may still occur, even on the scale of the rather one-sided Gulf War of 1991 or the wars of the Balkan states, which began that same year, but they will be infrequent and controversial.

More likely will be guerrilla warfare in its variety of forms, techniques, and degrees of effectiveness. Most of these are really civil wars. Their purpose is to wear down an unpopular or ineffective government through low-level, multiform (military, economic, psychological, etc.) attacks designed to destroy morale and call into question the legitimacy of the government. In addition, guerrilla fighters seek to break the links between the government and its people by killing low-level officials. When the hit-and-run tactics bring the government to a certain point of disarray, a major blow can then be struck to finish it off. With the end of the Cold War and its temptation to seek some advantage for one side over the other in such wars, other nations will be less inclined to get involved in them and work instead for their termination in the interests of regional peace. However, some of the techniques of guerrilla war have been adopted by people with another agenda. These techniques fall under the rubric of **terrorism.**

Whereas guerrilla wars are fought for the purpose of replacing one government with another (i.e., civil wars), terrorism has a more limited goal. Its purpose is aimed, in general, at forcing a change in the domestic or foreign policies of an existing government. The purpose of the violence is not to undermine directly the security of the government but, rather, to cause public opinion to rise up against the policy being contested out of fear of the terrorists. Indeed, terrorist activities are best directed at democratic governments subject to such public opinion.

Terrorist acts are, by nature, violent, random, indirect, dramatic, and secretive. The purpose is to induce a sense of helplessness in the minds of the citizens and, if possible, the government. The victims are usually not directly related to the policy or its makers. Innocent blood being shed is more scary than that of powerful people. What happens to your peaceful neighbor can happen to anybody! Whereas governmental, diplomatic, and military officials are targets of traditional warfare, the subjects of terrorism are more often businesspeople and private individuals. Geographically, most terrorism today comes about in the Middle East, followed by western Europe and Sub-Saharan Africa. The immediate future for terrorism also seems bright in eastern Europe, as new and inexperienced governments there must now confront old ethnic animosities and grievances long controlled and suppressed by the old pro-Soviet regimes.

In terms of actual physical harm, terrorism is a relatively minor problem when compared with other threats to individual security. Nevertheless, many people seem to have become overly concerned about the problem. This can be seen in the American response to the downing by terrorists of a Pan American jet over Lockerbie, Scotland, in 1988 and continuing concerns through the Gulf War period of 1990–91. Many Americans refused to fly on international flights and canceled their vacation plans out of their fear that all airlines were vulnerable to a repeat performance. Statistically, the likelihood is minuscule. Normal airline mishaps, even fatal ones, are much more likely to occur than are terrorist attacks.

Of more direct concern is the growing possibility of urban terrorism. One fear among many thoughtful law enforcement officers and others responsible for maintaining order in large municipalities is that organized groups may progress from the contemporary pattern of vandalism, sporadic and random violence, gang warfare, and street crime in general to something even worse. The problems associated with the existing levels of violence (poverty, joblessness, drugs, homelessness, low levels of education, etc.), if left to fester, could escalate to the level of terrorist causes. People with long-standing grievances and the lack of other means to express them in an effective way and others who seek attention, revenge, or an end to their frustrations may rather easily develop a nihilistic desire to lash out at an "unjust" world through the devices of terrorism. Their targets would be the fragile infrastructure of cities and the assumptions among citizens that they are safe in the urban environment. Through organized violence, terrorist groups could force policy changes more to their liking because these changes would be perceived as more economically desirable than continued violence and the slow strangulation of urban life. Frightening as it may be, this prospect will no doubt be addressed more and more in the near future by responsible governmental leaders around the world. Political solutions must be found to the problems of urban life all over the world lest terrorism becomes an attractive alternative to the status quo.

The reality of the nature of urban terrorism (if not the specific pattern previously discussed) dawned on Americans in 1993 when New York City's World Trade Center was car-bombed, apparently by Middle Eastern terrorists who objected to America's support of Israel and its hostility toward Iran. Many people were killed and injured, and countermeasures were instituted to protect the two buildings in the future. Then, in 1995, the federal building in Oklahoma City was car-bombed by U.S. citizens who seemed to be upset over American gun-control measures and who feared a government that they saw as inimical to their somewhat Neanderthal views of individual rights. One hundred and sixty-eight people were killed in that horror. What new forms of urban terrorism will emerge and what new issues will prompt them is unclear. That the problem is real and that serious attention needs to be paid to it now, here in America, is undeniable.

INTERNATIONAL POLITICS AND THE FUTURE

Returning to the theme of world peace among nations, from whence will come world peace if it ever comes? How could it happen? Some look for the solution in international law, in some kind of superior world military force, or perhaps in the emergence of a collection of regional governments, as in George Orwell's famous book *1984.* Unfortunately, all of these ideas seem to presuppose a rejection of the concept of state sovereignty, which defines the current order, and the creation of a true world government to replace it. It is that government that must bring about the international legal order, world police force, or reorganization of regional territories and peoples. Ultimately, then, the essential question is how to create such a world government.

Let us conclude this book by returning to the ideas contained in chapter 3, wherein we asked the question, whither the state? To begin with, it seems that the nation-state's major achievement (beyond providing the framework for an amazing variety of wars) was the stimulation and structuring of the Industrial Revolution. It took sovereign governments that could command large populations and resources and turn them toward the direction of industry and trade to provide the foundation for modern industrialization and thereby begin the mass production and distribution of goods that began in the late eighteenth century and continues to this day. The contemporary world economy, however, appears to have transcended the nation-states that helped produce it. It is rapidly evolving into a transnational and multinational phenomenon of worldwide corporations and financial institutions. Does not this suggest the need for some new political structure as well? Undoubtedly, there will be some kind of political evolution resulting from economic realities in the future, such as the European economic union of

1993 or the North American Free Trade Agreement (NAFTA) in 1995, and it is interesting to speculate upon how that might come about in other areas of the world.

Perhaps a crisis of some sort will focus the minds of world leaders on the necessity and benefits of a joint, worldwide cooperative institution of effective government over nation-states that can lay to rest ignorant prejudices about nationality, race, and ideology, just as the crisis of the Thirty Years' War enabled medieval Europeans to lay aside their deep feelings about religion and to coalesce into the nation-states that emerged from that war. We hope such a crisis will not be a major war. Nuclear weapons would seem to preclude that possibility as a rational and productive option. An environmental disaster, a new and devastating disease or some meteorological catastrophe will do. I would prefer the crisis to be merely a crisis of thought. No matter what the stimulation, there is one idea that will probably dominate the process when such a turning point occurs—the social contract. After all, it suggests that humankind created the state and that humankind can re-create it and determine its new structure and nature. The creation of a new world order may yet prove to be the greatest challenge of the twenty-first century. It may also be the only way for humankind to get to the twenty-second.

POINTS TO PONDER

How do you see the balance of power in the world today?

What changes would you suggest for the UN to be brought up to date?

List several reasons over which a rational nation-state might go to war today?

What factors of modern life make terrorism so pervasive today? Is an increase in terrorism inevitable?

Glossary

The following glossary contains terms used in the text that may not be familiar to the beginning student of politics. Each term is identified primarily as it is used in the book. There are other definitions for many of these terms. Further, some may disagree with the specific definitions offered. Again, the purpose of the glossary is to explain certain terms as they relate to the political theory contained herein.

Chapter

6 **Adjudication:** The process of hearing and settling a legal case through an established judicial procedure before an established court.

5 **Administration:** The process of carrying out policy; in other words, deciding what shall be done, when, by whom, and at what cost. It also involves the evaluation of the work done. (*See* Policy.)

3 **Aggression:** One state declaring war on another, committing an invasion or attack on another state's territory, executing a naval blockade, or supporting armed bands attacking another state. (League of Nations: 1933.)

4 **Anarchy:** Literally, *no government!* Either a condition of unbridled chaos within a society or a society based solely on voluntary cooperation without any coercion or interference with personal liberties.

6 **Appellate:** Pertaining to the process wherein the judgment of a lower court is taken to a higher court for review because of some error allegedly having been committed by the lower court.

12 **Arbitration:** The process of hearing and settling a controversy between states by judges of their own choice who decide on the basis of law by procedures agreed to by the parties. The decision is final. (*See* Comprom'is.)

6 **Arraignment:** Being called before a court to be formally charged or accused of a crime, or to answer to an indictment. (An indictment is a formal charge by a grand jury.)

11 **Australian ballot:** A voting ballot given to qualified voters at their polling places, listing all legal nominees and containing space for write-in candidates. Marking the ballot must be done in *secret!* The ballot is then placed in official ballot boxes.

7 **Authoritarian:** A system of government wherein the supreme power is in the hands of one person (or a small group) not responsible to the people for his or her actions, and wherein there is no legal method of changing the system or those who run it.

2 **Authority:** The right to use public power that has been deemed to be legitimately in the hands of those who are to use it in the execution of the functions of government.

12 **Balance of power:** The power relationship between or among nation-states expressed as an equation, usually in a state of flux. National power is made up of geographical, population, economic, industrial, military, psychological, and other lesser elements.

6 **Barrister:** A British lawyer who is fully qualified to plead a case in the formal courts and who can instruct students in the law or become a judge. (*See* Solicitor.)

11 **Bicameral:** Having two houses or chambers of government that are usually designated as being the upper and lower levels of a legislature.

10 **Block grant:** A grant-in-aid of national monies in the United States to states and their subdivisions for a variety of purposes within a designated functional area of government, for example, highways. (*See* Categorial grant.)

10 **Bureaucratic:** Pertaining to the organizations, officials, and procedures associated with an administrative undertaking. Often synonymous with rigidity, inefficiency, delay, and waste. (*See* Administration.)

4 **Bye-election:** A special election held between general elections to fill a vacancy in a parliament or legislature.

4 **Cabinet:** The executive portion of a parliamentary government that includes the prime minister (premier) and the heads (or ministers) of the most important administrative agencies; or, in the presidential system, those administrative heads (or secretaries) designated as collective advisors to the president.

8 **Capitalism:** An economic system based on the use of private property for profits in manufacturing or commerce regulated essentially by the law of supply and demand through the dynamics of competition.

10 **Categorial grant:** A grant-in-aid of national monies in the United States to states and their subdivisions for specific and clearly defined purposes that are governed by matching formulas and other strict rules with regard to quality of result and equal benefit. (*See* Block grant.)

12 **Central Intelligence Agency (CIA):** That organ of the executive branch of the American government that collects, through overt and covert means, information of use to the makers of foreign and defense policy, and assimilates and distributes it to proper authorities.

6 **Certiorari:** An order (writ) from an appellate court to a lower court ordering the records of a case to be sent up for review. (*See* Appellate and Writ.)

6 **Civil law:** Law between or among individuals (plaintiffs and respondents) that is compensatory and nonpunitive. Also a term referring to the Roman Law of continental Europe.

8 **Classic:** The established model that represents a kind of thing, encompassing its basic characteristics; the highest level of achievement; the superior version.

4 **Coalition:** A group of minority ministers, party members, or both in a parliament who come together to act as one party for the purposes of forming a majority that can govern; any combination of dissimilar groups that agree to act as one for common purposes.

6 **Codification:** A collecting and restatement of existing laws into a more systematic and precise form; the highest stage of the development of a legal system.

4 **Collegial executive:** A plural executive body, as in the cabinet of a parliamentary government, made up of a prime minister and other ministers. (*See* Parliamentary and Cabinet.)

8 **Communism:** An ideology based on the ideas of Karl Marx and Vladimir Lenin that envisions a totally collective economy leading ultimately to a stateless society. (*See* chapters 7 and 8.)

12 **Comprom'is:** A special agreement in an arbitration proscribing the membership of the court, defining the issues of the case, and laying down the rules of procedure to be followed in deciding the case. (*See* Arbitration.)

8 **Conservatism:** An approach to government that emphasizes order and authority as a check on the passions of ordinary people; an adherence to customs and constitutions; a resistance to rapid change. (*See* chapter 7.)

4 **Constitution:** A document of organic law defining and delimiting the major organs of government and assigning specific powers to each. It often includes a description of the basic rights of citizens. (*See* Organic law.)

6 **Criminal law:** Law covering offenses by people against the state that is punitive and noncompensatory and usually divided into felonies (serious crimes) and misdemeanors (petty offenses).

2 **Democracy:** Literally "rule for the people," accomplished either directly or through representatives, and assures the equality of all individuals in the process. (*See* chapter 6.)

8 **Dialectic:** According to Hegel, the process by which mankind moves through time, achieving progress through the cyclical clash of contradictory ideas about his or her mode of living.

5 **Diplomacy:** The act of communicating between or among sovereign governments by officially accredited representatives. (*See* chapter 12.)

7 **Economics:** Originally, the science of managing the household; with the advent of industrialization, it has come to refer to the production, distribution, and consumption of commodities.

2 **Egalitarian:** Adherence to the concept of absolutely equal economic and legal rights for all human beings through the application of governmental power.

3 **Egocentrism:** The self-centered view that one's ego or special group is the center, object, and norm of all experience. A typical attribute of ultranationalism.

6 **Equity:** Justice applied under circumstances not covered by law, based on fairness and impartiality.

6 **Ethics:** The specific moral code of individuals in their relationship to other people that can vary in terms of one's professional identity and the position he or she may currently occupy.

5 **Executive:** That function of government involved in the making of policy and the implementing of the will of the legislature. (*See* Policy.)

8 **Fascism:** An ideology that rejects equality in favor of hierarchy, looks to a supreme, charismatic leader whose will becomes law, sees all value derived from the state and appeals to emotion and militarism. Under fascism, the economy becomes a vast state corporation.

4 **Federalism:** A system wherein governing power is divided between a sovereign central government and regional governments possessing independent and inviolate powers of their own. Each sphere of activity is defined in the constitution of the state.

3 **Feudalism:** A political and economic system during the Middle Ages that was characterized by landed secular and religious hierarchies of nobles who had total control over ordinary people. These hierarchies were maintained through mutual obligations and pledges among the ruling classes.

11 **Franchise:** The right to vote as defined and regulated by statute.

11 **Gerrymandering:** Drawing representative districts in political bodies in such a way as to work to the advantage of one group or political party over another.

2 **Government:** An institution(s) whose purpose is to solve human disputes through law and enforce those solutions or laws through superior power (i.e., government is a regulator of society).

6 **Habeus corpus:** A writ or order to bring a person arrested for a crime before a court to test the validity of his or her arrest, in other words, to prevent an unfair arrest. (*See* Writ.)

4 **Head of government:** The chief executive officer of a government; the prime minister of a parliament or the president in a presidential system. (*See* Executive.)

4 **Head of state:** The highest ceremonial figure in a government whose function is to symbolize the sovereignty of the state and to ensure, under extraordinary circumstances, the existence of a government.

8 **Humanism:** The belief that human ideals (kindness, tolerance, loyalty, generosity, etc.) that occur in small groups (such as families) should also extend to the state.

1 **Hypothesis:** An as yet unproven assumption that is to be tested through evidence and scientific methods of inductive or deductive reasoning; also a tentative conclusion accepted for the moment (as in "a working hypothesis").

7 **Ideology:** A set of beliefs concerning the best way to organize governments and economies for dealing with the problems of the Industrial Revolution (Liberalism, Conservatism, Socialism, Communism, and Fascism).

12 **Immunity:** Being beyond or protected from the application of the laws of a state. (*See* chapter 12.)

11 **Initiative:** A petition by a prescribed number of voters that contains the wording of a proposed new law. When certified by competent authority, the law may be voted on directly by the voters in a referendum. (*See* Referendum.)

6 **Injunction:** A judicial writ or order to stop a practice or action deemed to be unfair. (*See* Writ.)

3 **Irridentia:** Literally unredeemed, referring to land that was once under the sovereignty of one state and now belongs to another; that land must be redeemed somehow, no matter what the cost.

12 **Joint Chiefs of Staff**: Chief policy-making and budgeting organization of the American Defense Department consisting of the military heads of the Army, Navy, Air Force and Marine Corps. It is headed by an officer of one of the first three branches.

4 **Judicial:** Pertaining to the application and interpretation of laws when they have been broken or when there is some dispute about their meaning; that which judges; that function that enforces the law.

4 **Judicial Review:** The power of the United States Supreme Court to delcare unconstitutional (and thus void) an act of the President, as state governor, the Congress, a state legislator, or any other court.

6 **Justice:** A standard for judging the legal order of a society that is satisfied when the best possible relationship among the people involved is seriously and actively sought, resulting in the highest possible degree of social happiness.

8 **Laissez-faire:** Literally leave us alone; a French term directed at governments imploring them to leave their people free to pursue their own economic interests in their own way, and to allow for competition in the marketplace.

6 **Law:** A code of conduct adopted and enforced by a state that seeks to determine solutions to public conflicts in advance and that also prescribes the behavior of people in certain areas of human conduct. It replaces customs and moral codes in seeking the rules whereby public order is achieved.

5 **Legislature:** That organ of government that writes the laws. Its duties may also include changing the constitution, electing the executive, supervising certain other functions of government, investigating public problems, and judging the performance of those people in the other organs of government; in other words, the center of a government.

2 **Legitimacy:** The popular perception of a justifiable and acceptable use of public power. That perception can be based on religion, wisdom, ideology, or a social contract. Without legitimacy, it is very difficult for a government to govern.

8 **Liberalism:** An ideology devoted to the freedom and equality before the law of each individual in a society. It espouses minimal governmental interference in the lives and property of citizens. It posits capitalism as the best economic system. (*See* Capitalism.)

8 **Libertarianism:** A political movement seeking to minimize government and extend the broadest civil and political rights to individuals. It seeks a pure market economy and rejects all but the most basic governmental services and taxes to pay for them.

9 **Lobbyist:** One who, on behalf of a special interest group or business, provides information and applies pressure on legislatures or administrative officials to influence legislation or public policy currently before them.

6 **Magistrate:** In America, a low-level official of the judiciary who adjudicates and administers the law for a small area (i.e., a county or city); a summary court judge. In Europe, the term may apply to major judicial officials. (*See* Adjudication.)

7 **Majoritarianism:** The idea that a numerical majority should rule, based solely on the fact that it is a majority, without any consideration of the basic values, concepts or organic laws of a society.

6 **Mandamus:** A judicial writ or order compelling a person or official to perform a specific action in the interest of fairness. (*See* Writ.)

8 **Maoism:** A radical form of Communism defined by Mao Tse-tung in China that includes the concepts of "humanism over industrialism" and "continuous revolution."

8 **Marxism:** A body of political and economic doctrine based on the ideas of Karl Marx seeking an egalitarian society based on "scientific socialism" to be achieved through revolution, followed by "the dictatorship of the proletariat," and leading ultimately to a communist (stateless) world. (*See* Socialism and Communism.)

12 **McCarthyism:** The reckless use, by a governmental official, of unsubstantiated accusations with regard to a person's patriotism or political loyalty, designed to engender fear and conformity to an established political orthodoxy—an aberration of the 1950s.

8 **Mercantilism:** A national economic policy aimed at maximizing gold holdings through strict governmental control over colonial and import/export policies that are designed to achieve a favorable balance of trade. (It was popular in the eighteenth century.)

7 **Meritocracy:** A government whose leaders are chosen and promoted because of personal achievement and ability.

7 **Moderate:** A person who is opposed to extreme or radical views of the political right or left; a centrist.

7 **Monism:** The doctrine or idea that the unity of authority, lifestyle, religion, and ideology are essential for social order; a mistrust of variety or pluralism. (*See* Pluralism.)

5 **Municipal:** Those things pertaining to a city, town, or other local self-government.

3 **Nation:** A people who share a common cultural, ethnic, or historic background (or all of these) and who wish to perpetuate this background politically within the context of the state.

3 **Nationalism:** People's identity with the nation as the perfect community and the insistence that its purposes be served by the system of nation-states. (*See* Nation).

12 **National Security Council:** That body of the executive branch of the American government that oversees the creation and implementation of policies that affect the security of the state. It consists of the president, the vice president, the secretaries of state and defense, the director of the CIA, the chairman of the Joint Chiefs of Staff, and other members requested by the president on an *ad hoc* basis.

6 **Natural law:** A system of basic rules and principles for human conduct that originate in man's reason, and do not have to be enacted positively. (*See* Normative.)

8 **Neoconservatism:** A political movement dating from the 1980s that opposes most of the leftist agenda and espouses an elitist control of government and the economy.

8 **Neoliberalism:** The assertion of a positive role for government in society wherein that government establishes minimum economic standards for its citizens, pushes for an expansion in civil rights for all, and advocates remedial programs to redress past injustices against minorities and the economically deprived.

8 **New Right:** A political movement, primarily of the middle class, that seeks to minimize governmental control over the economy and social structure while advancing governmental interference into the areas of religion and morality with a view toward establishing Christian norms of behavior for all citizens.

6 **Normative:** Pertaining to a norm or standard of behavior or condition, as in normative law, found in man's reason (natural law) or revealed by the divine. It does not change from time to time or from place to place. (*See* Natural law.)

12 **North Atlantic Treaty Organization (NATO):** Originally an alliance of fourteen nations, including the United States, which evolved during 1947–49 for the purpose of resisting, through military force, any Soviet expansion into western Europe. Today, it is an expanding organization whose basic purposes are, at best, unclear.

6 **Organic law:** The fundamental laws and principles of a government; those basic laws that give life to the state; constitutional law.

6 **Original jurisdiction:** The power of a court of record to hear a serious case for the first time; where a case begins.

10 **Parkinson's Law:** An observation about bureaucracy by C. Northcote Parkinson who notes that "work expands to fill the time available for its completion."

4 **Parliamentary:** Pertaining to a parliament and its rules and procedures; a governmental system that makes the executive dependent upon and responsible to a majority of the legislative assembly.

3 **Patriotism:** A rational and healthy appreciation for one's country or nation involving respect for its culture, symbols, and goals, obedience to its laws, financial support of its public activities, and physical support in times of crisis.

10 **Peter Principle:** An observation about bureaucracy by Laurence J. Peter who notes that a person in a career position within a bureaucracy is promoted until he or she reaches a personal level of incompetence, and remains there for the rest of his or her career.

6 **Plea bargain:** An agreement between a judge and prosecutor of a criminal case on the one hand, and an accused person on the other hand, to reduce the seriousness of the charge in exchange for an admission of guilt by the accused, thus avoiding the time and expense of a public trial.

7 **Pluralism:** The doctrine or idea that a variety of human expression and the freedom of the individual conscience are essential for a good society. An affirmation of multiparty political systems, many religions, and a variety of lifestyles. The opposite of Monism. (*See* Monism.)

5 **Policy:** A basic direction or attitude of a government aimed at the achievement of specific ends or goals, usually chosen from among alternatives.

4 **Policy making:** A choice among alternatives concerning the direction that a government or group should go; a decision about objectives or goals that a group sets for itself plus the means to be used to obtain them; an executive function.

9 **Political party:** In government, a group of people organized for the purpose of nominating and electing candidates for office, gaining control of a government thereby, and enacting a platform of commonly held goals and attitudes about the public policies of a state.

2 **Politics:** The peaceful resolution of public conflicts through compromise; a process involving governmental attention to relevant opinions and their conciliation through temporary law. (*See* chapter 2 for other definitions.)

8 **Populism:** An egalitarian movement of the 1880s that sought economic justice for midwestern farmers and workers of America as against the eastern monopolies of the day. Its agenda had a major effect on the modern Democratic Party, but its dedication to radical majoritarianism frightened most of the nation and resulted in its demise by the end of the 1940s.

6 **Positive law:** A kind of law that may vary from place to place and from time to time; law that is decided upon by people who must adapt it to their needs. A legal positivist rejects the assumption that law is normative. (*See* Normative.)

2 **Power:** The capacity to cause a thing to happen that would not happen without that capacity. Power may be military, economic, or psychological in nature.

12 **Precedent:** In law, a judicial decision used as a standard in subsequent similar cases. Precedent is used extensively in the Anglo-Saxon common law.

4 **Presidential system:** Pertaining to a system of government based upon the separation of the executive function and power from the legislative function and power; it can also be used to refer to the chief executive of such a system.

11 **Proportional representation:** An electoral system that ensures that each political party contesting for representatives will obtain a number of legislative seats in proportion to the number of votes cast for it. (*See* Political party.)

12 **Protocol:** The forms of ceremony and ritual used by diplomats to indicate existing relationships; diplomatic etiquette.

5 **Quasi:** Having a likeness to something, but not quite being that thing.

6 **Quo warrento:** A judicial writ or order that questions the authority of public officials to do a particular thing. It presents the unfair extension of the power of an official beyond that to which his or her office entitles him or her. (*See* Writ.)

7 **Radical:** That which looks to an extreme or revolutionary change in the political organization of the state or its policies.

7 **Reactionary:** That which opposes progress, idealizes the past, and seeks to move backwards in governmental policy and structure.

2 **Realpolitik:** An attitude toward public affairs that is based on the aggressive pursuit of personal or national interests without regard for ethical or philosophical considerations.

11 **Recall:** The removing of a public official before the expiration of his or her term through a process of petitioning for a special election on his or her continuance in office.

11 **Referendum:** A direct vote by the people of a nation state or lesser body (state, province, county, city, etc.) on a question of public policy such as a constitutional amendment, proposed law, or bond authorization. (*See* Initiative.)

3 **Reformation:** The movement for religious reform in Europe that began in 1517 and led to the division of the Roman Catholic Church and the Thirty Years' War (1618–48). Out of the latter came the modern nation-state.

11 **Representation:** The sending of persons to a legislative body to decide public issues on behalf of groups of people from predetermined geographical areas (districts, counties, states, wards, etc.); the process of indirect democracy.

10 **Revenue sharing:** The process of transferring national monies to states, counties, and other local governments to be used in any manner chosen by those lesser governments.

3 **Secondary interest:** A value or goal of a nation-state that is less than vital to its survival and can be approached through the process of negotiation and compromise.

12 **Secretariat:** The administrative department headed by a designated governmental secretary such as the Secretary General of the United Nations.

4 **Shadow cabinet:** The leadership of the largest minority party in a parliamentary government, which, upon becoming the majority, would become the operating cabinet of the new government. (*See* Cabinet and Parliamentary.)

11 **Single-Member district:** An election district (state, county, ward, or special district) from which only one representative is selected. (*See* Representation.)

3 **Social contract:** A mythical or actual document drawn up by representatives of the people of a state that creates a government for that state, and describes, delimits, or both, its powers; in modern terms, a constitution.

8 **Socialism:** Pertaining to an economic system wherein the manner of the production and distribution of goods and services is determined directly by the government. Its forms include Fabian, Classic, Militant, and Totalitarian socialism.

2 **Socialization:** The process of creating a psychological bond between a society (government) and individuals wherein people become loyal to and supportive of the laws and customs of that society.

6 **Solicitor:** A fully qualified British lawyer in general practice who can deal directly with clients and prepare cases for a barrister. In some American states, a solicitor is a prosecutor. (*See* Barrister.)

3 **Sovereignty:** The absolute, complete, and indivisible power of a government over the people within a state; that power of nation-states that makes them completely independent from each other.

6 **Stare decisis:** Literally let the decision stand, meaning, in Anglo-Saxon common law, one case may stand as a precedent for other similar cases. In Roman law, it meant that the decision of a court stood as law for that case no matter what happened in the future. (*See* Precedent.)

3 **State:** A bounded territory containing people who identify with that territory with a government that extends over that territory, and seeks, as its proper function, the common good of the people.

11 **Suffrage:** The right to vote as defined and regulated by legal enactments.

6 **Summary jurisdiction:** The power of a court to try cases for minor offenses (misdemeanors) wherein the punishments are limited, the procedures are informal, and no verbatim transcript is made (as in traffic courts, justice of the peace courts, and magistrate's court).

12 **Summit conference:** In diplomacy, a direct meeting of heads of governments designed to resolve some issue or to ceremonially conclude agreements reached by their respective diplomats.

8 **Syndicalist:** Pertaining to a labor movement in France (later in Spain and Italy) favoring direct attack on capitalists through sabotage, boycott, and general strikes, which would lead to a socialist state governed by a sort of craft union organization.

12 **Terrorism:** The indiscriminate and indirect use of violence, often against innocent citizens, by political or religious groups, for the purpose of forcing a change in governmental policy through resultant public pressure.

7 **Totalitarianism:** A governmental technique using modern technology to achieve a total social revolution wherein people are forcibly conditioned to an ideological system led by a single, elite party; as in communism or fascism.

4 **Tyranny:** The permission of monarchy wherein a monarch rules for his own benefit against the good of the people and is answerable to no one. Such a government is usually arbitrary and coercive.

3 **Ultranationalism:** An irrational and unhealthy attachment to one's country or nation involving a worshipful attitude toward its culture and symbols, and an unyielding quest for its goals, an unquestioning obedience to its laws and policies, and an aggressive assertion of its superiority over other countries or nations.

11 **Unicameral:** Referring to a legislature that has only one house or chamber (as in the state of Nebraska).

4 **Unitary:** Referring to a single government over a state which, though it may be decentralized to some extent, nevertheless, ultimately controls events throughout the state by its ability to coerce, negate, or withdraw the powers of local units.

8 **Utopian:** Pertaining to an ideal social, economic, and political society as described by Sir Thomas More in the sixteenth century. *Utopia* in Greek means *nowhere!*

3 **Vital interest:** A goal or value that is essential to the preservation of a state and for which a state will go to war; things affecting the security of a state's territory, government, people, and economy.

8 **Vocation:** One's occupation; the major thing one does to make a living; one's calling.

3 **WASP:** An acronym for White Anglo-Saxon Protestant; seen as the quintessential American of the first 150 years of the nation.

5 **Whip:** The assistant to a floor leader of a party in a legislature who maintains communication with his or her colleagues, canvasses his or her views, ensures votes, and otherwise enforces party discipline.

6 **Writ:** A judicial order that is written and commands a person to perform or cease to perform a specified act (the act usually having been deemed to be unfair).

12 **Xenophobia:** A fear, hatred, or both of foreigners or anything that is foreign.

Selected Bibliography

The following listing constitutes those works that include most of the ideas contained herein, both in terms of substance and significance. The list is not in any way a comprehensive one. Rather, it is my purpose both to indicate to you the source of many of my ideas and to provide to the serious student a basis for further study. In addition to the items listed on the following pages, students might also read as much as possible from those other truly primary source materials that are recognized by most political scientists to be basic in some fashion to the origins of our discipline. These include, among many others: Aristotle's *Politics* and *Nicomachean Ethics*; Cicero's *On the Commonwealth*; John Locke's *Second Treatise of Government*; Plato's *Apology, Crito*, and *Republic*; Thomas Hobbes' *Leviathan*; Machiavelli's *The Prince*; Marcus Aurelius' *Meditations*; Thomas Paine's *The Rights of Man*; and Rousseau's *The Social Contract*.

Finally, a word of encouragement to persons unduly put off by the erroneous assumption that such ancient writers as Cicero or Plato have little relevance for today. I would suggest that if Sir Isaac Newton were to reappear, he would be rather baffled by a modern text on nuclear physics. Further, if Galileo were suddenly reincarnated, he too would be lost in a world of black holes and quasars. However, if Aristotle should suddenly appear within our midst, I doubt if he would have a great deal of difficulty sensing the basic dimensions of our political difficulties. Whereas the issues themselves would be strange to him, the dynamics by which they are resolved would be as familiar to him as was the process of his own day. Our world has changed greatly since 500 B.C., but not humanity itself.

CHAPTER 1

De Vos, T. 1975. *Introduction to Politics*. Cambridge, Mass.: Winthrop Publishers, Inc.
Hamilton, C. V. 1982. *American Government*. Glenview, Ill.: Scott, Foresman and Company.
Ibele, O. H. 1971. *Political Science, An Introduction*. Scranton, Penn.: Chandler Publishing Company.
Kousoulas, D. G. 1979. *On Government and Politics*. 4th ed. Boston: Duxbury Press.

Masannat, G. S., and T. W. Madron. 1969. *The Political Arena*. New York: Charles Scribner's Sons.
Ranney, A. 1971. *The Governing of Men*. 3rd ed. New York: Holt, Rinehart and Winston, Inc.
Winter, H., and Bellows, T. J. 1977. *People and Politics, An Introduction to Political Science*. New York: John Wiley and Sons.

CHAPTER 2

Connolly, W. E. 1974. *The Terms of Political Discourse*. Lexington, Mass.: D.C. 1974. Heath & Company.
Crick, B. 1962. *In Defense of Politics*. London: Weidenfeld and Nicolson.
Deutsch, K. W. 1966. *The Nerves of Government*. New York: The Free Press.
Friedrich, C. J. 1963. *Man and His Government*. New York: McGraw-Hill.
Hacker, A. 1963. *The Study of Politics*. New York: McGraw-Hill.
Jards, D. 1973. *Socialization to Politics*. New York: Praeger Publishers.
Laswell, H. 1958. *Politics: Who Gets What, When, How*. Cleveland, Ohio: The World Publishing Company.
MacIver, R. M. 1965. *The Web of Government*. New York: The Free Press.
Pye, L. W., and S. Verba, eds. 1969. *Political Culture and Political Development*. Princeton, N.J.: Princeton University Press, 1969.
Renshon, S. A. 1977. *A Handbook of Political Socialization*. Riverside, N.J.: The Free Press.
Weiner, M. and S. Huntington. 1987. *Understanding Political Development*. Boston: Little, Brown & Company.
Zeigler, H. 1990. *The Political Community*. White Plains, New York: Longman.

CHAPTER 3

Barber, Sir Ernest. 1960. *Social Contract: Essays by Locke, Hume, and Rousseau*. Fair Lawn, N.J.: Oxford University Press.
Birch, A. H. 1989. *Nationalism and National Integration*. London & Boston: Unwin Hyman.
Contemporary Crisis of the Nation State. Oxford, United Kingdom: Blackwell Publishers, 1994.
Cox, R. H., ed. 1965. *The State in International Relations*. San Francisco: Chandler Publishing Company.
d'Entrèves, A. P. 1967. *The Notion of the State*. Oxford: The Clarendon Press.
Friedmann, W. G. 1945. *The Crisis of the Nation State*. New York: The Macmillan Company.
Herz, J. N. 1976. *The Nation State and the Crisis of World Politics*. New York: David McKay Co., Inc.
Kohn, H. 1965. *Nationalism: Its Meaning and History*. Princeton, N.J.: D. Van Nostrand Company.
Lowie, R. H. 1927. *The Origin of the State*. New York: Harcourt, Brace and World, Inc.
Ortega y Gasset, J. 1961. *History as a System (The Sportive Origin of the State)*. New York: W. W. Norton & Company, Inc.

CHAPTER 4

Hacker, A. 1963. *The Study of Politics*. New York: McGraw-Hill.
Hagopian, M. N. 1978. *Regimes, Movements, and Ideologies*. New York: Longman, Inc.
Ilbert, Sir Courtney. 1950. *Parliament: Its History, Constitution and Practice*. Fair Lawn, N.J.: Oxford University Press.
Macridis, R. C., and B.E. Brown, eds. 1961. *Comparative Politics: Notes and Readings*. Homewood, Ill.: The Dorsey Press.
Norton, P. 1991. *The British Polity*. White Plains, New York: Longman.
Peterson, P. E. 1995. *The Price of Federalism*. Washington, D.C.: The Brookings Institution.
Spiro, H. J. 1965. *Government by Constitution: The Political Systems of Democracy*. New York: Random House, Inc.
Strong, C. F. 1963. *A History of Modern Political Constitutions*. New York: Capricorn Books.
Verney, D. V. 1959. *The Analysis of Political Systems*. New York: The Free Press.

CHAPTER 5

Bock, E.A. 1965. *Government Regulation of Business, A Casebook.* Englewood Cliffs, N.J.: Prentice-Hall, Inc.
Fried, R.C. 1966. *Comparative Political Institutions.* New York: The Macmillan Company.
Karlen, D. 1967. *Anglo-American Criminal Justice.* New York: Oxford University Press.
Kornberg, A. 1973. *Legislatures in Comparative Perspective.* New York: David McKay Co., Inc.
Krislov, S., and L. Musolf 1964. *The Politics of Regulation.* Boston: Houghton Mifflin Company.
Morrison, H. 1960. *Government and Parliament.* London: Oxford University Press.
Murphy, W.F., and C.H. Pritchett, eds. 1961. *Courts, Judges, and Politics.* New York: Random House, Inc.
Rossiter, C. 1960. *The American Presidency.* New York: Harcourt, Brace and World.
Wahlke, J.C., et al. 1962. *The Legislative System.* New York: John Wiley & Sons, Inc.

CHAPTER 6

Abraham, H. J. 1986. *The Judicial Process.* 5th ed. New York: Oxford University Press.
Burkland, W. W., and A. D. McNair. 1936. *Roman Law and Common Law.* Cambridge, Mass.: Clarendon Press.
Diamond, A. S. 1951. *The Evolution of Law and Order.* London: Watts.
Frank, J. 1950. *Courts on Trial.* Princeton, N.J.: Princeton University Press.
Friedrich, C. J. 1958. *The Philosophy of Law in Historical Perspective.* Chicago: The University of Chicago Press.
Jenks, E. 1922. *A Short History of English Law.* Boston: Little, Brown & Company.
Mayers, L. 1964. *The American Legal System.* New York: Harper & Row, Publishers.
Murphy, W. F., and C. H. Pritchett, eds. 1961. *Courts, Judges, and Politics.* New York: Random House, Inc.
Pound, R. 1921. *The Spirit of the Common Law.* Boston: Marshall Jones.
Wolfe, C. 1986. *The Rise of Modern Judicial Review,* New York: Basic Books.

CHAPTER 7

Boudon, R. 1989. *The Analysis of Ideology.* Chicago: The University of Chicago Press.
Brzezinski, Z. B. 1962. *Ideology and Power in Soviet Politics.* 1962. New York: Frederick A. Praeger.
Dahl, R. T. 1985. *Controlling Nuclear Weapons: Democracy Versus Guardianship.* Syracuse, New York: Syracuse University Press.
Ebenstein, W. 1973. *Today's Isms.* 7th ed. Englewood Cliffs, N.J.: Prentice-Hall, Inc.
Friedrich, C. J., and Z. B. Brzezinski. 1965. *Totalitarian Dictatorship and Autocracy.* 2nd ed. New York: Frederick A. Praeger.
Girvetz, H. K. 1967. *Democracy and Elitism.* New York: Charles Scribner's Sons.
Guinier, L. 1994. *The Tyranny of the Majority: Fundamental Fairness in Representative Democracy.* New York: The Free Press.
Hagopian, M. N. 1978. *Regimes, Movements, and Ideologies.* New York: Longman, Inc.
Lipmann, W. 1955. *The Public Philosophy.* New York: Mentor—The New American Library.
Russell, B. 1934. *Freedom Versus Organization.* New York: W. W. Norton & Company, Inc.
Ward, B. 1959. *Five Ideas That Changed the World.* New York: W. W. Norton & Company, Inc.
Watkins, F. W. 1964. *The Age of Ideology.* Englewood Cliffs, N.J.: Prentice-Hall, Inc.

CHAPTER 8

Berki, R. N. 1975. *Socialism.* New York: St. Martin's Press, Inc.
Berlin, I. 1963. *Karl Marx.* New York: Oxford University Press.
Bottomore, T. B., ed. 1964. *Karl Marx, Early Writings.* New York: McGraw-Hill.

Cohen, C., ed. 1962. *Communism, Facism and Democracy: The Theoretical Foundations.* New York: Random House, Inc.

Collins, P. 1993. *Ideology After the Fall of Communism: The Triumph of Liberal Democracy.* London & New York: Boyars/Bowerdean.

DeRuggiero, G. 1959. *The History of European Liberalism.* Boston: Beacon Press.

Dishman, R. B. 1971. *Burke and Paine.* New York: Charles Scribner's Sons.

Dorrien, G. J. 1993. *The Neoconservative Mind: Politics, Culture, and the War of Ideology.* Philadelphia: Temple University Press.

Ebenstein, W. 1973. *Today's Isms.* 7th ed. Englewood Cliffs, N.J.: Prentice-Hall, Inc.

Engles, F., N. Lenin, and K. Marx. 1963. *The Essential Left.* New York: Barnes and NoNovel-Univin Books.

Girvin, B. 1994. *The Right in the Twentieth Century: Conservatism and Democracy.* London and New York: Pinter.

Gregor, A. J. 1969. *The Ideology of Fascism.* New York: The Free Press.

Jacobs, D. N., ed. 1979. *From Marx to Mao and Marchais.* New York: Longman, Inc.

Kirk, R. 1969. *The Conservative Mind: From Burke to Santayana.* New York: G. P. Putnam's Sons.

Laqueur, W. 1989. *The Long Road to Freedom: Russia and Glasnost.* New York: Scribner's.

Lowie, T. J. 1969. *The End of Liberalism.* New York: W. W. Norton & Company, Inc.

Mark, M. 1973. *Modern Ideologies.* New York: St. Martin's Press, Inc.

Mussolini, B. (January, 1935). "The Political and Social Doctrine of Fascism." *International Conciliation*, No. 306. New York: The Carnegie Endowment for International Peace.

Rossi-Landi, F. 1990. *Marxism and Ideology.* Oxford: Clarendon Press.

Sargent, L. T. 1975. *Contemporary Political Ideologies.* Homewood, Ill.: The Dorsey Press.

Shaffer, H. G., ed. 1967. *The Communist World.* New York: Appleton-Century-Crofts.

Viereck, P. 1962. *Conservatism Revisited.* New York: The Free Press.

CHAPTER 9

Beck, P. A. 1992. *Party Politics in America.* 7th edition. New York: Harper Collins.

Epstein, L. D. 1986. *Political Parties in the American Mold.* Madison: University of Wisconsin Press.

Flanigan, W. H. 1968. *Political Behavior of the American Electorate.* Boston: Allyn and Bacon, Inc.

Ginsberg, B. 1990. *Politics by Other Means: The Declining Importance of Elections in America.* New York: Basic Books, Inc.

Key, V. O., Jr. 1964. *Politics, Parties, and Pressure Groups.* 5th ed. New York: Thomas Y. Crowell Company, Publishers.

Lipset, S. M., and S. Rokkan, eds. 1967. *Party Systems and Voter Alignment.* New York: The Free Press.

Marti, J. 1989. *Political Parties and Elections in the United States.* Philadelphia: Temple University Press.

Neumann, S. 1956. *Modern Political Parties: Approaches to Comparative Politics.* Chicago: The University of Chicago Press.

Schattschneider, E. E. 1969. *Two Hundred Million Americans in Search of a Government.* New York: Holt, Rinehart and Winston.

Sorauf, F. J.1964. *Political Parties in the American System.* Boston: Little, Brown & Company.

Tocqueville, A., de. 1960. *Democracy in America.* New York: Alfred A. Knopf, Inc./Vintage.

CHAPTER 10

Bernstein, S. J., and P. O'Hara. 1979. *Public Administration: Organizations, People, and Public Policy.* New York: Harper and Row.

Denhardt, R. B. 1984. *Theories of Public Organization.* Monterey, Calif.: Brooks/Cole Publishing Company.

Downs, A. 1967. *Inside Bureaucracy.* Boston: Little, Brown & Company.

Gordon, G. J. 1982. *Public Administration in America.* New York: St. Martin's Press.

Lipsky, M. 1980. *Street-Level Bureaucracy.* New York: Russell Sage Foundation.

Lutrin, C. E., and A. K. Settle. 1976. *American Public Administration: Concepts and Cases*. Palo Alto, Calif.: Mayfield Publishing Company.

Meier, K. J. 1985. *Regulation*. New York: St. Martin's Press.

Nigro, F. A., and L. G. Nigro. 1984. *Modern Public Administration*. 6th ed. New York: Harper and Row.

Ripley, R. B., and G. A. Franklin. 1982. *Bureaucracy and Policy Implementation*. Homewood, Ill.: The Dorsey Press.

CHAPTER 11

Baker, G. E. 1966. *The Reapportionment Revolution*. New York: Random House, Inc.

Bone, H. A., and A. Ranney. 1963. *Politics and Voters*. New York: McGraw-Hill.

Gross, B. M. 1953. *The Legislative Struggle*. New York: McGraw-Hill.

Jewell, M. E. 1962. *The Politics of Reapportionment*. New York: Atherton Press.

Priven, F. F. 1988. *Why Americans Don't Vote*. New York: Pantheon Books.

Roelofs, H. M. 1976. *Ideology and Myth in American Politics*. Boston: Little, Brown & Company.

Rosenthal, A. 1974. *Legislative Performance in the States: Exploration of Committee Behavior*. New York: The Free Press.

Schattschneider, E. E. 1969. *Two Hundred Million Americans in Search of a Government*. New York: Holt, Rinehart and Winston.

Smith, E. R. A. N. 1989. *The Unchanging American Voter*. Berkley: The Univertsity of California Press.

CHAPTER 12

Brown, L. 1973. *World Without Borders*. New York: Vantage Books.

Claude, I. L., Jr. 1962. *Power and International Relations*. New York: Random House.

Eichelberger, C.M. 1977. *Organizing for Peace*. New York: Harper.

Grieves, F. L. 1977. *Conflict and Order*. Boston: Houghton Mifflin.

Ikle, F. C. 1964. *How Nations Negotiate*. New York: Harper and Row.

Kaplan, M. A. and N. Katzenbach. 1961. *The Political Foundations of International Law*. New York: Wiley.

Liska, G. 1962. *Nations in Alliance*. Baltimore: Johns Hopkins Press.

Luard, E. 1944. *The United Nations: How it Works and What it Does* (Revised by Derek Heater). New York: Saint Martins Press.

Morgenthau, H. J. 1967. *Politics Among Nations*. 4th ed. New York: Knopf.

Nicolson, H. 1955. *The Evolution of the Diplomatic Method*. New York: Macmillan.

Simon, J. D. 1994. *The Terrorist Trap: America's Experience with Terrorism*. Bloomington, Ind.: University Press.

Smith, B. L. 1994. *Terrorism in America: Pipe Dreams and Pipe Bombs*. Albany: The State University of New York Press.

Sutterlin, J. S. 1995. *The United Nations and the Maintenance of International Security*. Westport, Conn.: Praeger.

Watson, A. 1982. *Diplomacy*. New York: McGraw-Hill New Press.

Wright, Q. 1955. *Contemporary International Law: A Balance Sheet*. New York: Doubleday.

Index

Absolute monarchy, 39
Adams, John Quincy, 85
Adjudication, 98
  in international law, 276–277
Administrative law judge, 98
Advisory opinions, 99
Aggression, and nationalism, 54
Alien and Sedition Acts, 64
Allison, Graham, 225
Anarchy, 56
Anglo-Saxon Common Law, 106,
     119–123, 127, 131
Antigone, 38
Appellate Courts, 98, 130–133
Arbitration, 273, 275–276
Aristocracy, 56
Aristotle, 2, 9, 23, 29, 299
  government classifications by, 55–57
  on the natural origins of the state, 29
Arraignment, 105
Arthashastra, ancient political book, 2
Arthur, Chester A., 205
Articles of Confederation, the, 33,
     59–60, 239
Ataturk, Kemal, 153
Athenian Confederacy, 59
Australia, federalism in, 68
Australian ballot, 228–229
Authoritarian government, 152–154
Authority, defined, 13

Balance of Power, 278–279
Barristers, schooling of, 123
Battle of Hastings, 120
Behavioralists vs. traditionalists, 4–7

Bicameralism, 239–241
Blackstone, Sir William, 121
Block grants, 223
Bloodline, legitimacy of government
     via, 14
Bodin, Jean, 2, 39
Boorstin, Daniel, 141
Boren, James H., 226
Boundaries, national, 51
Boutros-Ghali, 284
Brezhnev, Leonid, 194
Bryan, William Jennings, 176
Brzezinski, Z. D., 159
Buchanan, James, 205
Buckley, William F., 178
Bureaucracy, 215–226
  evolution of, 217–218
  growth of, 220
  intergovernmental, 220–222
  public vs. private, 219–220
Bureaucratic politics model, 225
Burke, Edmund, 174–175
Bush, George, 124, 139, 179, 207
Bye-elections, 75

Cabinet
  dominance of, 80–81
  in Great Britain, 76–77
  origin of, 72
Calhoun, John C., 64
Calvin, John, 163–164, 166
Canada, federalism in, 68
Canon Law, 118
Carter, Jimmy, 99–100
Castro, Fidel, 23

Categorical grants, 223
Censureship, 86
Central Intelligence Agency (CIA), 264, 268
Certiorari, writ of, 129
Charismatic theory, of the origins of the
    state, 28–29
Charlemagne, 28
Charles I, of Great Britain, 29
Chiang Kai-shek, 196
China. *See* People's Republic
    of China
Church, and the feudal state, 36–38
Churchill, Winston, 23, 95, 176
Cicero, 2, 299
Cincinnatus, 22–23
Civil War, the, 23, 64, 66, 172
Clayton Act, 96
Cleveland, Grover, 205
Clinton, Bill, 71, 101, 139, 179, 207
Coalition, parliamentary, 78–79
Code
    of Draco, 118
    of Hammurabi, 118
    of Justinian, 118–119
    Napoleonic, 119
    of Solon, 118
Coke, Edward, 121
Cold War, 50, 263, 265, 277
Commentaries, 121–122
Committee System, Legislative, 253–256
Common Law, 106, 119–124, 127
Common Sense, book by Paine, 28, 166–167
Communism, 185–197
    Chinese, 195–197
    Soviet, 194–195
Compromis', 273
Compromise, as a political solution, 10
Confederacies, 59–60
Confucius, 2, 149
Connelly Amendment, 227
Consent orders, 99
Conservatism, 172–180
Constitution
    government classification by, 57–58
    as a social contract, 32–33
    of the U.S., 170–172
Constitutional Convention of 1787, 61–63,
    69, 170–171
Coren, Alan, 141

Corpus Juris Civilis, 119
Courts
    appellate, 98, 130–133, 135
    of original jurisdiction, 130
    Supreme, 130–133
    U.S. system of, 131–134
Creon, 38
Crick, Bernard, 16, 21, 23
Cuban Missile Crisis, 265
Custom, as a source of law, 276
Cyprus, 52

Dahl, Robert, 148–151
Darwin, Charles, 3
Decatur, Steven, 48
Declaration of Independence, 31, 142,
    164, 171
Democracy, 17, 57–58, 141–152
    direct, 220–232
    egalitarian forms, 17–21
    feedback in, 20
    inputs and outputs, 19–20
    political, 17–21
Democratic party, 64, 204–207
    origins of, 204–205
Deng Xiaoping, 197
Depression. *See* Great Depression
Deregulation, 100–101
Dialectic, Hegelian theory of, 186–188
Diplomacy, 270–274
Diplomatic conferences, 271–272
    summits, 272
Diplomatic methods
    conciliation, 272
    good offices, 272
    mediation, 272
Diplomatic terms
    immunity, 270–271
    protocol, 271
    rank, 271
Divine theory, of the origin of the
    state, 27–28
Draco, code of, 118
Due Process, 113

Easton, David, 19, 24
Economic policy-making, 91
Education and socialization, 15–16
Egalitarian democracy, 17–21
Egocentrism, as a problem in nationalism, 43

Eisenhower, Dwight, 176, 215
Elections, 144–145
   primary, 210
   recall, 230–231
Electoral College, and single member
       districting, 246–247
Employment Act of 1946, 91
Enclosure Movement, 160
Engels, Friedrich, 191
England. *See* Great Britain
Equal Rights Amendment, 145
Equality, and democracy, 18, 19
Equity, as a source of international law, 276
Equity Law, 128–129
Ethics and law, 114–115
Europe, political parties in, 208
Exclusionary rule, 113, 126
Executive
   collegial, 76–77
   functions of, 90–93

Fabians, 184
Falkland Islands, 52
Fascism, 197–201
Fealty Law, 118
Federal Register, 98
Federalism, 61–68
   non-American approaches, 68
Federalists, 204
Feudal state, 33–38
Fillmore, Millard, 204
Flag, as a symbol of nationalism, 47–48
Force, as a source of legitimacy, 13
Foreign policy, 259–261
Fortescue, Sir John, 121
Fourier, Charles, 181
France
   government of, 59, 77
   representation in, 251
Franco, Francisco, 154, 276
Franco-Prussian War, 191
Fremont, John C., 205
French Revolution, 135–137, 173–175
Freud, Sigmund, on personality, 45

Garfield, James, 205
General Assembly (of UN), 281–282
"General Will," 32
George I of Great Britain, 72
George II of Great Britain, 72

George III of Great Britain, 31, 40, 72, 126
German Federalism, 68
Germany, divided into East and West, 52
Gerry, Elbridge, 247–248
Gerrymandering, 247–249
Gibraltar, 52
Gideon v. Wainright, 126, 133
Gingrich, Newt, 179
Glasnost, 195
Glorious Revolution of 1688, The, 30
Gorbachev, Mikhail, 195
Government, 10–11
   Aristotle's classification of, 55–57
   authoritarian, 11, 152–154
   classification by constitutions, 55–58
   coalition, 78–79
   defined, 10
   Federal, 61–68
   inputs and outputs, 19–20
   legitimacy, 13–14
   parliamentary system of, 72–82
   political, 11
   power of, 11–13
   presidential system of, 69–72
   totalitarian, 154–159
Grant, Ulysses S., 205
Grants-in-aid, 222–224
Great Britain, 69
   American arbitrations with, 273
   government of, 72–73, 79
   judicial selection in, 122–123
   prime minister's powers in, 76–77
   representation in, 251
   socialism in, 184
Great Depression, 96, 170, 206
Grotius, Hugo, 275
Guardianship, 148–151
Gulf War, 284

Habeus corpus, writ of, 129
Hague Conference of 1899, 275
Hague Court of Arbitration, 275
Halpern, Morton, 225
Hamilton, Alexander, 3
Hammarskjold, Dag, 283
Hammurabi, code of, 118
Harrison, William Henry, 204
Hatch Act, 216–217
Head of state, 77–78

Hegel, Georg, 186–190
Hitler, Adolph, 13, 28, 156, 197–198
Hobbes, Thomas, 2, 29–30, 39, 268, 299
Hoover, Herbert, 206

Ideology (-ies), 135–141
    evolution of, 159–161
    as a source of legitimacy, 14
    terms of, 135–141
Impeachment, 22, 85–86
Independents, political, 207
Industrial Revolution, 160–161, 190
Initiative and referendum, 230–232
Injunction, writ of, 129
Input-outputs of government, 19–20
Interest groups, 211–213
International Court of Justice (ICJ),
        277–278, 282
International Law, 274–278
International organizations, 279–284
Interstate Commerce Commission, 96
Irridentia, 51–52
Italy, 52, 78, 197, 199

Jackson, Andrew, 64, 85, 216
Jay, John, 3
Jefferson, Thomas, 31, 69, 142, 172
Joint Chiefs of Staff, 264, 267, 268
John, of Great Britain, 72
Johnson, Andrew, 205
Johnson, Lyndon, 176
Judge(s). *See also* Judiciary
    in Great Britain, 122–123
    in the United States, 123–127
Judicial review, 71, 133–134, 148
Judiciary. *See also* Judge(s)
    function of, 93–94
Jurisdiction
    original, 130
    summary, 131
    superior, 131
Jus Civilis, 118
Jus Gentium, 118
Jus Natural, 118
Justice and law, 111–112
Justinian, code of, 118

Keynes, John Maynard, 3
Khrushchev, Nikita, 194
Kim Il Sung, 154, 156

King, Florence, 141
Kirk, Russel, 174–175
Koran, 103
Korea, 52, 265
Krasner, Stephen D., 225
Kristol, Irving, 180

Laissez faire, 165
Lasswell, Harold D., 24
Law
    Anglo-Saxon Common, 106, 119–122, 131
    canon, 118
    civil, 106, 108–109
    criminal, 106–108
    custom as a source of international law, 276
    defined, 11
    enforcement of, 63, 71, 109–110
    Equity, 128–129
    ethics and the law, 114–115
    Fealty, 118
    International, 274–278
    justice and the law, 111–112
    levels of law, 116
    morality and the law, 112–113
    natural, 38, 106
    normative, 103–104, 106
    organic, 116, 148
    positive, 103–106
    precedent as a source of, 121–122, 276
    principles as a source of, 276
    Roman, 41, 118–119
    rule of, 110–111, 148
    statutory, 122
    treaties as a source of, 276
    Tribal, 44–45, 116–117
    truth and the law, 113–114
"Lay Judges," 125
League of Nations, 276, 280
Legal systems, 116
    evolution of, 116–118
Legislators
    characteristics and qualifications of,
        249–251
    committee systems of, 254–256
    functions of, 84–88
Legitimacy
    defined, 13
    of government via politics, 14
    and socialization, 14–16

Lenin, Vladimir, 154, 192–195
Leviathan, The, book by Hobbes, 30
Liberalism, 163–172
   neo-, 170–172
Libertarianism, 177–178, 179
Lie, Trygve, 283
Lincoln, Abraham, 23, 48, 64, 121, 172, 205
Lippmann, Walter, 80
Lobbyists, 211–213, 239–240
Locke, John, 2, 164
   on the social contract, 31–32, 33
Louis XVI of France, 136, 137, 173

Machiavelli, Niccolo, 2, 299
Mackinder, Sir Harold, 3
Madison, James, 3, 69, 71
Magna Charta, The, 32
Major, John, 77, 179
Majoritarianism, 147–148
Majority
   defined, 145
   rule, 145–146
   simple, 145
Mandamus, writ of, 128–129
Mao Tse-tung, 154, 156, 195–197
Mapp v. Ohio, 126, 133
Marshall, John, 133
Marx, Karl, 3, 186, 188–192
Marxism, 188–192
Mayflower Compact, 33
McCarthy, Joseph, 86, 87, 88
McCarthyism, 146, 264
McKinley, William, 205
McNamara, Robert, 267
Mencken, H. L., 141
Mercantilism, 164–165
Merit selection, 216
Meritocracy, 149
Minority, 146
   in a parliamentary system, 75–76
Miranda v. Arizona, 126, 133
Missouri Plan, 125
Mob rule, 55–56, 148
Monarchy, 55
Montesquieu, 69, 83
Morality, and the law, 112–113
Morgenstern, Oskar, 3
Motor voter law, 67
Moynihan, Daniel Patrick, 257
Mussolini, Benito, 154, 197, 236

Nader, Ralph, 100
Napoleon, 28, 42, 174
Napoleonic Code, 119
Nation state, 40–55
   absolute monarchy in, 39
   boundaries of, 51
   divided nations, 52
   evolution of, 33–40
   identifying a, 50–51
   and irridentias, 51–52
National Academy of Sciences, 150
National anthems, 48
National economic policy-making, 91
National Industrial Recovery Act, 96
National interest, 44, 259–261
National Recovery Administration, 96, 200
National Security, 261–270
   basic problems in, 268–270
   organizational principles, 266–268
   policy-making, 91
   structures, 265–266
National Security Council, 264
Nationalism, 41–54
   and aggression, 54
   benefits of, 46
   evolution of, 42
   problems of, 43–46
   and self-determination, 49–50
   symbols, 47–49
Nationhood, 41–42
Natural Law, 38, 106
Natural theory, of the origins of the state, 29
Neotribalism, 44–45
Nepotism, 216
Neumann, John Von, 3
New Deal, 91, 137, 170, 176–177
New Right, The, 178–180
Newton, Sir Isaac, 7, 299
Nicomachean Ethics, The, book by Aristotle,
   23, 299
Nixon, Richard M., 22, 71, 86, 99, 100, 176,
   206, 223
Normative views of the law, 103–104
North, Oliver, 88
North American Free Trade Agreement,
   (NAFTA), 288
North American Treaty Organization,
   (NATO), 264
North Korea, 14, 17, 18, 154, 158
Northwest Ordinance of 1787, 60

Office of Management and Budget, 99
Oligarchy, 56
One-party political system, in U.S., 204–208
Organizational process model, 225
Orwell, George, 53, 157, 287
Owens, Robert, 181

Paine, Thomas, 28, 166–167, 171
  on the origin of the state, 28
Parkinson, C. Northcote, 224
Parkinson's Law, 224
Parliamentary system of government, 72–82
  characteristics of, 73–78
  coalition, 78–80
  compared to the presidential system,
    80–82
  evolution of, 72
Participation, in democracies, 20–21
Patriotism, 42–43
Pax Romana, 33, 41
Peace of Augsburg, 39
People's Republic of China
  communism in, 195–197
  democracy in, 17–18
  participation in, 20
  representation in, 252
  totalitarianism in, 154–159
Perestroika, 195
Perez de Cuellar, 284
Permanent Court of International Justice
  (PCIJ), 276
Peron, Juan, 153
Peter, Laurence J., 224
Peter Principle, 224
Pierce, Franklin, 204
Plato, 2, 13, 111, 149, 299
Plea bargaining, 105, 115
Plurality, 145
Podhoretz, Norman, 180
Poindexter, John, 88
Police powers, 63
Policy making, 71, 88–90
Politburo, 155
Political Action Committees, 213
Political democracy, 17–21
  future of, 256–257
  prerequisites for, 142–147
  problems in, 227–257
Political ethos, 15
Political parties

American approach to, 203–213
  defined, 203
  European, 208
  purposes of, 210
Political science, early approaches to, 2–3
Politicians, 25
Politics, 10, 16–17
  defined, 10, 23–25
  and democracy, 17
Politics, book by Aristotle, 2, 299
Polity, 56
Polk, James Knox, 204
Polycentrism, 219
Population, and representation, 251–252
Populist Party, 147
Positive law, 104–106
Power, 11–13, 260
  vacuums, 219
Precedent, as a source of law, 121–122, 276
Presidential system of government, 69–72
  compared to parliamentary system, 79–82
  policy-making areas, 90–93
Prince, The, book by Machiavelli, 2, 299
Principles, as a source of law, 276
Proportional representation, 241–245
Protestant Ethic, 110, 163–164
Proudhon, Pierre-Joseph, 181
Public ethos, 15
Punishment, 107–108

Quo warrento, writ of, 129

Reagan, Ronald, 67, 71, 99, 100, 139, 207,
  224, 233
"Reagan Revolution," 67
Realignment, 208
Recall, election, 230–231
Referendum, 230–232
Reformation, the, 37–38, 40
Registration, voting, 228
Regulatory agencies, 95–101
Regulatory independence, 99–100
Regulatory structures and procedures, 97–99
Religion, as a source of legitimacy, 13
Renaissance, 2, 59
Representation, 236–245
  geographical, 236–239
  and population, 251–253
  single member districts vs. proportional,
    241–245

Republic, The, book by Plato, 2, 13, 111, 149, 299
Republican party, 205–207
Research methods, 7–8
Revenue sharing, 223–224
Revolutionary War, 167
Reynolds v. Simms, 238
Ricardo, David, 190
Roman Empire, 33, 38, 39, 186
Roman Law, 116, 118–119
Roman Republic, 21
Roosevelt, Franklin D., 23, 73, 93, 96, 176, 206, 224
   and World War II, 23, 93
Rousseau, Jean Jacques, 2, 29, 31–32, 136
Rule making, 98–99
Rule of Law, 110–111
Rwanda, 51

Sabotage, 182
St. Augustine, 2, 27–28
Saint Simon, 182
St. Thomas Aquinas, 2
Scott, Sir Walter, 49
Second Treatis of Government, The, book by Locke, 31, 162, 299
Self-determination, 49–50
Self-incrimination, 113, 126
Senate, U.S., representation in, 236–237
Seniority system, 254–255
Shadow Cabinet, 75
Shaw, George Bernard, 141
Sherman Anti-Trust Act, 96
Simple majority, 145
Simpson, O. J., 106, 114
Single-member districts, 241–247
Smith, Adam, 164–166
Smith Act of 1940, 116, 146
Social Contract, 29–33, 288
Social Contract, The, book by Rousseau, 31, 299
Socialism, 180–185
   classic, 182
   Fabian, 184
   scientific, 185
   syndicalists, 181–182
   utopians, 181
   in Western countries, 183–185
Socialization, 14–16
   and legitimacy, 14
   and public education, 15–16

Solicitors, schooling of, 123
Solon, code of, 118
Solzhenitsyn, Alexander, 157
Sovereignty, 38–41
   time of, 21–23
Soviet Union
   arms race in, 6
   communism in, 194–195
   and national identity, 50–51
   totalitarianism in, 155
   treaties of, 277–278
Spoils system, 216–217
Stalin, Joseph, 154, 156, 194
Stare decisis, 121
State
   defined, 27
   feudal, 33–38
   future of, 53–54
   head of, 77–78
   origin of, 27–33
   regional, 53
   world, 53–54
Strauss, Leo, 6
Suffrage, women's, 227
Sullivan, William, 3
Sun Yat-sen, 195–196
Supreme courts, 131–133
Switzerland, confederalism in, 59
   federalism in, 68
Symbols, of nationalism, 47–49
Syndicalism, 181–182

Taboos, 44–45, 116
Taft, William Howard, 96
Tax structure, 65
Taylor, Zachary, 204
Tennyson, Alfred, Lord, 280
Thant, U, 284
Thatcher, Margaret, 77, 179, 227
Thirty Years' War, 37, 186, 288
Thomas, Clarence, 124
Thurmond, Strom, 246
Tilden, Samuel J., 85
Totalitarianism, 154–159
Totems, 44–45, 116
Trade practices conferences, 99
Traditionalists vs. behavioralists, 5–7
Treaties, 276
Treaty of Westphalia, 37, 39
Tribal Law, 44–45, 116–117
Truman, Harry, 176

Truth, and law, 113–114
Tyler, John, 204
Tyranny, 55

Ultranationalism, 43–46
Unicameralism, 239–241
Unitary government, 59
United Nations, 41, 46, 281–284
    as a confederacy, 60
    Economic and Social Council, 282
    General Assembly, 281–282
    images of, 283–284
    Secretariat, 281
    Security Council, 282
    Trusteeship Council, 282
Utopians, 181

Van Buren, Martin, 204
Verick, Peter, 178
Vico, Giovanni Battista, 2
Vietnam, 6, 22, 206–207, 265
    South Vietnam, 53
Vietnam war, 6, 22, 206–207
    and Richard Nixon, 22, 206–207
Vital interests, 44, 260
Voting, 143–146, 227–236
    behavior, 4, 232–236

Wallace, George, 246
Wallace, Henry, 246
War of 1812, 64
Warren Court, 71, 171
Washington, George, 48
WASP, 51
Watt, James, 160
Westphalia, Treaty of, 37, 39
Will, George, 178
William the Conqueror, 120
Wilson, Woodrow, 96, 205–206
Wisconsin v. Yoder, 16
Wisdom, as a source of legitimacy, 13
Writ
    of certiorari, 129
    of habeus corpus, 129
    of injunction, 129
    of mandamus, 128
    of quo warrento, 129

Yugoslavia, 52